AMANDA
TIDWELL

Grateful acknowledgment is made to the following publishers, authors, and agents for their permission to reprint copyrighted material. Any adaptations are noted in the individual acknowledgments and are made with the full knowledge and approval of the authors or their representatives. Every effort has been made to locate all copyright proprietors; any errors or omissions in copyright notice are inadvertent and will be corrected in future printings as they are discovered.

"America the Beautiful" from *Poems* by Katherine Lee Bates. First published, 1926, in the United States by E.P. Dutton. All rights reserved. Reprinted by permission of the publisher, E.P. Dutton, a division of Penguin Books USA Inc.

"Belinda's Challenge" abridged from *Belinda's Hurricane* by Elizabeth Winthrop. Text copyright © 1984 by Elizabeth Winthrop Mahony. Reprinted by permission of E.P. Dutton, a division of Penguin Books USA Inc.

"The Brooklyn Bridge: Emily's Triumph" by Charnan Simon, © 1989 by Silver, Burdett & Ginn Inc.

"Can She Sing?" excerpt from *Sarah, Plain and Tall* by Patricia MacLachlan, jacket art by Marcia Sewall. (A Charlotte Zolotow Book) Text copyright © 1985 by Patricia MacLachlan, art © 1985 by Marcia Sewall. Reprinted by permission of the American publisher, Harper & Row, Publishers, Inc., and the British publisher, Julia MacRae Books.

*The Comeback Dog* by Jane Resh Thomas, illustrations by Troy Howell. Copyright © 1981 by Jane Resh Thomas. Illustrations © 1981 by Troy Howell. Reprinted by permission of Clarion Books/Ticknor & Fields, a Houghton Mifflin Company.

*Dakota Dugout* by Ann Turner and illustrated by Ronald Himler is reprinted by permission of Macmillan Publishing Company, and of the author's agents, Curtis Brown Ltd. Text copyright © 1985 by Ann Turner. Illustrations copyright © 1985 by Ron Himler.

*Day of the Earthlings* by Eve Bunting, copyright © 1978 by Créative Education, Inc. Reprinted by permission of Creative Education, Inc.

Acknowledgments continue on pages 606–608, which constitute an extension of this copyright page.

# WORLD OF READING

# ·DREAM· CHASERS

P. DAVID PEARSON     DALE D. JOHNSON

THEODORE CLYMER     ROSELMINA INDRISANO     RICHARD L. VENEZKY

JAMES F. BAUMANN     ELFRIEDA HIEBERT     MARIAN TOTH

*Consulting Authors*

CARL GRANT     JEANNE PARATORE

## SILVER BURDETT & GINN

NEEDHAM, MA • MORRISTOWN, NJ
ATLANTA, GA • CINCINNATI, OH • DALLAS, TX
MENLO PARK, CA • NORTHFIELD, IL

# THE LAND OF THE FREE _____ 150

# IMAGINE A PLACE...

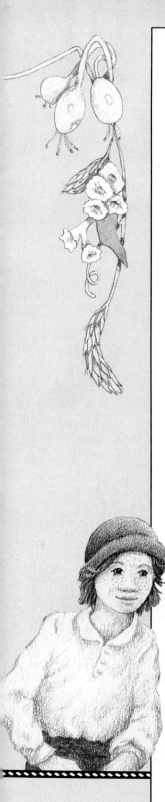

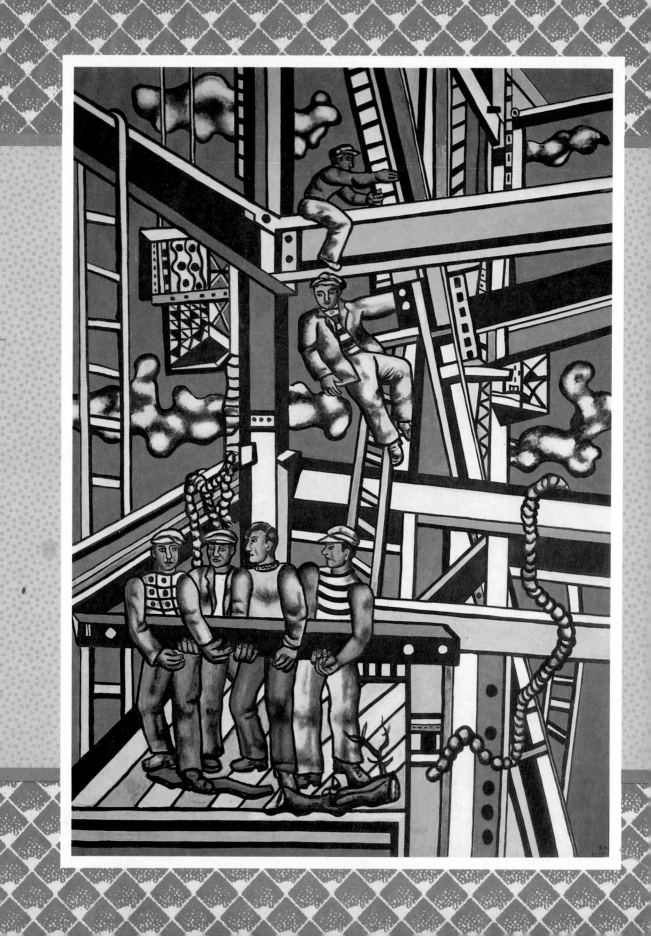

UNIT ONE

# A JOB WORTH DOING

*Building bridges or baby-sitting— why is work worth doing also worth reading about?*

LES CONSTRUCTEURS,
*oil on canvas by Fernand Léger, French, 1950*

*More than any-thing else, Leigh Botts wants to become a writer someday. Perhaps the advice of a famous author can help him.*

# Letters to Mr. Henshaw
## from <u>Dear Mr. Henshaw</u>

written by Beverly Cleary        illustrated by Paul O. Zelinsky

When Leigh Botts was in the second grade he wrote to author Boyd Henshaw to tell him how much he liked Mr. Henshaw's book, Ways to Amuse a Dog. *Mr. Henshaw did not respond, but Leigh continued to write to him. Finally, when Leigh was in the sixth grade, Mr. Henshaw responded with a suggestion that Leigh keep a diary. Now, although Leigh continues to write letters to Mr. Henshaw, he has begun to keep a diary as well. Out of habit, he begins each entry "Dear Mr. Henshaw."*

January 12

Dear Mr. Henshaw,

This is a real letter I am going to mail. Maybe I had better explain that I have written you many letters that are really my diary which I keep because you said so and because Mom still won't have the TV repaired. She wants my brain to stay in good shape. She says I will need my brain all my life.

Guess what? Today the school librarian stopped me in the hall and said she had something for me. She told me to come to the library. There she handed me your new book and said I could be the first to read it. I must have looked surprised. She said she knew how much I love your books since I check them out so often. I am on page 14 of *Beggar Bears*. It is a good book. I just wanted you to know that I am the first person around here to get to read it.

Your No. 1 fan,

Leigh Botts

January 19

Dear Mr. Henshaw,

Thank you for sending me the postcard with the picture of the lake and mountains and all that snow. Yes, I will continue to write in my diary even if I do have to pretend I am writing to you. You know something? I think I feel better when I write in my diary.

My teacher says my writing skills are improving. Maybe I really will be a famous author someday. She said our school along with some other schools is going to print (that means mimeograph) a book of work of young authors, and I should write a story for it. The writers of the best work will win a prize—lunch with a Famous Author and with winners from other schools. I hope the Famous Author is you.

I don't often get mail, but today I received two postcards, one from you and one from Dad in Kansas. His card showed a picture of a grain elevator. He said he would phone me sometime next week. I wish someday he would have to drive a load of something to Wyoming and would take me along so I could get to meet you.

That's all for now. I am going to try to think up a story. Don't worry. I won't send it to you to read. I know you are busy and I don't want to be a nuisance.

Your good friend,

Leigh Botts

February 15

Dear Mr. Henshaw,

I haven't written to you for a long time, because I know you are busy, but I need help with the story I am trying to write for the Young Writers' Yearbook. I got started, but I don't know how to finish it.

My story is about a man ten feet tall who drives a big truck, the kind my dad drives. The man is made of wax, and every time he crosses the desert, he melts a little. He makes so many trips and melts so much he finally can't handle the gears or reach the brakes. That is as far as I can get. What should I do now?

The boys in my class who are writing about monsters just bring in a new monster on the last page to finish off the villains with a laser. That kind of ending doesn't seem right to me. I don't know why.

Please help. Just a postcard will do.

Hopefully,

*Leigh Botts*

P.S. Until I started trying to write a story, I wrote in my diary almost every day.

February 28

Dear Mr. Henshaw,

   Thank you for answering my letter. I was surprised that you had trouble writing stories when you were my age. I think you are right. Maybe I am not ready to write a story. I understand what you mean. A character in a story should solve a problem or change in some way. I can see that a wax man who melts until he's a puddle wouldn't be there to solve anything and melting isn't the sort of change you mean. I suppose somebody could turn up on the last page and make candles out of him. That would change him all right, but that is not the ending I want.

   I asked my teacher Miss Martinez if I had to write a story for Young Writers, and she said I could write a poem or a description.

                    Your grateful friend,
                    Leigh

P.S. I bought a copy of your book *Ways to Amuse a Dog* at a garage sale. I hope you don't mind.

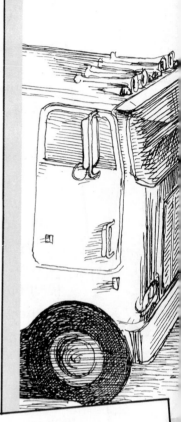

Tuesday, March 20

   Yesterday Miss Neely, the librarian, asked if I had written anything for the Young Writers' Yearbook, because all writing had to be turned in by tomorrow. When I told her I hadn't, she said I still had twenty-four hours and why didn't I get busy? So I did, because I really would like to meet a Famous Author. My story about the ten-foot wax man went into the wastebasket. Next I tried to start a story called "The Great Lunchbox Mystery," but I couldn't seem to turn my experience about food taken from my lunchbox into a story because I still don't know who the thief (thieves) was (were), and I don't want to know.

Finally I dashed off a description of the time I rode with my father when he was trucking the load of grapes down Highway 152 through Pacheco Pass. I put in things like the signs that said STEEP GRADE, TRUCKS USE LOW GEAR and how Dad down-shifted and how skillful he was handling a long, heavy load on the curves. I put in about the hawks on the telephone wires and about that high peak where Black Bart's lookout used to watch for travelers coming through the pass so he could signal to Black Bart to rob them, and how the leaves on the trees along the stream at the bottom of the pass were turning yellow and how good tons of grapes smelled in the sun. I left out the part about the waitresses and the video games. Then I copied the whole thing over in case neatness counts and gave it to Miss Neely.

Monday, March 26

Today wasn't the greatest day of my life. When our class went to the library, I saw a stack of Yearbooks and could hardly wait for Miss Neely to hand them out. When I finally got mine and opened it to the first page, there was a monster story, and I saw I hadn't won first prize. I kept turning. I didn't win second prize which went to a poem, and I didn't win third or fourth prize, either. Then I turned another page and saw Honorable Mention and under it:

A DAY ON DAD'S RIG
by
LEIGH M. BOTTS

19

There was my title with my name under it in print, even if it was mimeographed print. I can't say I wasn't disappointed because I hadn't won a prize, I was. I was really disappointed about not getting to meet the mysterious Famous Author, but I liked seeing my name in print.

Some kids were mad because they didn't win or even get something printed. They said they wouldn't ever try to write again which I think is pretty dumb. I have heard that real authors sometimes have their books turned down. I figure you win some, you lose some.

Then Miss Neely announced that the Famous Author the winners would get to have lunch with was Angela Badger. The girls were more excited than the boys because Angela Badger writes mostly about girls with problems like big feet or pimples or something. I would like to meet her because she is, as they say, a real live author, and I've never met a real live author. I am glad Mr. Henshaw isn't the author because then I would really be disappointed that I didn't get to meet him.

Friday, March 30

Today turned out to be exciting. In the middle of second period Miss Neely called me out of class and asked if I would like to go have lunch with Angela Badger. I said, ''Sure, how come?''

Miss Neely explained that the teachers discovered that the winning poem had been copied out of a book and wasn't original so the girl who submitted it would not be allowed to go and would I like to go in her place? Would I!

Miss Neely telephoned Mom at work for permission and I gave my lunch to my friend Barry because my lunches are better than his. The other winners were all dressed up, but I didn't care. I have noticed that authors like Mr. Henshaw usually wear old plaid shirts in the pictures on the back of their books. My shirt is just as old as his, so I knew it was OK.

Miss Neely drove us in her own car to the restaurant, where some other librarians and their winners were waiting in the lobby. Then Angela Badger arrived with Mr. Badger, and we were all led into the dining room which was pretty crowded. One of the librarians who was a sort of Super Librarian told the winners to sit at a long table with a sign that said Reserved. Angela Badger sat in the middle and some of the girls pushed to sit beside her. I sat across from her. Super Librarian explained that we could choose our lunch from the salad bar. Then all the librarians went off and sat at a table with Mr. Badger.

There I was face to face with a real live author who seemed like a nice lady, plump with wild hair, and I couldn't think of a thing to say because I hadn't read her books. Some girls told her how much they loved her books, but some of the boys and girls were too shy to say anything. Nothing seemed to happen until Mrs. Badger said, "Why don't we all go help ourselves to lunch at the salad bar?"

What a mess! Some people didn't understand about salad bars, but Mrs. Badger led the way and we helped ourselves to lettuce and bean salad and potato salad and all the usual stuff they lay out on salad bars. A few of the younger kids were too short to reach anything but the bowls on the first rows. They weren't doing too well until Mrs. Badger helped them out. Getting lunch took a long time, longer than in a school cafeteria, and when we carried our plates back to our table, people at other tables ducked and dodged as if they expected us to dump our lunches on their heads. All one boy had on his plate was a piece of lettuce and a slice of tomato because he thought he was going to get to go back for roast beef and fried chicken. We had to straighten him out and explain that all we got was salad. He turned red and went back for more salad.

I was still trying to think of something interesting to say to Mrs. Badger while I chased garbanzo beans around my plate with a fork. A couple of girls did all the talking, telling Mrs. Badger how they wanted to write books exactly like hers. The other librarians were busy talking and laughing with Mr. Badger who seemed to be a lot of fun.

Mrs. Badger tried to get some of the shy people to say something without much luck, and I still couldn't think of anything to say to a lady who wrote books about girls with big feet or pimples. Finally Mrs. Badger looked straight at me and asked, "What did you write for the Yearbook?"

I felt myself turn red and answered, "Just something about a ride on a truck."

"Oh!" said Mrs. Badger. "So you're the author of 'A Day on Dad's Rig'!"

Everyone was quiet. None of us had known the real live author would have read what we had written, but she had and she remembered my title.

"I just got honorable mention," I said, but I was thinking, She called me an author. A real live author called me an author.

"What difference does that make?" asked Mrs. Badger. "Judges never agree. I happened to like 'A Day on Dad's Rig' because it was written by a boy who wrote honestly about something he knew and had strong feelings about. You made me feel what it was like to ride down a steep grade with tons of grapes behind me."

"But I couldn't make it into a story," I said, feeling a whole lot braver.

"Who cares?" said Mrs. Badger with a wave of her hand. She's the kind of person who wears rings on her forefingers. "What do you expect? The ability to write stories comes later, when you have lived longer and have more understanding. 'A Day on Dad's Rig' was splendid work for a boy your age. You wrote like you, and you did not try to imitate someone else. This is one mark of a good writer. Keep it up."

I noticed a couple of girls who had been saying they wanted to write books exactly like Angela Badger exchange embarrassed looks.

"Gee, thanks," was all I could say. The waitress began to plunk down dishes of ice cream. Everyone got over being shy and began to ask Mrs. Badger if she wrote in pencil or on the typewriter and did she ever have books rejected and were her characters real people and did she ever have pimples when she was a girl like the girl in her book and what did it feel like to be a famous author?

I didn't think answers to those questions were very important, but I did have one question I wanted to ask which I finally managed to get in at the last minute when Mrs. Badger was autographing some books people had brought.

"Mrs. Badger," I said, "did you ever meet Boyd Henshaw?"

"Why, yes," she said, scribbling away in someone's book. "I once met him at a meeting of librarians where we were on the same program."

"What's he like?" I asked over the head of a girl crowding up with her book.

"He's a very nice young man with a wicked twinkle in his eye," she answered. I think I have known that since the time he answered my questions when Miss Martinez made us write to an author.

On the ride home everybody was chattering about Mrs. Badger this, and Mrs. Badger that. I didn't want to talk. I just wanted to think. A real live author had called me an author. A real live author had told me to keep it up. Mom was proud of me when I told her.

I'm glad tomorrow is Saturday. If I had to go to school I would yawn. I wish Dad was here so I could tell him all about today.

March 31

Dear Mr. Henshaw,

I'll keep this short to save you time reading it. I had to tell you something. You were right. I wasn't ready to write an imaginary story. But guess what! I wrote a true story which won Honorable Mention in the Yearbook. Maybe next year I'll write something that will win first or second place. Maybe by then I will be able to write an imaginary story.

I just thought you would like to know. Thank you for your help. If it hadn't been for you, I might have handed in that dumb story about the melting wax trucker.

Your friend, the author,

*Leigh Botts*

P.S. I still write in the diary you started me on.

## ◆ LIBRARY LINK ◆

*Does Leigh ever win a prize in the Young Writers' Yearbook, or meet Mr. Henshaw in person? Find out by reading the rest of* Dear Mr. Henshaw *by Beverly Cleary.*

## Reader's Response

Do you think Mr. Henshaw's advice helped Leigh become a better writer? Explain your answer.

# Letters to Mr. Henshaw

## ◆ Checking Your Comprehension

1. How did writing in his diary change Leigh?
2. Why did Leigh have a difficult time writing a story for the Young Writers' Yearbook?
3. How did Angela Badger help Leigh?
4. Do you agree with Angela Badger that a good writer develops his or her own style of writing?
5. What kind of a person was Leigh Botts? What examples in the story helped you learn about him?
6. If Leigh's work had not appeared in the Young Writers' Yearbook, what might have happened to his plans to become an author? Explain how you decided what might happen.

## ◆ Writing to Learn

**THINK AND RECORD**  In this story Boyd Henshaw told Leigh Botts to write a journal. What do you think might be written in Mr. Henshaw's journal or Leigh's journal? Here are some possible entries.

| Leigh Botts | Boyd Henshaw's Journal |
|---|---|
| *January 12*    I wrote a letter to Mr. Henshaw and told him I liked his book. | *January 15*    I heard from a young man named Leigh Botts. |
|  | *February 12*    I wrote to Leigh Botts and told him that I had trouble writing stories when I started out. |
|  |  |

**WRITE**  Write a journal entry that either Mr. Henshaw or Leigh Botts might write.

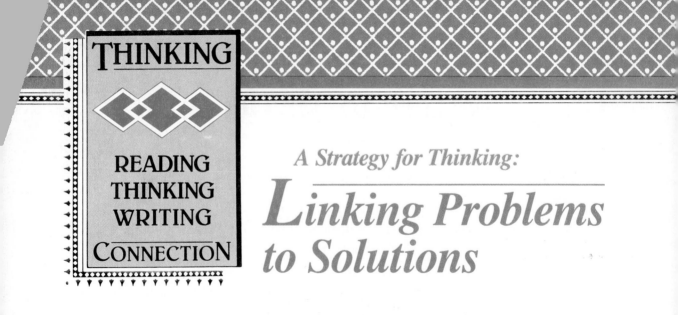

*A Strategy for Thinking:*

# Linking Problems to Solutions

**M**any stories center on a problem that must be solved. In some stories, a character goes on an adventure and encounters many problems along the way. Eventually, the character finds a solution that sweeps all the problems away. In other stories, a character may have a single problem to solve and has to come up with a tricky or inventive solution. You may get greater enjoyment out of a story if you learn to follow the events that link a problem in a story to its solution.

## Learning the Strategy

Do you remember the problems Leigh Botts had trying to write a story for the *Young Writers' Yearbook* in "Letters to Mr. Henshaw"? Here are the steps he followed to reach a solution.

> My story about the ten-foot wax man went into the wastebasket. Next I tried to start a story called "The Great Lunchbox Mystery," but I couldn't seem to turn my experience about food taken from my lunchbox into a story.... Finally I dashed off a description of the time I rode with my father when he was trucking the load of grapes down Highway 152 through Pacheco Pass.

To follow and appreciate a story like this, it may help if you trace the steps that lead from the problem to the solution. One useful strategy for tracing problems and solutions is to draw problem/solution steps. Problem/solution steps look like a staircase. You write the problem on the bottom step and the solution on the top step. Then you write the steps that lead from the problem to the solution on the steps going up the stairway.

Look at the problem/solution steps for the passage from "Letters to Mr. Henshaw."

**STEPS TO LEIGH'S SOLUTION**

| |
|---|
| **Solution: Leigh wrote about the truck ride.** |
| Step 2: He tried to write "The Great Lunchbox Mystery." |
| Step 1: He threw away the story about the wax man. |
| Problem: Leigh had to write a story. |

## Using the Strategy

In "Letters to Mr. Henshaw," Leigh's big dilemma, or problem, is how to become an author. By the end of the story, he has solved his problem: he feels he is finally an author.

Make problem/solution steps of your own, placing the following sentences in the correct order. Review the story if you want to refresh your memory.

◆ Mrs. Badger tells Leigh that she likes his writing.
◆ Leigh writes a description of a truck ride with his father.
◆ Leigh writes Mr. Henshaw for advice on a story.
◆ Leigh gets to go to lunch with a famous author.

## Applying the Strategy to the Next Story

During the next story, "The Emperor and the Kite," you will be asked to think about the main character's problem and the steps to the solution. Then you can write a set of problem/solution steps for the story.

◄◆► The writing connection can be found on page 87.

weller

*Djeow Seow, the daughter of an ancient Chinese emperor, is so small that she is often overlooked. But perhaps that will change.*

# The Emperor and the Kite

*by Jane Yolen*

Once in ancient China there lived a princess who was the fourth daughter of the emperor. She was very tiny. In fact she was so tiny her name was Djeow Seow,[1] which means "the smallest one." And, because she was so tiny, she was not thought very much of—when she was thought of at all.

Her brothers, who were all older and bigger and stronger than she, were thought of all the time. And they were like four rising suns in the eyes of their father. They helped the emperor rule the kingdom and teach the people the ways of peace.

Even her three sisters were all older and bigger and stronger than she.

They were like three midnight moons in the eyes of their father.

[1]Djeow Seow (jēōu shēōu)

They were the ones who brought food to his table.

But Djeow Seow was like a tiny star in the emperor's sight.

She was not even allowed to bring a grain of rice to the meal, so little was she thought of. In fact she was so insignificant, the emperor often forgot he had a fourth daughter at all.

And so, Djeow Seow ate by herself.

And she talked to herself.

◄❖►

Does Djeow Seow have a problem? What do you think her problem is?

And she played by herself, which was the loneliest thing of all. ◄❖►

Her favorite toy was a kite of paper and sticks.

Every morning, when the wind came from the east past the rising sun, she flew her kite. And every evening, when the wind went to the west past the setting sun, she flew her kite. Her toy was like a flower in the sky. And it was like a prayer in the wind.

In fact a monk who passed the palace daily made up a poem about her kite.

> *My kite sails upward,*
> *Mounting to the high heavens.*
> *My soul goes on wings.*

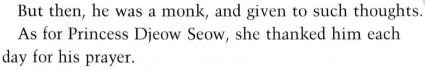

But then, he was a monk, and given to such thoughts.

As for Princess Djeow Seow, she thanked him each day for his prayer.

Then she went back to flying her toy.

But all was not peaceful in the kingdom, just as the wind is not always peaceful.

For the wind can trouble the waters of a still pond.

And there were evil men plotting against the emperor.

They crept up on him one day when he was alone, when his four sons were away ruling in the furthermost parts of the kingdom and his three daughters were down in the garden. And only Princess Djeow Seow, so tiny she seemed part of the corner where she sat, saw what happened. ◄◆►

The evil men took the emperor to a tower in the middle of a wide, treeless plain. The tower had only a single window, with an iron bar across the center. The plotters sealed the door with bricks and mortar once the emperor was inside.

Then they rode back to the palace and declared that the emperor was dead.

When his sons and daughters heard this, they all fled to a neighboring kingdom where they spent their time sobbing and sighing. But they did nothing else all day long.

All except Djeow Seow. She was so tiny, the evil men did not notice her at all.

And so, she crept to the edge of the wide, treeless plain.

And there she built a hut of twigs and branches.

Every day at dawn and again at dark, she would walk across the plain to the tower.

And there she would sail her stick-and-paper kite.

◄◆►

**Think about what is happening. Can this be a step toward solving Djeow Seow's problem?**

33

To the kite string she tied a tiny basket filled with rice and poppyseed cakes, water chestnuts and green tea. The kite pulled the basket high, high in the air, up as high as the window in the tower.

And, in this way, she kept her father alive. ◄◆►

**Think about what is happening. Can this be a step toward solving Djeow Seow's problem?**

So they lived for many days: the emperor in his tower and the princess in a hut near the edge of the plain.

The evil men ruled with their cruel, harsh ways, and the people of the country were very sad.

One day, as the princess prepared a basket of food for her father, the old monk passed by her hut. She smiled at him, but he seemed not to see her.

Yet, as he passed, he repeated his prayer in a loud voice. He said:

> *My kite sails upward,*
> *Mounting to the high heavens.*
> *My emperor goes on wings.*

The princess started to thank him. But then she stopped. Something was different. The words were not quite right.

34

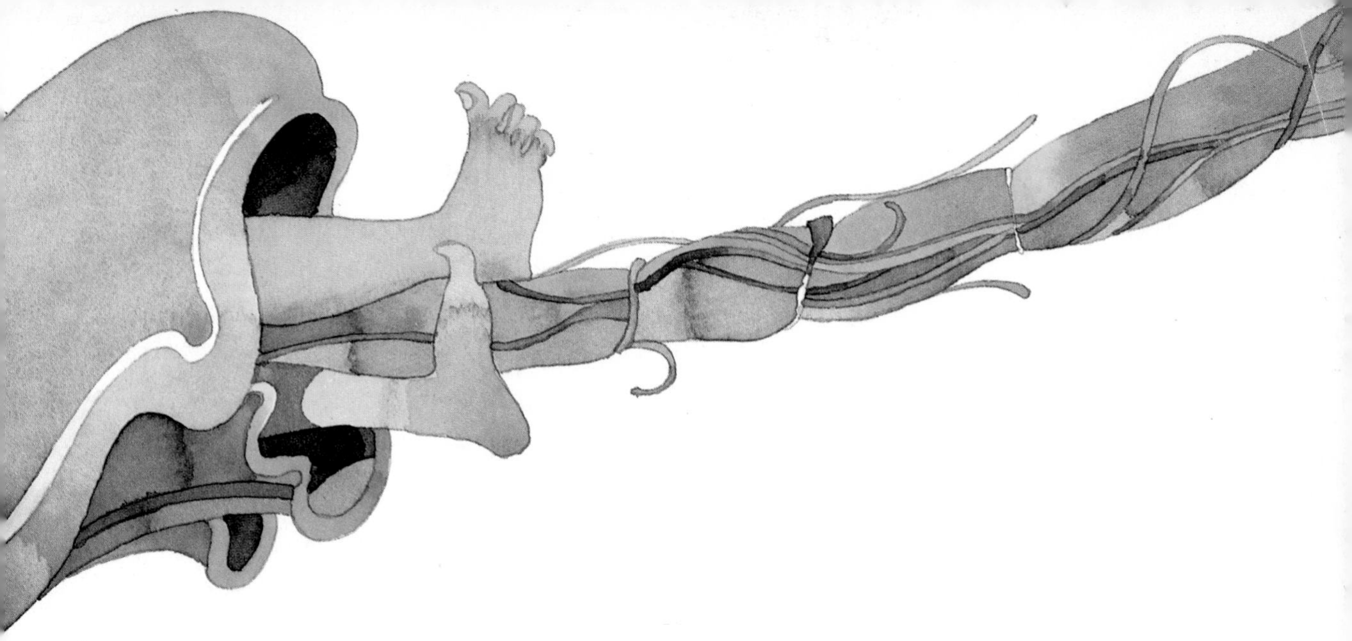

"Stop," she called to the monk. But he had already passed by. He was a monk, after all, and did not take part in things of this world.

And then Djeow Seow understood. The monk was telling her something important. And she understood.

Each day after that, when she was not bringing food to her father, Djeow Seow was busy. She twined a string of grass and vines, and wove in strands of her own long black hair. When her rope was as thick as her waist and as high as the tower, she was ready. She attached the rope to the string of the stick-and-paper kite, and made her way across the treeless plain.

When she reached the tower, she called to her father.

But her voice was as tiny as she, and her words were lost in the wind.

At last, though, the emperor looked out and saw his daughter flying her kite. He expected the tiny basket of food to sail up to his window as it had done each day. But what should he see but the strand of vines and grass and long black hair. The wind was raging above, holding the kite in its steely grip. And the princess was below, holding tight to the end of the rope. ◆◈◆

◆◈◆

Think about what is happening. Can this be a step toward solving Djeow Seow's problem?

35

Although the emperor had never really understood the worth of his tiniest daughter before, he did now. And he promised himself that if her plan worked she would never again want for anything, though all she had ever wanted was love. Then he leaned farther out of the tower window and grasped the heavy strand. He brought it into his tower room and loosened the string of the kite. He set the kite free, saying, "Go to thy home in the sky, great kite." And the kite flew off toward the heavens.

Then the emperor tied one end of the thick strand to the heavy iron bar across the window, and the other end stretched all the way down to Djeow Seow's tiny hands.

The emperor stepped to the window sill, slipped under the iron bar, saluted the gods, and slid down the rope. His robes billowed out around him like the wings of a bright kite.

When his feet reached the ground, he knelt before his tiny daughter. And he touched the ground before her with his lips. Then he rose and embraced her, and she almost disappeared in his arms.

With his arm encircling her, the emperor said, "Come to thy home with me, loyal child." He lifted the tiny princess to his shoulders and carried her all the way back to the palace.

At the palace, the emperor was greeted by wild and cheering crowds.

The people were tired of the evil men, but they had been afraid to act.

With the emperor once again to guide them, they threw the plotters into prison.

37

And when the other sons and daughters of the emperor heard of his return, they left off their sobbing and sighing, and they hurried home to welcome their father. But when they arrived, they were surprised to find Djeow Seow on a tiny throne by their father's side.

To the end of his days, the emperor ruled with Princess Djeow Seow close by. She never wanted for anything, especially love. ◄◆►

And the emperor never again neglected a person— whether great or small.

And, too, it is said that Djeow Seow ruled after him, as gentle as the wind and, in her loyalty, as unyielding.

◄◆►

**Write problem/ solution steps to show how Djeow Seow's problem was solved.**

**How could writing problem/solution steps be helpful to you?**

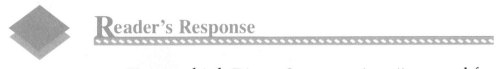

## Reader's Response

Do you think Djeow Seow was just "too good for words"? Explain.

# The *Emperor* and the *Kite*

## ◆ Checking Your Comprehension

1. Why was Djeow Seow like "a tiny star in the emperor's sight"?
2. List three things Djeow did that showed she was alone and lonely.
3. The emperor's other children fled when they heard he had died. What do you think of their actions?
4. What did Djeow do to change the emperor's opinion of her?
5. What did the emperor learn from his experience? How did you figure out the answer?
6. If the emperor had not been kidnapped, what do you think Djeow's life would have been like?

## ◆ Writing to Learn

**THINK AND ANALYZE**   Djeow Seow was a little person who accomplished a gigantic deed with the help of a kite. Read the kite-shaped poem below and notice how it is written.

| | |
|---|---|
| name of subject | Djeow Seow |
| two adjectives | Loyal and devoted |
| three active verbs | Kite flying, listening, wondering |
| adjective/noun; adjective/noun | Tiny star, youngest daughter |
| three active verbs | Watching, helping, planning |
| two adjectives | Gentle, brave |
| name of subject | Djeow Seow |

**WRITE**   Create a kite poem about a special person you know.

39

# READING FICTION

## Vocabulary:
# Connotations and Denotations

In "The Emperor and the Kite," you read how the emperor was captured:

> They *crept* up on him one day when he was alone, when his four sons were away ruling in the furthermost parts of the kingdom and his three daughters were down in the garden.

Go back and look again at the word *crept*. What does *crept* mean in that sentence? If you think it means "moved in a slow or sneaking way," you are right! The exact meaning of a word is called its *denotation*. If you are not sure of the denotation of a word, you can look up the word in the dictionary.

Why did the author decide to use the word *crept* instead of *moved?* Think about how the word *crept* made you feel. You probably felt that the emperor was in danger because the men were sneaking up on him and were about to surprise him. The feeling you get when you read a particular word is called that word's *connotation*. The word *crept* connotes certain feelings that give you a clearer picture of what is happening in the story.

## Identifying Connotations and Denotations

Here is another sentence from the same story:

> And there were *evil* men *plotting* against the emperor.

First, look at the word *evil.* The author might have used the word *naughty* instead. *Evil* and *naughty* have similar denotations: both mean "bad." However, *evil* and *naughty* have very different connotations. *Naughty* is a playful word that makes us think of mischievous children. The word *evil*, on the other hand, connotes wickedness and danger. The author chose the word *evil* to make you feel a certain way when you read the sentence.

Now look at the word *plotting.* Another word that might have been used in its place is *planning.* Both *plotting* and *planning* denote thinking about a way to do something. Which word connotes wickedness and secrecy? Again, the author has carefully chosen the word *plotting* to create a specific mood and to help you understand what is happening in the story.

## Using What You Have Learned

Write each sentence on a piece of paper, and use a word that connotes a more specific and powerful meaning than the word in italics. Base your answers on "The Emperor and the Kite."

**1.** The princess was *small.*
**2.** The evil men ruled in their *bad,* harsh way.
**3.** The wind was *blowing* above.
**4.** Djeow Seow built a *structure* out of sticks.

## As You Read

Now that you have practiced using connotations, you can appreciate how and why writers choose certain words over others. As you read the next story, "Belinda's Challenge," look for words that connote a specific meaning or feeling.

*Belinda and Granny May have always worked well together. But some jobs are for one person alone.*

# Belinda's Challenge

## by Elizabeth Winthrop

*Belinda has enjoyed a wonderful visit with her grandmother on Fox Island, off the coast of Maine. When a hurricane is predicted for her last day on the island, Belinda is both excited and fearful about the approaching storm. She is also upset that Granny May's grouchy neighbor, Mr. Fletcher, must abandon his unsafe house on the shore and join them. Worst of all, Mr. Fletcher will bring his bulldog Fishface, who has growled and snapped at Belinda all summer.*

When Belinda woke up the next morning, she missed the noisy screeching of the gulls and the warm sunlight on her face. Outside, the sky looked dark and stirred up. Everything that could blow in the wind was blowing, from the halyards on the few boats still in the harbor to Granny May's loose shutter.

Belinda dressed quickly and ran downstairs. Granny May was up and already listening to the radio. The bittersweet smell of coffee filled the kitchen.

"It's really coming, isn't it?" Belinda asked, kissing Granny May on the top of her head as she passed. "The sky looks so dark, and the gulls are all hiding away somewhere. I feel scared and excited all at the same time."

"That's the right way to feel," Granny May said. "The storm passed over New Haven and New York early this morning. Listen." She nodded at the radio.

"At five o'clock this morning, the winds at the center of the storm were clocked at 95 miles an hour. They are expected to decrease in velocity somewhat as long as the storm remains over land. At this time, the National Weather Service estimates that the storm will continue in a northeasterly direction at approximately 40 miles per hour. The full fury of the hurricane is expected to hit the Maine coast in the middle of the afternoon. And now, we have a report from John Davis on the cleanup operation in New Haven."

"Turn it off," Granny May said.

Belinda flipped the knob. It was a relief to have that grim voice shut off.

"We certainly don't need to hear what's happened to New Haven, since there's nothing we can do about it," Granny May said. "I spoke to your father this morning. He had heard the radio reports and wanted to make sure we were all battened down. He says to tell you that you are very lucky. He never did go through a hurricane on the island, and he always wanted to."

"What about them?" Belinda asked. "Will the hurricane hit them?"

"No, it passed to the east of them. All right now, let's worry about more important things, such as breakfast. I vote for scrambled eggs, bacon, fresh orange juice, muffins, and our very own blueberry jam. We'll make it a special hurricane feast."

Belinda nodded. She didn't feel much like eating, but she couldn't dampen Granny May's enthusiasm. "Are we going to be all right, Granny May?" she asked.

"It will be a little scary, Belinda, no doubt about it. The storm's turned out to be bigger than anyone predicted." Granny May came over and gave her a quick hug. "But this little house has been through some rougher weather than this and survived it. Don't worry too much."

The wind continued to rise, and the rain started soon after they had cleared away the breakfast dishes. The two of them put on their slickers and went out on the porch to secure the loose shutter. They had to shout at one another over the growing noise of the storm. Belinda could barely see the town dock through the deepening fog and the rain. The tide was running into the harbor, chased by the wind, so the bigger swells were already crashing up over the seawall.

Just then, Ed Fletcher parted the hedge and stumped across the lawn, carrying a flat black suitcase and Fishface's bed. His head was bent down against the rain, and the sides of his poncho billowed out with each gust of wind.

"He looks like a big yellow balloon," Belinda shouted into her grandmother's ear.

Mr. Fletcher turned once and made some noise that Belinda couldn't hear. In response to it, Fishface pushed his own way through the lower part of the hedge and trotted after the man.

"They even look alike," Belinda said out loud, knowing nobody could hear her.

Granny May motioned them all inside. There was no use trying to talk out on the porch.

"Water's already halfway up my porch steps," Mr. Fletcher said.

"Don't think we'll go out again till it's blown over," Granny May said cheerily. They all lifted off their wet slickers and hung them on the pegs by the door. "Ed, why don't you just take over the dining room and make that your place while you're here. There's a bathroom through that far door, and you can close both of the other doors if you need some privacy."

While Granny May was talking, Fishface was prowling along the edges of the room snuffling to himself. Belinda stood very still, hoping he would not recognize her as the lawn mower pusher, invader of his territory. He stopped when he got to her rubber boot and looked up. Belinda smiled hopefully, Fishface bared his teeth and growled.

Mr. Fletcher whistled. "Doesn't like being cooped up. Never has," he said. "I had to leave him out all last night. He slept under the porch."

"I heard him growling," Belinda said. "It sounded as if he wanted to have a good fight with a hurricane."

Mr. Fletcher took Fishface into the dining room with him and closed the door.

"Oh dear," Belinda said. "This is going to be a long day."

Standing there in the dim room, Belinda became aware of a steady moaning that sounded like Fishface in distress.

"What is that noise?" she asked, peering through the window.

"That's the wind. I remember that noise from the last bad storm," Granny May said. "It feels as if the storm has wrapped its arms around the house and is trying to squeeze us to death."

The wind was driving the rain at the house like a hose turned on full blast, and some of the windows had begun to leak from the force of the water. There were moments of clearing outside when Belinda could see beyond the porch railing. She was reminded of the sand walls she liked to build on the beach when the tide was rising. Eventually, a wave would wash over them, and when the water rushed back to the sea, there would be nothing left of her wall but a sodden lump of sand. For the first time, Belinda was really scared. She went and stood beside Granny May.

Granny May put her arm around Belinda's shoulders. "You come with me and help me find those flashlights. Then we'll start eating some of that food in the refrigerator."

They were sitting around the kitchen table, eating blueberry pie by the light of two candles, when Fishface began to howl. He had been pacing back and forth in the dining room, making strange noises and pawing at the rug for quite a while.

"It's the pressure falling as we get near the eye," Mr. Fletcher said. "Dogs can feel the change even more than humans. It makes him nervous."

The howling was awful. It said out loud all the fears that the people in the house were keeping inside.

Mr. Fletcher tried first to comfort the dog, and when that didn't work, he shouted at him.

"Fishface, quiet."

The howling subsided for a moment, but as soon as Mr. Fletcher left the dining room, it started again.

"Bring him in here, Ed," said Granny May. "I wouldn't want to be left all alone at a time like this either."

But Fishface began to go even crazier when Mr. Fletcher let him off the leash. He threw himself at the back door, whining and scratching. When they didn't open the door, he put up his head and howled again.

"I can't stand this," Mr. Fletcher muttered. "I'm going to take him out for just a minute. Maybe if he sees what's out there, he'll realize how lucky he is to be inside with us."

Belinda jumped up. "I've got the flashlight," she said quickly. "I'll get your slicker from the living room." Fishface was making her so nervous, she couldn't sit in the same room with him any longer.

The moment she got into the living room, she knew something was wrong. There was an ominous sound of splashing water. Her flashlight picked up the puddle coming in under the front door. It seemed to double in size as she stood there and stared. She grabbed their slickers and the ten perfect shells off the card table and ran back into the kitchen.

"Granny May," she cried. "The water's coming in under the porch door."

"Now we're in for it," Granny May said. "Go upstairs and throw down all the towels you can find. Hurry, Belinda. Ed, you'd better stay right here. If the water's up over the porch, it must have filled up the back yard by now."

But he didn't answer. He unlocked the back door and yanked it open against the pull of the wind. The storm burst into the kitchen like a wild uninvited guest, knocking over the vase on the table and blowing out the candles. Bending down against the rain, Mr. Fletcher pushed out the screen door, dragging a terrified Fishface behind him. Then the doors slammed, and Belinda and Granny May were alone for a moment.

"I'd like to take this hurricane over my knee and spank it," said Granny May. "What a lot of noise and trouble it's making."

Despite herself, Belinda had to smile at the picture of Granny May spanking the storm like a bad little boy. She ran upstairs to get the towels.

"Here they come," Belinda called as she leaned over the

bannister and dropped one pile and then another, straight out of the linen closet.

"Never mind," Granny May yelled. "It's too late. Come down and we'll try to save some of what's in here."

They took off their shoes and sloshed around in the rising water, taking the pictures off the walls and the drawers out of Granny May's desk.

"Where is that Ed Fletcher now that we really need him?" Granny May said as she piled another chair on the couch. "All right, abandon ship. Let's take some food upstairs."

"Shouldn't we go over to Mrs. Greenstone's house?" Belinda said.

"Too late now, Belinda. I'm afraid we'd have to swim over, and I don't think this old lady has the strength. Now where is Ed and that blasted dog?"

Just then the kitchen door blew open again, and Mr. Fletcher reappeared. He pushed the door shut behind him and leaned against it, breathing heavily.

"Ed, where's the dog?" Granny May said.

"He's gone," he said. "One minute he was there, and then the leash was yanked out of my hand and I didn't see him again. The water's coming up so fast. He was just swept away."

"I'm sure he'll be all right," Belinda said, touching Mr. Fletcher's wet sleeve. "I bet he was swept right over to Mrs. Greenstone's house. She'll take him until the storm is over."

Mr. Fletcher put one hand over his eyes and began to cry. Granny May took his arm.

"Ed, we've got to get upstairs now. There's two feet of water in the living room, and it's begun to seep in here."

"My tools," he cried, suddenly. "I've got to get my tools."

He pulled away from the two of them and rushed into the dining room.

"What tools?" Belinda said, but Granny May did not answer. She was filling up a box with food.

"Take this upstairs, Belinda, and come down as quickly as you can for the next one."

They moved into the two bedrooms upstairs. Granny May lit the candles and set all the food in one corner on the book-shelves.

"There now," she said. "Just like home."

They both glanced at Mr. Fletcher, who had not said a word. He was sitting on the bed, staring out the window, one hand on his black briefcase. He looked so sad and lost that Belinda wanted to go up and hug him, but she didn't dare.

Every so often the house shook as a piece of floating debris crashed into it. The water was filled with all kinds of surprises: pieces of boats, mattresses, roofs of houses, furniture, clothing. On one of her trips to the bottom of the stairs to check the level of the water, Belinda saw a box of dolls floating by the window.

Late in the afternoon, in the middle of a game of gin rummy, Granny May said, "Listen, I hear the change. Here comes the hole in the doughnut."

Belinda put down her cards. The wind had subsided, and there was an eerie calm around the house. Belinda walked down the hall and looked out the back window. The yard had turned into a small pond, and she could just make out the door of the garage across the water. In one corner, where the fence connected to the wall of the garage, there was a pile of debris. She looked closer. Something was moving around on top of a table.

"Mr. Fletcher," she screamed. "Come here quickly. I see Fishface. He's alive. Hurry."

The two old people came racing down the hall.

"Where?" Mr. Fletcher said.

"There," Belinda said, pointing. "By the garage."

"I'm going to get him," Mr. Fletcher said.

"No you don't, Ed Fletcher. With that bum leg, you won't get beyond the back porch," Granny May said, grabbing the old man by the arm. "And if you were stranded out there, we couldn't save you. Fishface has done just fine up till now. He's in a protected spot. The storm will wear itself out soon."

While the two of them argued, Belinda turned back to the window. Fishface was pacing around and around on the table-top, as if trying to decide whether or not to jump.

"We can't leave him out there the whole time," Belinda cried. "I'll go."

She twisted away and ran down the stairs before Granny May could say no. The water in the kitchen was up to the seats of the chairs. The sight of it stopped her. Mr. Fletcher came down behind her. He was carrying a life preserver and a coil of rope.

"What's left of the wind is blowing in the right direction, towards the garage," he said as he put the life preserver over her

head and fastened it. He tied the rope around her waist, leaving a few feet to dangle. "As soon as you get a hold of his collar, tie this end of the rope to it, and I'll pull you both back. Your granny will be watching from upstairs, and if she thinks you're having any trouble, she'll yell at me to pull you back."

For a moment, Belinda wished she had never offered.

"He doesn't like me, Mr. Fletcher," she said. "What if he tries to bite me?"

"Then leave him," Mr. Fletcher said without looking at her.

They pushed their way through the water in the kitchen. He opened the door, and she launched herself quickly before she had time to get scared. The water felt cold at first. The hardest thing was trying to swim with the heavy life preserver, but as Mr. Fletcher had said, the current and the wind blew her in the right direction. A plastic box brushed her shoulder and floated away.

Halfway across the back yard, she put her feet down and, to her surprise, she touched ground. Then she half swam, half

walked to the corner. Fishface saw her and began to whimper,
pacing back and forth on his tabletop. As she drew closer, the
whining changed to a low growl.

"Now listen to me, you stupid dog, I'm not going to get near
you if you start that," she shouted. "I came all the way out here
to save you, and if you don't want to spend the rest of this hurricane out here, then you'd better just be quiet and listen." The
tone of her voice shut him right up, so she kept on talking to
him just that was as she pushed aside the garbage cans and the
chair that were bumping up against his table. "I hope you know
how to swim, Fishface, because if you don't, you're in big trouble." He let her tie the rope around his collar without a sound.

"All right," she yelled waving back at the house. "Let's go."

The rope tightened so quickly that it pulled her off her feet.
Fishface skidded off his table and into the water with a splash.
He soon recovered and was paddling up next to her, the rope
slack between them. At one point, a large piece of wood came
up between them and caught on the rope.

"Hold your breath," Belinda shouted as she pulled the rope down. The dog disappeared for a moment and came back up, spluttering, but free of the wood. After that, he seemed to get tired, because he paddled less energetically and slipped behind her.

The wind was rising again, and Belinda had a hard time keeping her head above the water and watching for obstacles at the same time. At last, she was back at the kitchen door, and Mr. Fletcher pulled them both inside with one enormous yank on the rope.

Granny May was waiting on the landing. "Well now," she said, folding Belinda into her arms. "Look what the storm swept in." When Belinda looked up, she saw tears in Granny May's eyes. Belinda began to cry too, now that she was safe inside. Mr. Fletcher put a towel around her and helped her upstairs to bed. She vaguely remembered Granny May changing her into her nightgown, and then she fell asleep.

♦ LIBRARY LINK ♦

*To find out more about Belinda's interesting summer on Fox Island, read all of the book* Belinda's Hurricane *by Elizabeth Winthrop.*

## Reader's Response

Would you have tried to save Fishface if you were Belinda? Explain your answer.

# Belinda's Challenge

## Checking Your Comprehension

1. How did Belinda feel about the approaching hurricane?
2. Why did Mr. Fletcher and Fishface come to stay with Granny May and Belinda?
3. What events showed that the storm was intensifying? How did you arrive at your answer?
4. Why did Mr. Fletcher take Fishface outside during the storm?
5. How do you know Mr. Fletcher cared about Fishface?
6. Describe Belinda's rescue of Fishface.

## Writing to Learn

**THINK AND PLAN**   Belinda, her grandmother, Mr. Fletcher, and Fishface survived the storm because they had food, supplies, and courage. If you knew your home stood in the path of a hurricane, how would you prepare for the storm? List the supplies you would assemble.

---

### HURRICANE EMERGENCY LIST

**food:** _____

**safety and health equipment:** _____

**light supply:** _____

**communication equipment:** _____

**books and games:** _____

---

**WRITE**   Use your emergency supply list. Make a plan to survive the hurricane and display it on your first draft of a hurricane safety poster.

# Harry's Drawings

## by Mary Riskind

*Learning to communicate well is always challenging. For Harry and his friends communicating involves learning the specific skills and techniques of sign language. Before Harry's story begins, the author explains some facts about sign language.*

# A Note to the Reader from Mary Riskind

I am a hearing person, but I grew up in a family with deaf parents. To communicate with my parents, I learned to talk with my hands before I learned to talk with my voice. The characters in this story are deaf, like my mother and father, and they are using sign language, just as we did at home. As you read this story, you will find that what Harry and his friends say to each other is not like everyday speech. One of the problems I discovered in writing about deaf children is that it is hard to translate sign language into English, so I would like to tell you a little bit about how I have done that here.

56

One of the things you will notice is that words in the dialogue sometimes are spelled out, or fingerspelled. In the manual alphabet each letter is represented by a particular hand-shape. Some of them look like the written letter: *O* and *C* are examples. But the letter *S* is made by a fist. You can say anything you want with the manual alphabet, but people usually fingerspell only at certain times: if there is no sign for a word; to say the proper name of a person or place, such as a city (although there are a few common signs for big cities like Chicago and Washington, D.C.); or to give emphasis to a word—a little like raising your voice.

AMERICAN

LIBRARY

ASSOCIATION

1981

Deaf people typically use some combination of signs and fingerspelling. A person who speaks sign language well can go as fast as (even faster than) you can say the same things out loud. Signs are what make it possible to go so fast.

There are different kinds of signs. Some signs act out, or pantomime, the ideas they are supposed to represent. Hold your first two fingers over your ear and wiggle them backward. Does that make you think of rabbit ears? You have just said the word *rabbit*. Some signs do not look at all like what they mean but they belong to groups of signs all made in a similar way. Let me give

you an example. Signs that have to do with being female (*mother, sister, daughter, aunt, girl*) are all made by touching the lower half of the face.

Some signs are initializations, made by shaking the first letter of the word, such as *g* for *green*. There are also signs deaf people learn, depending on where they grew up or go to school. For instance, I've noticed that people from different areas use a different sign for *candy*.

How you say a sign is important. Signs can change meaning if they are repeated, or if they are said slower or faster, or if you point the sign away from or toward yourself. You turn your hand away to say 'catch-him' and toward yourself to say 'catch-me.' Your facial expression is also part of making a sign. It should match the sign. If you frown as you form the sign for *pleased*

57

or *happy*, a deaf person would find you difficult to understand.

Sign language is very condensed, or telegraphic. Oftentimes word endings (*-s, -ly, -ed, -ing*) and little words (*is, am, are, has, had, I, the*) are omitted, and a single sign will do the work of two or more English words to communicate

an idea. In the dialogue you will also see many hyphenated words, like 'thank-you' and 'show-me.' These are words said by a single sign.

Word order in sign language often is not the same as its English translation. 'See before that finish' said in sign language becomes "I've already seen that before" in English. I wanted to give you a feeling for sign language, but without confusing you, so I stayed with English word order through most of the story, and sometimes I added little words or endings.

Sign language is changing today. My parents learned sign and they taught it to me the way Harry speaks in this story. But to help younger deaf people learn English more easily new signs are being developed and introduced. For example, there are now signs for the words *is, am,* and *are,* and their use is spreading.

I hope you enjoy getting to know Harry.

*Mary Riskind*

## Harry's Drawings

*It is the 1890s when Harry arrives at a Philadelphia school for the deaf to learn a trade. Harry, who loves to draw, carries with him his father's gift of special drawing supplies.*

After dinner Harry unpacked a pair of trousers and a couple of shirts from his locker and hung them on the hooks above his bed—he guessed he'd need them now that he was staying—and he collected his charcoal pencils and paper to take with him to study hour.

His friend Landis took a seat across from him at the table and nodded a greeting. Harry's head bobbed shyly.

He rolled the pencils between his fingers. They were smooth, well-balanced, better than the ones he usually had. His father must have been eager to please him. He folded and unfolded the knife. He whittled the end of one of the pencils to a fine point, and played with the shavings until they crumbled and scattered. Then he huddled over a sheet of the paper.

He rubbed the charcoal in short, even strokes. Soon the form of a building emerged, then out of that two long arms and a wide brick portico with stairs that swept around either side and met in front. A cobblestone walkway extended from the building through the trees to a high brick fence and iron gate. He penciled in the sign he remembered hanging in the front: THE BERTIE SCHOOL FOR THE DEAF.

Landis reached over for his attention. 'Jealous,' he said. 'You draw very good.' He made his signs small to escape the study proctor's notice.

Harry felt his ears burn. 'For my brother. Never saw school.'

'Can you draw something for me?'

'Maybe. What?'

'Anything. Think idea yourself.'

Harry hesitated. 'Will try.' He started once, discarded the paper, started again and discarded that piece, too. Suddenly he fell to work. When he was finished he kicked Landis's foot, then passed his picture under the table.

Landis examined the drawing in his lap. His face broke into a smirk. Landis gave the picture to his neighbor on the right and fingerspelled 'H-a-r-r-y.' The boy looked over, winked his approval, and passed it to the person next to him, and so on, until the paper traveled full circle round the table.

All of a sudden the study proctor swooped beside Landis and ripped the drawing out of his hands. 'Whose? Yours?' All eyes in the long room turned.

Landis declined to say anything. The rest sat rigid.

The proctor spied Harry's pencils and the small sheaf of paper. 'Yours.' She pursed her lips as if she'd tasted something bitter, and stabbed a finger at the sketch. It was an outrageous caricature of Mr. Thomas with a great walrus mustache and heart-shaped head. 'Study. Not play.' She scooped up the drawing materials and returned with them to her desk.

Harry looked desperately to Landis.

'Not worry,' Landis said. 'Lady not cross.'

Harry was not persuaded. He was miserable.

When the hour was finished, Landis and Harry walked together to the proctor's desk. 'New boy?' the proctor asked. 'Drawings very good.' She handed over Harry's art supplies but held back the pictures of Mr. Thomas and of the school. 'I keep pictures. Want show. What your name?'

'H-a-r-r-y B-e-r-g-e-r.' Harry's heart pounded. 'Pictures for brother.'

'Will give-back later.' She packed up her belongings, including the pictures. There was nothing for Harry to do but leave.

For the next few days Harry made it a practice to bury himself in the thick of the lunchroom crowd or any line, and Landis delivered his mail. He hoped if Mr. Thomas didn't see him he'd forget to be angry about the picture.

In time he'd nearly forgotten the drawing himself, so it came as a rude jolt one afternoon when Mr. Thomas strode directly to him in the print shop. 'Come,' he motioned and led the way to the corridor. Harry's stomach fluttered.

'B-e-r-t-i-e want see-you,' Mr. Thomas said. The flutter turned to cold fear.

Mr. Thomas accompanied him to the headmaster's office, ushered him to the overstuffed chair opposite Mr. Bertie, then gazed out the window.

Mr. Bertie reached in a drawer and placed two sheets of paper on the desk blotter. There were his drawings. The bloated walrus-face lay on top. He stiffened.

'Drawing perfect,' Mr. Bertie flourished. 'You like draw?'

'Yes. Since little,' Harry signed weakly.

'Who teach-you?'

'Mother. And myself,' he answered, confused. These weren't the kinds of questions he expected.

'Want learn more?'

Now he was truly confused. He didn't know what to say. Mr. Bertie repeated his question. Hesitant, he nodded yes.

Mr. Bertie leaned over his desk. 'Wonder maybe you change. No-more printing. Go to t-a-i-l-o-r-i-n-g. Study clothing design. Study much more drawing. Cutting. Sewing. Think you like?'

Harry began to relax. What he'd learned in the print shop so far was tedious, though he enjoyed reading the finished copy.

'Well?' Mr. Bertie prodded.

He didn't know about tailoring, except his mother did do mending and sewing for townspeople in Muncy. On the other hand, he knew he loved drawing. 'Try?' Harry said.

The elderly man beamed. 'Fine. Settled. Mr. Thomas lead-you now.' He spoke a few words to Mr. Thomas, then he rose and handed over the sketch of the school to Harry. He held on to the other one. 'Allow-me keep this? Face very funny.'

Harry looked to Mr. Thomas, who had stopped before the coat-closet mirror. He was giving the tips of his mustache a satisfied twist. Mr. Bertie winked at Harry.

Harry grinned.

When Harry arrived at the textile room, he was surprised to see mostly girls—there were none in the print shop—and a handful of the older boys, who he knew slept in the third-floor dormitory. A few people paused from their work and smiled or gestured hello.

A short, quick man wearing a pincushion strapped to his wrist and a green visor showed him to a slant-top desk beside the windows. 'Since first day, you look, try new things. To-morrow work. Any questions, ask—' He fingered the other pupils watching their exchange. 'I-f they not know, come see me.' And he was gone.

Harry hopped aboard the stool. The desk was arrayed with leads, pen points, holders, rulers, jars of ink, and other interesting items he didn't recognize. He reached first for a wood figurine. To his surprise it was flexible. The arms, the knees, the torso, bent. He twisted the form into a series of improbable positions—legs wrapped around the neck, crawling on all fours upside-down, or rolled into a ball.

A curly head grinned at him above the top of his board. The girl caught his eye. 'Silly,' he remarked, referring to the wood doll. 'What for?'

'Copy. Move any, how you want, then copy,' she said. 'Paper in drawer. Down right.'

In the drawer he found several kinds: heavy coarse sheets, satin smooth sheets, and thin translucent skins. He selected a pen point and holder and a piece of the heavy paper. After fumbling with the point, he finally jammed it into the cork handle. He was opening a jar of ink when the curly head peered over again.

'Shake first,' she said.

He shook. Black ink slopped out the sides and spattered on his fresh sheet of paper.

The girl laughed. 'No. No. Push-down-top first. Then shake. Better smooth paper for i-n-k. Rough good for black pencil,' she lectured.

Harry mopped up with a handkerchief. He was starting to feel irked with this know-it-all girl. He pointedly flipped the coarse paper clean side up and slid the edges under two thin slats hinged to the board. He wondered if she'd noticed he figured out how to hold the papers without her.

Then the pen dragged and ink oozed outward. The line he drew spread into a blotch. Phooey! The print shop was never like this.

The instructor stopped at Harry's table. 'Mistake.' He reached in the drawer and pulled out a smoother, harder sheet of paper. 'Best for i-n-k.' He whisked past.

Harry hunched down low, keeping his paper out of view of the curly-headed girl. He made a tiny mark with his pen. The ink behaved and stayed in its place. This was better. He unwound the figurine and molded it to resemble a person running; he sketched a front view first, then a side view.

'Good. Good. Perfect.' The instructor was at his side again. Harry sat a little straighter. The teacher gestured to the other side of his drawing board. 'A-g-n-e-s, show new boy sewing machine. And materials.' Agnes obediently climbed off her stool to stand next to him.

Agnes, Harry thought. His mother had an aunt named Agnes. He liked her pictures but he didn't like this Agnes.

Agnes stole a look at Harry's drawings. 'Nice,' she said. Harry scowled.

When Agnes led the way to the cutting tables, Harry loitered as far back as he could. The tables were heaped with fabrics. Agnes handed Harry several scraps. The material was soft, yet tightly woven and strong. It was finer than anything he had seen before.

'Man's coat, pants,' Agnes explained, 'for rich.' She extended the sign for 'rich' to suggest an awesome stack of money. It wasn't easy, but Harry managed not to smile.

Next she showed him to an empty machine. Agnes spun the wheel with her right hand. She pedaled the treadle and guided two pieces of material under the needle. 'Careful fingers. I-f needle in. Ouch.'

She halted a moment and reached for his hand. He pulled it away. She looked angry. 'Want show something.' He yielded reluctantly. She placed his hand on the sewing machine, then resumed her stitching. The machine hummed into his fingertips with the light rumble of a satisfied cat under his hand. He smiled in spite of himself.

'Now me,' he begged. Agnes moved over on the bench.

The machine spun a couple of times, then stopped abruptly. 'What wrong?' he asked.

'Feet.' Agnes showed him how to keep his feet in rhythm with the wheel.

He made one or two false starts, but at last he had it. His feet rocked back and forth, back and forth, while the sewing machine purred. They took turns working the treadle the remainder of the afternoon and Harry listened with his fingers.

'Feel wonderful! Feel wonderful!' he said.

♦ LIBRARY LINK ♦

*If you enjoyed "Harry's Drawings," you might want to read the entire book,* Apple Is My Sign, *by Mary Riskind.*

**R**eader's Response

Did you learn anything about people in this story? Explain.

# Harry's Drawings

## Checking Your Comprehension

1. What are some of the different kinds of signs used in sign language?
2. Why do you think Harry drew the caricature of Mr. Thomas?
3. Why was Harry surprised at Mr. Bertie's questions about his drawing?
4. What kind of person was Mr. Bertie? What clues in the story told you this?
5. If Agnes had not helped Harry on his first day at the tailor shop, what might have happened?
6. What did you enjoy most about the story?

## Writing to Learn

**THINK AND PLAN**   A scene from a story can be turned into "Reader's Theater" by rewriting it as a play script. In this scene from "Harry's Drawings," notice how the narrator helps tell what is happening.

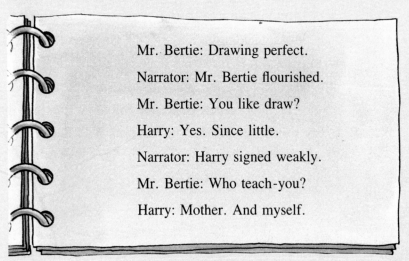

Mr. Bertie: Drawing perfect.

Narrator: Mr. Bertie flourished.

Mr. Bertie: You like draw?

Harry: Yes. Since little.

Narrator: Harry signed weakly.

Mr. Bertie: Who teach-you?

Harry: Mother. And myself.

**WRITE**   Find another scene from "Harry's Drawings." Write a "Reader's Theater" version of the scene you choose.

## How Writers Write

▲ The Greeks thought poets had to be inspired by one of the nine Muses, the goddesses of the arts.

Your teacher says that you are to write a story, and your first draft is due next week. What, you wonder, are you going to write about? Wouldn't it be wonderful to be like "real" authors? "Real" writers must never have any trouble writing, you think. The truth is that sometimes they do. They work very hard to think of ideas for their stories, and often they don't like what they have written. One famous writer, Isaac Bashevis Singer, whom you will read about in Unit 3, says, "The wastebasket is a writer's best friend. Mine is on a steady diet." Can't you just see him and his wastebasket overflowing with crumpled up papers from starting over and over to get his story just right?

Most writers have a special place and a special time for writing. Even if they don't have a great idea to write about, they still write. That's the only way to make a good idea come along sooner or later. Isaac Bashevis Singer writes for three hours every morning, in bed. As soon as he wakes up he begins to " . . . scribble immediately," as he says. In the afternoon, he types the parts he likes.

◄ A great deal of travel helped inspire many of Agatha Christie's mysteries.

Virginia Hamilton makes use of
family gossip and stories. ▶

Agatha Christie wrote mystery stories such as
*Murder on the Orient Express*. Getting a book started was the
hardest part for her. She would go to her room and stare at her
typewriter or bite on her pencils until she figured out exactly
what she wanted to write. Sometimes it took her a whole month
before her story really got going and became fun for her to do.

Where do writers get their stories? Many times it's from
listening to stories that other people in their families and neighborhoods tell. Virginia Hamilton, who wrote *The House of Dies
Drear*, used to listen to her parents and her aunts and uncles and
cousins tell stories and gossip about one another and even about
their ancestors. Now she uses those stories when she writes
her books.

In her books, Yoshiko Uchida uses folk tales she heard
when she was a little girl. These folk tales serve as the
basis for her stories.

Being a writer means listening for stories to tell.
It means finding a special time and place to write, and
doing a great deal of writing. And it means sticking with
an idea even if you fill a whole wastebasket before your
story is done. You can do those things. You can be a
"real" writer, too.

Mark Twain,
the author of
*Tom Sawyer*,
was another
writer who
found a
wastepaper
basket very
important! ▼

◀ Yoshiko Uchida is inspired by
folk tales from her childhood.

71

# I Hear America Singing

I hear America singing, the varied carols I hear,
Those of mechanics, each one singing his as it should
    be blithe and strong,
The carpenter singing his as he measures his plank or
    beam,
The mason singing his as he makes ready for work, or
    leaves off work,
The boatman singing what belongs to him in his boat,
    the deck-hand singing on the steamboat deck,
The shoemaker singing as he sits on his bench, the
    hatter singing as he stands,
The wood-cutter's song, the ploughboy's on his way in
    the morning, or at noon intermission or at
    sundown,
The delicious singing of the mother, or of the young
    wife at work, or of the girl sewing or washing,
Each singing what belongs to him or her and to none
    else,
The day what belongs to the day—at night the party of
    young fellows, robust, friendly,
Singing with open mouths their strong melodious songs.

Walt Whitman

# A Time to Talk

When a friend calls to me from the road
And slows his horse to a meaning walk,
I don't stand still and look around
On all the hills I haven't hoed,
And shout from where I am, "What is it?"
No, not as there is a time to talk.
I thrust my hoe in the mellow ground,
Blade-end up and five feet tall,
And plod: I go up to the stone wall
For a friendly visit.

Robert Frost

73

*When it comes to finding jobs and getting favors at home,*
*Martin's sister Marietta seems to have all the good luck.*

# A Paying Job

by Mary Stolz
from The Explorer
of Barkham Street

On a drizzly day late in March, Martin came in the house as the telephone started ringing. His mother, who had Saturday off from work but not Sunday, was home and upstairs running the vacuum, so Martin answered.

"Is Marietta there?" a woman's voice asked.

Might've known, thought Martin. "Just a sec," he said to the caller, putting the receiver on the hall table. "Mom!" he shouted.

"Hey, is Marietta anywhere around?" No answer. Just the steady, sort of irritable, hum of the vacuum. He climbed the stairs. "Mom, I said is Marietta here? Somebody's calling her."

Mrs. Hastings turned off the vacuum and shook her head. "She's taking a guitar lesson."

"*Guitar* lesson! Since when has she—"

"Later, Marty. I'm busy. Don't you think you'd better tell whoever it is, in case they're still waiting?"

Martin stumped down the stairs, scowling, picked up the receiver, and said, "You still there?"

"Just."

"Yeah. Well, I'm sorry. I had to ask my mother and she's upstairs, vacuuming."

"Is Marietta there or not? I really need to know."

"Not. I mean, she isn't. She's—she's out." He could not bring himself to say the other. Guitar lessons! He couldn't have a saxophone, but Marietta, just like that, was taking guitar lessons!

"Now what am I going to do?" the woman was saying.

"I could give her a message," Martin said, choking. Guitar lessons!

"Do you know when she'll be back?"

"Nope."

"Well, I guess that's that. I'll just have to cancel my appointment. Thank you—"

"Hey, just a minute . . . this's Mrs. Weaver, isn't it?"

"Yes. And you're Martin, of course."

"Right. And you wanted Marietta to baby-sit Ryan, huh?"

"Yes, only I want her right now. I have a dentist appointment, and I don't want to take Ryan out in this weather. He just got over a cold. I should have called Marietta sooner, but yesterday was so pleasant, I thought I'd be able to take him with me. And now this rain, and he'd have to sit around in the waiting room—"

From what he'd heard, Martin didn't think Ryan would be good at sitting around.

"I could come over," he said.

Silence.

Then Mrs. Weaver said, "Well, Martin—I wouldn't offend for the world, but—" She cleared her throat and stopped speaking.

"Mrs. Weaver," he said, "I don't know why nobody around here has noticed it, but I am—I'm not how I used to be. Always in trouble, I mean. I'm just about never in trouble anymore, if anybody'd take the trouble to look and find out."

"Now, Martin. Actually, I have noticed some improvement in you."

Well, whoopty-do, thought Martin. He said, "My Mom's home, if anything—not that there'd be anything, but just in case, she's here, and you're only six houses down the street, and I don't see why—"

"How old are you, Martin?"

"Thirteen. Marietta started baby-sitting, around the neighborhood, when she was thirteen."

"Fourteen, surely. I was the first person to use her, when Ryan was just two. She was fourteen."

"Guess I made a mistake," said Martin.

"Martin, tell me the truth—you've never baby-sat in your life, now have you?"

Martin took a chance on fact. He tried to recall what his sister had said the job entailed. "No, I never have. But I could do it easily, Mrs. Weaver. Really. Just read to him and play games and get his supper and bathe him and put him to bed—"

"Martin!" She was laughing. "It's the middle of the morning, and I'll only be gone a couple of hours. You'd just have to stay with him. A game or a book would be fine."

"Then I can do it?" he said happily.

"Well, if your mother's really there—"

For Pete's sake, he thought, I *said* she was, didn't I?

"—and if she says you can, why then—all right, let's give it a try."

Assuring her that he'd be there in two minutes, Martin bounded up the stairs to his mother with the news.

"Baby-sit?" she said. "I shouldn't think a boy—"

"Mom. That's sexist."

She smiled. "It is. Of course it is, and very wrong of me. Well, go along and yes, I'll be here, but I hope to heaven—"

"Nothing'll go wrong. It'll be fine. Oh, boy. I wonder how much Marietta makes." Thinking of his sister, he frowned. "What's this about guitar lessons? Where'd she get a guitar, I'd like to know. You never said anything about getting her a guitar, and I think it's rotten when I—"

"Marty! That Mrs. Zimmerman that she sits for, who's bringing up those two children of hers alone, *she* gave it to Marietta. She had a couple extra left over from when her husband died. He was a music teacher, and now she has his guitar school downtown. She heard Marietta plucking at the strings one day, to amuse the children, and gave her one."

"Just gave it to her? A guitar? Do you know what a guitar costs?"

"Yes. Marietta's lucky. She always has been. Mrs. Zimmerman is giving her lessons in exchange for baby-sitting time. Things do seem to fall into her lap, don't they?"

"Yeah," Martin said dully. "They sure do."

"Don't go feeling sorry for yourself, Martin. It's a terrible habit you have. And being envious of other people's luck. What good does it do?"

It does no good at all, Martin said to himself, walking down Barkham Street to the Weaver house. Still, he was often envious of other people. Of their looks, their luck, their superior position in life.

Martin didn't think he was the only one in the family that suffered from self-pity. Probably he'd inherited it. It had been handed down to him along with his father's nose and crooked front tooth.

Mrs. Weaver was already in her raincoat when he arrived. She looked him over critically. "Well, I hope I'm doing the right thing," she said.

Martin assumed a reliable expression and assured her that she was. "Where's Ryan?"

"Behind the sofa." She sighed. "He's put out that it's not to be Marietta." Apparently Ryan did not know Marietta's opinion of him. "Not that he has anything against you," Mrs. Weaver went on.

"Don't see how he could have. We haven't even been introduced. Ha-ha. No, really, Mrs. Weaver. I like kids. I get along with them fine. You go along. I'll get him out from behind that sofa, all right." This seemed to alarm her, so he added, "I'll lure him out, like. With a story," he added, inspired.

"Oh, you like to tell stories?"

Do I! thought Martin, but decided she might take that wrong, too. "I'll read him one. I see you have books right there on the table. No, you go and get your teeth fixed and don't worry."

"Tooth," she said, still wavering. "A little filling. Well." She walked over to the sofa, leaned across the top of it. "Come on, now, Ryan. Martin's here, and he wants to read to you. Won't that be nice? He can read you some of the *Noisy* books, all about Muffin." Silence from behind the sofa. "This is Marietta's brother, isn't that practically as good?" No sound. "Oh, dear," she said, turning away. "I guess I'll have to cancel after all, Martin. I'm sorry."

Feeling rejected, feeling really *hurt*, by a little kid that didn't know any better, Martin felt his face flush. That always happened when he felt humiliated, which made things worse because then people knew how he was feeling.

"That's okay," he said, swallowing hard. It had been a dumb idea anyway. Baby-sitting, for Captain Cook's sake. He didn't know any other guy who did that, so probably it was just as well that Ryan had—

Ryan's head came up from behind the sofa. "I don't care if you read to me," he said.

Martin glanced at Mrs. Weaver. "Does that mean I can? I mean, I should?"

"It means he'd like it. Ryan hasn't a notion of good manners. We're thinking of devoting the summer to teaching him the basics. Like please and thank you." She took up her umbrella and handbag. "Then it's all set?"

"Sure thing," said Martin, not nearly as confident as he'd been a few minutes ago. Well, there was always his mother. If the kid got out of hand, he'd yell for Mama. Oh boy, he thought. I hope I can stick it out for a couple of hours. There'd be no living with Marietta, if—

Just this once, he thought. Get through it this time, and then don't try such a dumb stunt again.

Mrs. Weaver kissed her son, who'd come right out into the living room, nodded to Martin, and said, "Don't let Greensleeves out."

"Okay. Who's Greensleeves?"

"Parakeet. In there—" She gestured toward the living room and in a moment was gone.

While the sound of her car dwindled away, Martin and Ryan stood eyeing each other.

"Cookies, I think," said Ryan.

"Huh?"

"I want some cookies."

Martin glanced at the clock on the mantel. 10:30 A.M. Marietta, he was pretty sure, had told him that the people left instructions, long lists of do's and don'ts, for their baby-sitters. They left telephone numbers for emergency purposes. Why hadn't Mrs. Weaver done these things for him? Probably, he decided, because she was in a hurry to get to the dentist. Probably because she figured it was just a couple of hours, so what the heck. Probably because she knew Martin's mother was on tap. Well, I'm not going to call and ask if this tyke can have cookies, he thought, and said, "Sure thing. In the kitchen?"

"Not in the bathroom."

"Wow. How old are you, Ryan?"

"Five."

"Five." Don't look me up when you're ten. "Okay, cookies. And then the books?"

Ryan didn't answer. He walked to the kitchen, got a pan of brownies from the sideboard and said, "You pour some milk."

Martin looked at the brownies. Homemade. That inner voice which everyone is supposed to have, but which rarely addressed itself to Martin, now just about shouted. Those brownies were not for morning consumption by Ryan and his sitter. Even if the sitter, who hadn't had anything like a brownie in weeks, found that his mouth was watering.

"Hey, now. Wait," he said. "Cookies—that's one thing. But these're made for a—a purpose. They're probably for your dinner tonight. You can't have them," he said, surprised at his own firmness.

Ryan reached a hand toward the brownies, his eye on Martin.

"I said no! Look, haven't you got some store cookies around? Your mother made the brownies, I bet, for a special treat. Probably you're going to have them with ice cream tonight. Come on, Ryan. It's too early for cookies anyway."

Ryan regarded him pensively, then withdrew his hand. "Okay. Let's read."

Martin experienced a true thrill of triumph.

Back in the living room, sitting together on the sofa, Greensleeves mute on his perch as a stuffed bird, he read the *Winter Noisy Book* and then the *Seashore Noisy Book*. Ryan had them all memorized and said the words along with him. He also pointed out each thing in each drawing. In the Seashore book, he put a finger on the whale and said, "I had a whale once."

"Followed you home, did he?"

Ryan grinned. "Most people say, 'Oh, a toy whale, Ryan, how nice.'"

"I know about these things."

"Did you ever have a whale?"

"Had a walrus. Not for long, of course."

"What did you feed him?"

"Pizza. What did you feed your whale?"

"Chocolates."

They grinned at each other, and then Martin went on reading. Later, they put Ryan's electric tracks together. It was a tricky job. When you got one section of tracks firmly snapped together, another section detached itself. Still, working together, they finally had a respectable length of looping track with overhead spans supported by small building blocks. Then they ran the two race cars, one blue and one red, around the course at breakneck speed.

Martin couldn't believe it when he heard the front door open and Mrs. Weaver's voice calling, "Ryan and Martin, where are you?"

Martin, at the door of Ryan's room, said, "Here. We've been having a race. Is your tooth all right?"

"It's fine. How did things go?"

"Fine. I mean, we had a good time, didn't we, Ryan?"

Ryan nodded. "Come on back and play, Marty," he said impatiently.

"I can't, Ryan. I have to get home for lunch." Ryan's lower lip pushed out and it was plain that he was preparing to yell. "Ryan! I'll come see you again, real soon. Okay?"

"How soon?"

"Very. No, I mean it. I will. I want to."

"My goodness," said Mrs. Weaver. "You certainly made a hit."

"He's nicer than Marietta," said Ryan. "I like him lots better."

Filled with pleasure, but trying to sound offhand, Martin said, "Ryan's a good kid. We got along just great."

"You know what I miss," Mrs. Weaver said, getting out her wallet. "I miss the word 'children.' All you ever hear now is 'kid.' *Kids.* Whatever happened to 'child' and to 'children,' do you suppose?"

"Gobbled by goats?" Martin said, and gave a snort of self-admiration.

Mrs. Weaver smiled at him. "Maybe. But I think it's too bad. Well, here you are, Martin." She handed him three dollars.

Martin stepped back. "No. No, really, Mrs. Weaver. I don't want it. I had a swell time, and I didn't have anything else to do anyway—"

"Martin. You'll have to work it out with Marietta, but it's obvious that Ryan's happy in your company, so when I need a sitter, I'd be glad to call on you, only not if you refuse payment. This is a business arrangement. Evenings, it's two dollars an hour."

"Gee. Well, thanks. That's swell. See you, Ryan."

"You remember, Marty! You *said*."

"I'll remember."

Walking home, he felt good, really great. Just like that he'd won a little kid's heart. *Child's* heart. And here he was, practically guaranteed a paying job. If Marietta didn't kick up a stink. What with the other jobs she got, not to mention guitars thrown in and lessons, he didn't see how she could begrudge him Ryan. He felt so good he forgot to resent the guitar.

And who knew, maybe the Weavers had a saxophone tucked away in the attic, going to waste . . .

"Can't tell," he said to himself cheerfully, and went into his house whistling.

## ♦ LIBRARY LINK ♦

*Does Martin continue to baby-sit for Ryan? Does he ever get a saxophone? You can find out by reading the rest of* The Explorer of Barkham Street *by Mary Stolz.*

**R**eader's Response

Do you think that Mrs. Weaver made the right choice in allowing Martin to baby-sit for Ryan? Explain your answer.

# A Paying Job

## Checking Your Comprehension

1. How did Martin feel when he found out that his sister was taking guitar lessons? Why did he feel this way?
2. Why did Martin want to baby-sit for Ryan?
3. Why do you think Martin wouldn't accept money from Mrs. Weaver for baby-sitting for Ryan that day? How did you reach that conclusion?
4. List three reasons why Martin felt good walking home from Mrs. Weaver's house.
5. Suppose Ryan had not gotten along so well with Martin. How do you think the story might have turned out?
6. Which scene seemed most real to you during Martin's baby-sitting time with Ryan? Explain your answer.

## Writing to Learn

**THINK AND ANALYZE** Martin has a problem; he feels sorry for himself. He reaches a solution; he learns to be successful at something. What steps, or events, in the story, led Martin to his solution? Copy and complete the problem/solution steps below. Use as many steps as you need.

Solution: *Martin is a success at baby-sitting.*

Step 3:

Step 2:

Step 1: *He talks Mrs. Weaver into letting him try baby-sitting.*

Problem: *Martin feels sorry for himself.*

**WRITE** Have you ever had a problem to solve? Draw problem/solution steps showing the steps you took to reach a solution. Then write a paragraph telling about your problem and how you solved it.

*Here are some ways to make money—and to have fun at the same time!*

# Jobs for You

## by Larry Belliston & Kurt Hanks

### ～ Kids: Read This First! ～～～～～

How do you decide which job will work best for you? The first thing to do is find out what kind of work the job involves. Will you be selling, or making something, or cleaning up, or what? What do you most enjoy doing? Do you think you'd like to talk to someone about buying Christmas cards, or would you rather change the oil in a car? Would you prefer to clean out a basement, or to make dried flower arrangements? The first and most important question you can ask in picking a job is: *What would I most enjoy doing?*

Picking a job is like buying a suit of clothes—you don't just grab the first thing that's handy. Instead you

**As a tutor, you are able to earn while another student learns.**

look at the sizes, think about colors, compare prices. Only after finding a style that you like—and only after you're sure you have a good fit—do you pay for the clothes and wear them to school.

It's not hard to find a suit of clothes you're satisfied with. And it's not hard to find a job that will be fun. All you have to do is take a good look before you leap!

## Tutoring

If you have information other people would like to have, or if you have a skill or expertise you could share, maybe you could sell it by being a tutor. But you must know something well enough to teach it to another person.

Here are some things you might teach:

- games—chess, checkers, video games, backgammon, billiards
- sports—basketball, baseball, volleyball, football, tennis, racquetball, Ping-Pong, bowling, badminton
- singing
- dancing
- art
- musical instruments—guitar, drums, piano, recorder, violin, saxophone, and others
- the three Rs—reading, writing, 'rithmetic
- science
- penmanship
- foreign languages
- sewing

The key is to find something you know about that others *wish* they knew about. And then teach them.

To get started as a tutor, try one or all of these approaches:

- talk to your teacher and principal to see if they know of students who could benefit from your help
- talk to the community education people to see if they'll let you set up a class
- spread the word among your friends and ask them to spread the word farther
- distribute flyers in the areas where there are lots of kids
- put a notice in your school newspaper

Most of your tutoring will be done at home (either yours or the student's), and you'll probably tutor only one person at a time. Check with your teacher or principal to see how much tutors in your area charge.

## Washing Cars

People can go down to the car wash, put in a handful of quarters, and get a clean car for three dollars or so. But if it's a cold day, it's a miserable job. And if the day is nice, they have to wait in line forever. Sometimes it's just easier to drive a dirty car.

And then there's the interior—after they use the car wash, they still have to worry about cleaning the inside. It's all a nuisance for some car owners. They wish their cars were clean, but it's hardly worth the hassle

**Teaching tennis provides good exercise.**

**Washing cars produces fast results.**

**Teaching piano may be a rewarding experience.**

to dust the dash, wash the floor mats, and vacuum the crumbs from yesterday's oatmeal cookies.

Then you come to the door. You offer to wash their car for a couple of dollars, which is just about what they'd have to pay at the car wash—and you're bringing the job to them. You'll clean the interior for another dollar. Some people won't be interested—they'd rather have a dirty car. And some will think you're an angel from heaven.

Take your own hose, in case they don't have one. Also take rags, bucket, sponges, towels, window washer, and, if you can, a friend! If you can take a portable vacuum, your work will go even more smoothly.

## Spring Clean-up

Help people clean their houses, basements, attics, and garages.

No matter how hard people try, their houses still get dirty! They can clean every day, but by the time the year is over, there's still more cleaning to do than they have time for.

**A good way to get new business is to call on neighbors and tell them about your cleaning services.**

Then spring rolls around. It's warmer outside, so people can open the windows of their houses, fling the doors open, and really dig in and push the dust *out*. But spring cleaning is a big job, and many people put it off, just because it takes so much time and energy. Those people would welcome a little help, and they'd be willing to pay for it.

But your help doesn't just have to come in the spring. The need for cleaning is year-round. And you can get paid for making it happen.

### How to Do It

Find customers. There are plenty of homeowners and apartment dwellers who would love to get some

**Working outdoors is a good advertisement for your services.**

assistance in their cleaning. They just don't know where to go for help.

A little advertising will go a long way. Make up some flyers and pass them out to people you know. You'll almost certainly get a bunch of calls asking you to come help.

Once you've worked for someone it will be easier for you to get a job with them the next time. To keep the business going year-round, you'll need to do some follow-up work. Call the people you've worked with and ask if you can come help again. Pass out flyers again, until gradually you've built up enough customers that you have steady work.

Set a price. The best way to charge for your services is by the

**A flyer is one way to advertise.**

house. Check around in your area to find out how much people get paid for cleaning services. You can charge a little less than adults are getting paid. But don't expect to get more than the current minimum wage.

Learn to clean. Much of your work will be under the direct supervision of the homeowner. In

**Neighbors may hire you to move large items for them.**

that case, he or she will tell you what to do and how to do it. Your task will be to follow directions carefully.

But sometimes you'll be put in a room and told to go at it. "Clean this room," you'll be told, and that's about it.

Before you go, then, it's a good idea to know how to clean a room. Learn how to effectively pick up junk, how to clean floors, how to clean windows, how to clean walls. Learn

how to handle your equipment and supplies.

Books that answer a lot of questions on cleaning are easy to find in the library or at the bookstore. Be sure you do your homework before you try to go out and clean someone else's house.

Some of the jobs you may be asked to do:

- wash walls and windows
- sweep, mop, wax, or scrub hardwood, tile, or linoleum floors
- clean carpets, beat rugs
- clean the bathroom—toilets, tub, sink, walls
- pick up, sort through, or haul junk outside
- clean out closets and drawers
- polish silverware
- wash dishes
- dust furniture
- rearrange furniture

### Shining Shoes

Take a shoeshine kit from door to door, or office to office, and shine people's shoes.

Most people like their shoes to look clean, shiny, and well-groomed. But they often don't have time to keep their shoes shined.

If a neighborhood child came to the door and offered to shine shoes for a reasonable price, many people would take him or her up on it in a minute. It's a valued service, one that many people can't get easily elsewhere.

### How to Do It

Put together a kit. Start by making a shoe-shine kit. Buy a few basic kinds of polish. Buy colored as well as clear, for standard leather as well as patent-leather shoes. Paste polish is generally better than liquid.

Buy some paste applicators. You can get cloths or little brushes for this purpose. The brushes usually work better.

Get some brushes to buff up the shoes, and some soft cloths to give them the final polish.

Learn how to shine shoes. If you can, find a shoeshine stand in your area and go and just watch for a while. See how the shiner does his job.

Here are the basic steps to shining shoes:

1. Clean the shoe off, removing mud and dust.
2. Put the polish on with a little brush. Don't put it on too thick, just a thin layer over the part of the shoe you need to polish. Don't get any polish on the bottom of the shoe. It will come off where it's least wanted, on the customer's carpet, for example.
3. Get out your polishing brush and rub with light strokes back and forth over the area you polished. The brush will take off the excess polish and put a shine on the shoe.
4. Get out the polishing cloth and give the shoe a final rubdown.

Set a price. When you visit the shoeshine stand, make a note of how much the shiner is charging. You can charge a comparable price. But you're giving added service by going to the customers. Keep that in mind when you set your price. Also keep this in mind: If you can tell the customer you're cheaper than other local shoe shiners, you'll probably pick up more business.

Find customers. Your customers are all over the place. All you have to do is let them know you're available.

Shining shoes is one business that you may do in your own home.

A shoe shine person delivers finished work to neighborhood businesses.

Probably the best approach is to go around your neighborhood with your kit. Tell people what you're up to and see if they'll let you shine their shoes on the spot. You can:

1. Shine them right on their feet. (Be sure to take some newspaper with you to protect the floor.)
2. Take them out onto their porch and shine them there.
3. If it's cold, take them home and deliver them later in the day. Be prepared by taking a sack with you. Be sure to check to see how long you can keep them.

Another place you might try is an office building. Get permission from the office manager first. Then pull out your newspapers and go to work.

Set a schedule. Once you have happy customers, keep them happy. The best way is to get on a regular schedule for shining the shoes. Agree to come back the last Saturday morning of the month, or every other Wednesday evening, or every Monday just after school.

## A Success Story

With some kids, shoe shining is more than just a job—it's a rung on their ladder to success. A boy once set up a shoeshine outside a bank. The bank people didn't mind, and it was a good place to meet customers.

One day the bank president came by. "I could use a shine," he said. "Can you do a good job really quick?"

"You bet," the boy said enthusiastically. He got out his shoe-shining stuff and had the job done in nothing flat. The bank president was so pleased that he gave the boy a nice tip.

A week later, the president stopped again. "You did a great job, but with these feet of mine it just didn't last. How about another shine?"

The boy grinned and shined the shoes again—and got another tip.

The banker started to make it a habit after that. Every week he'd have the boy shine his shoes. And every week he'd offer a generous tip.

After working by the bank for a couple of years, the boy closed down his shoeshine stand and went to work someplace else. But here's the best part: years later the boy decided to make a career of banking.

He went back to the same bank to see if they would offer him a job. The bank president was still there—and he remembered his old shoeshine boy.

"I know your work," the president said. "And I believe it would be to this bank's advantage to have a person like you working here."

When you do good work, people notice. And they're usually willing to let you work for them again.

◆ LIBRARY LINK ◆

*If you are interested in reading stories about kids with clever ideas for jobs, try* Eddie, Incorporated *by Phyllis Naylor and* Kid Power *by Susan Pfeffer.*

## Reader's Response

What do you think about getting a job and earning some spending money?

# Jobs for You

## Checking Your Comprehension

1. In this article, you've read about different kinds of jobs. Name three of them.
2. How did the boy who shined the bank president's shoes get a job at the bank?
3. How can you decide what kind of job is for you?
4. Describe three ways you can look for customers.
5. What might be another title for this article? How did you arrive at this suggestion?
6. What do you think was the best advice in this article? Explain why.

## Writing to Learn

**THINK AND DISCOVER**   Would you like to earn extra spending money? Draw a picture. Show yourself doing a job you enjoy.

**WRITE**   Write a ''Help Wanted'' ad for someone to do the kind of work you showed in your drawing. Explain in detail what skills or qualifications this job requires.

**READING FICTION**

*Comprehension:*

# *Predicting Outcomes*

After Martin's disastrous introduction to Ryan, did you ever think that Martin would succeed in "A Paying Job"? Once you saw how well Martin was getting along with Ryan, you probably guessed that Martin's first job would turn out well. Predicting outcomes may help you gain a better understanding of the characters and events in a story.

To predict the outcome of a story, think about the characters and review the events that have already occurred. These are called story clues. Next, think about similar experiences that you have had. These are called experience clues. Then, make your predictions based on both kinds of clues. Continue reading and evaluate your predictions.

## *Predicting Outcomes in "A Paying Job"*

By going through the thinking process just explained, you could have predicted one of the major decisions in "A Paying Job." Mrs. Weaver telephoned to ask Martin's sister, Marietta, to baby-sit for little Ryan. Martin told Mrs. Weaver that Marietta could not baby-sit.

At this point, a story clue and an experience clue could have helped you form a prediction about what Martin would do next. You knew from the story that Martin wanted to earn money. You also know from experience that many thirteen-year-olds want more spending money and that they are old enough to baby-sit. Putting these clues together, you could have predicted that Martin would offer to baby-sit for Ryan. The diagram shows the clues used to make this prediction.

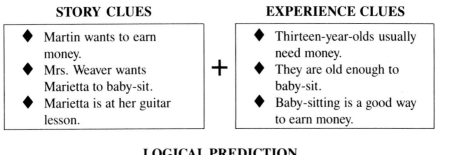

| STORY CLUES | | EXPERIENCE CLUES |
|---|---|---|
| ◆ Martin wants to earn money.<br>◆ Mrs. Weaver wants Marietta to baby-sit.<br>◆ Marietta is at her guitar lesson. | **+** | ◆ Thirteen-year-olds usually need money.<br>◆ They are old enough to baby-sit.<br>◆ Baby-sitting is a good way to earn money. |

**LOGICAL PREDICTION**

Martin will offer to baby-sit.

## Using What You Have Learned

Read the end of the story. Then make logical predictions by answering the questions that follow.

> Walking home, he felt good, really great. Just like that he'd won a little kid's heart. *Child's* heart. And here he was, practically guaranteed a paying job. If Marietta didn't kick up a stink. What with the other jobs she got, not to mention guitars thrown in and lessons, he didn't see how she could begrudge him Ryan. He felt so good he forgot to resent the guitar.
>
> And who knew, maybe the Weavers had a saxophone tucked away in the attic, going to waste. . . .

**1.** Do you think that Mrs. Weaver will ask Martin to baby-sit again?
**2.** How do you think Marietta will respond if this should happen?
**3.** How do you think Martin will feel about Marietta's response?

## As You Read

After you have read two or three pages of the next story, "Keplik, the Match Man," stop and predict the outcome. Then continue reading to find out whether your prediction was correct.

*There are some people who take such pride in a hobby that they become completely absorbed in it. One such person is Mr. Keplik.*

# the
# Match Man

## by Myron Levoy

There once was a little old man who lived in a big old tenement on Second Avenue. His name was Mr. Keplik and he had once been a watchmaker. In the window of his tiny watch-repair shop he had put up a sign that read: WHEN YOUR WRIST WATCH WON'T TICK, IT'S TIME FOR KEPLIK. Keplik loved watches and clocks and had loved repairing them. If a clock he was repairing stopped ticking he would say to himself, "Eh, eh, eh, it's dying." And when it started ticking again he would say, "I am *gebentsht.*[1] I am blessed. It's alive."

Whenever an elevated train[2] rumbled by overhead, Keplik would have to put down his delicate work, for his workbench and the entire shop would shake and vibrate. But Keplik would close his eyes and say, "Never mind. There are worse things. How many people back in Lithuania wouldn't give their right eye to have a watch-repair shop under an el train in America."

While he worked Keplik never felt lonely, for there were always customers coming in with clocks and watches and complaints.

[1]gebentsht (gə bensht')

[2]elevated train: a train that runs above street level, also called "the el"

"My watch was supposed to be ready last week," a customer would say. "I need my watch! Will you have it ready by tonight, Keplik?"

And Keplik would answer, "Maybe yes, maybe no. It depends on how many el trains pass by during the rush hour." And he would point his finger up toward the el structure above.

But when Keplik grew very old, he had to give up watch repairing, for he could no longer climb up and down the three flights of stairs to his apartment. He became very lonely, for there were no longer any customers to visit him and complain. And his hands felt empty and useless for there were no longer any gears or pivots or hairsprings or mainsprings to repair. "Terrible," said Keplik, to himself. "I'm too young to be old. I will take up a hobby. Perhaps I should build a clock out of walnut shells. Or make a rose garden out of red crepe paper and green silk. Or make a windmill out of wooden matchsticks. I'll see what I have in the house."

There were no walnuts and no crepe paper, but there were lots and lots of burned matchsticks, for, in those days, the gas stoves had to be lit with a match every time you wanted a scrambled egg or a cup of hot cocoa. So Keplik started to build a little windmill out of matches.

Within a month's time, the windmill was finished. Keplik put it on his kitchen table and started to blow like the east wind. The arms turned slowly, then faster, just like a real windmill. "I'm gebentsht," said Keplik. "It's alive."

Next, Keplik decided to make a castle, complete with a drawbridge. But the matches were expensive; he would need hundreds and hundreds for a castle. So he put a little sign outside his apartment door, and another in his window:

USED MATCHSTICKS BOUGHT HERE. A PENNY FOR FIFTY.
IF YOU HAVE A MATCHSTICK, SELL IT TO KEPLIK.

The word spread up and down the block very quickly, and soon there were children at Keplik's door with bags and boxes of used matches. Keplik showed them the windmill on the kitchen table and invited them to blow like the east wind. And Keplik was happy, because he had visitors again and lots of work for his hands.

Day after day, week after week, Keplik glued and fitted the matches together. And finally the castle stood completed, with red and blue flags flying from every turret. The children brought toy soldiers and laid siege to the castle, while Keplik pulled up the drawbridge.

Next, Keplik made a big birdcage out of matches, and put a real canary in it. The bird sang and flew back and forth while the delicate cage swung on its hook. "Ah ha," said Keplik. "The cage is alive. And so is the canary. I am double gebentsht."

Then he made little airplanes and jewelry boxes from matchsticks and gave them to the boys and girls who visited him. And the children began calling him "the Match Man."

One day, Keplik decided that it was time for a masterpiece. "I am at my heights as an artist," Keplik said to himself. "No more windmills. No more birdcages. I am going to make the Woolworth Building. Or the Eiffel Tower. Or the Brooklyn Bridge. Eh . . . eh . . . but which?"

And after much thought, he decided that a bridge would be better than a tower or a skyscraper, because if he built a bridge he wouldn't have to cut a hole in the ceiling. The Brooklyn Bridge would be his masterpiece. It would run across the living room from the kitchen to the bedroom, and the two towers would stand as high as his head. "For this I need matches!" Keplik said aloud. "Matches! I must have matches."

And he posted a new sign: MATCH FOR MATCH, YOU CANNOT MATCH KEPLIK'S PRICE FOR USED MATCHES. ONE CENT FOR FIFTY. HURRY! HURRY! HURRY!

Vincent DeMarco, who lived around the corner, brought fifty matches that very afternoon, and Cathy Dunn and Noreen Callahan brought a hundred matches each the next morning. Day after day, the matches kept coming, and day after day, Keplik the Match Man glued and fixed and bent and pressed the matches into place.

The bridge was so complicated that Keplik had decided to build it in separate sections, and then join all the sections afterward. The bridge's support towers, the end spans, and the center span slowly took shape in different parts of the room. The room seemed to grow smaller as the bridge grew larger. A masterpiece, thought Keplik. There is no longer room for me to sit in my favorite chair. But I must have more matches! It's time to build the cables!

Even the long support cables were made from matchsticks, split and glued and twisted together. Keplik would twist the sticks until his fingers grew numb. Then he would go into the kitchen to make a cup of coffee for himself, not so much for the coffee, but for the fact that lighting the stove would provide him with yet another matchstick. And sometimes, as he was drinking his coffee, he would get up and take a quick look at his bridge, because it always looked different when he was away from it for a while. "It's beginning to be alive," he would say.

And then one night, it was time for the great final step. The towers and spans and cables all had to be joined together to give the finished structure. A most difficult job. For everything was supported from the cables above, as in a real bridge, and all the final connections had to be glued and tied almost at the same moment. Nothing must shift or slip for a full half hour, until the glue dried thoroughly.

Keplik worked carefully, his watchmaker's hands steadily gluing and pressing strut after strut, cable after cable. The end spans were in place. The center span was ready. Glue, press, glue, press. Then suddenly, an el train rumbled by outside. The ground trembled, the old tenement shivered as it always did, the windows rattled slightly, and the center span slid from its glued moorings. Then one of the end cables vibrated loose, then another, and the bridge slipped slowly apart into separate spans and towers. "Eh, eh, eh," said Keplik. "It's dying."

Keplik tried again, but another train hurtled past from the other direction. And again the bridge slowly slipped apart. I am too tired, thought Keplik. I'll try again tomorrow.

Keplik decided to wait until late the next night, when there would be fewer trains. But again, as the bridge was almost completed, a train roared past, the house shook, and everything slipped apart. Again and again, Keplik tried, using extra supports and tying parts together. But the bridge seemed to enjoy waiting for the next train to shake it apart again.

Ah me, thought Keplik. All my life those el trains shook the watches in my hands, down below in my shop. All my life I said things could be worse; how many people back in Lithuania wouldn't give their left foot to have a watch-repair shop under an el train in America.

But why do the el trains have to follow me three flights up? Why can't they leave me alone in my old age? When I die, will there be an el train over my grave? Will I be shaken and rattled around while I'm trying to take a little well-deserved snooze? And when I reach heaven, will there be an el train there, too, so I can't even play a nice, soothing tune on a harp without all this *tummel*, this noise? It's much too much for me. This is it. The end. The bridge will be a masterpiece in parts. The Brooklyn Bridge after an earthquake.

At that moment, another el train roared by and Keplik the Match Man called toward the train, "One thing I'll *never* do! I'll never make an el train out of matches! Never! How do you like *that*!"

When the children came the next afternoon, to see if the bridge was finished at last, Keplik told them of his troubles with the el trains. "The bridge, my children, is *farpotshket.*[3] You know what that means? A mess!"

The children made all sorts of suggestions: hold it this way, fix it that way, glue it here, tie it there. But to all of them, Keplik the Match Man shook his head. "Impossible. I've tried that. Nothing works."

Then Vincent DeMarco said, "My father works on an el station uptown. He knows all the motormen, he says. Maybe he can get them to stop the trains."

---

[3]farpotshket (far puch′kət)

Keplik laughed. "Ah, such a nice idea. But not even God can stop the Second Avenue el."

"I'll bet my father can," said Vincent.

"Bet he can't," said Joey Basuto. And just then, a train sped by: raketa, raketa, raketa, raketa, raketa. "The trains never stop for anything," said Joey.

And the children went home for dinner, disappointed that the bridge made from all their matchsticks was farpoot . . . farbot . . . *whatever* that word was. A mess.

Vincent told his father, but Mr. DeMarco shrugged. "No. Impossible. Impossible," he said. "I'm not important enough."

"But couldn't you *try*?" pleaded Vincent.

"I know *one* motorman. So what good's that, huh? One motorman. All I do is make change in the booth."

"Maybe he'll tell everybody else."

"*Assurdità*[4]. Nonsense. They have more to worry about than Mr. Keplik's bridge. Eat your soup!"

But Mr. DeMarco thought to himself that if he did happen to see his friend, the motorman, maybe, just for a laugh, he'd mention it. . . .

Two days later, Vincent ran upstairs to Keplik's door and knocked. *Tonight* his father had said! Tonight at one A.M.! Keplik couldn't believe his ears. The trains would stop for his bridge? It couldn't be. Someone was playing a joke on Vincent's father.

But that night, Keplik prepared, just in case it was true. Everything was ready: glue, thread, supports, towers, spans, cables.

A train clattered by at five minutes to one. Then silence. Rapidly, rapidly, Keplik worked. Press, glue, press, glue. One cable connected. Two cables. Three. Four. First tower finished. Fifth cable connected. Sixth. Seventh. Eighth.

[4]assurdità (u soor'dē tä')

110

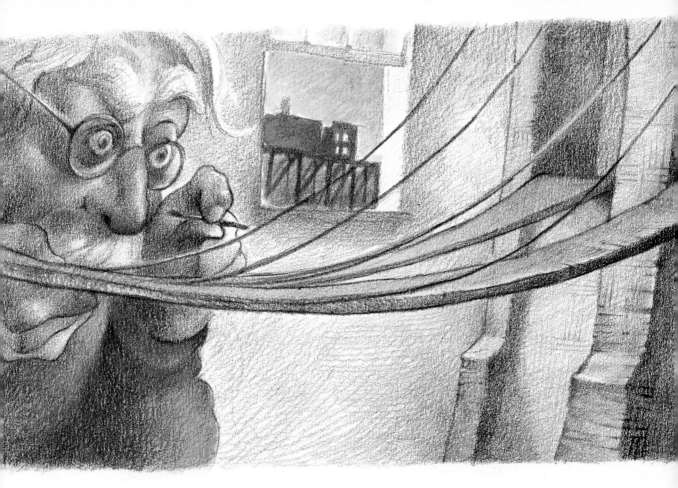

Other tower in place. Now gently, gently. Center span in
position. Glue, press, glue, press. Tie threads. Tie more
threads. Easy. Easy. Everything balanced. Everything supported. Now please. No trains till it dries.

The minutes ticked by. Keplik was sweating. Still no
train. The bridge was holding. The bridge was finished.
And then, outside the window, he saw an el train creeping
along, slowly, carefully: cla . . . keta . . . cla . . . keta . . .
cla . . . keta . . . cla . . . keta . . . Then another, moving
slowly from the other direction: cla . . . keta . . . cla . . .
keta . . . .

And Keplik shouted toward the trains, "Thank you, Mister Motorman! Tomorrow, I am going to start a great new
masterpiece! The Second Avenue el from Fourteenth Street
to Delancey Street! Thank you for slowing up your trains!"

And first one motorman, then the other, blew his train whistle as the trains moved on, into the night beyond. "Ah, how I am gebentsht," said Keplik to himself. "In America there are kind people everywhere. All my life, the el train has shaken my hands. But tonight, it has shaken my heart."

Keplik worked for the rest of the night on a little project. And the next morning, Keplik hung this sign made from matches outside his window, where every passing el train motorman could see it:

## ◆ LIBRARY LINK ◆

*The story of Keplik is from* The Witch of Fourth Street and Other Stories *by Myron Levoy. Look for it at the library.*

## Reader's Response

How would you feel about having Keplik as a friend? Explain your answer.

# Keplik, the Match Man

## Checking Your Comprehension

1. What was the setting for this story?
2. Keplik stopped working but took up a hobby. How were the two activities alike? How were they different?
3. At what point in the story did it seem that Keplik might not finish his masterpiece? How did you identify this part of the story?
4. How did Keplik complete his project?
5. Imagine a different hobby for Keplik. What situation might Keplik get into with this new hobby?
6. What do you think was Keplik's biggest problem in building his masterpiece?

## Writing to Learn

**THINK AND CREATE**   What kind of sign do you think Keplik will make *after* he finishes the Second Avenue el from Fourteenth Street to Delancey Street? Review below some of the signs Keplik made in the past.

**WRITE**   Draw the sign Keplik might make after he finishes the el. On it, write the message you think he will write on his sign.

# PHILBERT PHLURK

*written by Jack Prelutsky*
*illustrated by Victoria Chess*

The major quirk of Philbert Phlurk
was tinkering all day,
inventing things that didn't work,
a scale that wouldn't weigh,
a pointless pen that couldn't write,
a score of silent whistles,
a bulbless lamp that wouldn't light,
a toothbrush with no bristles.

114

He built a chair without a seat,
a door that wouldn't shut,
a cooking stove that didn't heat,
a knife that couldn't cut.
He proudly crafted in his shop
a wheel that wouldn't spin,
a sweepless broom, a mopless mop,
a stringless violin.

He made a million useless things
like clocks with missing hands,
like toothless combs and springless springs
and stretchless rubber bands.
When Phlurk was through with something new,
he'd grin and say with glee,
"I know this does not work for you,
but ah! it works for me."

# READING
## AND STUDYING

*Study Skill:*

# Taking Notes

**I**magine that you have to write a newspaper story about jobs for young people. How might you begin the assignment? The article "Jobs for You" would be a good starting point. You could read the article and take notes to help you organize the information. Read the following paragraph from "Jobs for You" about starting a shoeshine business.

> Start by making a shoeshine kit. Buy a few basic kinds of polish. Buy colored as well as clear, for standard leather as well as patent-leather shoes. Paste polish is generally better than liquid. Buy some paste applicators. You can get cloths or little brushes for this purpose.

Now look at the notes you might take about this paragraph.

Make a shoeshine kit: ———————————— | head |

- buy polish
- buy both clear and colored polish
- paste is better than liquid
- get cloths or little brushes

| list supporting details |

Whenever you read a selection in which there are many facts and ideas, taking notes can help you understand and remember what you read. Not only can you use notes to write an article, you can also use them when you study.

## Steps for Taking Notes

1. Skim the selection. List the boldfaced heads and subheads. They usually state the main ideas. Leave space under each of those items so you can list any supporting details.
2. Read the entire passage. Look for details that support the main ideas. They can often be found in the topic sentence of each paragraph. For each main idea, ask yourself, "What kind of details would support the main idea?" Then look to see if you can find them. You will probably want to include these details in your notes.
3. Write down the key words and phrases in your own words. Using your own words will help you to understand and remember what you have read.

## Using What You Have Learned

Take notes in list form on the following passage from "Jobs for You." Follow the steps for taking notes.

### Spring Clean-up—How to Do It

Find customers. There are plenty of homeowners and apartment dwellers who would love to get some assistance in their cleaning. They just don't know where to go for help.

A little advertising will go a long way. Make up some flyers and pass them out to people you know. . . .

To keep the business going year-round, you'll need to do some follow-up. Call the people you've worked with and ask if you can come help again.

# The Brooklyn Bridge:

## EMILY'S TRIUMPH

### by Charnan Simon

*In the mid-1800s, many doors were closed to women. But when something was important to Emily Warren, she didn't give up. Emily found a way to open doors for herself.*

Emily Warren Roebling was a person to be reckoned with. As a girl growing up in Cold Spring, New York, she would lean out her bedroom window, see the busy, hurrying Hudson River, and think about all the places that it visited.

Emily could only yearn to visit these places herself. It wasn't easy for girls to go places in America in the middle of the nineteenth century, not by themselves, at any rate.

Emily first found this out when it came to her education. Emily was good in math, languages, and history. When she finished the convent school in Georgetown, D.C., she wanted to study further.

Her older brother Gouverneur said it was out of the question. Gouverneur had been head of the family since Emily's father died in 1859. He always decided family matters. He said she had gone to school long enough.

Emily thought that was nonsense. But Gouverneur was thirty and she was sixteen, and in the 1850s sixteen-year-old girls didn't argue with their thirty-year-old brothers. Instead, Emily kept on studying by herself—even going so far as to borrow some of Gouverneur's own army engineering books!

When the Civil War began, Gouverneur was a major general in the Union Army. Emily wanted to help her country, too. In the spring of 1864 she visited her brother's Army Corps' camp on the banks of the Potomac River.

She firmly told Gouverneur that she wanted to be a nurse. She reminded him that Clara Barton and her Red Cross workers needed all the help they could get. She appealed to him on the grounds that she was another Warren who wanted to fight for the Union cause.

But her brother wouldn't listen. He thought a field hospital was no place for a respectable young woman. Emily fumed on the train ride home. She couldn't go against her brother's decision, though she thought it was unfair.

## Emily learns about bridge building

During her short stay at the Army Camp, Emily had met a young lieutenant named Washington Roebling. Gouverneur had described him as one of his best engineers, a young man with a good head on his shoulders. Emily thought so, too. She had enjoyed talking to Lieutenant Roebling more than anyone she'd ever met. He seemed to enjoy talking with her, too. In fact, six weeks

**Emily Warren, twenty years old at the time of this photograph, was determined to learn all she could about bridge building.**

after they had met, he asked Emily to marry him. They were married on January 18, 1865.

After the Civil War, Washington was discharged from the Army. The young couple headed immediately for Kentucky to join Washington's father, John Roebling. He was a brilliant engineer who was now building the world's longest single-span bridge over the Ohio River.

Emily had heard a lot about Washington's father, and how he had carefully raised Washington to be his partner. Now she was glad of the hours she'd stolen to read Gouverneur's engineering books. It helped her understand what Washington was talking about— and sometimes it seemed that all he *did* talk about was bridges!

# The Brooklyn Bridge begins

For two years Washington and his father worked on the Ohio River Bridge. Then, in the spring of 1867 came the big news the Roeblings had been waiting for. After years of debate, the New York legislature had authorized the building of a bridge over the East River from New York to Brooklyn. The Chief Engineer of this bridge was to be John Roebling.

It was the beginning of a hectic time for Emily and Washington. First they made a year-long trip to Europe, so Washington could study how bridges were built there. Washington especially wanted to learn more about the new method of digging bridge foundations in *pneumatic caissons*. A pneumatic caisson was a huge, waterproof box that opened on the bottom. After a caisson was placed in a river, air was pumped in to drive the water out. The caisson was weighted down so it rested on the river bottom, and men worked inside it to dig out the foundation for the bridge towers.

Emily shared Washington's excitement over the bridge he was going to build. There would be two towers for the bridge, one on the Brooklyn side, and one on the New York side. Each tower would have to be dug deeply enough to rest on solid bedrock. Only then would the towers be secure enough to hold up the weight, 5,000 tons, that would be suspended between them.

Most bridges were supported by piers, but this would be a suspension bridge. Cables strung between the towers would have to support the full weight of the roadway.

The roadway had to be stiff enough not to shake. For this, girders and trusses were necessary, as well as stays above and below the floor of the road. To further strengthen the 1600-foot-long bridge, Washington decided to use steel instead of iron wire. Only the Roebling Wire Company itself could be counted on to produce the high quality steel wire needed.

Emily and Washington came home from Europe with much new information about building bridges—and with a newborn son, named John Augustus Roebling II after his grandfather. The next few months were busy ones. Washington and his father still had to convince doubters that a suspension bridge this size could be built. Emily listened and offered suggestions, but mainly she took care of her family.

Everything seemed to be going smoothly. The doubters had been silenced, and money—over five million dollars—had been raised to start construction. The engineers had begun surveying locations for the Brooklyn tower. Then disaster struck. A ferry boat hit the pier where John Roebling was standing and badly crushed his foot. Two weeks later, on July 22, 1869, the Chief Engineer was dead.

There wasn't time to mourn. Washington knew that it was up to him to realize his father's dream. Several weeks later came the official word— Washington Roebling would succeed his father as Chief Engineer.

Now Washington and Emily committed themselves completely to the bridge. Final plans had to be made,

Newspaper illustrations from 1870 show the caisson in detail. *Left,* men wait for pressure within the caisson to be equalized. *Right,* workers enter the bottom hatchway leading to the caisson.

machines and materials purchased, and workmen and assistant engineers hired. Finally, on January 2, 1870, the construction began on the Brooklyn tower.

First, the giant caisson had to be built and placed in the river. The caissons depended on air pressure inside the box being great enough to keep water from rushing in around the bottom. Sometimes workers could suffer a bad reaction to the pressure—a painful and sometimes fatal reaction known as the "bends," or "caissons disease."

Washington made sure everyone was careful when working in the caisson. Slowly, slowly, the work proceeded despite many setbacks.

Several times fire threatened to destroy the caisson. Once it nearly flooded. Emily watched proudly as the Brooklyn tower gradually rose seventy-five feet above the river.

By the spring of 1872, work could start on the New York tower. The Brooklyn caisson rested on bedrock at forty-four feet. The New York caisson would have to go down to seventy-eight feet. This called for greater air pressure inside the caisson—and the first cases of the bends occurred. Three men died that spring—and one early summer afternoon Washington Roebling was carried out of the New York caisson unconscious.

*Left,* men in the caissons broke up rocks and boulders found on the river bottom. *Right,* fragments were then hauled to a water shaft where they were lifted to the surface by a clamshell scoop.

## Emily oversees the construction of the bridge

For weeks Washington drifted in and out of consciousness, while Emily did all she could to nurse him to health. When it became obvious that Washington would remain an invalid, he began feverishly writing exact directions for finishing the bridge. If he couldn't supervise the work himself, at least he could spell out precisely what was to be done! All winter he worked, but when spring came he despaired. He told Emily he would have to resign as Chief Engineer, because he was unable to work on the site of the bridge.

Immediately Emily asked to become his assistant. She told him she could visit the bridge site for him and do what was needed to finish the bridge. Washington wearily reminded her she was not an engineer. He felt that, in any case, women didn't belong at construction sites. But Emily had lived with the bridge for five years and wasn't ready to give it up. She finally convinced her husband, and they both continued work on the Brooklyn Bridge.

For weeks Emily pored over Washington's engineering books, just as she'd pored over Gouverneur's so many years before. She studied Washington's plans for building the anchorages, for stringing the cables, and for suspending the spans. She learned how to determine the stress various materials could stand and how to read and understand bridge specifications. Then she set out.

At first she acted as Washington's messenger. She carried his instructions to the workers and relayed their messages back to him. But soon that wasn't enough. Emily had to start making judgments about men and materials on the spot. She smoothed the way between city officials and rival engineers. She dealt with dishonest contractors and corrupt politicians who saw the bridge as a means of making personal fortunes.

Every day she made critical decisions about the specifications and stability of the bridge—and more than once stopped substandard materials from being built into it. She visited the construction site two or three times each day. At home she worried about so many visitors coming to see Washington. Emily spoke with each caller herself, so carefully and skillfully that they felt honored to speak with her instead. An editorial of the day called Emily the "chief engineer of the work,"

admired and respected by everyone connected with the bridge.

Perhaps Emily's most triumphant moment was on December 11, 1881, when she led the way across the newly completed floor system of the bridge. It was a glorious feeling to walk from Brooklyn to New York on a bridge that *she* had helped construct!

Or perhaps her greatest triumph took place in 1882, when Emily became the first woman to speak before the American Society of Civil Engineers. There she defended her invalid husband's ability to continue as Chief Engineer. In an age when the idea of a woman engineer was laughed at as unthinkable, Emily won a standing ovation!

Finally, on the sun-washed morning of May 24, 1883, the opening of the Brooklyn Bridge was officially celebrated. On the Brooklyn side, Emily Roebling and many officials started toward the bridge. On the Manhattan side, the President of the United States, Chester A. Arthur, led the ceremonial march to Brooklyn. Then the President officially opened the span to traffic. Thousands of well-wishers cheered the bridge as the Eighth Wonder of the World. Later, Abram S. Hewitt, the

Observers such as the man shown above often watched the construction of the Brooklyn Bridge from a temporary slat-floored footbridge. Also shown in this photograph are the steel deck beams that formed the base for the bridge roadway.

main speaker, hailed both John and Washington Roebling as the geniuses behind the bridge.

Hewitt concluded his remarks by saying, ". . . One name, which may find no place in the official records, cannot be passed over here in silence . . . The name of Mrs. Emily Warren Roebling will thus be inseparably associated with all that is admirable in human nature, and with all that is wonderful in the constructive world of art."

Yes, Emily Warren Roebling was a person to be reckoned with!

### ◆ LIBRARY LINK ◆

*For enjoyable stories about nineteenth-century girls and women as adventurous as Emily, read* Little Women *by Louisa May Alcott and* Lucy Makes a Match *by Patricia Beatty.*

### Reader's Response

What do you admire most about Emily Warren Roebling? Explain your answer.

# The Brooklyn Bridge:
# EMILY'S TRIUMPH

## Checking Your Comprehension

1. What did Emily do about her education in spite of her brother's refusal to let her continue her studies?
2. Why was working inside the caisson dangerous?
3. Name three ways in which Emily contributed to the building of the bridge.
4. Which event do you think was Emily's greatest triumph? How did you choose this event?
5. Why did the author say Emily Warren Roebling was "a person to be reckoned with"?
6. If Washington had not become ill, how might Emily's life have been different?

## Writing to Learn

**THINK AND REMEMBER** Emily accomplished a small miracle because she was an unusually talented and dedicated person. Name three people you know who are able to do difficult things.

**WRITE** Share the accomplishments of one of the people you chose. Write a brief biography, and tell about a challenging problem that your friend or relative solved.

127

## Literature:
# Characterization

**O**ne day you're waiting in the lunch line, and suddenly Celeste bumps into you. Milk goes flying across the tray, into your macaroni, and all over your shoes. The lunch line lady glares. Celeste doesn't even apologize; she rushes past and runs out of the cafeteria.

"That's not like her," you think. Or maybe you're thinking, "That's just like her. She never looks where she's going."

How you would react depends on what kind of person you think Celeste is. It would depend on how she usually acts. You get to understand people through clues that you see time and time again. The clues come from what people say and how they act.

## Understanding Characters

Characters are the people an author creates in a story, play, or poem. You can understand characters the same way you understand people—through clues in what they say and what they do. Sometimes that's easy. In the poem "Philbert Phlurk," for example, Philbert Phlurk's "major quirk" is that he invents useless things. All those silly inventions are clues to his character. Another clue comes at the end of the poem, when you hear how satisfied Phlurk is with his work, even if everyone else finds it foolish.

In "The Emperor and the Kite," you meet the tiny daughter of the emperor. The story emphasizes her smallness at first. Once her father is imprisoned, though, you see other characteristics. She is clever. She is brave, for she helps her father despite the nearness of the enemy. She is loyal, for she returns day after day to the same spot, out of love.

## Believable Characters

Most characters in literature are more complicated—and therefore more believable—than Princess Djeow Seow and Philbert Phlurk. Sometimes it's hard to know what the clues to their personalities mean. These clues are there, though, so that you can understand characters just as you understand your friends. In fact, understanding characters can help you understand your friends.

Take Leigh Botts in "Letters to Mr. Henshaw." The story is in the form of a diary; you learn about Leigh from what he says. You also learn about him from his reports of what other people say to him or about him. For instance, he says that the librarian stopped him in the hall to tell him she had Mr. Henshaw's newest book. The incident shows that he really is an eager reader.

What else do you know about Leigh Botts? He wants to be a writer. He tries hard. When he comes up with the story about the wax man driving the truck across the desert, you learn that he takes criticism well. Instead of getting upset, he understands why Mr. Henshaw doesn't like his wax man. "A character in a story should solve a problem or change in some way," Mr. Henshaw advises, and Leigh realizes that his wax man can't do either.

You also learn that Leigh notices everything around him. He notices the rings on Mrs. Badger's forefingers. He notices the hawks on the telephone wires. He notices how good the truckload of grapes smelled in the sun. His awareness of detail is consistent with his ambition to be a writer. "You made me feel what it was like to ride down a steep grade with tons of grapes behind me," Mrs. Badger says when she calls Leigh Botts an "author."

## Read and Enjoy

As you read "Working with Al," think about the two characters you meet, Sarah Ida and Al. What do you learn about their personalities in the story?

*A summer job is important to Sarah Ida, but so are the things she begins to learn about herself.*

# WORKING WITH

## by Clyde Robert Bulla

*Sarah Ida Becker is spending the summer with her Aunt Claudia because Sarah Ida's mother is ill. Sarah Ida feels lonely, unhappy and bored so she decides to find a summer job. Al is the only person in town who will hire a ten-and-a-half-year-old girl. He agrees to give Sarah Ida a job helping him at his shoeshine stand.*

Aunt Claudia was waiting on the porch. "Sit down," she said, when Sarah Ida came up the steps. "I want to talk to you."

Sarah Ida sat in the porch swing.

"You must never do this again," said Aunt Claudia. "You must always let me know where you're going. Do you understand?"

"Yes," said Sarah Ida.

"Where have you been?"

"On the avenue."

"What were you doing?"

"Looking for a job. And I found one."

"You found one?"

"Yes, I did."

"Where?"

"On Grand Avenue. Working for the shoeshine man."

"*Who?*"

"Al Winkler, the shoeshine man."

Aunt Claudia looked dazed. "How did you know him?"

"I didn't know him. He had a 'Help Wanted' sign and I stopped."

"Al Winkler," said Aunt Claudia, as if she were talking to herself. "I remember him so well. He came to the library when I worked there. He hadn't gone to school much, and he wanted to learn more. I helped him choose books." She asked, "Does he want you to work at his stand?"

"He said to talk to you about it."

"Do you want to work for him?" asked Aunt Claudia.

"I told you, I want some money of my own."

"This might be a good way to earn some," said Aunt Claudia.

"You *want* me to shine shoes on Grand Avenue?"

"If it's what you want to do," said Aunt Claudia.

131

Sarah Ida started down the steps. Aunt Claudia didn't call her back. There was nothing for her to do but go.

She found Al sitting in one of his chairs.

"What did she say?" he asked.

"She said yes."

"You want to start now?"

"I don't care," she said.

He opened a drawer under the platform and took out an old piece of cloth. "Use this for an apron. Tie it around you."

She tied it around her waist.

A man stopped at the stand. He was a big man with a round face and a black beard. He climbed into a chair and put his feet on the shoe rests.

"How are you, Mr. Naylor?" said Al.

"Not bad," said the man. "Who's the young lady?"

"She's helping me," said Al. "She needs practice. You mind if she practices on you?"

"I don't mind," said Mr. Naylor.

Al said to Sarah Ida, "I'm going to shine one shoe. You watch what I do. Then you shine the other one."

He took two soft brushes and brushed the man's shoe.

"That takes off the dust," he said. "Always start with a clean shoe."

He picked up a jar of water with an old toothbrush in it. With the toothbrush he sprinkled a few drops of water on the shoe.

"That makes a better shine." He opened a round can of brown polish. With his fingers he spread polish on the shoe.

"Now you lay your cloth over the shoe," he said. "Stretch it tight—like this. Pull it back and forth—like this. Rub it hard and fast. First the toe—then the sides—then the back."

When he put down the cloth, the shoe shone like glass. He untied the man's shoelace. He drew it a little tighter and tied it again.

He asked Sarah Ida, "Did you see everything I did?"

"Yes," she said.

"All right. Let's see you do it."

She picked up the brushes. She dropped one. When she bent to pick it up, she dropped the other one. Her face grew hot.

She brushed the shoe. She sprinkled the water.

"Not so much," Al told her. "You don't need much."

133

She looked at the brown polish. "Do I have to get this on my fingers?"

"You can put it on with a rag, but it's not the best way. You can rub it in better with your fingers."

"I don't want to get it on my hands."

"Your hands will wash."

She put the polish on with her fingers. She shined Mr. Naylor's shoe. She untied his shoelace, pulled it tight, and tried to tie it again.

Al tied it for her. "It's hard to tie someone else's shoe when you never did it before."

Mr. Naylor looked at his shoes. "Best shine I've had all year," he said. He paid Al. He gave Sarah Ida a dollar bill.

After he had gone, she asked Al, "Why did he give me this?"

"That's your tip," said Al. "You didn't earn it. He gave it to you because you're just getting started."

"Will everybody give me a dollar?" she asked.

"No," he said, "and don't be looking for it."

Others stopped at the stand. Sometimes two or three were there at once. Part of the time Sarah Ida put polish on shoes. Part of the time she used the polishing cloth.

Toward the end of the day she grew tired. She tried to hurry. That was when she put black polish on a man's brown shoe.

The man began to shout. "Look what you did!"

"It's not hurt," said Al. "I can take the black polish off. Sarah Ida, hand me the jar of water."

She reached for the jar and knocked it over. All the water ran out.

"Go around the corner to the filling station," Al told her. "There's a drinking fountain outside. Fill the jar and bring it back."

Sarah Ida brought the water. Al washed the man's shoe. All the black polish came off.

"See?" he said. "It's as good as new."

"Well, maybe," said the man, "but I don't want *her* giving me any more shines."

He went away.

Sarah Ida made a face. "He was mean."

"No, he wasn't," said Al. "He just didn't want black polish on his brown shoes."

"Anyone can make a mistake," she said.

"That's right. Just don't make too many." He said, "You can go now." He gave her a dollar. "This is to go with your other dollar."

"Is that all the pay I get?"

"You'll get more when you're worth more," he said. "You can come back tomorrow afternoon. That's my busy time. Come about one."

She didn't answer. She turned her back on him and walked away.

In the morning she told Aunt Claudia, "I'm going to the drugstore."

"Aren't you working for Al?" asked Aunt Claudia.

"Maybe I am, and maybe I'm not," said Sarah Ida.

In the drugstore she looked at magazines. She looked at chewing gum and candy bars. None of them seemed to matter much. Her money was the first she had ever worked for. Somehow she wanted to spend it for something important.

She went home with the two dollars still in her pocket.

She and Aunt Claudia had lunch.

"If you aren't working for Al," said Aunt Claudia, "you can help me."

"I'm going to work," said Sarah Ida. Working for Al was certainly better than helping Aunt Claudia.

She went down to the shoeshine stand.

"So you came back," said Al.

"Yes," she said.

"I didn't know if you would or not."

Customers were coming. Al told Sarah Ida what to do. Once she shined a pair of shoes all by herself.

They were busy most of the afternoon. Her hair fell down into her eyes. Her back hurt from bending over.

Late in the day Al told her, "You've had enough for now. You can go. You got some tips, didn't you?"

"Yes," she said. "Do you want me to count them?"

"No. You can keep them. And here's your pay." He gave her two dollars. "And I want to tell you something. When you get through with a customer, you say 'thank you.' "

"All right," she said.

"One more thing. You didn't say yesterday if you were

coming back or not. This time I want to know. Are you coming back tomorrow?"

"Yes," she said.

"Come about the same time," he said. "I'm going to
bring you something."

What he brought her was a white canvas apron. It had
two pockets. It had straps that went over her shoulders and
tied in the back. There were black letters across the front.

"Why does it say 'Lane's Lumber Company'?" she
asked. "Why doesn't it say 'Al's Shoeshine Corner'?"

"Because it came from Lane's Lumber Company," he
said. "Fred Lane is a friend of mine, and he gave it to me."

It was nothing but a canvas apron. She didn't know why
she should be so pleased with it. But it was a long time since
anything had pleased her as much. She liked the stiff, new
feel of the cloth. The pockets were deep. She liked to put her
hands into them.

That night she thought about the apron. She had left it locked up at the stand. She almost told her mother and father about it in the letter she wrote them. She had promised to write twice a week—to make Aunt Claudia happy. But she didn't think they would care about her apron. All she wrote was:

Dear Mother and Father,
    I am all right. Everything is all right here.
It was hot
today. Good-by,
         SARAH IDA

She didn't tell Aunt Claudia about her apron. She didn't feel too friendly toward Aunt Claudia.

There were times when she didn't even feel too friendly toward Al.

There was the time when she shined an old man's shoes. He paid her and went away.

Al said, "I didn't hear you say 'thank you.'"

"He didn't give me any tip," she said. "The old stingy-guts."

They were alone at the stand. Al said, "What did you call him?"

"Old stingy-guts," she said. "That's what he is."

"Don't you ever say a thing like that again," said Al in a cold, hard voice. "He didn't have to give you a tip. Nobody has to. If he wants to give you something extra, that's his

138

business. But if he doesn't, that's his business, too. I want to hear you say 'thank you' whether you get any tip or not."

It scared her a little to see him so angry. She didn't speak to him for quite a while.

But that evening he said, as if nothing had happened, "I could use some help in the morning, too. You want to work here all day?"

"I don't know," she said.

"You can if you want to. Ask your aunt."

She started home. On the way, a boy caught up with her. His arms and legs were long, and he took long steps. He looked ugly, with his lower lip pushed out. He asked, "What are you doing working for Al?"

She walked faster. He kept up with her. "How much is he paying you?"

"I don't see why I should tell you," she said.

"You've got my job, that's why."

The light turned green, and she crossed the street. He didn't follow her.

All evening she thought about what the boy had said. In the morning she asked Al about it.

"Was he a skinny boy?" asked Al. "Did he have light hair?"

"Yes," she said.

"That was Kicker."

"His name is *Kicker*?"

"That's what he called himself when he was little. Now we all call him that. He's my neighbor."

"What did he mean when he said I had his job?"

"I don't know. Once I asked him if he wanted to work for me. He said he did. Then he never came to work. He didn't want the job, but I guess he doesn't want you to have it, either."

"Maybe he changed his mind," she said. "Maybe he wants to work for you now."

"Maybe," said Al. "I'll have a talk with him. I don't think you'll see him any more."

Every evening, after work, Sarah Ida was tired. But every morning she was ready to go back to Shoeshine Corner. It wasn't that she liked shining shoes, but things *happened* at the shoeshine stand. Every customer was different. Every day she found out something new.

Some things she learned by herself. Like how much polish to use on a shoe. A thin coat gave a better and quicker shine. Some things Al told her. "When a customer comes here, he gets more than a shine," he said. "He gets to rest in a chair. When you rub with the cloth, it feels good on his feet. When you tie his shoelaces a little tighter, it makes his shoes fit better. My customers go away feeling a little better. Anyway, I *hope* they do."

One warm, cloudy afternoon, he said, "We might as well close up."

"Why?" she asked. "It's only three o'clock."

"It's going to rain. Nobody gets a shine on a rainy day."

He began to put away the brushes and shoe polish. She helped him.

"Maybe you can run home before the rain," he said. A few big drops splashed on the sidewalk. "No, too late now."

They sat under the little roof, out of the rain.

"Hear that sound?" he said. "Every time I hear rain on a tin roof, I get to thinking about when I was a boy. We lived in an old truck with a tin roof over the back."

"You *lived* in a truck?"

"Most of the time. We slept under the tin roof, and when it rained, the sound put me to sleep. We went all over the South in that truck."

"You and your mother and father?"

"My dad and I."

"What were you doing, driving all over the South?"

"My dad sold medicine."

"What kind?"

"Something to make you strong and keep you from getting sick."

"Did you take it?"

"No. I guess it wasn't any good."

She had never heard him talk much about himself before. She wanted him to go on.

"Was it fun living in a truck?"

"Fun? I wouldn't say so. Riding along was all right. Sometimes my dad and I stopped close to the woods, and that was all right, too. But I never liked it when we were in town selling medicine. Dad would play the mouth harp, and he made me sing. He wanted me to dance a jig too, but I never could."

She tried to imagine Al as a little boy. She couldn't at all. "Why did he want you to sing and dance?" she asked.

"To draw a crowd. When there was a crowd, he sold medicine. We didn't stay anywhere very long. Except once. We stayed in one place six months. My dad did farm work, and I went to school."

He told her about the school. It was just outside a town. The teacher was Miss Miller. The schoolhouse had only one room.

"There was this big stove," he said, "and that winter I kept the fire going. Miss Miller never had to carry coal when I was there."

"Did you like her?" asked Sarah Ida. "Was she a good teacher?"

"Best teacher I ever had. Of course, she was just about the *only* one. I hadn't been to school much, but she took time to show me things. Do teachers still give medals in school?"

"Sometimes. Not very often."

"Miss Miller gave medals. They were all alike. Every one had a star on it. At the end of school you got one if you were the best in reading or spelling or writing or whatever it was. Everybody wanted a medal, but I knew I'd never get one because I wasn't the best in anything. And at the end of school, you know what happened?"

"What?"

"She called my name. The others all thought it was a joke. But she wasn't laughing. She said, 'Al wins a medal for building the best fires.' "

"And it *wasn't* a joke?" asked Sarah Ida.

"No. She gave me the medal. One of the big boys said, 'You better keep that, Al, because it's the only one you'll ever get.' "

"And did you keep it?"

He held up his watch chain. Something was hanging from it—something that looked like a worn, old coin.

"That's what you won?" asked Sarah Ida.

He nodded.

"That's a medal?" she said. "That little old piece of tin?"

She shouldn't have said it. As soon as the words were out, she was sorry.

Al sat very still. He looked into the street. A moment before, he had been a friend. Now he was a stranger.

He said, "Rain's stopped. For a while, anyway."

He slid out of his chair. She got up, too.

"I—" she began.

He dragged the folding door across the stand and locked up.

"Go on. Run," he said. "Maybe you can get home before the rain starts again."

She stood there. "I didn't mean what you think I did," she said. "That medal—it doesn't matter if it's tin or silver or gold. It doesn't matter *what* it's made of, if it's something you like. I said the wrong thing, but it wasn't what I *meant*. I—"

He had his back to her. She didn't think he was listening. She said, *"Listen* to me!"

He turned around. "You like ice cream?"

"Yes," she said.

"Come on. I'll buy you a cone."

She went with him, around the corner to Pearl's Ice Cream Shack.

"What kind?" he asked.

"Chocolate," she said.

They sat on a bench inside the Shack and ate their chocolate cones.

"It's raining again," he said.

"Yes," she said.

Then they were quiet, while they listened to the rain. And she was happy because the stranger was gone and Al was back.

## ◆ LIBRARY LINK ◆

*Do you want to know what happens to Sarah Ida after the summer is over? You can find out by reading the entire book* Shoeshine Girl *by Clyde Robert Bulla.*

## Reader's Response

During the summer, Sarah Ida gets to know Al by working with him. Is Al the kind of boss for whom you would like to work?

## *Writing an Explanation*

In this unit you met characters who did work that was important to them. For people who love what they do, like Keplik, the reward doesn't come from the money earned. The reward comes from the pleasure of doing a job well.

Now you will write an explanation for your classmates of one kind of work that interests you. Explain why it interests you.

### *Prewriting*

Before you begin writing, make a cluster like the one below. Write five different kinds of work that interest you. Then draw a box around the circle in the center.

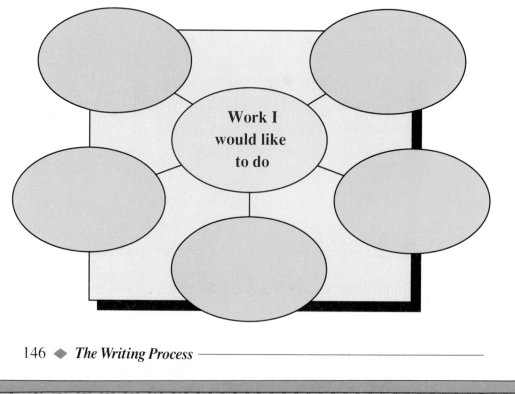

**Work I would like to do**

Now answer the following questions. Your answers will give you more information about the job that interests you.

♦ What kind of work would you most want to do?

♦ Whom would you want to work with?

♦ Where would you work?

♦ When would you work?

*Writing*

Get ideas from both your answers and your cluster. Use the ideas to write two paragraphs explaining what kind of work you would most like to do. Try to give an idea of some of the talents and abilities that the work would require. Then explain why you chose that kind of work.

*Revising*

Read what you have written. Are your sentences and paragraphs organized in an order that makes sense? Have you explained your ideas clearly?

*Proofreading*

Correct spelling, grammar, and punctuation errors. Then make a neat copy of your essay.

*Publishing*

Make a class booklet called *The Joy Is in the Doing*.

# WORKING TOGETHER

## *Creating an Advertisement for a Job*

**I LIKE KIDS!**

Thirteen-year-old boy who gets along very well with children will baby-sit. Available: Monday-Thursday, 3:00-5:00 P.M. Friday and Saturday evenings. Reasonable hourly rates. Call Martin at 555-1234.

The characters in this unit discovered special things about themselves through the work they did. After Martin's experience with Ryan in the story "A Paying Job," Martin could have placed this advertisement in his local newspaper. Notice how the first line of the ad gets the reader's attention. The ad also tells the kind of job Martin wants, when he is available, and how to contact him.

Your group will write a job advertisement for a story character in this unit. To help the group work well together, group members should be responsible for one or more of these tasks:

♦ Encourage everyone in the group to share ideas.

♦ Record the group's ideas.

♦ Remind group members to listen carefully.

♦ Keep the group on the subject.

As a group, recall the characters from the stories in this unit. Agree on one character for whom you will write a job advertisement. Think about the job the character might want. Then suggest ways to begin the ad, and make a list of facts to include.

Work together to use the group's ideas to write a job advertisement. When everyone is finished, post ads on the bulletin board.

148 ◆ *Cooperative Learning*

# BOOKS TO ENJOY

***The High King*** by Lloyd Alexander *(Holt, Rinehart & Winston, 1968)* Taran, the Assistant Pig-Keeper in the land of Prydain, has long yearned to be a hero. If he can triumph in battle against the evil Arawn, he will suceed beyond his dreams.

***The Pushcart War*** by Jean Merrill *(Harper & Row, 1964)* It all begins when a truck runs into his pushcart and pitches Morris the Florist headfirst into a pickle barrel. The pushcart peddlers then unite to defy the big truckers who are trying to put them out of business.

***The Trumpet of the Swan*** by E. B. White *(Harper & Row, 1973)* Dismayed at being a trumpeter swan who cannot make a sound, Louis is determined to learn to play the trumpet.

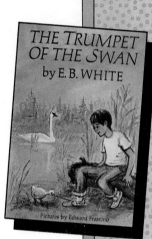

***Ordinary Jack*** by Helen Cresswell *(Macmillan, 1977)* Everyone in his family is talented—except for Jack. When he tests out his ability as a prophet, Jack turns the whole zany household topsy-turvy.

***Mysteriously Yours, Maggie Marmelstein*** by Marjorie Sharmat *(Harper & Row, 1982)* Her talent wins her a position as columnist on the school paper, but Maggie must still find a way to keep her identity a secret.

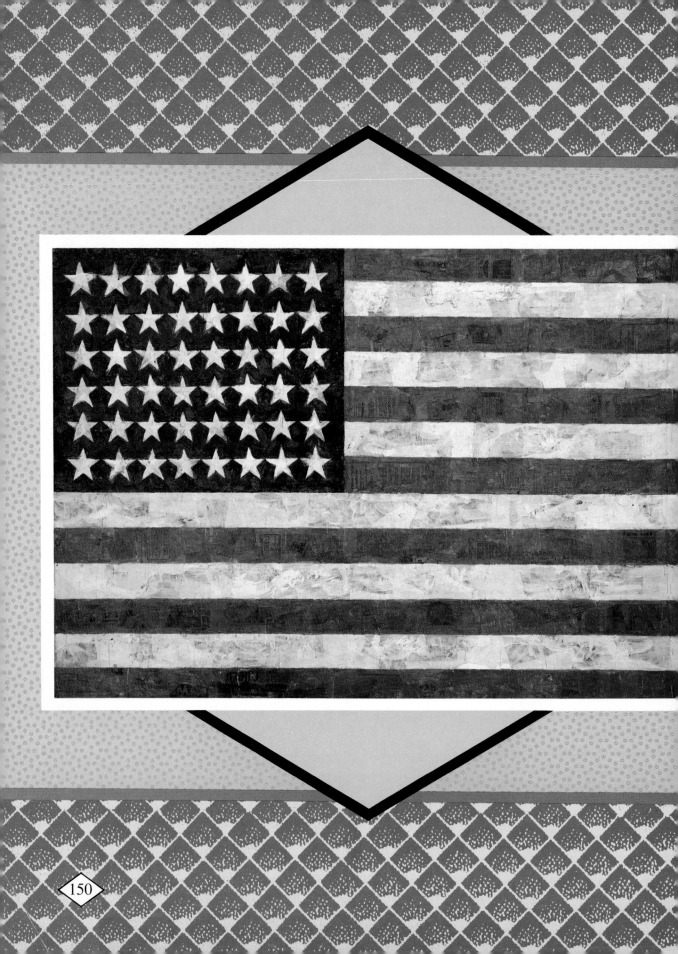

# THE LAND —OF— THE FREE

*S*ome writers capture
the dynamic spirit
of America in words.

What are some
elements of that
lively spirit?

FLAG,
*encaustic, oil, and collage on canvas by Jasper Johns,
American, 1955*

# TONWEYA
## AND THE
# EAGLES

## a Lakota Indian Tale
## retold by Rosebud Yellow Robe

*The feather of the red-winged eagle represents
bravery to the Lakotas. This Native American
legend explains why.*

It was the summer when the big ball of fire fell from the sky. A band of Lakotas had set up a camp. Among them was a young man whose name was Tonweya.[1] He was not only good to look upon, but he was a great runner and hunter. He was very brave in the face of danger. Everyone said that someday he would be a chief. Brave and good chiefs are always needed in every tribe.

One day Tonweya went out hunting. He found a small herd of buffalo grazing near the hills, and, picking out a young fat cow, sent an arrow straight into her heart. While he was skinning the buffalo, he noticed a large eagle circling above him. Watching her flight he saw that she settled on a ledge of rock projecting from a high, steep cliff about a quarter mile away. Tonweya knew there must be a nest there. He was determined to find it. If there were young eaglets, he could capture them and raise them for their feathers.

He looked carefully at the ledge. He saw it would be impossible to climb up to it from the plain below. The only way was from above and getting down would be very dangerous. After skinning the buffalo, Tonweya cut the green hide into one long narrow strip. Then he stretched and twisted the strip through the dust until he had a long strong rope of hide.

[1]Tonweya (tōn wā′ yu)

153

Coiling this about him, he made his way to the tip of the cliff right above the eagle's nest on the ledge. Fastening one end of this rawhide rope to a jack pine, he let the other fall over the ledge. Looking down he saw that it hung within a few feet of the nest. His plan was to slide down the rope and tie the eaglets to the end. Then after he had pulled himself up again, he could draw them up after him. Great honor would come to him. A pair of captive eagles would supply feathers for many warriors.

Tonweya carefully lowered himself over the edge of the cliff and soon stood on the ledge. There were two beautiful young eaglets in the nest, full feathered, though not yet able to fly. He tied them to his rope and prepared to climb up. But just as he placed his weight on the rope, to his great surprise, it fell down beside him. The green hide had been slipping at the knot where he had tied it to the tree; when he pulled on it to go up again, the knot came loose and down came the rope.

Tonweya realized immediately that he was trapped. Only Wakan-tanka,[2] the Great Mystery, could save him from a slow death by starvation and thirst. He looked below him. There was a sheer drop of many hundreds of feet with not even the slightest projection by which he might climb down. When he tried to climb up, he could find neither handhold nor foothold. Wanbli,[3] the eagle, had chosen well the place for a nest.

Despite his brave heart terror gripped Tonweya. He stood looking off in the direction he knew his people to be. He cried out, *Ma hiyopo! Ma hiyopo!*[4] Help me!" but only the echo of his own voice answered.

As the sun was setting, the mother eagle returned to her nest. She screamed in rage when she saw a man with her eaglets. Round and round she flew. Now and then she would charge with lightning speed toward Tonweya and the young

[2]Wakan-tanka (wa' kän täng' kä)   [3]Wanbli (wän' blē)
[4]Ma hiyopo (mä' hē yō' pō): help me

154

birds. The two eaglets flapped their wings wildly and called out to her. Finally in despair the mother eagle made one more swoop toward her nest, and then screaming defiantly, flew off and disappeared. Night fell and the stars came out. Tonweya was alone on the ledge with the two little birds.

When the sun came up, Tonweya was very tired. He had not slept during the night. The ledge was so narrow, he was afraid he might roll off if he fell asleep. The sun rose high in the heavens and then started its descent into the west. Soon it would be night. Tonweya looked forward with dread to the lonely vigil he must again keep. He was very hungry and so terribly thirsty.

The second day Tonweya noticed a small spruce growing in a cleft of the rocks some four feet above him. He tied a piece of his rope to this tree and he fastened the other end around his waist. That way even if he stumbled, he would not fall off the ledge. More important still, he could chance some sleep, which he needed badly.

The third day passed as the others had; heat, hunger, unquenchable thirst. The hope that some of his people might come in search of him was gone. Even if they came, they would never think of looking for him on the cliffs. The mother

155

of the eaglets did not return. Tonweya's presence had frightened her away.

By this time the two eaglets, seeing that Tonweya had no intention of hurting them, had made friends with him. They allowed Tonweya to touch them at will.

Tonweya could see that they were as hungry as he was, so taking out his knife he cut small pieces from the rawhide rope and fed them. This act of kindness removed the last vestige of fear they might have had. They played all about him. They allowed him to hold them aloft. They flapped their wings bravely as he lifted them toward the sun. As he felt the upward pull of their wings, there came to him an idea. Since he had no wings of his own, why could he not make use of the wings of his eagle brothers? He raised his arms toward the sky and called upon Wakan-tanka for wisdom.

The night of the third day, the one on which he had fed the eaglets for the first time, was raw and chill. When Tonweya stretched out for what little sleep he could get, he shivered with the cold. As if understanding his need, the two little eaglets left their nest and, coming over to where he lay, nestled their warm, fluffy bodies close beside him. In a few moments Tonweya was asleep.

While he was asleep, he dreamed. In his dream Wakan-tanka spoke to him. He told him to be brave, the two eaglets would save him. Tonweya awoke suddenly. The eagles were still beside him. As they felt him move, they nestled even closer to him. He placed his arms around them. He knew that his time to die had not yet come. He would once more see his people. He was no longer afraid.

For days thereafter Tonweya fed the rawhide rope to his eagle friends. Luckily it was a long rope, for it was, of course, almost a whole buffalo hide. But while the eaglets thrived on it and grew larger and stronger each day, Tonweya grew thinner and weaker. It rained one day and water gathered in the hollows of the rocks on the ledge. Still he was very hungry and thirsty. He tried to think only of caring for the eaglets.

Each day Tonweya would hold them up by their legs and let them try their wings. Each day the pull on his arms grew stronger. Soon it was so powerful it almost lifted him from his feet. He knew the time was coming for him to put his idea into action. He decided he must do it quickly, for weak as he was he would be unable to do it after a few more days.

The last of the rawhide was gone, the last bit of water on the ledge was drunk. Tonweya was so weak, he could hardly stand. With an effort he dragged himself upright and called his eagle brothers to him. Standing on the edge of the ledge he called to Wakan-tanka for help. He grasped the eaglets' legs in each hand and closing his eyes he jumped.

For a moment he felt himself falling, falling. Then he felt the pull on his arms. Opening his eyes he saw that the two eagles were flying easily. They seemed to be supporting his weight with little effort. In a moment they had reached the ground. Tonweya lay there too exhausted, too weak to move. The eagles remained by his side guarding him.

After resting awhile Tonweya slowly made his way to a little stream nearby. He drank deeply of its cool water. A few berries were growing on the bushes there. He ate them ravenously. Strengthened by even this little food and water, he started off in the direction of the camp. His progress was slow, for he was compelled to rest many times. Always the eaglets remained by his side guarding him.

On the way he passed the spot where he had killed the buffalo. The coyotes and vultures had left nothing but bones. However, his bow and arrows were just where he had left them. He managed to kill a rabbit upon which he and his eagle friends feasted. Late in the afternoon he reached the camp, only to find that his people had moved on. It was late. He was very tired so he decided to stay there that night. He soon fell asleep, the two eagles pressing close beside him all night.

The sun was high in the sky when Tonweya awoke. The long sleep had given him back much strength. After once more giving thanks to Wakan-tanka for his safety he set out after his people. For two days he followed their trail. He lived on the roots and berries he found along the way and what little game he could shoot. He shared everything with his eagle brothers, who followed him. Sometimes they flew overhead, sometimes they walked behind him, and now and then they rested on his shoulders.

Well along in the afternoon of the second day he caught up with the band. At first they were frightened when they saw him. Then they welcomed him with joy.

They were astonished at his story. The two eagles who never left Tonweya amazed them. They were glad that they had always been kind to Wanbli and had never killed them.

The time came when the eagles were able to hunt food for themselves and though everyone expected them to fly away, they did not. True, they would leave with the dawn on hunting forays, but when the evening drew near, they would fly back fearlessly and enter Tonweya's tipi, where they passed the night. Everyone marveled at the sight.

But eagles, like men, should be free. Tonweya, who by now understood their language, told them they could go. They were to enjoy the life the Great Mystery, Wakan-tanka, had planned for them. At first they refused. But when Tonweya said if he ever needed their help he would call for them, they consented.

The tribe gave a great feast in their honor. In gratitude for all they had done, Tonweya painted the tips of their wings a bright red to denote courage and bravery. He took them up on a high mountain. He held them once more toward the sky and bidding them good-bye released them. Spreading their wings they soared away. Tonweya watched them until they disappeared in the eye of the sun.

159

Many snows have passed and Tonweya has long been dead. But now and then the eagles with the red-tipped wings are still seen. There are always two of them and they never show any fear of people. Some say they are the original sacred eagles of Tonweya, for the Wanbli lives for many snows. Some think they are the children of the sacred ones. It is said whoever sees the red-tipped wings of the eagles is sure of their protection as long as he is fearless and brave. And only the fearless and brave may wear the eagle feather tipped with red.

## ◆ LIBRARY LINK ◆

*If you found Tonweya's adventure fascinating, read more in the book* Tonweya and the Eagles and Other Lakota Indian Tales, *retold by Rosebud Yellow Robe.*

## Reader's Response

Do you think Tonweya's courage helped him survive, or do you think he was just fortunate?

# TONWEYA AND THE EAGLES

### Checking Your Comprehension

1. Why did Tonweya want to find the eagle's nest?
2. Why was the ledge on which the eagle's nest was located a trap for Tonweya?
3. In what two ways was the rawhide rope useful to Tonweya?
4. List the brave actions of Tonweya and of the eaglets.
5. If Tonweya's plan to capture the eaglets had worked, how might the story have turned out?
6. Do you agree with the Lakotas that an eagle feather is a good symbol of bravery? How did you decide?

### Writing to Learn

**THINK AND RECALL**   Can you remember Tonweya's adventure with the eagles? Copy and complete the flow chart below. Write the most important parts of the story in the order that they happened. Use as many spaces as you need.

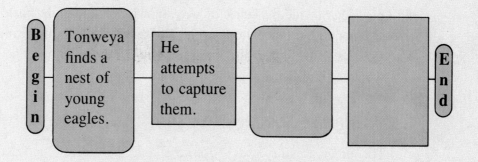

Begin → Tonweya finds a nest of young eagles. → He attempts to capture them. → □ → □ → End

**WRITE**   Choose the part of the story you liked best. Write a paragraph that summarizes what happened in that part.

*A Strategy for Thinking:*

# Using What You Know

**R**eading is easier and means more if you already know something about the topic of a story. Think about choosing a book to read at the library. Sometimes a book just seems to jump out and say, "Read me!" Why is that? Often, a book attracts you because of its title. A title can trigger your thoughts and get you to use your past knowledge. This puts you in the proper mind-set for reading. Then you can apply your past knowledge to new information as you read.

This is one of the ways the mind works. New knowledge and ideas mean more and are remembered better if they are hooked onto old knowledge or ideas. Think of new knowledge as a little boat. If you have nothing to hook it on, it may drift away. Before you read, it is a good idea to bring to the front of your mind any knowledge or ideas you may already have about the topic.

## Learning the Strategy

The previous story was "Tonweya and the Eagles—a Lakota Indian Tale" by Rosebud Yellow Robe. When you read the title, you might have thought, "I've already read some Indian tales," or "I saw a TV show about the Lakota tribe," or "Eagles are magnificent birds!" It's amazing how much you already know and how much you can anticipate about what will be in a story before you even read it.

One way to get ready to read a story or article is to make a list of what you already know about the title or the topic. Before you begin a story or book, take out a piece of paper and list what you think the story might be about, based on the title. The list below is one you might write about "Tonweya and the Eagles"

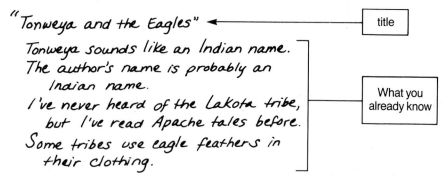

"Tonweya and the Eagles" ← title

Tonweya sounds like an Indian name.
The author's name is probably an
    Indian name.
I've never heard of the Lakota tribe,
    but I've read Apache tales before.
Some tribes use eagle feathers in
    their clothing.

What you already know

Can you think of any other things you knew before you read "Tonweya and the Eagles" that you could have added to this list?

## Using the Strategy

The next selection you will read is titled "What Is an American?" Before you read it, write the title "What Is an American?" on the top of your paper. List as many answers to that question as you can in five minutes.

## Applying the Strategy to the Next Selection

Save the list you made. As you read "What Is an American?" you will be asked to think about the author's answers to the title question. After you read, you will be asked to add any new ideas to the list you made. You may want to consider whether listing your own ideas helped you understand the author's ideas.

The writing connection can be found on page 217.

You can learn about the American spirit by reading Robert Frost's poems, which celebrate nature, or by listening to the effortless grace of Ella Fitzgerald (inset) singing.

# What Is An
# American?

## by Loren Gary

*America is made up of people from a variety of backgrounds. They have drawn on their backgrounds to make contributions that are original, diverse—and valuable to the growth of a nation.*

What is an American? That is a question almost too big to answer.

What is an American? Whom do we mean when we speak of Americans? There are the Native Americans whose ancestors inhabited the land before the European explorers. An American is the descendant of the early colonists who settled the East and Southwest. An American is the great-great-great grandchild of the rugged western pioneers. An American is the grandchild of immigrants from anywhere on the globe. An American is a brand-new citizen from another land.

What is an American? There are so many millions of Americans—the question has as many answers as there are people in this great land.

What is an American? Who can answer the question best? A young person? An old person? A factory worker? A traveling salesman? A dreamer? A speaker of English or Spanish or Yiddish or Khmer or Polish or Swahili or Swedish or Arabic or Creole or Japanese? A housewife? A teacher? An inventor? A basketball player? A farmer? A legislator? An artist? . . . ◄◆►

An artist! Perhaps an artist can answer the question. After all, a work of art can often mirror the artist's society. A work of art can help people see who they are.

What is an American? Here are some American artists: architects, writers, and musicians. Think of each artist's work as holding up a little mirror to America, each mirror reflecting a part of the answer.

◄◆►
**What is an American? What ideas would you add to your list?**

165

# Architects

Frank Lloyd Wright was born in 1869 in Madison, Wisconsin. He was the son of Welsh parents who had immigrated to the United States in the 1840s. Even as a boy, Wright knew that he wanted to become an architect. At age nineteen, he went to work in an architectural firm in Chicago. Six years later, he left the firm, eager to design buildings on his own.

Wright believed that American architecture needed to break free from traditional designs. At the time, most American architects were building homes that looked like massive Greek or Roman temples, or like the towering cathedrals of the Middle Ages. Wright thought that houses should be built on a smaller, more human scale. He also believed that a building should be as close to nature as possible. It should have plenty of open spaces. It should blend in with its natural surroundings and should even be built out of materials taken from those surroundings.

**Frank Lloyd Wright (inset) gave the Robie House a low, horizontal design to make it seem closer to its surroundings.**

In 1909, Wright had a chance to put his ideas into practice when he designed a house in Chicago for Frederic Carleton Robie. Wright made the Robie House long and horizontal, rather than tall and vertical. He eliminated interior walls and ran rooms together, so that it was possible to look through from front to back with nothing blocking the view. Such a design, Wright reasoned, would be more in keeping with the openness of the Midwestern prairies which stretched out to the south of the house when it was built.

Frank Lloyd Wright worked as an architect for over fifty years. By the time of his death in 1959, he had permanently changed American architecture with his fresh visions and his bold designs.

I. M. Pei is another bold designer. In fact, he is one of the most acclaimed architects in America. But Pei's style is very different from Wright's. Pei is a promoter of modernist architecture, which can be recognized by its simplicity of design and by the use of such building materials as steel and glass.

Pei was born in 1917, in Canton, China. He came to America in 1935 to attend college. When he graduated in 1939, he was unable to return to China because of the outbreak of World War II. So he stayed and worked as an architect. Later he became a professor at the Graduate School of Design at Harvard University in Cambridge, Massachusetts. In 1955, he formed his own architectural firm.

Pei's firm designed the John Hancock Building in Boston. This striking tower, which was completed in 1976,

**The Hancock Building, by I. M. Pei (inset) and Partners.**

rises some sixty stories high. No two sides have the same length, so the building looks noticeably different depending on the angle from which a person views it. The building's exterior is made of pale blue glass. On a clear day, the surrounding buildings can be seen brilliantly reflected in the Hancock's glass sides.

Laurinda Spear and Bernardo Fort-Brescia, like I. M. Pei, consider themselves modernists. Spear was born in Miami. Fort-Brescia was born in Peru. He came to America to attend school and stayed here to work after he had finished. The two are married and make their home in Miami. Their firm, Arquitectonica—the Spanish word for "architectural"—is known for buildings that imaginatively use color and design.

In 1980, Spear and Fort-Brescia designed Atlantis, a condominium development in Miami. One side of the building is curved. A prism-shaped structure, painted bright red, sits on top of the roof. In the middle of the building and twelve stories up is a hole known as the "skycourt." With a whirl-pool, a spiral staircase, and a palm tree, it is a place where the residents of the building can relax. ❖❖

◆❖▸
**What is an American? What ideas would you add to your list?**

**Atlantis, designed by Spear and Fort-Brescia, has a red prism on top and a skycourt (inset) in the middle.**

168

## Writers

Laura Ingalls Wilder was born in Lake Pepin, Wisconsin, in 1867. She and her family lived in a log cabin at the edge of a large wood. In later years, they moved to Kansas, Minnesota, and eventually to the Dakota Territory.

Wilder wrote eight books that tell the story of her life and travels. At least one of the books, *Little House on the Prairie*, is probably familiar to most Americans. The books tell of the hard work that was required to build a new life out on the frontier. They bring alive the hard times that the pioneers endured, but they also record the simple joys of farm life and celebrate the courage and independence of the pioneer spirit. Laura Ingalls Wilder died in 1957, in Missouri.

**Laura Ingalls Wilder's Kansas home has been rebuilt on its original site.**

Robert Frost was not a pioneer, but he knew about the self-reliance that goes with rural life. He was born in San Francisco but spent most of his life in New England.

**For Frost, something as ordinary as watching woods fill up with snow was an occasion for poetry.**

169

**Frost's poetry captures the simple beauty of New England.**

He started writing poetry early on. One of his most famous volumes is entitled *North of Boston*. Frost's poems show a deep love of nature. Their earthy wisdom and simple language reflect the lean and hardy New England spirit. Frost was awarded the Pulitzer Prize for poetry four times. He died in 1963.

**August Wilson, Pulitzer Prize-winning playwright**

August Wilson says he got his start as a writer in 1965, when he wrote an essay on Robert Frost. Today, people are writing about Wilson. He is one of the most respected playwrights in America. He was born in 1945 in Pittsburgh. Later he moved to St. Paul, Minnesota, where he has written some of his best plays.

Wilson's best-known plays include: *Joe Turner's Come and Gone, The Piano Lesson,* and *Fences.* For *Fences* he was awarded the 1987 Pulitzer Prize for drama. *Fences* belongs to a series of ten plays that Wilson plans to write. His goal is to portray the history of black life in the twentieth century. In his view, "black Americans have the most dramatic story of all mankind to tell." For Wilson's characters, the struggle to maintain dignity continues even when dreams have been shattered. ◄◆►

◄◆►
**What is an American? What ideas would you add to your list?** ʼ

# Musicians

Jazz is perhaps America's greatest gift to the world of music. Jazz is not so much a kind of music as it is a way of playing music. Improvisation is an important part of jazz. Jazz musicians often improvise, or make up notes, while they are playing or singing. And when it comes to improvisation, few people can match Ella Fitzgerald.

**Ella Fitzgerald has been a jazz singer for over fifty years.**

Ella Fitzgerald has been singing for over fifty years. No other jazz singer has been able to sing so well for so long. Fitzgerald is a master at "scat" singing—improvising with the voice. Scatting is done by making up and singing nonsense syllables to go with the music. For instance, instead of humming a few notes, a scat singer might sing, "De zat zoo zat, de zat zoo zat." Hearing Ella Fitzgerald scat is a very special musical experience. Her voice is so smooth, it's almost like honey.

When Fitzgerald was just a teenager growing up in New York City's Harlem in 1934, a drummer and bandleader named Chick Webb heard her at an amateur singing contest. He invited her to join his jazz band. Five years later Ella Fitzgerald was a star, and she has been shining ever since.

Aaron Copland is a composer who is no stranger to jazz. Works such as his "Jazz Concerto" for piano show very clearly that he understands what jazz is all about. At the time Copland composed the concerto, jazz was considered to be merely a popular art form—not the kind of material to be used by serious composers. But Copland's musical genius enabled him to use that popular art in a more formal composition.

171

Copland's parents were Russian Jews who immigrated to New York City around the beginning of the twentieth century. Copland himself was born in Brooklyn in 1900. He studied music for several years in France, where he learned to compose according to the latest theories. Yet at the same time, he experimented with adding bits of popular songs and folk music to his compositions. The results have been a fresh and powerful blend of the traditional and the modern. ◄◆►

◄◆►

**What is an American? What ideas would you add to your list?**

What is an American? That is a question with about 245,000,000 answers! Like the artists we've read about, Americans come from many different backgrounds and have many different interests. Despite such diversity, these artists' work points to characteristics that we all may share.

An American may love our natural world as did Robert Frost and Frank Lloyd Wright. An American may share with Laura Ingalls Wilder an adventurous and pioneering spirit. An American may have the courage to break with tradition and explore new ideas as I. M. Pei, Laurinda Spear, and Bernardo Fort-Brescia have done with their buildings. An American may have the lively creativity of Ella Fitzgerald scat singing, or may combine the old and the new as Aaron Copland has done. An American can be one who cherishes the dignity of the individual as August Wilson does.

◄◆►

**Add some new ideas to your list on "What is an American?"**

**Could topic lists help you with your other school work? How?**

What is an American? American artists can suggest some answers. Fresh, proud, independent, and bold—their work is a mirror of the American spirit. ◄◆►

## Reader's Response

You have read about several architects, writers, and musicians. Which one of these individuals would you most like to meet? Why?

# What Is An
# Americans?

## Checking Your Comprehension

1. What is unusual about the building in Miami designed by Laurinda Spear and Bernardo Fort-Brescia?
2. Which sentence below is a fact and which one is an opinion? "His goal is to portray the history of black life in the twentieth century. In his view, 'black Americans have the most dramatic story of all mankind to tell.'"
3. What is one way in which Frank Lloyd Wright's work differed from I. M. Pei's? How did you arrive at this answer?
4. Make up another title for this selection.
5. In your opinion, why were the people in this essay so different from each other?

## Writing to Learn

**THINK AND EXPLAIN**   There are many good ideas about what it means to be an American. On a sheet of paper, make a list of the things that you would put into your definition of an American.

· loves the land
· stands for freedom and justice
· is adventurous and independent

**WRITE**   Using your list, write your definition of what an American is. Explain why you think the things in your definition are important.

# THE WHITE HOUSE

### by June Swanson

This engraving shows the White House partially repaired after the 1814 British attack.

*To many Americans the White House, the official home of the President, is a symbol of the presidency and the American government. But the White House wasn't always known by that name.*

On June 18, 1812, President James Madison approved an act of Congress declaring war on Great Britain. The British had been stopping American ships on the high seas and illegally searching them. They often carried off American sailors who they claimed were deserters from the British navy. The United States felt it had to put a stop to this, so Congress declared war.

In the summer of 1814, a British fleet sailed into the Chesapeake Bay. A large party of soldiers went ashore. The American forces were not strong enough to hold them back, and the British were soon marching on Washington, D.C. They burned much of the city, including the Capitol bulding, the Library of Congress, and the president's house.

President Madison was away at the time on an inspection tour of American troops, but through the bravery and quick thinking of his wife, Dolley, many of America's historical documents and other items were saved. Into an old wagon she loaded her husband's official papers, the original Declaration of Independence (which had been framed and placed under glass), silver from the dining room, and a famous portrait of George Washington painted by Gilbert Stuart.

Dolley Madison then dressed herself and her maid in clothes that a farmer's wife and her servant might have worn. She took along a friend and a soldier who also dressed as farmers. In this way they were able to leave the burning city in safety.

After the burning of Washington, D.C., the British moved on to Baltimore, but that city was defended by Fort McHenry. Both the British army and the British naval fleet were driven back, and Baltimore was saved.

As soon as it was safe, members of the U.S. Government returned to Washington, and President Madison ordered the rebuilding of the city. The president's house had been badly burned. Only the blackened shell of its walls remained standing. The house probably would have been completely destroyed if the fire hadn't been put out by a summer thunderstorm during the night of the burning.

As it was, the president's house had to be rebuilt practically from the bottom up. The inside had been totally destroyed, and all of the furnishings were gone. The rebuilding took almost four years.

For a few months the Madisons lived in a private house just west of the old president's house. Then in 1815 they moved to a house on the corner of Pennsylvania Avenue and 19th Street, where they lived until the end of Madison's term of office.

The White House is shown here, in the background, as it appeared immediately after the British attack.

*Above*, this famous portrait of George Washington was among the items saved from burning by Dolley Madison, *right*.

When James Monroe became president in 1817, the house still was not ready. The Monroes lived in their own house in Washington for nine months. Finally the president's house was finished, and on New Year's Day in 1818, President and Mrs. Monroe held a reception to reopen it. At that time its name was officially declared to be the Executive Mansion.

Because workmen had applied numerous coats of white paint to hide the smoke-blackened walls, the outside of the Executive Mansion was now a dazzling white. For this reason, in spite of its new official name, it was often called simply the white house.

Its official name changed several times throughout the next 80 years, to the President's Mansion, the President's Home, and even the President's Palace. To most people, though, it was still the white house.

Then in 1902 President Theodore Roosevelt authorized this popular name as the official title of the president's home, and it has been the White House ever since.

An 1801 painting shows Georgetown and surroundings.

# Designing Washington, D.C.

## by Lillie Patterson

*The White House is only one part of the plan for Washington, D.C. The story of the plan involves drama, confusion, mystery—and a man named Benjamin Banneker.*

On a blustery afternoon, Benjamin Banneker rode down the hill to Ellicott's Lower Mills. He tied his horse to a hitching post in front of the store and hurried inside.

George Ellicott rushed to meet him, waving a letter in welcome. "Here it is," Ellicott called out, his eyes reflecting the excitement in his voice. "My cousin Major Ellicott writes that he will come in a few days to take you with him."

"It seems beyond belief," Banneker said in a voice equally animated. "This will be the greatest adventure of my life."

The two men moved to a small room that served as an office. Sitting near a stove that glowed because of the icy chill, they talked about the letter that had come from Major Andrew Ellicott.

Their voices quickened as they talked over the events that had led to the receipt of the letter. The surveying task was part of a new undertaking by the young United States. Until this time the Congress had temporarily been sitting in first one city, then another—eight cities in all. Now Congress decided that the nation should have a permanent capital city.

But where? Congress left the choice to the President. In 1790 George Washington selected a centrally located spot near the majestic Potomac River, between the states of Maryland and Virginia. Each state donated a parcel of land for the project.

This ten-mile-square federal district had to be surveyed before the city could be built. In January, 1791, President Washington decreed that this survey should be made, and Andrew Ellicott was the logical choice.

Ellicott, in turn, needed an assistant with skills in both astronomy and mathematics. The President and Thomas Jefferson, who was then secretary of state, readily agreed that Benjamin Banneker should be appointed for this position.

Banneker and Ellicott made a good team. Ellicott decided to supervise the workmen in the field, while Banneker made the astronomical observations and mathematical calculations they needed. Their measurements had to be precise.

By the end of February the surveying was well under way. In March the engineer-architect began his work of designing the city. President Washington appointed Major Pierre Charles L'Enfant for this task. L'Enfant had come to America from his native France as a volunteer to fight with the American colonies during the War for Independence. He adopted the United States as his home and began a career of designing buildings and medals. It was L'Enfant who designed the Order of the Purple Heart, the medal awarded to American soldiers wounded in combat.

In addition to L'Enfant, the President also appointed three men to serve as commissioners to supervise the city planning. The day came when Ellicott began meeting with these commissioners. He persuaded Banneker to go along.

When they entered the room for that first meeting, the faces of the commissioners registered their surprise. What?—their expressions asked—should a black man sit at discussions regarding the most important project in the nation?

It did not take long, however, for Banneker's quick mind and imaginative ideas to change their doubts to praise. After the first meeting, the men accepted him as a regular member of the planning team.

**A medallion depicts engineer Pierre Charles L'Enfant.**

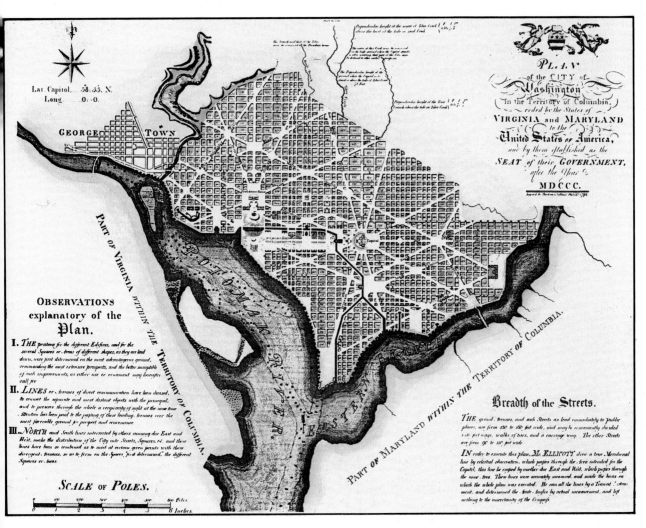

Ellicott's 1792 map shows L'Enfant's plan for the city.

In late March, George Washington rode down from Philadelphia to examine the surveying. He spoke of his pleasure at the progress being made.

Another dramatic moment came when Ellicott and Banneker determined the central point of the city. Working with their notes, they plotted a perfect line running due north and south. This line they crossed with another running east and west. On the hill where the two lines crossed, a hill covered with dense trees, they marked the center of the city.

Pierre L'Enfant looked at the hill and described it in a letter to Thomas Jefferson: "a pedestal waiting for a monument." On his plans he drew a fitting monument—the Congress House, or Capitol. On a second hill, covered by an orchard, he marked the site of the President's palace, later called the White House.

L'Enfant put his heart into the city planning. He studied plans of all the major cities of Europe and vowed to make the American capital the "City Beautiful." In a letter to the President, he reminded him of the unique venture. "No nation ever before had the opportunity offered them of deliberately deciding upon the spot where their Capital City should be fixed."

In his planning, the architect drew a grid of city blocks, with streets laid out in checkerboard fashion. Streets running north and south were named for numbers. Broad avenues, called by states' names, were planned to fan out from central points like spokes in a giant wheel. Most streets during these times were less than fifty feet across. L'Enfant planned for streets over one hundred feet wide and for one grand avenue four times wider. To add to the symmetrical beauty of the city, the architect planned public parks, fountains, circles, and monuments.

Benjamin Banneker thrilled to the idea of these grand plans. He liked L'Enfant, and whenever he got a chance to talk with him or to learn details of his plans, he made the most of the opportunity.

**Banneker published an almanac in 1795.**

Unfortunately, the commissioners did not share this admiration. "Good land is being wasted to make wide avenues," they complained. "There are too many public parks."

"Make no little plans when building the capital," L'Enfant said in answer. "The city must be magnificent enough to grace a great nation."

The commissioners demanded maps of the plans so that lots could be sold. L'Enfant refused, knowing that land speculators would buy up choice spots.

The friction came to a crisis when the nephew of one of the commissioners began building a manor house on a spot that would block a major avenue.

"The streets and avenues must be laid out before houses go up helter-skelter," L'Enfant insisted.

The powerful landowner refused to move the structure. So L'Enfant sent a crew of workmen to dismantle the half-finished house and move the materials out of the way.

This was too much for the city commissioners. They complained to President Washington. At that time the President and Jefferson were busy with problems of running the country. The two sided with the commissioners. Reluctantly, the President notified L'Enfant that his services were at an end.

Deeply hurt and heartbroken, L'Enfant left, taking most of his completed plans with him. With his departure, Washington and Jefferson were left with a ten-mile square of muddy land and no plans for changing it into a city. If the project took too long, Congress might well withdraw support and not vote the funds they needed.

The two leaders turned to Andrew Ellicott for help. Could he finish the surveying and map the city as well?

Major Ellicott agreed and turned to his faithful assistant. "Will you help me?" he asked Benjamin Banneker.

"I will assist in every way I can," Banneker readily agreed. Working together, he and Ellicott were able to draw new plans, based upon their knowledge of the designs of Pierre L'Enfant. Their task was not insurmountable because they could use notes from their actual survey of the ground. Fortunately for America, the plans were eventually completed.

In later years, many people have insisted that it was Banneker who saved the city by drawing L'Enfant's plans from memory. Some scholars believe that this story is only part fact and the rest legend.

The bulk of Banneker's notes, which might have given full details, were lost in a tragic fire. Many of Major Ellicott's papers were lost or stolen during another misunderstanding with the commissioners.

What is known beyond the shadow of a doubt is that Banneker assisted in laying out both the federal territory that became the District of Columbia and the capital called Washington City. As he had envisioned, Washington, D.C., developed into one of the most elegant and symmetrical capitals in the world. Visitors from all over the world find pleasure in its spacious, graceful charm. Benjamin Banneker helped to create this historic loveliness.

 **Reader's Response**

How do you feel about L'Enfant's statement that Washington, D.C. "must be magnificent enough to grace a great nation"?

# THE WHITE HOUSE   Designing Washington, D.C.

## ◆ Checking Your Comprehension

1. What happened to the president's house in 1814?
2. What was done to rebuild the president's house? How did you decide on your answer?
3. Which name mentioned in the article do you think is the best one for the president's house? Explain your answer.
4. What was the "greatest adventure" of Benjamin Banneker's life?
5. What might have happened if Andrew Ellicott and Benjamin Banneker had been unable to complete L'Enfant plans for the new capital?

## ◆ Writing to Learn

**THINK AND INVENT**  The White House is a symbol of the presidency of the United States of America. Look at other symbols on this page and tell what they represent.

**WRITE**  Invent a symbol for your school, class, club, or athletic team. Draw a picture of the new symbol. Write an explanation of how it represents your school, class, club, or athletic team.

# What Presidents Read

Not many people are busier each day than the president of the United States. Yet some presidents have managed to make time in their busy schedules for personal reading. For them it has been a way to escape from the pressures of the presidency and relax.

Thomas Jefferson was, perhaps, the greatest of all presidential readers. Jefferson found pleasure in reading any book he felt could teach him something new. He read books about history, art, architecture, law, religion, philosophy, music, and science. By the time he left the presidency, Jefferson had built his own personal library of 6,400 books.

Another president who was an enthusiastic reader didn't learn to read until after he was married! Andrew Johnson became president after Abraham Lincoln was assassinated. He had never had any regular education at all. His wife, Eliza, taught him to read, write, and do arithmetic. He especially liked to read poetry, history, and famous speeches. He once amazed his secretary by talking for half an hour about Chinese

▲ Thomas Jefferson sometimes had twenty different books spread out on his library floor. He would refer to one and then to another.

Late in life, Andrew Johnson said, "I missed my ▶ vocation. If I had been educated in early life, I would have been a schoolmaster."

186

history, which he had learned about from his reading.

John F. Kennedy was one of the greatest readers of all the presidents. He liked almost every kind of book, from serious books about history to mysteries and adventure stories. His love of reading started when he was a young boy. He was often sick and entertained himself by reading. *King Arthur and His Knights* became one of his favorite books. As an adult, he became most interested in biographies and history books about people who were leaders. Only three years before he became president, he wrote his own book, *Profiles in Courage*, about six United States senators who showed special courage and leadership. The book won the Pulitzer Prize for biography.

Some days it seems almost impossible to find time to read a book for pleasure. But some of our presidents have found that reading can be an important part of any person's life.

President Kennedy autographs his book, *Profiles in Courage.*
▼

◀ Eliza Johnson, wife of the seventeenth president, opened the world of books to her husband.

# America The Beautiful

## by *Katherine Lee Bates*

O beautiful for spacious skies,
For amber waves of grain,
For purple mountain majesties
Above the fruited plain!
America! America!
God shed His grace on thee,
And crown thy good with brotherhood
From sea to shining sea!

O beautiful for pilgrim feet,
Whose stern, impassioned stress
A thoroughfare for freedom beat
Across the wilderness!
America! America!
God mend thine every flaw,
Confirm thy soul in self-control,
Thy liberty in law!

O beautiful for heroes proved
        In liberating strife,
Who more than self their country loved,
        And mercy more than life!
            America! America!
        May God thy gold refine
Till all success be nobleness
        And every gain divine!

O beautiful for patriot dream
        That sees beyond the years
Thine alabaster cities gleam
        Undimmed by human tears!
            America! America!
        God shed His grace on thee
And crown thy good with brotherhood
        From sea to shining sea!

**READING FICTION**

*Vocabulary:*
# Multiple Meanings

**M**any words have more than one meaning. Think of the word *band*. It can mean "musicians who play together," "a wedding ring," "a colored stripe," or "a group of people." *Band* is a word with at least four meanings! This kind of word is called a multiple-meaning word.

In "Tonweya and the Eagles," you read that "A *band* of Lakotas had set up a camp." Which meaning of the word *band* fits this sentence? How can you tell?

If you don't know which meaning of a word is the correct one in a particular sentence, you need to look for clues in the rest of that sentence. Who or what would be most likely to set up a camp? Which meaning makes the most sense? In this case, "a group of people" fits best. This way of figuring out a word's meaning is called looking for context clues.

Sometimes there will not be a context clue that indicates which meaning of a multiple-meaning word fits a sentence. In such cases, you should look up the word in a dictionary. For example, try to figure out the meaning of *hide* in this sentence:

> After skinning the buffalo, Tonweya cut the green hide into one narrow strip.

One meaning for the word *hide* is "to conceal." Does it mean that in this sentence? No; in this sentence, *hide* means "the skin of an animal." Look up *hide* in the dictionary for other definitions of this multiple-meaning word.

## Finding the Right Meaning

Here is another sentence from "Tonweya and the Eagles."

There was a sheer *drop* of many hundreds of feet with not even the slightest projection by which he might climb down.

Here are two meanings of the word *drop:*
1. a bit of liquid that is rounded in shape
2. the distance down

The phrases *many hundreds of feet* and *climb down* are context clues. From these clues, you can figure out that in this sentence the word *drop* means "the distance down."

Can you find other words in the sentence that might have multiple meanings? How about the words *feet* and *projection?* In the dictionary, find more than one meaning of each word.

## Using What You Have Learned

Write the meaning of each word in italics as it is used in each sentence. Then write another meaning for each word. Use a dictionary if you need to.

1. He was very brave in the *face* of danger.
2. He *saw* that he could not climb up to the eagle's nest from the *plain* below.
3. He would make a rope of buffalo hide and slide *down* many *feet* to the nest.
4. Now and then she would *charge* with lightning speed toward Tonweya and the young birds.

## As You Read

In the next story, "The Thanksgiving Play," there are some multiple-meaning words. See if you can find three of them.

*At Thanksgiving, being with family and friends can be wonderful—and sometimes surprisingly painful.*

# The Thanksgiving Play

## by
## Nicholasa Mohr

Felita was glad when her family decided to move back to the old neighborhood. She would be near her friends again, especially her best friend, Gigi. Felita's grandmother, Abuelita, who always seemed to understand her, would also be close by.

A wonderful thing happened this new school year. Gigi, Consuela, Paquito, and I were put in the same class. It had never happened before. It was too good to be true! Of course knowing Gigi and I were in the same class made me the happiest.

Our teacher, Miss Lovett, was friendly and laughed easily. In early October, after we had all settled into our class and gotten used to the routine of school once more, Miss Lovett told us that this year our class was going to put on a play for Thanksgiving. The play we were going to perform was based on a poem by Henry Wadsworth Longfellow, called "The Courtship of Miles Standish." It was about the Pilgrims and how they lived when they first landed in America.

We were all so excited about the play. Miss Lovett called for volunteers to help with the sets and costumes. Paquito and I agreed to help with the sets. Consuela was going to work on makeup. Gigi had not volunteered for anything. When we asked her what she was going to do, she shrugged and didn't answer.

Miss Lovett said we could all audition for the different parts in the play. I was really interested in being Priscilla. She is the heroine. Both Captain Miles Standish and the handsome, young John Alden are in love with her. She is the most beautiful maiden in Plymouth, Massachusetts. That's where the Pilgrims used to live. I told my friends how much I would like to play that part. Everyone said I would be perfect . . . except Gigi. She said that it was a hard part to do, and maybe I wouldn't be able to play it. I really got annoyed and asked her what she meant.

"I just don't think you are right to play Priscilla. That's all," she said.

"What do you mean by right?" I asked. But Gigi only shrugged and didn't say another word. She was beginning to get on my nerves.

Auditions for the parts were going to start Tuesday. Lots of kids had volunteered to audition. Paquito said he would try out for the brave Captain Miles Standish. Consuela said she was too afraid to get up in front of everybody and make a fool of herself. Gigi

didn't show any interest in the play and refused to even talk to us about it. Finally the day came for the girls to read for the part of Priscilla. I was so excited I could hardly wait. Miss Lovett had given us some lines to study. I had practiced real hard. She called out all the names of those who were going to read. I was surprised when I heard her call out "Georgina Mercado." I didn't even know Gigi wanted to try out for Priscilla. I looked at Gigi, but she ignored me. We began reading. It was my turn. I was very nervous and kept forgetting my lines. I had to look down at the script a whole lot. Several other girls were almost as nervous as I was. Then it was Gigi's turn. She recited the part almost by heart. She hardly looked at the script. I noticed that she was wearing one of her best dresses. She had never looked that good in school before. When she finished, everybody clapped. It was obvious that she was the best one. Miss Lovett made a fuss.

"You were just wonderful,

Georgina," she said, "made for the part!" Boy, would I have liked another chance. I bet I could have done better than Gigi.

Why hadn't she told me she wanted the part? It's a free country, after all. She could read for the same part as me. I wasn't going to stop her! I was really angry at Gigi.

After school everyone was still making a fuss over her. I decided I wasn't walking home with them.

"I have to meet my brothers down by the next street," I said. "See you." They hardly noticed. Only Consuela said goodbye. The rest just kept on hanging all over Gigi. Big deal, I thought.

Just before all the casting was completed, Miss Lovett offered me a part as one of the Pilgrim women. All I had to do was stand in the background like a zombie. It wasn't even a speaking part.

"I don't get to say one word," I protested.

"Felicidad Maldonado, you are designing the stage sets and you're assistant stage manager. I think that's quite a bit. Besides, all the speaking parts are taken."

"I'm not interested, thank you," I answered.

"You know"—Miss Lovett shook her head—"you can't be the best in everything."

I turned and left. I didn't need to play any part at all. Who cared?

Gigi came over to me the next day with a great big smile all over her face. I just turned away and made believe she wasn't there.

"Felita,[1] are you taking the part of the Pilgrim woman?" she asked me in her sweetest voice, just as if nothing had happened.

"No," I said, still not looking at her. If she thought I was going to fall all over her like everyone else, she was wasting her time.

"Oh," was all she said, and walked away. Good, I thought. I don't need her one bit!

At home Mami[2] noticed something was wrong.

"Felita, what's the matter? You aren't going out at all. And I haven't seen Gigi for quite a while. In fact I haven't seen any of your friends."

"Nothing is the matter, Mami. I just have lots of things to do."

"You didn't go having a fight with Gigi or something? Did you?"

"Now why would I have a fight with anybody!"

"Don't raise your voice, miss," Mami said. "Sorry I asked. But you just calm down."

The play was going to be performed on the day before Thanksgiving. I made the drawings for most of the scenery. I made a barn, a church, trees and grass, cows, and a horse. I helped the others make a real scarecrow. We used a broom and old clothes.

By the time we set up the stage, everything looked beautiful. Gigi had tried to talk to me a few times. But I just couldn't be nice back to her. She acted as if nothing had happened, as if I was supposed to forget she hadn't told me she was going to read for the part! I wasn't going to forget that just because she was now Miss Popularity. She could go and stay with all her newfound friends for all I cared!

The morning of the play, at

[1]Felita (fe lē' tu)

[2]Mami (mä'mē): mother

196

breakfast, everybody noticed how excited I was.

"Felita," Papi[3] exclaimed, "stop jumping around like a monkey and eat your breakfast."

"She's all excited about the school play today," Mami said.

"That's right. Are you playing a part in the play?" Papi asked.

"No," I replied.

"But she's done most of the sets. Drawing and designing. Isn't that right, Felita?"

"Mami, it was no big deal."

"That's nice," said Papi. "Tell us about it."

"What kind of sets did you do?" Johnny asked.

[3]Papi (pä′pē): father

"I don't know. Look, I don't want to talk about it."

"Boy, are you touchy today," Tito said with a laugh.

"Leave me alone!" I snapped.

"Okay." Mami stood up. "Enough. Felita, are you finished?" I nodded. "Good. Go to school. When you come back, bring home a better mood. Whatever is bothering you, no need to take it out on us." Quickly I left the table.

"Rosa," I heard Papi say, "sometimes you are too hard on her."

"And sometimes you spoil her, Alberto!" Mami snapped. "I'm not raising fresh kids."

The play was a tremendous hit. Everybody looked wonderful and played their parts really well. The stage was brilliant with the color I had used on my drawings. The background of the country-side, the barn, and just about everything stood out clearly. Ernesto Bratter, the stage manager, said I was a good assistant. I was glad to hear that, because a couple of times I'd had to control my temper on account of his ordering me around. But it had all worked out great.

No doubt about it. Gigi was perfect as Priscilla. Even though the kids cheered for the entire cast, Gigi got more applause than anybody else. She just kept on taking a whole lot of bows.

Afterward Miss Lovett had a party for our class. We had lots of treats. There was even a record player and we all danced. We had a really good time.

Of course Priscilla, alias Gigi, was the big star. She just couldn't get enough attention. But not from me, that was for sure. After the party Gigi spoke to me.

"Your sets were really great. Everybody said the stage looked wonderful."

"Thanks." I looked away.

"Felita, are you mad at me?"

"Why should I be mad at you?"

"Well, I did get the leading part, but . . ."

"Big deal," I said. "I really don't care."

"You don't? But . . . I . . ."

"Look," I said, interrupting her, "I have to go. I promised my mother I'd get home early. We have to go someplace."

I rushed all the way home. I didn't know why, but I was still furious at Gigi. What was worse was that I was unhappy about having those feelings. Gigi and I had been real close for as far back as I could remember. Not being able to share things with her really bothered me.

We had a great Thanksgiving. The dinner was just delicious. Afterwards, Abuelita[4] asked me if I wanted to go home with her that evening. Boy, was I happy to get away from Mami. I just couldn't face another day of her asking me questions about Gigi, my friends,

[4]Abuelita (ä bwe lē' tu): grandmother

and my whole life. It was getting to be too much!

It felt good to be with Abuelita in her apartment. Abuelita never questioned me about anything really personal unless I wanted to talk about it. She just waited, and when she sensed that I was worried or something, then she would ask me. Not like Mami. I love Mami, but she's always trying to find out every little thing that happens to me. With my abuelita sometimes we just sit and stay quiet, not talk at all.

This time we sat quietly for a while, then Abuelita spoke.

"You are getting to be a big girl now, Felita. You just turned eleven years old. My goodness!

"Tell me, how have you been? It seems like a long time since we were together like this." She smiled her wonderful smile at me. Her dark, bright eyes looked deeply into mine. I felt her warmth and happiness.

"I'm okay, Abuelita."

"Tell me about your play at school. Rosa tells me you worked on the stage sets. Was the play a success?"

"It was. It was great. The stage looked beautiful. My drawings stood out really well. I never made such big drawings in my life. There was a farm in the country, a barn, and animals. I made it the way it used to be in the olden days of the Pilgrims. You know, how it was when they first came to America."

"I'm so proud of you. Tell me about the play. Did you act in it?"

"No." I paused. "I didn't want to."

"I see. Tell me a little about the story."

I told Abuelita all about it.

"Who played the parts? Any of your friends?"

"Some."

"Who played the part of the girl both men love?"

"Oh, her? Gigi."

"Gigi Mercado, your best friend?" I nodded. "Was she good?"

"Yes, she was. Very good."

"You don't sound too happy about that."

"I don't care." I shrugged.

"But if she is your best friend, I should think you would care."

"I . . . I don't know if she is my friend anymore, Abuelita."

"Why do you say that?"

I couldn't answer. I just felt awful.

"Did she do something? Did you two argue?" I nodded. "Can I ask what happened?"

"Well, it's hard to explain. But what she did wasn't fair."

"Fair about what, Felita?"

I hadn't spoken about it before. Now with Abuelita it was easy to talk about it.

"Well, we all tried out for the different parts. Everybody knew what everybody was trying out for. But Gigi never told anybody she was going to try out for Priscilla. She kept it a great big secret. Even after I told her that I wanted to try for the part, she kept quiet about it. Do you know what she did say? She said I wasn't right for it . . . it was a hard part and all that bunch of baloney. She just wanted the part for herself, so she was mysterious about the whole thing. Why shouldn't she let me know that she wanted to be Priscilla? I wouldn't care. I let her know my plans. I didn't go sneaking around."

"Are you angry because Gigi got the part?"

It was hard for me to answer. I thought about it for a little while. "Abuelita, I don't think so. She was really very good in the part."

"Were you as good when you tried out for Priscilla?"

"No." I looked at Abuelita. "I stunk." We both laughed.

"Then maybe you are not angry at Gigi at all."

"What do you mean?"

"Well, maybe you are a little bit . . . hurt?"

"Hurt?" I felt confused.

"Do you know what I think? I think you are hurt because your best friend didn't trust you. From what you tell me, you trusted her, but she didn't have faith in you. What do you think?"

"Yes." I nodded. "Abuelita, yes. I don't know why. Gigi and I always tell each other everything. Why did she act like that to me?"

"Have you asked her?"

"No."

"Why not? Aren't you two speaking to each other?"

"We're speaking. Gigi tried to be friendly a few times."

"Don't you want to stay her friend?"

"I do. Only she came over to me acting as if nothing ever happened. And something did happen! What does she think? That she can go around being sneaky and I'm going to fall all over her? Just because she got the best part, she thinks she's special."

"And you think that's why she came over. Because she wants to be special?"

"I don't know."

"You should give her a chance. Perhaps Gigi acted in a strange way for a reason."

"She wasn't nice to me, Abuelita. She wasn't."

"I'm not saying she was. Or even that she was right. Mira,[5] Felita, friendship is one of the best things in this whole world. It's one of the few things you can't go out and buy. It's like love. You can buy clothes, food, even luxuries, but there's no place I know of where you can buy a real friend. Do you?"

I shook my head. Abuelita smiled at me and waited. We were both silent for a long moment. I wondered if maybe I shouldn't have a talk with Gigi. After all, she had tried to talk to me first.

"Abuelita, do you think it's a good idea for me to . . . maybe talk to Gigi?"

[5]Mira (mē' ru): look

202

"You know, that's a very good idea." Abuelita nodded.

"Well, she did try to talk to me a few times. Only there's just one thing. I won't know what to say to her. I mean, after what's happened and all."

"After so many years of being close, I am sure you could say 'Hello, Gigi. How are you?' That should be easy enough."

"I feel better already, Abuelita."

"Good," Abuelita said. "Now let's you and I get to sleep. Abuelita is tired."

I kept thinking of what Abuelita had said, and on Monday I waited for Gigi after school. It was as if she knew I wanted to talk. She came over to me.

"Hello, Gigi," I said. "How are you?"

"Fine." Gigi smiled. "Want to walk home together?"

"Let's take the long way so we can be by ourselves," I said.

We walked without saying anything for a couple of blocks. Finally I spoke.

"I wanted to tell you, Gigi, you were really great as Priscilla."

"Did you really like me? Oh, Felita, I'm so glad. I wanted you to like me, more than anybody else. Of course it was nothing compared to the sets you did. They were something special. Everybody liked them so much."

"You were right, too," I said. "I wasn't very good for the part of Priscilla."

"Look." Gigi stopped walking and looked at me. "I'm sorry about . . . about the way I acted. Like, I didn't say anything to you or the others. But, well, I was scared you all would think I was silly or something. I mean, you wanted the part too. So, I figured, better not say nothing."

"I wouldn't have cared, Gigi. Honest."

"Felita . . . it's just that you are so good at a lot of things. Like, you draw really well. You beat everybody at hopscotch and kick-the-can. You know about nature and animals, much more than the rest of us. Everything you do is always better than . . . what I do! I just wanted this part for me. I wanted to be better than you this time. For once I didn't want to worry about you. Felita, I'm sorry."

I was shocked. I didn't know Gigi felt that way. I didn't feel better than anybody about anything I did. She looked so upset, like she was about to cry any minute. I could see she was miserable and I wanted to comfort her. I had never had this kind of feeling before in my whole life.

"Well, you didn't have to worry. 'Cause I stunk!" We both laughed with relief. "I think I was the worst one!"

"Oh, no, you weren't." Gigi laughed. "Jenny Fuentes was the most awful."

"Worse than me?"

"Much worse."

"And how about Louie Collins? I didn't think he read better than Paquito."

"Right," Gigi agreed. "I don't know how he got through the play. He was shaking so much that I was scared the sets would fall right on his head."

It was fun, Gigi and I talking about the play and how we felt about everybody and everything. It was just like before, only better.

♦ LIBRARY LINK ♦

*If you are interested in reading more about friendship, try* Soup *or* Soup for President *by Robert Newton Peck, and* Me and the Terrible Two *by Ellen Conford.*

**Reader's Response**

Would you rather have Gigi or Felita as a friend? Explain your answer.

# The Thanksgiving Play

## Checking Your Comprehension

1. Why did Felita become angry with Gigi?
2. Explain how Felita and Gigi mended their friendship.
3. Suppose Abuelita had not had a talk with Felita. What might have happened to Felita and Gigi's friendship? How did you think out your answer to this question?
4. Do you think Gigi should have told Felita that she wasn't right for the part of Priscilla? Explain your answer.
5. Is Abuelita someone with whom you could share a problem? Explain your answer.

## Writing to Learn

**THINK AND DECIDE**   Did you understand why the friendship of Felita and Gigi got into difficulty? Why did they have trouble making up? Read and think about some of the advice below based on the story.

---

**Advice on Friendship**

- You can't excel at everything.
- Friendship is something you can't go out and buy.
- Best friends should trust each other.

---

**WRITE**   What is the best way to stay friends with your friends? Write an ''advice column'' for an imaginary newspaper. Tell how you think friends can keep their friendships alive.

## READING FICTION

*Comprehension:*

# Fact and Opinion

**A**s you read the opening of "The Thanksgiving Play" it's easy to sense Felita's happiness as she writes:

> A wonderful thing happened this new school year. Gigi, Consuela, Paquito, and I were put in the same class. It had never happened before. It was too good to be true!

Part of this statement is fact and another part is opinion. It is a fact that this is the first time Gigi, Consuela, Paquito, and Felita are in the same class. How can you prove this fact? Imagine that you are a character in the story. You could check the school records to verify Felita's statement.

It is Felita's opinion, however, that this is "a wonderful thing," "too good to be true." Felita is expressing what she thinks or feels about being in the same class with Gigi, Consuela, and Paquito.

In your reading, you come across many statements that are facts or opinions. When you recognize that a statement is a fact, you are able to judge whether what happened in a story can be proven to be true. On the other hand, when you recognize that a statement is an opinion, you can understand what someone thinks or feels about something.

206

## Identifying Fact and Opinion

Sometimes a writer may include a signal word that indicates that the statement is an opinion. When Gigi said to Felita, "I just don't think you are right to play Priscilla," Gigi was stating an opinion. As you read on, you found out just how strong an opinion it really was. It puzzled Felita and hurt her.

It was, however, only what Gigi thought about Felita's ability to play Priscilla. It was not a fact. It was neither true nor false. The word *think* in this sentence signals that this is an opinion.

Certain words, such as *think*, as well as phrases such as *it appears*, signal that a statement expresses an opinion. Common signal words and phrases for an opinion are *I think, I believe, it seems, I suppose, probably, maybe.* When you read words such as these, you can be fairly sure that the author, or a character in the story, is expressing an opinion.

As you read on in "The Thanksgiving Play," you found out that Felita did not get the part in the play. Do you remember how disappointed Felita was when she did not get the part?

Here is what Miss Lovett, Felita's teacher, told her. See if you can tell which statement gives facts and which gives an opinion.

"Felicidad Maldonado, you are designing the stage sets and you're assistant stage manager. I think that's quite a bit."

Read the first sentence again. Can it be tested or proven? Yes, it can. First, a character in the story could ask someone else in the story about it. Second, a character could observe Felicidad to see whether she did both jobs. This is something real that can be proven true. Therefore, this first sentence gives factual statements.

Read the second sentence again. Is there anything in it that can be proven correct or incorrect, true or false? No, there isn't. It is simply Miss Lovett's opinion, because no one knows for sure how much quite a bit is. Also, the signal words *I think* are clues to tell you it is an opinion.

The following diagram shows a way that can help you figure out whether a statement is a fact or an opinion.

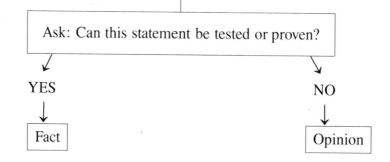

When you read a selection, ask yourself whether a statement can be tested or proven. If the answer is yes, the statement is probably a fact. If the answer is no, the statement is probably an opinion.

## Using What You Have Learned

Read the following passage from "The Thanksgiving Play." Think about which statements are facts and which are opinions. Then answer the questions.

Miss Lovett said we could all audition for the different parts in the play. I was really interested in being Priscilla. She is the heroine. Both Captain Miles Standish and the handsome, young John Alden are in love with her. She is the most beautiful maiden in Plymouth, Massachusetts. That's where the Pilgrims used to live. I told my friends how much I would like to play the part. Everyone said I would be perfect . . . except Gigi. She said that it was a hard part to do, and maybe I wouldn't be able to play it.

1. What are the facts in the passage? Suggest a way to tell why these statements are facts.
2. What are the opinions in the passage? Identify any signal words that indicate these statements are opinions.
3. Give your opinion of Gigi's comments in this passage. Use a signal word to express your opinion.
4. Copy one statement of fact from the selection "The White House." Then write your own opinion about that fact.

## As You Read

Next you will read a selection called "The Liberty Bell." As you read, look for facts and opinions. Ask yourself whether a statement can be observed or proven. If the answer is no, then look for signal words to indicate that the statement is an opinion. Remember that you may not always find signal words in each opinion that you read.

# The Liberty Bell

## by James Cross Giblin

*Today the Liberty Bell is cracked and silent, but once it was the voice of a brave new nation.*

To many people, nothing symbolizes American independence as much as the Liberty Bell. Fourth of July fireworks often trace the outline of the Liberty Bell against the night sky. And almost every Independence Day parade includes a replica of the Bell on one of the floats.

The Liberty Bell wasn't known by that name when it arrived from England in September 1752. It was called the State House Bell, since it had been ordered for the new State House in Philadelphia.

Before the bell was raised to the top of the State House tower, it was hung from a temporary stand in the yard. People wanted to hear it ring, so one morning the bell was tested. While a crowd looked on, a smiling bellringer stepped up to the bell and swung its heavy clapper. A loud *bong* resounded through the air, but almost at once the bellringer's smile changed to a worried frown. For a crack had split the rim and raced up the side of the bell.

Everyone was horrified. Some wanted to send the ruined bell back to England and order a replacement. Others thought that would take too long. At last it was decided to recast the bell in Philadelphia. John Stow, who owned a brass foundry that made everything from candlesticks to kettles, was hired to do the job. He took on John Pass as his assistant.

Pass and Stow broke the original bell into small pieces with sledgehammers so they could melt down the metal. Then they made new molds, poured in the metal, and recast the bell in Stow's foundry.

However, this first recasting wasn't a success. When the new bell was hung in the State House tower in April 1753, it made only a dull *bonk* when struck. Someone said it sounded like two coal scuttles[1] being banged together.

So Pass and Stow took down the bell and started all over again. They worked quickly, and the third bell was ready by June. It was hung in the State House tower, and everyone in the yard below waited breathlessly as it was struck. They smiled when the bell gave out a loud, echoing *bong-g-g*.

On the side of the bell there is an inscription from the Bible: "Proclaim Liberty throughout the land to all the Inhabitants Thereof." Many people think this refers to the Declaration of Independence. But of course it couldn't, since it was carved on the bell twenty-three years before the Declaration was written. It refers instead to the freedom of religion that all citizens of Pennsylvania enjoyed.

Also on the bell is a statement that it was ordered for the State House of Pennsylvania, the names of Pass and Stow, and the year the bell was made. Someone made a mistake, though, and misspelled the word *Pennsylvania*. To this day it appears as "Pensylvania" on the side of the Liberty Bell.

From 1753 until 1776, the bell summoned public officials to meetings at the State House. It was rung often during sessions of the Second Continental Congress. But there is no record that it was rung on July 4, 1776, the day the Declaration of Independence was adopted.

Many people mistakenly believe that the Liberty Bell did ring loud and long on that day because of a story that was published in 1846. According to

---

[1]coal scuttle: a metal pail for carrying coal

the story, an old, white-haired bellringer waited all afternoon in the steeple of the State House for word that the Declaration had been adopted. As he waited, he kept muttering to himself, "They'll never do it, they'll never do it!"

Suddenly a boy came racing up the tower steps. "They've signed!" he shouted. "Ring, Grandfather! Ring for Liberty!"

The old man's face broke into a huge smile. He grasped the bell ropes and gave them a mighty tug. The sound of the State House Bell rang out, carrying the glad news to everyone in Philadelphia.

It makes a good story, but there is no evidence that it really happened on July 4, 1776. We do know, however, that the State House Bell rang on July 8 to announce the first public reading of the Declaration. And that night it rang in celebration with all the other bells of Philadelphia.

When the British army approached Philadelphia in September 1777, the State House Bell was hastily removed from the building. People were afraid the British would melt down the bell for ammunition. Its 2,080 pounds of metal would have given them nearly 33,000 rounds at one ounce per shot.

The State House Bell and ten other large city bells were loaded onto sturdy farmers' wagons and covered with straw. Then they were smuggled out of Philadelphia in the middle of the night so that British spies wouldn't know what was going on.

The wagons carrying the bells joined a convoy of 700 wagons loaded with refugees and goods. All of them headed northwest, away from the British army. Just as the convoy reached Bethlehem, Pennsylvania, on September 24, the wagon with the

State House Bell broke down under its great weight.

The bell was transferred to another wagon and taken on to Allentown. There it was hidden in the basement of the Zion High German Reformed Church. The church itself was used as a military hospital for wounded soldiers from George Washington's army.

The State House Bell stayed in Allentown until the British left Philadelphia in June 1778. Then it was shipped back to Philadelphia along with the other city bells, and was rehung in the State House steeple. It rang when General Cornwallis of Great Britain surrendered to George Washington at Yorktown in 1781. It rang when the United States signed a peace treaty with Britain in 1783. And it rang over and over again when the U.S. Constitution was adopted in 1788.

The State House Bell kept on ringing on important occasions until July 8, 1835. On that morning it was tolling for the funeral procession of John Marshall, chief justice of the U.S. Supreme Court, when suddenly it cracked for the second time. Strangely enough, it was fifty-nine years to the day since the bell had rung out to celebrate the first reading of the Declaration of Independence.

The bell remained silent until 1846. Then the edges of the crack were filed down so that they wouldn't vibrate against each other, and the bell was rung on George Washington's birthday. At first it gave out loud, clear notes, but then the crack spread. After that, the bell could never be rung again.

But even though it was now silent for good, the bell lived on as a national symbol. It was first called "the Liberty Bell" in an antislavery booklet published in 1839. The new name

quickly took hold. In 1852, on the 100th anniversary of its arrival in Philadelphia, the Liberty Bell was put on display in the State House, which was now known as Independence Hall. The bell was placed on a pedestal with thirteen sides to represent the thirteen original states.

Why did the Liberty Bell become such a strong symbol of American freedom and independence? Perhaps because, unlike the Declaration of Independence, it was a three-dimensional object that could be seen and touched. Thousands of Americans and people from other countries came to view the bell when it was displayed at the great Centennial Exhibition in Philadelphia in 1876.

After that exhibition closed, the Liberty Bell traveled to many other cities. It was shown in New Orleans in 1885, in Chicago in 1893, in Boston in 1903, and in St. Louis in 1904.

Millions of people saw the bell on its tours around the country. It rode on a flat, open railroad car surrounded by a protective railing. The bell was

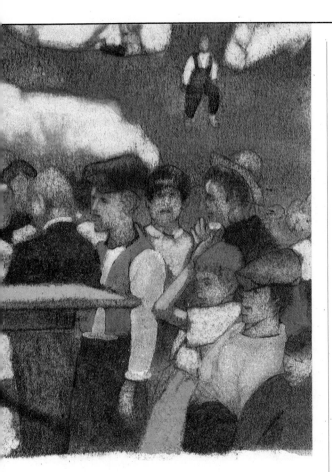

suspended from a wooden yoke with the words "1776—Proclaim Liberty" lettered on it. Flowers, ribbons, and evergreen wreaths decorated the yoke and the flatcar.

As the Liberty Bell traveled on, people back in Philadelphia became more and more concerned about its safety. They feared that the bumping and jolting of the railroad would lengthen the crack in its side.

In 1915 the bell made one final trip to an exposition in San Francisco after 200,000 schoolchildren signed a petition asking that it be sent. Upon its return to Philadelphia, the bell was examined carefully. When it was discovered that the crack had widened, word went out: The Liberty Bell will travel no more. It has stayed in Philadelphia ever since.

Meanwhile, other bells rang in the Liberty Bell's place. As part of the Centennial celebrations of 1876, a wealthy merchant, Henry Seybert, gave money for a new bell to be installed in the tower of Independence Hall. The bell weighed 13,000 pounds—a thousand for each of the thirteen colonies—and was made from four Civil War cannons, melted down. It chimed for the first time at 12:01 A.M. on July 4, 1876.

To honor the 200th anniversary of the Declaration of Independence, Queen Elizabeth II of England presented a Bicentennial Bell to the people of the United States in July 1976. It was made in the Whitechapel Foundry in London, the same foundry that cast the original Liberty Bell. On its side are inscribed the words "Let Freedom Ring!"

At the presentation, Queen Elizabeth said: "It seems to me that Independence Day, the Fourth of July, should be celebrated as much in

Britain as in America. Not in rejoicing at the separation of the American colonies from the British crown, but in sincere gratitude to the Founding Fathers of this great Republic for having taught Britain a very valuable lesson . . . We learned to respect the right of others to govern themselves in their own ways."

The Bicentennial Bell now hangs in a simple brick belfry that is part of the Independence Park Visitors Center in Philadelphia. It is rung every day at 11:00 A.M. and 3:00 P.M., and on special occasions.

But it is the silent Liberty Bell to which hundreds of thousands of visitors still flock every year. Since New Year's Eve 1976, it has been displayed in a modern pavilion on the grassy mall below Independence Hall. Guides in the pavilion encourage people to touch the smooth surface of the bell and feel a part of it.

Now, on the Fourth of July, descendants of the men who signed the Declaration of Independence gather at the Liberty Bell pavilion. Often they are children. Promptly at two o'clock they tap the Liberty Bell gently with rubber-tipped hammers. At the same time the Centennial Bell atop Independence Hall chimes thirteen times, once for each of the thirteen colonies.

## ◆ LIBRARY LINK ◆

*To learn more about symbols of Independence Day, try reading other chapters in the book* Fireworks, Picnics, and Flags *by James Giblin.*

## Reader's Response

The Liberty Bell rang out to celebrate many important moments in history. In which event would you have wanted to participate? Explain your answer.

# The Liberty Bell

## Checking Your Comprehension

1. What is the most important physical feature of the Liberty Bell?
2. The author writes, ''Nothing symbolizes American independence as much as the Liberty Bell.'' Is this statement a fact or an opinion? Explain your choice.
3. Why was the name of the State House Bell changed to the Liberty Bell?
4. Queen Elizabeth II said that America's Founding Fathers taught Britain a valuable lesson. What was that lesson? How did you figure out your answer?
5. The Liberty Bell has a special meaning for each American. What meaning does the Liberty Bell have for you?

## Writing to Learn

**THINK AND DECIDE**   Think of a new title for the article you have just read about the Liberty Bell. Then list the information and ideas that readers might think about if they read your title before reading the article.

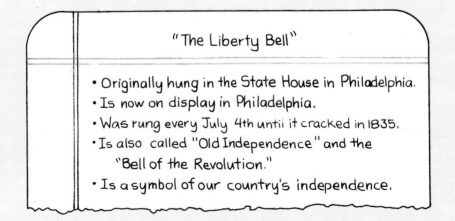

"The Liberty Bell"

• Originally hung in the State House in Philadelphia.
• Is now on display in Philadelphia.
• Was rung every July 4th until it cracked in 1835.
• Is also called "Old Independence" and the
     "Bell of the Revolution."
• Is a symbol of our country's independence.

**WRITE**   Write several sentences explaining how your new title would help people prepare to read the article on the Liberty Bell.

217

# Miss Louisa
## and
# the Outlaws

*by Frances Watts*

*Miss Louisa, a determined schoolteacher in the old West, believes in order and discipline. When uninvited visitors burst into her classroom, everybody learns a lesson or two!*

## CHARACTERS:

**MISS LOUISA:** *the schoolteacher*      **REGINA:** *other pupil*

**THEODORE:** *pupil*     **BENNY:** *outlaw*

**ANNABELLE:** *pupil*     **DEAD-EYE DAN:** *outlaw*

**WILLIAM:** *pupil*     **SHERIFF**

**CLARA:** *other pupil*     **SHERIFF'S ASSISTANT**

**TIME:** *A day in May, at the turn of the century.*

**SETTING:** *A one-room schoolhouse.*

*At Rise:* MISS LOUISA *is standing at her desk. The pupils sit at attention, with their hands folded.*

**MISS LOUISA:** For our history lesson this afternoon you all were to learn the first three stanzas of "Paul Revere's Ride." Theodore, would you come to the front of the room and recite, please?

**THEODORE:** (*Rises uneasily from his desk and walks slowly to front. Recites haltingly*) Uh—uh— "Listen, my—children and you—shall hear." Uh—uh—

**MISS LOUISA:** (*Sternly*) I see that you haven't studied your lesson, Theodore. You will stay after school and learn the lines before you leave this afternoon. Do you understand?

219

**THEODORE:** (*Mumbles as he slinks back to his seat*) Yes.

**MISS LOUISA:** Remember your manners! Yes, *what,* Theodore?

**THEODORE:** (*Straightens up and speaks with respect*) Yes, *Miss Louisa.*

**MISS LOUISA:** Annabelle, let's see how well you have learned the stanzas.

**ANNABELLE:** (*Stumbles to front, stares up at ceiling and recites slowly*) Uh—uh. "Listen, my children, and you shall hear." Uh—uh. "Of the midnight ride of Paul Revere." Uh—uh—(*fidgets*)

**MISS LOUISA:** Annabelle, you will join Theodore after school. Do you understand?

**ANNABELLE:** (*Mumbles as she returns to her seat*) Yes.

**MISS LOUISA:** Yes, *what,* Annabelle?

**ANNABELLE:** (*With respect*) Yes, *Miss Louisa.*

**MISS LOUISA:** (*Sighs*) Boys and girls, I asked you to memorize it in hopes that you will recognize the courage and strength some of our forefathers possessed when they founded our great country. Do you know what courage is?

**CLASS:** (*After a moment's hesitation*) No, Miss Louisa.

**MISS LOUISA:** Well, courage is behaving bravely when you are most afraid. All of us, at some time, have been afraid. Those who discipline themselves and control fear in times of stress are exhibiting courage. Is that clear?

**CLASS:** Yes, Miss Louisa.

**ANNABELLE:** (*In a whispered aside to* THEODORE) I'll bet Miss Louisa has never been afraid in her life!

**THEODORE:** (*Aside*) You said it.

**MISS LOUISA:** William, do you think you can recite the lines for us?

**WILLIAM:** Yes, Miss Louisa. (*He goes confidently to front and recites*) "Listen, my children, and you shall hear of the midnight ride of Paul Revere."

(*He recites first two verses. Then outlaws enter down right.*)

**BENNY:** Stay where you are!

**THEODORE:** (*Fearfully*) Outlaws! It's Benny the Kid and Dead-Eye Dan! The ones that robbed Dodge City Bank last week!

**ANNABELLE:** It is! It is! Their pictures are up in the Post Office. Wanted, dead or alive! A hundred dollars reward! (*The children scream with terror. Some of them run to the back of the room.*)

**MISS LOUISA:** (*Rapping on desk with a ruler. Speaks sternly*) Back to your seats, everyone! How often have I told you never to leave your seats without permission! (*Timidly, but obediently, children return to seats.*)

**DAN:** Nobody's going to get hurt, kiddies, as long as you set there quiet.

**MISS LOUISA:** (*With great dignity*) Watch your grammar in front of my pupils, sir. The proper expression is—*sit there quietly*—not—*set there quiet.*

**DAN:** (*Baffled*) Huh? Oh. As long as you *sit there quietly.*

**BENNY:** Just in case somebody tipped off the Sheriff in town, my pal Dan and me are going to hide out here till the two-thirty freight train comes through. Then we'll make our getaway. So don't anybody get any bright ideas like yelling out the window or running for help, see?

**DAN:** (*Nodding at two vacant desks in row nearest to audience*) Let's take a load off our feet, Benny. May as well be comfortable till train time.

**MISS LOUISA:** (*Firmly*) Just a moment, Daniel! I believe that is your name. You and Benjamin will kindly wipe your feet on this mat before you sit down. (*Points to mat in doorway*)

**BENNY:** (*In confusion*) Say, what is this? Dan and me is outlaws. We don't take orders from you.

**MISS LOUISA:** It's Dan and *I are* outlaws, sir. And as long as you and Benjamin take refuge here, I shall insist that you obey the rules of our schoolhouse. Kindly wipe your feet, gentlemen!

**DAN:** (*Grudgingly*) All right. All right. We'll wipe our feet.

**MISS LOUISA:** Mind your manners, sir. When I speak to you, you are to answer, ''Yes, Miss Louisa.'' Do you understand?

**BENNY** *and* **DAN:** (*Meekly*) Yes, Miss Louisa. (*They wipe their feet, then tiptoe to the vacant desks.*)

**BENNY:** (*Aside to* DAN, *seems puzzled*) I don't know why we let this schoolteacher lead us around by the nose. By all rights we ought to tie her up in the closet.

**MISS LOUISA:** (*Brisk and efficient*) Well, boys and girls, we shall continue our history lesson tomorrow. It is now time for music. Let's have a song. A jolly one. How about "Old MacDonald Had a Farm"?

**REGINA:** We can't sing, Miss Louisa. We—we're too scared! (*Lays head on desk and sobs*)

**MISS LOUISA:** Afraid, Regina? Of what is there to be afraid? As far as we are concerned, we simply have two extra pupils in our room. We will follow our usual schedule. (*Coolly takes pitch pipe from her pocket and sounds the key. Class begins to sing "Old MacDonald." MISS LOUISA interrupts song by rapping with ruler. Speaking to outlaws*) Benjamin and Daniel, why aren't you singing?

**DAN:** (*Bewildered*) Huh? Why should we sing?

**CLARA:** (*Earnestly*) Because, when we have music in this school, everybody sings.

**WILLIAM:** (*Nods*) And that means *everybody*. It's a school rule.

**MISS LOUISA:** (*To children*) Clara and William, this is not your affair. (*To outlaws, firmly*) When we start to sing again, you will sing. Do you understand?

**BENNY:** (*Mumbles*) Yes.

**MISS LOUISA:** Yes, *what*, Benjamin.

**BENNY:** Yes, Miss Louisa. (MISS LOUISA *blows pipe again and waves her arms as she leads the song. The children's spirits rise noticeably as they progress through the various animal sounds of the song. The faces of the outlaws are comically serious as they sing along with the children. When song ends,* MISS LOUISA *crosses over to window and gazes out with a worried frown.*)

**BENNY:** Stay away from that window, ma'am. We're not giving you the chance to signal for help.

**DAN:** You may be a schoolmarm, but you can't outsmart us. Nobody has ever outsmarted Benny the Kid and Dead-Eye Dan.

**MISS LOUISA:** (*Stays at window. Speaks matter-of-factly*) It looks a bit like rain. Annabelle, will you and Theodore please go out and bring in the flag? (ANNABELLE *and* THEODORE *rise to obey.*)

**BENNY:** (*To* MISS LOUISA) Do you think we're stupid? Why, the minute those kids leave this room they'll run for the Sheriff.

**ANNABELLE:** (*Nervously*) Don't insist that we go, Miss Louisa! It really doesn't look like rain.

**MISS LOUISA:** There are cumulus clouds forming in the west. It is May; showers begin suddenly in spring. (*To outlaws*) It is a rule in our school that we never allow the American flag to become wet. One of you may accompany Annabelle and Theodore, if you wish. But our flag must not be rained upon! Do you hear? (*The outlaws exchange exasperated looks, then finally nod agreement.*)

**BENNY:** Oh, all right then.

**MISS LOUISA:** (*Sternly*) What did you say?

**BENNY:** (*Meekly*) Yes, Miss Louisa. (*He heads toward the door and motions to* ANNABELLE *and* THEODORE *to precede him. They exit.*)

**MISS LOUISA:** Now, boys and girls, we will have a spelling bee. Regina and Clara may be captains. You may start choosing teams, girls. (*CLARA and REGINA proceed to choose sides, calling out various children's names. The teams line up on opposite sides of the stage and face audience. BENNY, THEODORE, and ANNABELLE enter. They wipe their feet carefully. ANNABELLE hands flag to* MISS LOUISA, *who folds it and puts in on her desk.*)

**REGINA:** (*Continuing with the choosing*) I choose Theodore for my team. (THEODORE *takes his place.*)

**CLARA:** I choose Annabelle. (ANNABELLE *takes her place.*)

**REGINA:** I choose Daniel.

**CLARA:** I choose Benjamin.

**BENNY:** Say, what is this? What's going on?

**DAN:** (*With enthusiasm*) A spelling bee, pal. Ain't you never been in a spelling bee before?

**MISS LOUISA:** *Haven't you ever,* Daniel. Watch your grammar!

226

**DAN:** Haven't you ever been in a spelling bee before?

**BENNY:** No, and I'm not going to now. Besides, it'll be train time soon. We have to stay on the alert.

**MISS LOUISA:** (*Pauses, then nods sympathetically*) Very well, Benjamin. I will excuse you from participating in the spelling bee. Naturally, it would be most embarrassing for you to be spelled down by a group of young children.

**BENNY:** (*Blustering*) Who's scared of being spelled down? Look, maybe I haven't had much schooling, but I'm not so dumb that a bunch of little kids can lick me at spelling.

**MISS LOUISA:** I admire your spirit, Benjamin. You won't mind joining Clara's team then. (*Waits patiently for* BENNY *to line up*)

**BENNY:** (*Sighs in resignation*) Oh, all right.

**MISS LOUISA:** (*Severely*) What's that, Benjamin?

**BENNY:** Yes, Miss Louisa. (*He takes his place at the end of* CLARA's *line.* MISS LOUISA *stands with a spelling book at center stage and calls out words for the children to spell.* DAN *and*

227

BENNY *are caught up in the spirit of competition. They cheer and applaud the spellers along with the others. All spell correctly until* BENNY's *turn.* )

**MISS LOUISA:** Now, Benjamin, I would like you to spell the word "thief."

**BENNY:** (*Raises eyes to ceiling*) Uh-uh. Let me see. T—h. T-h-e-i-f.

**MISS LOUISA:** That is wrong, Benjamin. The correct spelling is t-h-i-e-f. You may take your seat.

**ANNABELLE:** (*Aside*) Gee whiz! He *is* a thief, and he can't even spell it!

**BENNY:** (*Stomps sulkily to his desk*) Aw, so what if I'm not a good speller. I still make a good living. (*Sound of a train whistle is heard. It gradually increases in volume.*)

**DAN:** (*Rushes to window*) Yeow! There goes the two-thirty train!

**BENNY:** (*Running over to window, stamping angrily*) I told you it was time to get out of here! But you had to let that crazy school-teacher talk us into a spelling bee!

**DAN:** All right. All right. So at least *I* didn't miss my spelling word. (*The children still stand in their lines, but they buzz with excitement.* SHERIFF *and* ASSISTANT *enter suddenly.*)

**SHERIFF:** (*Draws gun, catching outlaws off guard*) Hands up! (*Outlaws raise hands.* SHERIFF *and* ASSISTANT *steer them toward the door, as children cheer.*)

**THEODORE:** Sheriff, how did you know the outlaws were here?

**SHERIFF:** I didn't know, son. But I gathered something was wrong when I happened to look out of my office window and saw that the school flagpole was bare. Why, you know as well as I do, that unless it's raining, Miss Louisa never lowers the flag until sundown. It's a rule of the school. Remember, Miss Louisa was my teacher, too.

**MISS LOUISA:** (*To* SHERIFF) I was hoping you'd notice that the flag was down, and would remember that rule, Rodney. Apparently my pupils remember *some* things that I teach them.

**WILLIAM:** (*Laughing*) Miss Louisa was just like Paul Revere's friend. She used a signal to tell about the enemy!

228

**MISS LOUISA:** That's right.

**WILLIAM:** (*To* outlaws) And if you gentlemen were the slightest bit educated about the ways of the weather, you would have known that cumulus clouds in the west rarely mean immediate rain.

**BENNY:** (*To* DAN) I had a hunch that we should have tied that teacher up in the closet the moment we came in!

**DAN:** Could *you* have tied her up?

**BENNY:** (*Scratches his head in bewilderment*) No, I guess I couldn't have done that. There's something about Miss Louisa. Well, you just can't imagine tying her up in a closet. (*Pauses*) She doesn't scare easy, and before you know it, you're half-scared of *her*.

**MISS LOUISA:** The proper grammar, Benjamin, is—She doesn't scare easily.

**BENNY:** Yes, Miss Louisa.

**SHERIFF:** Well, we'll take these scoundrels down to jail where they belong. You'll receive the hundred dollars reward in a few days, Miss Louisa.

**MISS LOUISA:** Thank you, Rodney. I believe it will be just enough money to take the children on an outing to the Dodge City music festival. (*The children shout with delight.* SHERIFF *and* ASSISTANT *exit with outlaws.*)

**MISS LOUISA:** And now, children, I believe that I will dismiss you for the rest of the afternoon.

**CLASS:** Hooray! Hooray for Miss Louisa! (*They exit noisily.* ANNABELLE *and* THEODORE *remain in their seats.*)

**MISS LOUISA:** (*Sitting down limply at her desk. She holds her head in her hands. In a few minutes she looks up and sees* ANNABELLE *and* THEODORE) Well, children, why are you still here?

**THEODORE:** You asked us to stay and learn the first three stanzas of ''Paul Revere's Ride,'' Miss Louisa.

**MISS LOUISA:** Oh, so I did. Well, I will excuse you just this once. You see, I'm feeling a bit shaky. (*Rubs forehead*)

**ANNABELLE:** (*Thoughtfully*) Miss Louisa, you were afraid when the outlaws were here, weren't you?

**MISS LOUISA:** Oh, yes. Very much afraid. I did everything in my power to delay them, so that they might miss the train and be captured. Yet, I longed for them to leave before anyone was hurt.

**THEODORE:** Well, you didn't act scared. Not one bit!

**ANNABELLE:** (*Stoutly*) Naturally, she didn't! She behaved bravely when she was most afraid. That's *courage*. Remember?

**MISS LOUISA:** (*Smiling*) Perhaps I taught you something today after all. (*She takes the flag from the desk and hands it to* ANNABELLE.) Before you leave, children, please hoist the flag again. It's several hours yet until sundown. We must abide by the rules of the school, you know.

**ANNABELLE:** (*With admiration*) Yes, Miss Louisa.

**THEODORE:** (*With a quick bow of respect*) Yes, indeed. Good-by, Miss Louisa. (ANNABELLE *and* THEODORE *exit, as curtain falls.*)

## Reader's Response

Would you like to be a student in Miss Louisa's classroom? Explain why.

# Miss Louisa
### and
# the Outlaws

## Checking Your Comprehension

1. When and where does this play take place?
2. Why was this day not a typical one for Miss Louisa and the schoolchildren?
3. What was the real reason Miss Louisa wanted the flag taken down? How did you figure this out?
4. Why do you think there was a school rule that did not allow the flag to be flown in the rain?
5. If Miss Louisa had not had the flag taken down, what might have happened?
6. What was the most important lesson learned in Miss Louisa's class the day the outlaws appeared?

## Writing to Learn

**THINK AND ANALYZE** You can't *see* things like courage or love or loyalty. So how do you know they are there? People like Miss Louisa have a way of making invisible qualities visible. Read these statements.

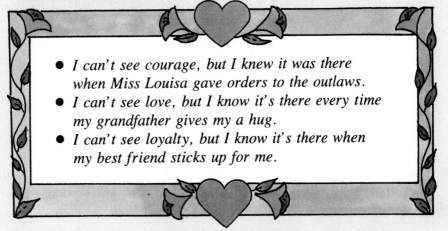

- *I can't see courage, but I knew it was there when Miss Louisa gave orders to the outlaws.*
- *I can't see love, but I know it's there every time my grandfather gives my a hug.*
- *I can't see loyalty, but I know it's there when my best friend sticks up for me.*

**WRITE** Write two short poems about things you can't see but know are there. Write about things such as friendship, generosity, curiosity, or joy.

233

# Using SQR

When you read a social studies textbook, you read about people, places, and events. It is important to realize that these details are part of a larger idea. Using a study plan called SQR will help you see both the details and the main ideas.

## What Is SQR?

SQR stands for *Survey, Question*, and *Read*.

♦ Survey: First, skim the section to get a general idea of the topic.
♦ Question: Then, list questions to answer as you read. Also, look at any questions that are in the book.
♦ Read: Finally, read carefully to answer your own questions and those provided in the book.

## Learning SQR

♦ **Survey**

Survey the pages by skimming the headings, questions, and list of vocabulary words. Recall what you already know about the words in the list. Look at illustrations and captions to get a clearer idea of the topic.

What, would you say, is the topic of the social studies chapter on the next page?

234

# Spain Builds an Empire in the New World

*What areas of the Americas did Spain explore?*

By surveying the elements of this chapter, you can see that the topic is the Spanish exploration of America. You haven't read any of the paragraphs in this chapter, but surveying has given you a broad view of the topic.

### ♦ Question

Notice the question in the example, "What areas of the Americas did Spain explore?" This question is an important clue to the content of the chapter. Ask yourself other questions, such as "Are the two capitalized words in the vocabulary box names of people or of places? Why are they important? What kinds of *exploration* or *colonies* will this chapter tell about?" Often, vocabulary lists, titles, and the lesson preview questions will help you form your own questions. Make a list of these questions so that you remember them.

### ♦ Read

Once you have formed questions, read the chapter for answers. Record any answers that you think are especially important. You may find that additional questions come to mind as you read.—

What questions might you have when you finish reading about colonies?

> **Colonies.** You have already learned that Christopher Columbus was one of Spain's early explorers. After Columbus's explorations, Spain began to build an empire in the Americas. Columbus started Spain's first colony in the Americas on the island of Hispaniola. A colony is land that is ruled by another country. Within one hundred years after Columbus's first voyage, Spain had built a great empire.

You might ask, "What were the colonies like? Where were they? Who built them? Are they still there?" Make a note of questions you think are important. Further reading might help you to answer such questions. You may want to reread parts of the chapter as new questions arise.

**As You Read—Survey**   Survey the following lesson from a social studies textbook. Then turn to the questions on page 241.

# Immigration

## VOCABULARY

| | |
|---|---|
| immigrant | zoning |
| ghetto | settlement house |
| tenement | social work |

**A Land of Opportunity**    The United States was an exciting place to be in the 1800s. There were new jobs, new land, and new opportunities here because of the Industrial Revolution. Many people in other parts of the world wanted a new chance in life. Beginning in the 1830s, **immigrants** came to the United States by the thousands. Immigrants are people who come into and settle in another country.

People had many different reasons for coming to the United States. Hardships at home, chances for work on farms and in factories in this country, and a desire for greater freedom were their chief reasons for leaving their old homes and traveling so far.

Unfortunately, there were so many immigrants coming so rapidly that many Americans did not welcome them. The immigrants were seen as outsiders who did things differently. Sometimes there was ill-feeling between immigrants and life-long Americans. Still, the immigrants came. Their hard work and belief in democracy helped to shape the United States.

**Immigration Grows**    Fewer than 1 million immigrants came to the United States between 1790 and 1840. About 17 million immigrants came here between 1840 and 1900. About 180 million entered between 1900 and 1920.

From 1840 to the 1870s, most of the immigrants came from the northern and western parts of Europe. Many came from Great Britain, Germany, and Scandinavia. Most of these people settled on farms and in the West. Many Irish settled in such cities as Boston, Massachusetts, and New York City. Some Germans settled in such western cities as Cincinnati, Ohio; St. Louis, Missouri; and Milwaukee, Wisconsin.

More and more people came from the southern and eastern parts of Europe between 1880 and 1920. Most of these immigrants were from Italy, Austria-Hungary, Russia, Poland, and Greece. Some people in the United States did not feel comfortable with these new immigrants. Their ways of living seemed so foreign and strange. Movements grew to close the doors of the United States and not let people come in as freely as before.

**Passengers get ready to leave for America.**

■ How, do you think, did these immigrants feel as they left their homeland?

**Tenements in New York City are pictured above. Tenements were built quickly. People living in them lived under poor conditions.**

■ What are some of the poor conditions of the tenements in this picture?

**Controlling Immigration**     From 1776 until 1882, there were no laws dealing with immigration. All people could come here to live and work. In 1882 a law stopped Chinese laborers from entering the United States. That year there was also a law that banned criminals. Insane people, very poor people, and those who were sick were also banned. A law in 1917 kept out people who could not read. Under this law, all immigrants 16 years or older had to prove that they could read 30 to 80 words in English or any other language. Today, immigrants may come from any country. There are, however, strong rules about the number of immigrants that may enter each year.

**Ghettos**     During the 1800s, the new immigrants came to the United States to work in the factories or in the mines. Most of these immigrants settled in the cities. The people mainly settled together in sections of the city where they could live among people from their homelands. This kept their customs and native languages alive. The immigrants drew comfort from living near and taking care of one another. Such neighborhoods where people of the same backgrounds lived were often called **ghettos**. Big cities, such as New York City and Chicago, Illinois, had large immigrant neighborhoods. Today when people speak of ghettos they often mean a place where people with low incomes live.

**Problems in the Cities**     The cities grew rapidly between 1850 and 1900, with little planning. This caused problems. **Tenements** were built quickly for the many people moving to the cities. Tenements were apartment houses with poor safety, sanitation, and comfort conditions. These apartments had little air or light. The plumbing was poor. Factories dirtied the water and the air. Cities did little to help

**Central Park in New York City was built to keep some open spaces for city residents.**
■ **What are some of the activities taking place in the park?**

control these conditions. Little land was set aside for parks, open spaces, and recreation areas. The was little **zoning**, or dividing of the cities into parts. The result was that factories, stores, and houses were all built together in the same area. Overcrowded housing, lack of recreation, and boredom led to more family problems and crime in the cities.

**Reforms**     Efforts were made to reform the cities, or to change them for the better. One way was to build parks to keep open spaces. Frederick Law Olmsted built Central Park in New York City in 1858. He also designed and built parks in other cities in the United States. He made up a name for his work—landscape architecture. He made American cities more beautiful and livable with the parks he built.

Laws were passed to improve housing and sanitation in the cities. Buildings had to have a certain number of windows for better light and better air. Sewers and waste disposal plants were built. Pigs no longer roamed in New York City to clean up the garbage in the streets.

**Settlement Houses**     In 1889, Jane Addams began Hull House in Chicago, Illinoís. It was the most famous **settlement house** in the United States. A settlement house provides services for the people who live in a crowded city neighborhood. At Hull House, workers ran a nursery for young children of working mothers. Hull House workers taught English to immigrants. Workers helped to get the unemployed jobs. Hull House gave people in the neighborhood a place to come to play

An early assembly line in Pittsburg, Pennsylvania.
■ How did the assembly line speed up production?

games from checkers to basketball. Milk and other foods were provided for poor families. Another famous settlement house was the Henry Street Settlement House in New York City. Settlement workers like Jane Addams were doing **social work**. Social work is a job in which people help other people.

**Growth in Labor Supply**    As more and more immigrants poured onto the shores of the United States, the supply of labor increased greatly. Many farmers were leaving the farms to look for jobs in factories. As factories grew, so did the labor supply to fill the new jobs made by new businesses. Some workers managed to improve their conditions, but many others did not. Workers whose skills were replaced by machines felt less important. At the end of a day's work, a factory worker did not feel a sense of satisfaction. A factory worker could not say, "I did that. It is a result of my own skill and my own

effort." Many employers began to think of workers simply as costs of production. They thought that costs of the workers could be lowered more easily than could costs for the machines, especially since there was a large labor supply. Many employers tried to keep the costs of labor— the workers' wages—as low as possible. To get a fair wage, many workers grouped together. Next you will learn about farm groups and labor groups.

**CHECKUP**

1. Where did most of the immigrants come from between 1840 and the 1870s?
2. Why did the immigrants who came between 1880 and 1920 have a hard time fitting in?
3. Why were ghettos formed?
4. What were some of the problems that developed as cities grew quickly?
5. **Thinking Critically**   If you were an immigrant coming to the United States in the 1800s, what would you have done first when you arrived?

## Using What You Have Learned

**Question:** After you have surveyed the lesson, answer the first four questions below.

1. What is the topic of the lesson?

2. What period of time does the lesson cover? How do you know?

3. Write three questions that you thought of while you were surveying this lesson.

4. What do you think is the purpose of asking questions before you read?

**Read:** Now, go back and carefully read the social studies lesson on pages 237–240. After reading, answer the following questions.

5. Answer the three questions you wrote for question 3.

6. List three things you learned in reading this lesson.

7. Exchange your questions with those of a partner, and write answers to each other's questions.

Examples and excerpts are from *The United States: Yesterday and Today, Silver Burdett & Ginn Social Studies,* © 1988.

# John Henry

## *A Ballad from Southern United States*

1. When John Henry _____ was just a lit - tle ba - by,
Sit - tin' on his dad - dy' knee,
He _____ gave one long and _____ lone - some cry,
Said, "A ham - mer be the death of me."
me."

2. Well, the cap - tain _____ said to John _____ Hen - ry,
"Gon - na bring that steam drill round,
Gon - na take that steam drill _____ out on the job,
Gon - na whop that steel ____ on ____ down."
down."

3. John Henry told his captain,
"Well, a man ain't nothin' but a man,
But before I let your steam drill beat me down,
I'll die with a hammer in my hand.
I'll die with a hammer in my hand."

4. Oh, the man that invented the steam drill,
   He thought that he was mighty fine,
   But John Henry drove his steel fifteen feet,
   And the steam drill drove only nine.
   And the steam drill drove only nine.

5. John Henry kept hammerin' on the mountain,
   There was lightnin' in his eye.
   He drove so hard that he broke his heart,
   And he laid down his hammer and he died.
   And he laid down his hammer and he died.

6. They carried him off to the graveyard,
   They buried him in the sand.
   And people came from near and far
   To praise that steel-drivin' man.
   To praise that steel-drivin' man.

*Nothing gets the better of the mighty Paul Bunyan, but in this tale, Paul and his men find out just how hot the sun can get!*

# The POPCORN Blizzard

## by Dell J. McCormick

When Paul Bunyan had cut down all the trees in North Dakota, he decided to go west. It was summertime, and the forest was sweet with the smell of green trees. The spreading branches cast their cool shadows on the ground.

"We must cross vast plains" said Paul to his men, "where it is so hot that not even a blade of grass can grow. You must not become too thirsty as there will be very little water to drink."

Paul knew it would be a long, hard journey, so he decided to send all the heavy camp equipment by boat down the Mississippi River and around the Horn to the Pacific Ocean. Paul told Billy Whiskers, a little bald-headed logger with a bushy beard, to take a crew of men and build a boat. Billy had once been a sailor. In a short time the boat was finished and loaded with all the heavy camp tools.

Everyone cheered as Billy Whiskers and his men started down the Mississippi River on their long trip. Billy wore an admiral's hat and looked every inch the sailor, although he hadn't been on board a ship for thirty-five years.

With Paul and Babe the Blue Ox leading the way, the rest of the camp then started across the plains on their long journey west. In a few days they had left the woods and were knee deep in sand that stretched out before them for miles and miles. The sun became hotter and hotter!

"I made some vanilla ice-cream," said Hot Biscuit Slim one day as he gave the men their lunch, "but the ice became so hot under this boiling sun that I couldn't touch it!"

Tiny Tim, the water boy, was so hot and tired that Paul had to put him up on Babe's back where he rode the rest of the trip. Every time Babe took a step forward, he moved ahead two miles, and Tiny Tim had to hold on with all his might. Even Ole the Big Swede, who was so strong he could carry a full-grown horse under each arm, began to tire.

There was not a tree in sight. Paul Bunyan's men had never before been away from the forest. They missed the cool shade of the trees. Whenever Paul stopped to rest, thirty or forty men would stand in his shadow to escape the boiling sun.

"I won't be able to last another day," cried Brimstone Bill, "if it doesn't begin to cool off soon!"

Even Paul Bunyan became tired finally and took his heavy double-bitted axe from his shoulder and dragged it behind him as he walked. The huge axe cut a ragged ditch through the sand that can be seen to this day. It is now called the Grand Canyon, and the Colorado River runs through it.

It became so hot that the men were exhausted and refused to go another step. Hot Biscuit Slim had complained that there was very little food left in camp. That night Paul took Babe the Blue Ox and went on alone into the mountains to the north. In the mountains Paul found a farmer with a barnful of corn.

"I will buy your corn," said Paul to the farmer. So he loaded all the corn on Babe's back and started for camp. By the time he arrived there, the sun was shining again and the day grew hotter as the sun arose overhead. Soon it became so hot that the corn started popping. It shot up into the air in vast clouds of white puffy popcorn.

It kept popping and popping and soon the air was filled with wonderful white popcorn. It came down all over the camp and almost covered the kitchen. The ground became white with popcorn as far as the eye could see. It fell like a snowstorm until everything was covered two feet deep with fluffy popcorn.

"A snowstorm! A snowstorm!" cried the men as they saw it falling. Never had they seen anything like it before. Some ran into the bunkhouses and put on their mittens and others put on heavy overcoats and woolen caps. They clapped each other on the back and laughed and shouted for joy.

"Let's make snowshoes!" cried Ole the Big Swede. So they all made snowshoes and waded around in the white popcorn and threw popcorn snowballs at each other, and everybody forgot how hot it had been the day before.

Even the horses thought it was real snow, and some of them almost froze to death before the men could put woolen blankets on them and lead them to shelter.

Babe the Blue Ox knew it was only popcorn and winked at Paul.

Paul Bunyan chuckled to himself at the popcorn blizzard and decided to start west again while the men were feeling so happy. He found them all huddled around the kitchen fire.

"Now is the time to move on west," said Paul, "before it begins to get hot again." So they packed up and started. The men waded through the popcorn and blew on their hands to keep them warm. Some claimed their feet were frostbitten, and others rubbed their ears to keep them from freezing.

After traveling for a few weeks more, they saw ahead of them the great forest they had set out to reach. They cheered Paul Bunyan who had led them safely over the hot desert plains. Babe the Blue Ox laughed and winked at Paul whenever anyone mentioned the great blizzard.

## ◆ LIBRARY LINK ◆

*More adventures of Paul Bunyan and other American tall-tale heroes can be found in* American Tall Tales *by Adrien Stoutenberg.*

## Reader's Response

Would you like to have Paul Bunyan as a neighbor? Why or why not?

# The POPCORN Blizzard

## Checking Your Comprehension

1. Why did Paul Bunyan decide to go west?
2. Name two problems the men had while crossing the plains.
3. List three events in this tale that really could have happened. Then list three events that really could not have happened.
4. How did you know that Paul Bunyan was giant-sized? What clues told you so?
5. If Paul had not told his men to pack up and move on after the popcorn blizzard, what might have happened?
6. Which part of the tall tale did you enjoy most? Explain your answer.

## Writing to Learn

**THINK AND IMAGINE**  Paul was the biggest man in America, and he told the tallest tales. How well has he taught *you* to exaggerate? Practice with the ''starters'' below.

When Paul opened his umbrella, it . . . .

Once, a smart sailor used Paul's shoes for . . . .

The tailor who made Paul's shirt used . . . .

**WRITE**  Write an original Paul Bunyan story. For example, think about how Paul might eat, where he might sleep, how he might travel, or what job he might have to do. Be sure to exaggerate!

# READING FICTION

## Literature:
# Motivation

Imagine these two similar situations. First imagine that it is Saturday morning. You have to get up and cut the lawn, but you just can't seem to get out of bed. Then imagine a different Saturday morning. You hop out of bed early. You have only one thing in mind. You can't wait to go to the amusement park for a day of rides.

What is the difference between these two situations? In the second one, you have a strong reason for getting up early. This reason is called *motivation*. Just as you act for certain reasons or causes, so do the characters in a story. Writers create characters with motives— those inner feelings and desires that cause a character to act in a certain way. When you recognize a character's motivation, you can make predictions about what will happen and why.

## Recognizing Motivation

Sometimes a writer has a character explain his or her motivation. In "The Thanksgiving Play," Gigi reveals the inner feelings that motivate her. When she and Felita finally have a heart-to-heart talk, Gigi explains what motivated her to act in such a secretive way.

> "Everything you do is always better than what I do! I just wanted this part for me. I wanted to be better than you this time. For once I didn't want to worry about you."

Once Felita understood Gigi's motivation, their friendship was saved.

A writer does not always directly tell you what motivates a character. Sometimes you infer, or figure out, a character's motivation from what a character wants, experiences, or feels.

250

In the Indian tale "Tonweya and the Eagles," Tonweya searches for the eagles because he wants to capture them and raise them for their feathers. The writer tells us about Tonweya.

> Great honor would come to him. A pair of captive eagles would supply feathers for many warriors.

You can infer that Tonweya is motivated to capture the eagles because he feels he will get recognition for his brave deed.

Sometimes events in a story cause a character's motivation to change. You can see this happen when Tonweya is trapped on the ledge. At first he feeds the eaglets out of kindness.

> Tonweya could see that they were as hungry as he was, so taking out his knife he cut small pieces from the rawhide rope and fed them.

After he dreams that they will save him, Tonweya's motive for feeding the eaglets changes. He wants them to grow quickly and be strong enough to fly him to safety.

Both story characters and people in real life have reasons for acting the way they do. Increasing your awareness of what motivates characters in a story may help you understand the motivation of people you know.

## Read and Enjoy

The next selection, "Ezra, the Baseball Fan," is about a boy and his father. As you read, try to recognize why Ezra is motivated to become a good chess player.

*For Ezra Feldman, a trip to the Baseball Hall of Fame in Cooperstown, New York, is a dream come true. Baseball is not only America's national pastime, it is also Ezra's personal passion.*

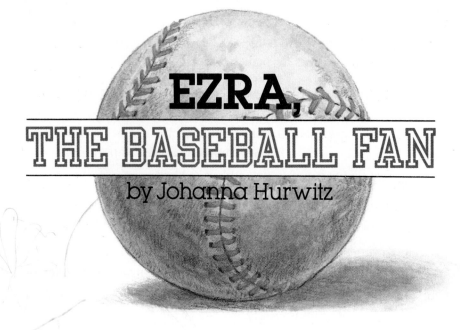

# EZRA, THE BASEBALL FAN
## by Johanna Hurwitz

*Ezra and his father agree about many things, but not about baseball. While his older brother Harris understands Ezra's enthusiasm for baseball, it only puzzles Mr. Feldman. He wishes that Ezra shared his interests in chess and in history. He is certainly surprised when Professor Strauss, a history teacher and a baseball fan, urges the Feldmans to visit a baseball museum.*

"Who would have thought I would be driving to Cooperstown?" Mr. Feldman said the next morning, as they started on their way. What he was really thinking, Ezra imagined, was who would have thought a man like Professor Strauss would care about baseball.

The person who was driving Ezra to the Baseball Hall of Fame on Sunday morning was very different from the one who had driven him to Albany the day before. The dinner and conversation with Professor Strauss had completely changed Mr. Feldman's mood. He whistled as he drove, and when he spoke, his voice was cheerful.

Ezra was delighted that they were heading toward Cooperstown. He hoped the professor would agree to his father's lecture series. He tried to think of something to say or do to show his appreciation to his father. Then he remembered what Harris had said about how pleased his father would be if Ezra played chess with him more often.

"Dad," said Ezra, "yesterday afternoon, while you were at your meeting, I played a couple of games on the chess computer."

"How did you make out?" asked Mr. Feldman.

"I lost," said Ezra. "But it was fun. I bet I could beat that machine one of these days."

"I bet you could too, if you played more," said Mr. Feldman.

"Do you think I'll ever beat you?" asked Ezra.

"You might," conceded his father, "but only if you work at it."

"Dad, if I beat you at a game of chess, will you come with me to see a live game at Shea Stadium?"

Mr. Feldman laughed. "Here I am driving you to a baseball museum, of all places, and as if that isn't enough you want me to take you to a baseball game too," said Mr. Feldman. But his voice wasn't angry. He sounded amused.

"Well, will you?" asked Ezra. "If I beat you, of course."

"Sure. You beat me at a game of chess, and I'll take you to a two-timer. No, what do they call it when they play two games one right after the other?"

"Doubleheader," Ezra corrected his father. "It's a deal!" Ezra knew they had made a real agreement, and he felt very good.

"This is a funny, out-of-the-way place to have a baseball museum," Mr. Feldman commented, as they approached Cooperstown.

"It's here because it's also the home of Abner Doubleday. Some people say that he invented baseball," Ezra explained to his father.

They parked their car between one with a license plate from Michigan and another with plates from Florida.

"Imagine! People seem to travel here from all over the country," Mr. Feldman marveled aloud. This observation didn't surprise Ezra at all.

Inside, the museum was like a treasure chest full of wonderful things for Ezra to see. There were huge enlarged photographs of all the record-making events in baseball history. And enclosed in glass cases were the very balls and gloves and uniforms that had taken part in the major events of the game.

Ezra didn't know which way to look first, whether to start upstairs and work his way down or downstairs and work his way up. He wanted to be everywhere at once, seeing everything at the same time.

Ezra and Mr. Feldman waited while a family of six people read an inscription, and when they moved on, they were able to see the locker in which Stan Musial of the Cardinals had stored his uniform. There was a glass door on the locker so Ezra could look inside and see Musial's old uniform with the number six on it. Musial's old playing shoes were there too, worn and dirty. They looked as if any moment the baseball player would return and put them on.

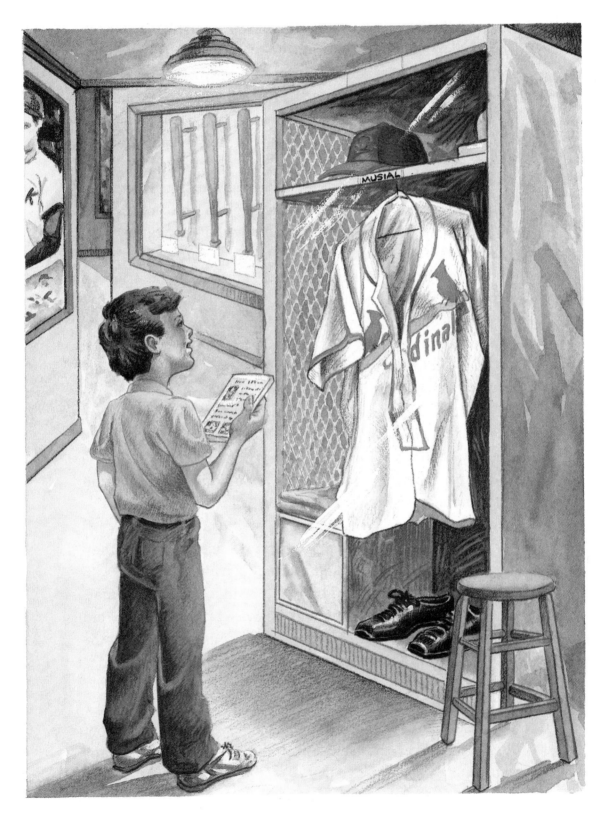

"Look! There's the bat Musial used when he became the first major-league player to hit five home runs in a double-header," Ezra read aloud. "It was on May 2, 1954."

"May 2, 1954," said Mr. Feldman. "That was the day Prime Minister Jawaharlal Nehru of India concluded his first Asian conference with the rulers from Ceylon, Pakistan, Burma, and Indonesia."

Ezra looked at his father with amazement. How could somebody say so many words in English and not make a single bit of sense? He didn't know what his father was talking about. Then he remembered how often his father had said the very same thing to him when he tried to explain a baseball game to him.

"It's amazing," said Mr. Feldman. "Who remembers that conference now?"

Mr. Feldman was still thinking about India, and as far as Ezra knew India didn't have a single baseball team.

"Oh, look at that!" Ezra said, pointing to still another exhibit. "That baseball is really old. It's the ball from opening day at the Polo Grounds on April 12, 1911."

"April 12, 1911," mused Mr. Feldman. "That was the fiftieth anniversary of the firing on Fort Sumter. It was the beginning of the Civil War."

"Oh, Dad! When people are at a baseball game, they don't think about wars and killing," Ezra protested.

"Now that was a real tragedy," said a gray-haired man to Mr. Feldman. Ezra thought he was talking about Fort Sumter, but the man was pointing to an enlarged photograph of the old Giants team leaving the field after the final game at the Polo Grounds on September 29, 1957.

"Imagine! They pulled down the stadium and built apartment houses there in its place," said the man. "New York was never the same after the Giants left," he said sadly.

"What about the Dodgers?" asked another man, who had overheard him. "There never was and there never will be another team like those old Brooklyn Dodgers."

People gathered around and began debating the merits of the New York Giants and the Brooklyn Dodgers. Ezra wanted to listen to them, but he was worried that his father would insist upon relating some historic event that took place on September 29, 1957. Imagine having a father who spoke as if he were a cross between a newspaper and a history book. Ezra didn't think that the baseball fans would understand. He pulled his father away from the discussion and toward some old benches from the Polo Grounds and from Ebbetts Field.

There was a picture of Harvey Haddix of the Pittsburgh Pirates. He had pitched the first twelve-inning, no-hit perfect game against the Braves at Milwaukee on May 26, 1959.

Mr. Feldman read the caption under the picture. Ezra waited for the computer inside his father's head to respond. In a way, his father's brain was like the electronic chess set. He had programmed himself to think in terms of world history. His photographic memory reacted automatically. Sure enough, within seven seconds Mr. Feldman said, "Why that's just two days after John Foster Dulles died. He was Secretary of State under President Eisenhower."

"President Eisenhower was a baseball fan," said Ezra. "He always threw out the first ball at the beginning of the baseball season, and he attended games whenever he could. I've seen pictures of him."

"I wonder why he bothered doing a thing like that," said Mr. Feldman.

"It's probably the reason he wanted to become president in the first place," said Ezra. "All presidents are invited to throw out the first ball, and it's one of the best jobs they get to do. They sit in box seats in the very front,

and they can shake hands with all the players." He thought for a moment. "If I don't become a baseball statistician, maybe I'll become president of the United States."

"That," said Mr. Feldman, "I've got to live to see."

The baseball season was in full swing. Every day new games were played and new records were made all over the country. The newspapers were filled with photographs and news articles. Ezra went to his birthday doubleheader with Bruce and Louis. The Mets won one game and lost one game. The outcome could have been worse. Attending the game, Ezra thought about his baseball-chess bargain with his father.

Two weeks after they returned from Albany Mr. Feldman received a letter from Professor Strauss accepting his proposal. So now Mr. Feldman was very busy. He was home just as many hours as in the past, but much of his time was spent writing letters to others and notes to himself about the lecture series that was to take place the following autumn. He was so busy that he didn't notice when Ezra stayed up past eleven o'clock on a school night to watch the end of a baseball game.

Mrs. Feldman had said, "Ezra, will you be able to get out of bed tomorrow morning?"

"Sure," said Ezra.

"OK, then just this once," his mother said. She was very easygoing. Ezra hoped she wouldn't be too disappointed when he grew up and didn't win those famous prizes that Harris had told him about.

But Ezra was determined that he would win a chess game from his father. On evenings when there wasn't a baseball game, he often played a couple of games against the chess computer. The machine kept beating him, but Ezra didn't worry. It was a secret between the two of them. Besides, the machine let him think as long as he wanted to. Ezra would try out several positions until he found the one that seemed the strongest. And then, when he decided what to do, he entered his moves into the machine and waited for its response.

One evening Ezra won two games in a row against the machine. Of course, it was set at the simplest level, but still beating it gave him confidence. He went to his father. "How about a game of chess?" he asked.

Mr. Feldman looked up from his notes. "As a matter of fact, I'm ready for a break," he said. So the two of them sat at the dining room table with the chessboard between them. It was the first game they had played together in a long time. "Don't forget, if I win, you're going to take me to a baseball game," Ezra reminded his father.

"Sure," his father said. He picked up a black pawn and a white pawn in his hands and held them behind his back.

259

Ezra chose the right hand. It held the white pawn, which meant that Ezra would go first. This way of deciding was fair. If they decided the way they did at a baseball game, his father would never be first, since this was his house. In chess, unlike baseball, the player who goes first has an advantage.

Ezra moved. And then his father. Playing a game against a real person wasn't easy. You had to keep wondering what they thought of what you did. And Mr. Feldman usually said out loud what he thought. "That's a foolish move. You left your queen unprotected," he said.

What was worse, serious chess players always insist upon "touch move," which means that whatever piece you touch has to be moved, even if in the midst of the move you have a better idea. In baseball, if the pitcher winds up for a pitch and then doesn't throw the ball to the batter, it is considered a balk.

Ezra could see the sense of the rule in baseball, but not in chess. Often when he played with his father the touch-move rule cost him the game. He would put his hand out and start to move a piece and then suddenly see a better move. It was too late. "You touched the rook," Mr. Feldman would remind him. "Now you've got to move it." The chess machine never noticed if Ezra touched a piece and then changed his mind. No wonder it was easier to win against a machine than against his father. They played two games, and Ezra lost them both.

"Keep practicing," his father said, as they put the chess pieces back into their box. "If you don't beat me this year, maybe you'll beat me next."

That was no consolation to Ezra. He was determined to get a win before the current baseball season ended.

A few days later Harris phoned to speak to his parents. He had registered for two summer courses so he was still in Princeton, even though it was July.

Mr. and Mrs. Feldman had gone to a concert, and so Ezra and Harris had a long conversation together. The Dodge was up to 143,500 miles. "I drove to Rhode Island one weekend, and Roger drove to Cambridge the next," said Harris. "But mostly, when we don't feel like studying, we just drive around and around here."

"Isn't the gas awfully expensive?" Ezra asked.

"It sure is," agreed Harris. "Why do you think I always call collect?"

They spoke some more. Of course Harris already knew about things like the successful trip to Albany and the trip to the Baseball Hall of Fame. "I lost two chess games to Dad the other evening," admitted Ezra. "I don't think I'll ever beat him. Especially when he plays touch move."

"That always did me in too," Harris remembered. "He's very strict about it because a good chess player thinks with his head and not with his fingers. You should be able to visualize the board without having to move pieces around to see what they will look like."

"I know," Ezra said. "But my hand always seems to shoot out before I can stop it."

"Right," Harris sympathized. "I don't remember how I trained myself to control it."

Two days later Harris remembered, and he sent Ezra a letter. The letter contained only one sentence—not even "Dear Ezra" or "Love, Harris"—just one sentence, four words long. But it was very important, and it was the turning point in Ezra's chess career. The sentence said: "Sit on your hands."

The idea was so simple that Ezra was amazed that it hadn't occurred to him earlier. Now, whenever he played chess, even with the machine, he sat on his hands until he was absolutely ready to move. If he made a bad move, at least it was the bad move he wanted to make and not one he was forced into because he had thought with his fingers.

Ezra decided it was like thinking out loud when you answered a question quickly at school. Sometimes you might say the right thing, but more often you wished you had kept your mouth shut.

Ezra lost the next few games he played against his father, but not once was he forced to make a move because he had accidentally or deliberately touched a piece he hadn't intended to move. And then, on the first Sunday in August, on a day when heavy rains cancelled baseball games in seven states, Ezra sat down to play still another chess game with his father.

Ezra chose white once again, and so he opened with the first move. The next few moves were routine, but then Ezra sacrificed his knight. He permitted his father to take the piece when it could have been avoided, the same way a baseball player makes a sacrifice hit in order to advance a base runner.

"Why did you do that?" asked Mr. Feldman, as he took the knight. "Now you are behind a piece."

However, two days before the chess computer had made that same move when Ezra was playing with it. At the time, Ezra had wondered about the move too. It was an unusual one. And yet, within a few more moves, the machine had won the game. Now Mr. Feldman made the same move that Ezra had made two days before. Ezra copied what the machine had done. Again the game was over within a few moves, and this time Ezra was the winner.

"I can't believe it," said Mr. Feldman. "That was so clever! Let me see it again." He rearranged the pieces on the board and then quickly replayed the white and black moves. "I went here, you went here, I went here, you went here. . . ." he mumbled to himself.

"Ezra, that was brilliant! I would never have thought of that sequence of moves."

"I learned it from the machine," admitted Ezra. "But it counts as winning, doesn't it?"

"It sure does!" Mr. Feldman beamed and held out his hand to shake Ezra's.

"Why are you sitting on your hands?" he asked.

"Oh, it's just a trick I learned from Harris," said Ezra, as he shook hands with his father.

Mrs. Feldman looked up from her Sunday crossword puzzle. "I knew you would do it." She smiled at Ezra.

"Did you know that now Dad is going to take me to a baseball game?" asked Ezra, smiling proudly.

"In the rain?" asked both his parents together.

"Not in the rain. But the next sunny home game," said Ezra. "I'll teach you how to become a baseball fan," he promised.

## Reader's Response

How did you feel about the way in which the problem between Ezra and his father was resolved?

## Writing an Interview

Life in America today is different in many ways from the way it was in the past. As you read the selections in this unit, you learned about the diverse Americans who have helped shape our history.

If you could step back into American history, where would you go? To whom would you most want to speak? Would you try to interview a famous resident of the White House? Or would you prefer to interview a successful inventor or scientist? If you could speak with Benjamin Banneker, what would you discuss? If you met Miles Standish and the other Pilgrims, what would you ask them about their experiences?

Use your imagination to write a brief account of an interview with the historical figure whom you select. You will plan questions and write answers to your questions for your classmates to read.

### Prewriting

Begin preparing for writing by doing two things: select the time period in American history that you would like to visit, and choose a historical figure who interests you.

Use the stories in this unit, a history or social studies textbook, or a library book to obtain information about the historical figure you selected. As you read, prepare five questions and take notes for five answers. On your paper, make a chart like the one that follows. It may help you organize your thoughts.

| Information about the person | Questions to ask | Possible answers |
|---|---|---|
| | | |

### Writing

Give your paper the title "An Interview with. . ."and add the name of the historical figure you choose. Record a time and a date for the interview. Then identify yourself as the interviewer.

Bobby Jones: Mr. Banneker, you once said that your participation in the designing of Washington, D.C., would be the greatest adventure of your life. Do you still feel that way?

Skip a space and write the name of your historical figure and his or her response. Remember to capitalize names. Also, include a colon before writing the response. Follow this format for all five questions and responses.

### Revising

Reread the interview. Did you make the answers of the historical figure seem lifelike and conversational? See if you can add a phrase that might have been popular at the time your historical character lived.

### Proofreading

Correct spelling, grammar, and punctuation mistakes. Make a neat copy of your interview.

### Publishing

Make a class book entitled *Meet Famous Americans*. Bind the book and place it in your school library.

# WORKING TOGETHER

## *Inventing a New Holiday*

The stories in this unit told about the heroes and events that helped shape this country. Some of these heroes and events are remembered on national holidays such as Thanksgiving and the Fourth of July. What other people or events might deserve a holiday? Paul Bunyan and his men probably would think that there should be a "Great Popcorn Blizzard Day."

Work as a group to invent a new holiday and write a description of it. Group members should share these responsibilities:

◆ Encouraging others to talk

◆ Recording the group's ideas

◆ Showing appreciation for other people's ideas

◆ Agreeing or disagreeing in a pleasant way

As a group, review the stories in this unit. Talk about the people and events in the stories, and think about the holidays you could invent for them. Agree on one person or event to celebrate. Then, write a description of the holiday. Is it an important event in our history? Would it celebrate one person's achievements? How would the holiday be celebrated? What would you call it? Would you send cards? Would stores close? Each of you should be able to explain *why* you would celebrate and *what* you would do on the special holiday.

# BOOKS TO ENJOY

***In the Year of the Boar and Jackie Robinson*** by Bette Bao Lord *(Harper, 1984)* Emigrating from China, Shirley Temple Wong arrives in New York City eager to learn about America. When she discovers baseball, her happiness is complete.

***The Pilgrims of Plimouth*** by Marcia Sewall *(Atheneum, 1986)* The Pilgrims' journey and first year in Plimouth come alive as described here by the men, women, and children of 1620.

***The Double Life of Pocahantas*** by Jean Fritz *(Putnam, 1983)* Pocahantas was a beautiful and brave Native American princess. Her fascination with the English settlers in Jamestown changed her world forever.

***The Glorious Fourth at Prairietown*** by Joan Anderson *(Morrow, 1986)* In 1836, the Carpenters, traveling west by covered wagon, arrived in Indiana in time to join a rollicking Fourth of July celebration.

***Ida Early Comes Over the Mountain*** by Robert Burch *(Avon, 1982)* When tall and merry Ida Early rapped on the door of their Georgia home, no one in the Sutton family could have guessed what tall tales, treats, and good times were in store for them.

# IMAGINE
A
PLACE...

*A* traveler might journey
anywhere on Earth—
or even beyond Earth.

*Is a journey merely
a change in location,
or does it change the
traveler, too?*

KHUSRAW LISTENING TO BARBAD
PLAYING THE LUTE,
*painting by Mirza-'Ali, Safavid, Persian, ca. 1540*

Shlemiel, a most unusual man, starts out on a journey
to Warsaw. The results are surprising and confusing.

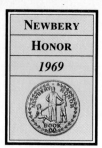

# When Shlemiel Went to Warsaw

## by Isaac Bashevis Singer

CHEL

**T**hough Shlemiel[1] was a lazybones and a sleepyhead and hated to move, he always daydreamed of taking a trip. He had heard many stories about faraway countries, huge deserts, deep oceans, and high mountains, and often discussed with Mrs. Shlemiel his great wish to go on a long journey. Mrs. Shlemiel would reply, "Long journeys are not for a Shlemiel. You better stay home and mind the children while I go to market to sell my vegetables." Yet Shlemiel could not bring himself to give up his dream of seeing the world and its wonders.

A recent visitor to Chelm had told Shlemiel marvelous things about the city of Warsaw.[2] How beautiful the streets were, how high the buildings and luxurious the stores. Shlemiel decided once and for all that he must see this great city for himself. He knew that one had to prepare for a journey. But what was there for him to take? He had nothing but the old clothes he wore. One morning, after Mrs. Shlemiel left for the market, he told the older boys to stay home from cheder[3] and mind the younger children. Then he took a few slices of bread, an onion, and a clove of garlic, put them in a kerchief, tied it into a bundle, and started for Warsaw on foot.

There was a street in Chelm called Warsaw Street and Shlemiel believed that it led directly to Warsaw. While still in the village, he was stopped by several neighbors who asked him where he was going. Shlemiel told them that he was on his way to Warsaw.

"What will you do in Warsaw?" they asked him.

Shlemiel replied, "What do I do in Chelm? Nothing."

He soon reached the outskirts of town. He walked slowly

[1]Shlemiel (shlǝ mēl')

[2]Chelm (khelm), Warsaw: cities in Poland

[3]cheder (khā' dǝr): a Jewish religious school for young children

because the soles of his boots were worn through. Soon the houses and stores gave way to pastures and fields. He passed a peasant driving an ox-drawn plow. After several hours of walking, Shlemiel grew tried. He was so weary that he wasn't even hungry. He lay down on the grass near the roadside for a nap, but before he fell asleep he thought, When I wake up, I may not remember which is the way to Warsaw and which leads back to Chelm. After pondering a moment, he removed his boots and set them down beside him with the toes pointing toward Warsaw and the heels toward Chelm. He soon fell asleep and dreamed that he was a baker baking onion rolls with poppy seeds. Customers came to buy them and Shlemiel said, "These onion rolls are not for sale."

"Then why do you bake them?"

"They are for my wife, for my children, and for me."

Later he dreamed that he was the King of Chelm. Once a year, instead of taxes, each citizen brought him a pot of strawberry jam. Shlemiel sat on a golden throne and nearby sat Mrs. Shlemiel, the queen, and his children, the princes and princesses. They were all eating onion rolls and spooning up big portions of strawberry jam. A carriage arrived and took the royal family to Warsaw, America, and to the river Sambation, which spurts out stones the week long and rests on the Sabbath[4].

[4]Sabbath: traditional day of rest for Jewish people

Near the road, a short distance from where Shlemiel slept, was a smithy. The blacksmith happened to come out just in time to see Shlemiel carefully placing his boots at his side with the toes facing in the direction of Warsaw. The blacksmith was a prankster, and as soon as Shlemiel was sound asleep he tiptoed over and turned the boots around. When Shlemiel awoke, he felt rested but hungry. He got out a slice of bread, rubbed it with garlic, and took a bit of onion. Then he pulled his boots on and continued on his way.

He walked along and everything looked strangely familiar. He recognized houses that he had seen before. It seemed to him that he knew the people he met. Could it be that he had already reached another town, Shlemiel wondered. And why was it so similar to Chelm? He stopped a passerby and asked the name of the town. "Chelm," the man replied.

Shlemiel was astonished. How was this possible? He had walked away from Chelm. How could he have arrived back there? He began to rub his forehead and soon found the answer to the riddle. There were two Chelms and he had reached the second one.

Still, it seemed very odd that the street, the houses, the people were so similar to those in the Chelm he had left behind. Shlemiel puzzled over this fact until he suddenly remembered something he had learned in cheder: "The earth is the same everywhere." And so why shouldn't the second Chelm be exactly like the first one? This discovery gave Shlemiel great satisfaction. He wondered if there was a street here like his street and a house on it like the one he lived in. And indeed, he soon arrived at an identical street and house. Evening had fallen. He opened the door and to his amazement saw a second Mrs. Shlemiel with children just like his. Everything was exactly the same as in his own household. Even the cat seemed the same. Mrs. Shlemiel at once began to scold him.

"Shlemiel, where did you go? You left the house alone. And what have you there in that bundle?"

The children all ran to him and cried, "Papa, where have you been?"

Shlemiel paused a moment and then he said, "Mrs. Shlemiel, I'm not your husband. Children, I'm not your papa."

"Have you lost your mind?" Mrs. Shlemiel screamed.

"I am Shlemiel of Chelm One and this is Chelm Two."

Mrs. Shlemiel clapped her hands so hard that the chickens sleeping under the stove awoke in fright and flew out all over the room.

"Children, your father has gone crazy," she wailed. She immediately sent one of the boys for Gimpel the healer. All the neighbors came crowding in. Shlemiel stood in the middle of the room and proclaimed, "It's true, you all look like the people in my town, but you are not the same. I came from Chelm One and you live in Chelm Two."

"Shlemiel, what's the matter with you?" someone cried.

"You're in your own house, with your own wife and children, your own neighbors and friends."

"No, you don't understand. I come from Chelm One. I was on my way to Warsaw, and between Chelm One and Warsaw there is a Chelm Two. And that is where I am."

"What are you talking about. We all know you and you know all of us. Don't you recognize your chickens?"

"No, I'm not in my town," Shlemiel insisted. "But," he continued, "Chelm Two does have the same people and the same houses as Chelm One, and that is why you are mistaken. Tomorrow I will continue on to Warsaw."

"In that case, where is my husband?" Mrs. Shlemiel inquired in a rage, and she proceeded to berate Shlemiel with all the curses she could think of.

"How should I know where your husband is?" Shlemiel replied.

Some of the neighbors could not help laughing; others pitied the family. Gimpel the healer announced that he knew of no remedy for such an illness. After some time, everybody went home.

Mrs. Shlemiel had cooked noodles and beans that evening, a dish that Shlemiel liked especially. She said to him, "You may be mad, but even a madman has to eat."

"Why should you feed a stranger?" Shlemiel asked.

"As a matter of fact, an ox like you should eat straw, not noodles and beans. Sit down and be quiet. Maybe some food and rest will bring you back to your senses."

"Mrs. Shlemiel, you're a good woman. My wife wouldn't feed a stranger. It would seem that there is some small difference between the two Chelms."

The noodles and beans smelled so good that Shlemiel needed no further coaxing. He sat down, and as he ate he spoke to the children:

"My dear children, I live in a house that looks exactly like this one. I have a wife and she is as like your mother as two peas are like each other. My children resemble you as drops of water resemble one another."

The younger children laughed; the older ones began to cry. Mrs. Shlemiel said, "As if being a Shlemiel wasn't enough, he had to go crazy in addition. What am I going to do now? I won't be able to leave the children with him when I go to market. Who knows what a madman may do?" She clasped her head in her hands and cried out, "What have I done to deserve this?"

Nevertheless, she made up a fresh bed for Shlemiel; and even though he had napped during the day, near the smithy, the moment his head touched the pillow he fell fast asleep and was soon snoring loudly. He again dreamed

277

As the crowd came in, one of the elders, Dopey Lekisch, was saying, "Maybe there really are two Chelms."

"If there are two, then why can't there be three, four, or even a hundred Chelms?" Sender Donkey interrupted.

"And even if there are a hundred Chelms, must there be a Shlemiel in each one of them?" argued Shmendrick Numskull.

Gronam Ox, the head elder, listened to all the arguments but was not yet prepared to express an opinion. However, his wrinkled, bulging forehead indicated that he was deep in thought. It was Gronam Ox who questioned Shlemiel. Shlemiel related everything that had happened to him, and when finished, Gronam asked, "Do you recognize me?"

"Surely. You are wise Gronam Ox."

"And in your Chelm is there also a Gronam Ox?"

"Yes, there is a Gronam Ox and he looks exactly like you."

"Isn't it possible that you turned around and came back to Chelm?" Gronam inquired.

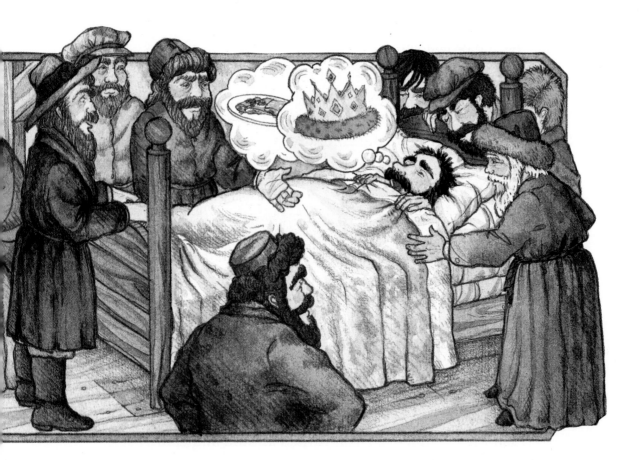

overcoming his bashfulness, he decided to get up. He threw off the covers and put his bare feet on the floor. "Don't let him run away," Mrs. Shlemiel screamed. "He'll disappear and I'll be a deserted wife, without a Shlemiel."

At this point Baruch the baker interrupted. "Let's take him to the elders. They'll know what to do."

"That's right! Let's take him to the elders," everybody agreed.

Although Shlemiel insisted that since he lived in Chelm One, the local elders had no power over him, several of the strong young men helped him into his pants, his boots, his coat and cap and escorted him to the house of Gronam Ox. The elders, who had already heard of the matter, had gathered early in the morning to consider what was to be done.

As the crowd came in, one of the elders, Dopey Lekisch, was saying, "Maybe there really are two Chelms."

"If there are two, then why can't there be three, four, or even a hundred Chelms?" Sender Donkey interrupted.

"And even if there are a hundred Chelms, must there be a Shlemiel in each one of them?" argued Shmendrick Numskull.

Gronam Ox, the head elder, listened to all the arguments but was not yet prepared to express an opinion. However, his wrinkled, bulging forehead indicated that he was deep in thought. It was Gronam Ox who questioned Shlemiel. Shlemiel related everything that had happened to him, and when finished, Gronam asked, "Do you recognize me?"

"Surely. You are wise Gronam Ox."

"And in your Chelm is there also a Gronam Ox?"

"Yes, there is a Gronam Ox and he looks exactly like you."

"Isn't it possible that you turned around and came back to Chelm?" Gronam inquired.

"Why should I turn around? I'm not a windmill," Shlemiel replied.

"In that case, you are not this Mrs. Shlemiel's husband."

"No, I'm not."

"Then Mrs. Shlemiel's husband, the real Shlemiel, must have left the day you came."

"It would seem so."

"Then he'll probably come back."

"Probably."

"In that case, you must wait until he returns. Then we'll know who is who."

"Dear elders, my Shlemiel has come back," screamed Mrs. Shlemiel. "I don't need two Shlemiels. One is more than enough."

"Whoever he is, he may not live in your house until everything is made clear," Gronam insisted.

"Where shall I live?" Shlemiel asked.

"In the poorhouse."

"What will I do in the poorhouse?"

"What will you do at home?"

"Who will take care of my children when I go to market?" moaned Mrs. Shlemiel. "Besides, I want a husband. Even a Shlemiel is better than no husband at all."

"Are we to blame that your husband left you and went to Warsaw?" Gronam asked. "Wait until he comes home."

Mrs. Shlemiel wept bitterly and the children cried, too. Shlemiel said, "How strange. My own wife always scolded me. My children talked back to me. And here a strange woman and strange children want me to live with them. It looks to me as if Chelm Two is actually better than Chelm One."

"Just a moment. I think I have an idea," interrupted Gronam.

"What is your idea?" Zeinvel Ninny inquired.

"Since we decided to send Shlemiel to the poorhouse, the town will have to hire someone to take care of Mrs. Shlemiel's children so she can go to market. Why not hire Shlemiel for that? It's true, he is not Mrs. Shlemiel's husband or the children's father. But he is so much like the real Shlemiel that the children will feel at home with him."

"What a wonderful idea!" cried Feivel Thickwit.

"Only King Solomon could have thought of such a wise solution," agreed Treitel Fool.

"Such a clever way out of this dilemma could only have been thought of in our Chelm," chimed in Shmendrick Numskull.

"How much do you want to be paid to take care of Mrs. Shlemiel's children?" asked Gronam.

For a moment Shlemiel stood there completely bewildered. Then he said, "Three groschen[5] a day."

"What?" screamed Mrs. Shlemiel. "What are three groschen nowadays? You shouldn't do it for less than six a day." She ran over to Shlemiel and pinched him on the arm. Shlemiel winced and cried out, "She pinches just like my wife."

The elders held a consultation among themselves. The town budget was very limited. Finally Gronam announced: "Three groschen may be too little, but six groschen a day is definitely too much, especially for a stranger. We will compromise and pay you five groschen a day. Shlemiel, do you accept?"

"Yes, but how long am I to keep this job?"

"Until the real Shlemiel comes home."

[5]groschen (gru' shən): a German coin no longer in use

Gronam's decision was soon known throughout Chelm, and the town admired his great wisdom and that of all the elders of Chelm.

At first, Shlemiel tried to keep the five groschen that the town paid him for himself. "If I'm not your husband, I don't have to support you," he told Mrs. Shlemiel.

"In that case, since I'm not your wife, I don't have to cook for you, darn your socks, or patch your clothes."

And so, of course, Shlemiel turned over his pay to her. It was the first time that Mrs. Shlemiel had ever gotten any money for the household from Shlemiel. Now when she was in a good mood, she would say to him, "What a pity you didn't decide to go to Warsaw ten years ago."

"Don't you ever miss your husband?" Shlemiel would ask.

"And what about you? Don't you miss your wife?" Mrs. Shlemiel would ask.

And both would admit that they were quite happy with matters as they stood.

Years passed and no Shlemiel returned to Chelm. The elders had many explanations for this. Zeinvel Ninny believed that Shlemiel had crossed the black mountains and had been eaten alive by the cannibals who live there. Dopey Lekisch thought that Shlemiel most probably had come to the Castle of Asmodeus, where he had been forced to marry a demon princess. Shmendrick Numskull came to the conclusion that Shlemiel had reached the edge of the world and had fallen off. There were many other theories; for example, that the real Shlemiel had lost memory and had simply forgotten that he was Shlemiel. Such things do happen.

Gronam did not like to impose his theories on other people; however, he was convinced that Shlemiel had gone to the other Chelm, where he had had exactly the same experience as the Shlemiel in this Chelm. He had been hired by the local community and was taking care of the other Mrs. Shlemiel's children for a wage of five groschen a day.

As for Shlemiel himself, he no longer knew what to think. The children were growing up and soon would be able to take care of themselves. Sometimes Shlemiel would sit and ponder, Where is the other Shlemiel? When will he come home? What is my real wife doing? Is she waiting for me, or has she got herself another Shlemiel? These were questions that he could not answer.

Every now and then Shlemiel would still get the desire to go traveling, but he could not bring himself to start out. What was the point of going on a trip if it led nowhere? Often, as he sat alone puzzling over the strange ways of the world, he would become more and more confused and begin humming to himself:

*Those who leave Chelm end up in Chelm.*
*Those who remain in Chelm are certainly in Chelm.*
*All roads lead to Chelm. All the world is one big Chelm.*

## ♦ LIBRARY LINK ♦

*For more tales about the wise men of Chelm and other unusual heroes, read the rest of the book* When Shlemiel Went to Warsaw and Other Stories *by Isaac Bashevis Singer.*

## Reader's Response

What tickled your funny bone about this story?

# When Shlemiel Went to Warsaw

## Checking Your Comprehension

1. Why do you think Mrs. Shlemiel said that long journeys are not for a Shlemiel? What led you to your conclusion?
2. What happened to make Shlemiel think he had arrived in a new town?
3. How did Shlemiel's family react when he first returned home?
4. If you were one of Shlemiel's children, how would you have tried to convince Shlemiel that he was really in his own home?
5. How wise do you think the elders of Chelm were? Explain your answer.

## Writing to Learn

**THINK AND REMEMBER**   Shlemiel was confused and didn't know where he was. People are often faced with similar problems. Can you remember a time when you misinterpreted directions, or a time when you lost your way?

**WRITE**   Share an autobiographical experience. Write about a time when you may have been confused about directions or a plan. If you wish, tell about a time when you were lost and didn't know where you were.

# Isaac Bashevis Singer

"I was born in Poland, on July 14, 1904, and grew up in Warsaw. My father was an orthodox rabbi; my mother was the daughter of the Rabbi of Bilgoray. I studied in Cheder, a religious school, and only studied one subject, religion," stated Isaac Bashevis Singer.

286

His family included a younger brother, Mosha, and an older brother and sister, Israel Joshua and Hinde Esther.

One can read about Mr. Singer's childhood years in the author's own words in *A Day of Pleasure: Stories of a Boy Growing Up in Warsaw,* a book that won the 1970 National Book Award for Children's Literature.

Although Singer was a student at the Rabbinical Seminary in Warsaw, he chose not to become a rabbi. "I do not deserve to be a rabbi. In our Orthodox household every second word was 'forbidden.' In my later years, I'm practicing many of the things that were forbidden!"

Instead he went to work as a journalist for the Yiddish[1] press in Poland after completion of his studies. In 1935 Mr. Singer came to the United States and worked as a journalist and book reviewer for New York's *Jewish Daily Forward.*

"In 1935, when I came here, I got a job on the *Forward.* I said to my editor, 'What I want is a steady job.' He replied, 'A steady job? In a language that will die in ten years?' Yet, you see, Yiddish is still with us."

And indeed it is. Mr. Singer has done much to make the culture, customs, and idiomatic language of the Jewish people familiar the world over. Although he originally wrote in Hebrew,[2] he long ago adopted Yiddish as his medium of expression; he personally supervises the translation of his works into the English language.

His first book for children was *Zlateh the Goat and Other Stories.* I asked Mr. Singer why he turned to writing for children. "Because I felt I could do it," he answered. "I still believe there is no basic difference in writing for grown-ups or for children."

[1]Yiddish: a language written in Hebrew characters with words borrowed from Hebrew, Russian, Polish, and English
[2]Hebrew: the official language of Israel

*Zlateh the Goat* is a collection of seven tales set in Chelm, a village of fools where the seven elders are the most foolish of all the inhabitants. The book's illustrations, done by the Caldecott Award-winning artist Maurice Sendak, beautifully capture the bittersweetness of Jewish folklore and perfectly depict what Mr. Singer's text is all about. In 1967 *Zlateh the Goat* was designated a Newbery Honor Book.

The same year *The Fearsome Inn* appeared, as well as *Mazel and Shlimazel or the Milk of a Lioness,* a handsome picture book illustrated by Margot Zemach. This tale was inspired by Singer's memory of a story his mother told when he was a boy.

His fourth book for children, *When Shlemiel Went to Warsaw*, also illustrated by Margot Zemach, was a 1969 Newbery Honor Book. Mr. Singer relates eight stories, some inspired by traditional Jewish tales, ranging from hilarious trickery in ''Shrewd Todie and Lyzer the Miser'' to the tender ''Menaseh's Dreams.''

In 1970 the author received the National Book Award for his unforgettable *A Day of Pleasure*. The stories in this volume actually took place during the first fourteen years of his life. The last story, ''Shosha,'' deals with a later time.

In a brief foreword to the text, the author wrote: ''I have a good deal more to tell about myself, my family, and the Poland of days gone by. I hope to continue these memoirs and reveal a world that is little known to you, but which is rich in comedy and tragedy, rich in its individuality, wisdom, foolishness, wildness, and goodness.''

In preparing his books, Mr. Singer told me, ''I write the stories, translate them, and edit them together with another translator. If they are bad, the critics let me know.''

The author is not worried about the Yiddish language slowly disappearing. "I should worry? I put all my capital, you might say, in Yiddish. But I'm not at all worried. Declining it is. But you know that in our history there is a long way between declining and dying."

In addition to his writing, he does a great deal of lecturing. "I also steal chickens," he jested. He lives with his wife in an apartment house on New York's Upper West Side. His favorite possessions are his books. In his spare time he enjoys "working and walking and visits with his son and three grandchildren."

Since the 1960's, Singer has created over fifteen books for girls and boys; his works have earned him much praise. In 1978, he won the Nobel Prize for Literature, the most distinguished award a writer can receive.

Of all that has been said of Isaac Bashevis Singer, perhaps the *Chicago Tribune* sums up his work best with the statement:

"(His) tales are no more for Jewish children than Andersen's fairy tales are for Danish children. They have the sweep, the direct voice-to-ear simplicity, the easy familiarity which make all folk literature universal."

## Reader's Response

What did you find remarkable about Isaac Bashevis Singer? Explain your answer.

## LEE BENNETT HOPKINS INTERVIEWS

# Isaac Bashevis Singer

### Checking Your Comprehension

1. Did Mr. Singer's education prepare him for his career? Explain your answer.
2. Why does Mr. Singer write in the Yiddish language?
3. What do you think Mr. Singer would have done if the Yiddish language had died, as his editor had predicted?
4. Where does Mr. Singer get his ideas for his stories?
5. Why do you think Mr. Singer says that writing for children is no different from writing for grown-ups? How did you think of your answer?
6. Do you think adults would like Isaac Bashevis Singer's children's books? Explain your answer.

### Writing to Learn

**THINK AND INTERPRET** To *interpret* means to explain the meaning of something. You have read a story by Isaac Bashevis Singer, "When Shlemiel Went to Warsaw." You also have read an interview with the author. Now think about this quotation from the last part of the interview.

> "(Singer's) tales are no more for Jewish children
>
> than Andersen's fairy tales are for Danish children."

**WRITE** Write a paragraph to explain your interpretation of the quotation. End by saying whether you agree or disagree with the quotation.

**THINKING**

READING
THINKING
WRITING
CONNECTION

*A Strategy for Thinking:*

# Recognizing Expectations

When you read, it often helps to have expectations about the material you are going to read. If you are in the right mind-set for a story, you may understand it better and enjoy it more. Your expectations may not always be correct, but you will be thinking about the story and using clues to help you anticipate events.

## Learning the Strategy

Where do expectations come from? They are a combination of clues from the beginning of a story and clues from your own experience. When you start a story, you should read the title and the first paragraph. Then ask yourself, "What do I expect will happen in this story?"

Often, there are other clues to use as well. Do the pictures at the beginning tell you anything? Have you ever read anything by this author before? What about the type of story? You will have different expectations for a science fiction story than for a fable.

One way to keep track of your expectations is to make an expectations chart. Read the beginning of "When Shlemiel Went to Warsaw," and look at the following chart.

**When Shlemiel Went to Warsaw**
by Isaac Bashevis Singer

Though Shlemiel was a lazybones and a sleepyhead and hated to move, he always daydreamed of taking a trip. He had heard many stories about faraway countries, huge deserts, deep oceans, and high mountains, and often discussed with Mrs. Shlemiel his great wish to go on a long journey.

## EXPECTATIONS CHART

| Clues | Expectation |
|---|---|
| What does the title lead you to expect? | The story is about a trip to Warsaw, a city in Poland. |
| What do you expect based on the first page? · | The story is about Shlemiel's trip. |
| Does the type of story make you expect anything? | Stories about journeys often turn into adventures. |

## *Using the Strategy*

Read the first page of the next story, "The Search for the Magic Lake." Then make an expectations chart for the story using clues from the title, the first few paragraphs, and the type of story. Remember to use information from your own experience as well.

## *Applying the Strategy to the Next Story*

Save your expectations chart to use when you read "The Search for the Magic Lake." You will be asked at several points whether the story followed your expectations.

◄◆► The writing connection can be found on page 369.

*Journeys may be undertaken out of curiosity or for pleasure. Or, they may be taken as a quest—a daring search for something of great importance.*

# The Search for the
# MAGIC

*an Inca Tale retold
by Genevieve Barlow*

Long ago there was a ruler of the vast Inca[1] Empire who had an only son. This youth brought great joy to his father's heart but also a sadness, for the prince had been born in ill health.

As the years passed the prince's health did not improve, and none of the court doctors could find a cure for his illness.

One night the aged emperor went down on his knees and prayed at the altar.

"Oh Great Ones," he said, "I am getting older and will soon leave my people and join you in the heavens. There is no one to look after them but my son, the prince. I pray you make him well and strong so he can be a fit ruler for my people. Tell me how his malady can be cured."

[1]Inca (ing' ku): an ancient people of South America

LAKE

The emperor put his head in his hands and waited for an answer. Soon he heard a voice coming from the fire that burned constantly in front of the altar.

"Let the prince drink water from the magic lake at the end of the world," the voice said, "and he will be well."

At that moment the fire sputtered and died. Among the cold ashes lay a golden flask.

But the emperor was much too old to make the long journey to the end of the world, and the young prince was too ill to travel. So the emperor proclaimed that whosoever should fill the golden flask with the magic water would be greatly rewarded.

Many brave men set out to search for the magic lake, but none could find it. Days and weeks passed and still the flask remained empty.

In a valley, some distance from the emperor's palace, lived a poor farmer who had a wife, two grown sons, and a young daughter.

One day the older son said to his father, "Let my brother and me join in the search for the magic lake. Before the moon is new again, we shall return and help you harvest the corn and potatoes."

The father remained silent. He was not thinking of the harvest, but feared for his sons' safety.

When the father did not answer, the second son added, "Think of the rich reward, Father!"

"It is their duty to go," said his wife, "for we must all try to help our emperor and the young prince."

After his wife had spoken, the father yielded.

"Go if you must, but beware of the wild beasts and evil creatures," he cautioned.

With their parents' blessing, and an affectionate farewell from their young sister, the sons set out on their journey.

They found many lakes, but none where the sky touched the water.

Finally the younger brother said, "Before another day has passed we must return to help father with the harvest."

"Yes," agreed the other, "but I have thought of a plan. Let us each carry a jar of water from any lake along the way. We can say it will cure the prince. Even if it doesn't, surely the emperor will give us a small reward for our trouble." ❖

"Agreed," said the younger brother.

On arriving at the palace, the deceitful youths told the emperor and his court that they brought water from the magic lake. At once the prince was given a sip from each of the brothers' jars, but of course he remained as ill as before.

Do you expect their plan will work?

"Perhaps the water must be sipped from the golden flask," one of the high priests said.

But the golden flask would not hold the water. In some mysterious way the water from the jars disappeared as soon as it was poured into the flask.

In despair the emperor called for his magician and said to him, "Can you break the spell of the flask so the water will remain for my son to drink?"

"I cannot do that, your majesty," replied the magician. "But I believe," he added wisely, "that the flask is telling us that we have been deceived by the two brothers. The flask can be filled only with water from the magic lake."

When the brothers heard this, they trembled with fright, for they knew their falsehood was discovered.

So angry was the emperor that he ordered the brothers thrown into chains. Each day they were forced to drink water from their jars as a reminder of their false deed. News of their disgrace spread far and wide.

Again the emperor sent messengers throughout the land pleading for someone to bring the magic water before death claimed him and the young prince.

Sumac,[2] the litle sister of the deceitful youths, was tending her flock of llamas when she heard the sound of the royal trumpet. Then came the voice of the emperor's servant with his urgent message from the court.

Quickly the child led her llamas home and begged her parents to let her go in search of the magic water.

Do you predict Sumac will be successful?

"You are too young," her father said. "Besides, look at what has already befallen your brothers. Some evil spirit must have taken hold of them to make them tell such a lie."

And her mother said, "We could not bear to be without our precious Sumac!"

"But think how sad our emperor will be if the young prince dies," replied the innocent child. "And if I can find the magic lake, perhaps the emperor will forgive my brothers and send them home."

"Dear husband," said Sumac's mother, "maybe it is the will of the gods that we let her go."

Once again the father gave his permission.

"It is true," he murmured, "I must think of our emperor."

[2]Sumac (soo mäk)

Sumac was overjoyed, and went skipping out to the corral to harness one of her pet llamas. It would carry her provisions and keep her company.

Meanwhile her mother filled a little woven bag with food and drink for Sumac—toasted golden kernels of corn and a little earthen jar of *chicha,*[3] a beverage made from crushed corn.

The three embraced each other tearfully before Sumac set out bravely on her mission, leading her pet llama along the trail.

The first night she slept, snug and warm against her llama, in the shelter of a few rocks. But when she heard the hungry cry of the puma, she feared for her pet animal and bade it return safely home.

The next night she spent in the top branches of a tall tree, far out of reach of the dreadful puma. She hid her provisions in a hole in the tree trunk.

At sunrise she was aroused by the voices of gentle sparrows resting on a nearby limb.

"Poor child," said the oldest sparrow, "she can never find her way to the lake."

"Let us help her," chorused the others.

"Oh please do!" implored the child, "and forgive me for intruding in your tree."

"We welcome you," chirped another sparrow, "for you are the same little girl who yesterday shared your golden corn with us."

"We shall help you," continued the first sparrow, who was the leader, "for you are a good child. Each of us will give you a wing feather, and you must hold them all together in one hand as a fan. The feathers have magic powers that will carry you wherever you wish to go. They will

[3]chicha (chē chä)

also protect you from harm." Each sparrow then lifted a wing, sought out a special feather hidden underneath, and gave it to Sumac. She fashioned them into the shape of a little fan, taking the ribbon from her hair to bind the feathers together so none would be lost.

"I must warn you," said the oldest sparrow, "that the lake is guarded by three terrible creatures. But have no fear. Hold the magic fan up to your face and you will be unharmed."

Sumac thanked the birds over and over again. Then, holding up the fan in her chubby hands, she said politely, "Please, magic fan, take me to the lake at the end of the world."

A soft breeze swept her out of the top branches of the tree and through the valley. Then up she was carried, higher and higher into the sky, until she could look down and see the great mountain peaks covered with snow.

At last the wind put her down on the shore of a beautiful lake. It was, indeed, the lake at the end of the world, for, on the opposite side from where she stood, the sky came down so low it touched the water.

Sumac tucked the magic fan into her waistband and ran to the edge of the water. Suddenly her face fell. She had

left everything back in the forest. What could she use for carrying the precious water back to the prince?

"Oh, I do wish I had remembered the jar!" she said, weeping.

Suddenly she heard a soft thud in the sand at her feet. She looked down and discovered a beautiful golden flask—the same one the emperor had found in the ashes.

Sumac took the flask and kneeled at the water's edge. Just then a hissing voice behind her said, "Get away from my lake or I shall wrap my long, hairy legs around your neck."

Sumac turned around. There stood a giant crab as large as a pig and as black as night.

With trembling hands the child took the magic fan from her waistband and spread it open in front of her face. As soon as the crab looked at it, he closed his eyes and fell down on the sand in a deep sleep.

Once more Sumac started to fill the flask. This time she was startled by a fierce voice bubbling up from the water.

"Get away from my lake or I shall eat you," gurgled a giant green alligator. His long tail beat the water angrily.

Sumac waited until the creature swam closer. Then she held up the fan. The alligator blinked. He drew back.

Slowly, quietly, he sank to the bottom of the lake in a sound sleep.

Before Sumac could recover from her fright, she heard a shrill whistle in the air. She looked up and saw a flying serpent. His skin was red as blood. Sparks flew from his eyes.

"Get away from my lake or I shall bite you," hissed the serpent as it batted its wings around her head.

Again Sumac's fan saved her from harm. The serpent closed his eyes and drifted to the ground. He folded his wings and coiled up on the sand. Then he began to snore.

Sumac sat for a moment to quiet herself. Then, realizing that the danger was past, she sighed with great relief.

"Now I can fill the golden flask and be on my way," she said to herself.

When this was done, she held the flask tightly in one hand and clutched the fan in the other.

"Please take me to the palace," she said.

Hardly were the words spoken, when she found herself safely in front of the palace gates. She looked at the tall guard.

"I wish to see the emperor," Sumac uttered in trembling tones.

"Why, little girl?" the guard asked kindly.

"I bring water from the magic lake to cure the prince."

The guard looked down at her in astonishment.

"Come!" he commanded in a voice loud and deep as thunder.

In just a few moments Sumac was led into a room full of sadness. The emperor was pacing up and down in despair. The prince lay motionless on a huge bed. His eyes were closed and his face was without color. Beside him knelt his mother, weeping.

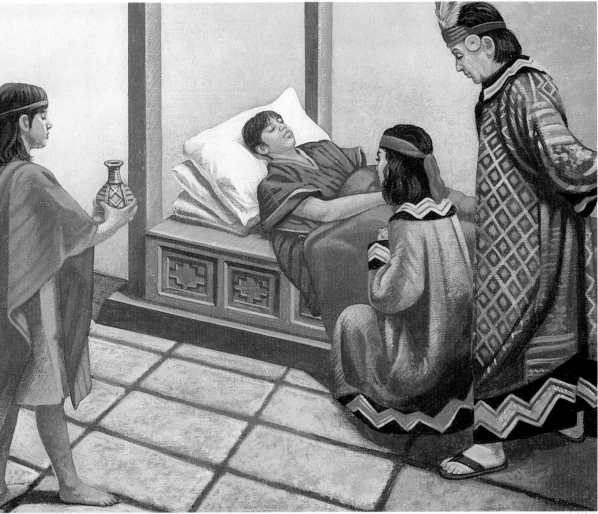

◆◆◆

**Did you expect the prince to get better?**

Without wasting words, Sumac went to the prince and gave him a few drops of magic water. Soon he opened his eyes. His cheeks became flushed. It was not long before he sat up in bed. He drank some more. ◆◆◆

"How strong I feel!" the prince cried joyfully.

The emperor and his wife embraced Sumac. Then Sumac told them of her adventurous trip to the lake. They praised her courage. They marveled at the reappearance of the golden flask and at the powers of the magic fan.

"Dear child," said the emperor, "all the riches of my empire are not enough to repay you for saving my son's life. Ask what you will and it shall be yours."

"Oh, generous emperor," said Sumac timidly, "I have but three wishes."

"Name them and they shall be yours," urged the emperor.

"First, I wish my brothers to be free to return to my parents. They have learned their lesson and will never be false again. I know they were only thinking of a reward for my parents. Please forgive them."

"Guards, free them at once!" ordered the emperor.

"Secondly, I wish the magic fan returned to the forest so the sparrows may have their feathers again."

This time the emperor had no time to speak. Before anyone in the room could utter a sound, the magic fan lifted itself up, spread itself wide open, and floated out the window toward the woods. Everyone watched in amazement. When the fan was out of sight, they applauded.

"What is your last wish, dear Sumac?" asked the queen mother.

"I wish that my parents be given a large farm and great flocks of llamas, vicuñas, and alpacas, so they will not be poor any longer."

"It will be so," said the emperor, "but I am sure your parents never considered themselves poor with so wonderful a daughter."

"Won't you stay with us in the palace?" ventured the prince.

"Yes, stay with us!" urged the emperor and his wife. "We will do everything to make you happy."

"Oh thank you," said Sumac blushing happily, "but I must return to my parents and to my brothers. I miss them as I know they have missed me. They do not even know I am safe, for I came directly to your palace."

The royal family did not try to detain Sumac any longer.

"My own guard will see that you get home safely," said the emperor.

When she reached home, she found that all she had wished for had come to pass: her brothers were waiting for her with their parents; a beautiful house and huge barn were being constructed; her father had received a deed granting him many acres of new, rich farm land.

Sumac ran into the arms of her happy family. ◆❖◆

◆❖◆

**Did your expectations for the story come true? How did your expectations help you make sense of the story?**

**R**eader's Response

How did you feel about the wishes that Sumac made? Explain your answer.

# The Search for the
# MAGIC LAKE

## Checking Your Comprehension

1. Why did the emperor want water from the magic lake?
2. Why did the two brothers deceive the emperor?
3. How were Sumac's reasons for looking for the magic lake different from her brothers' reasons?
4. Could Sumac have found the lake without the sparrows' help? Explain your answer.
5. What did the emperor's actions at the end of the story tell you about his feelings? How did you arrive at your answer?
6. What do you think was Sumac's bravest act? Explain your answer.

## Writing to Learn

**THINK AND IMAGINE**  When Sumac was granted three wishes, she did not wish for anything for herself. Think about the three wishes Sumac made for others.

**Sumac's Wishes**
- that her brothers be set free
- that the fan be returned to the forest
- that her parents never be poor again

**WRITE**  If you could make three wishes for others, what would they be? Write three wishes. Then choose one of them and write a paragraph explaining why it is your most important wish.

307

# The Way Through The Woods

## by Rudyard Kipling

They shut the road through the woods
Seventy years ago.
Weather and rain have undone it again,
And now you would never know
There was once a road through the woods
Before they planted the trees.
It is underneath the coppice and heath,
And the thin anemones.
Only the keeper sees
That, where the ring-dove broods,
And the badgers roll at ease,
There was once a road through the woods.

Yet, if you enter the woods
Of a summer evening late,
When the night-air cools on the trout-ringed pools
Where the otter whistles his mate
(They fear not men in the woods,
Because they see so few),
You will hear the beat of the horse's feet,
And the swish of a skirt in the dew,
Steadily cantering through
The misty solitudes,
As though they perfectly knew
The old lost road through the woods . . .
But there is no road through the woods.

# Snowshoe Trek To Otter River

## By David Budbill

*Twelve-year-old Daniel packs his gear before setting out on a day's hike. He is ready for any emergency . . . or so he thinks.*

Early in the morning after Daniel finished breakfast, he took his backpack off the wall and unpacked it. He had packed everything carefully last night, but now that it was time to go, he had to be sure everything was there, ready, in case he needed it. Daniel could see his mother moving about the kitchen, watching him out of the corner of her eye. He knew she was laughing to herself about the way he fussed over his equipment. But the gear was important. If he got caught out there in a blizzard, or if something happened to him and he

couldn't get back, his life might depend on the few things he carried on his back.

He spread the backpack's contents on the kitchen floor. Nested cookpots: one 8-inch skillet with folding handle, one 6-inch plate, one quart pail with lid, a metal cup, a fork and spoon. His pocketknife would do the cutting. A bunch of waterproof matches wrapped in tinfoil. Two fire starters he had made by rolling paper tightly, tying it with string, and soaking it in hot paraffin. A compass, a hatchet, and a sleeping bag. Daniel

cut three thick slices of his mother's homemade bread, buttered them, then took two chunks of bacon and three eggs from the refrigerator. He wrapped everything carefully and put it in the backpack with a bag of nuts and raisins, a little salt, a small jar of sugar, and a handful of tea in a small bag. As far as Daniel was concerned, bacon and eggs, bread, and tea was the perfect campfire lunch for a winter's day of snowshoeing.

Daniel was only twelve, but he knew a lot about getting along in the woods. His parents were dairy farmers. Although they lived surrounded by the wilderness, they never really were a part of it. But down the road from Daniel's house there was an old man, a Frenchman by the name of Mr. Bateau, who had come down from Canada years ago. Mr. Bateau was Daniel's favorite person. He was a man of the woods—a logger, a hunter, a fisherman, and a trapper. Mr. Bateau had taught Daniel all he knew about the wild world. He had shown him how to fish, build wilderness camps, identify wild flowers and animal tracks, how to talk to birds, call foxes, make coyotes howl. But most of all Mr. Bateau had given Daniel a love of the wilderness that drew Daniel out now into the white, cold world beyond his house.

Daniel's plan was to strike out across the high swamp behind his farm and continue down the mountain to Otter River in the valley below. Last summer he and his best friend, Seth, had built a lean-to on the far side of Otter River. Daniel planned to have his lunch at the camp, check the supplies they had stashed there, and return home before dark.

When the backpack was packed again, Daniel put on two pairs of heavy wool socks and pulled his rubber-bottom, leather-top winter boots over them. He wore long underwear and wool pants. Over a long-sleeved undershirt he wore a cotton shirt and over that a wool shirt and over that another, heavier wool shirt. If he got hot, he could peel off a layer or two, but he doubted he'd get hot. He looked out the window at the thermometer. It said ten degrees below zero. By noon it might be ten above.

He was ready. He slipped his backpack on, kissed his mother good-bye, and went onto the porch. He pulled his wool cap down over his ears, put on his mittens, picked up his snowshoes, and stepped out into the snow. He slipped his boots into the snowshoe harnesses and adjusted the bindings carefully.

It was a clear, bright, still day. The spruce and fir trees on the horizon made a deep green band that separated the bright blue sky from the white, pure white earth. As Daniel struck out across the pasture behind the house, the cold air stung his face. It felt good. It was the perfect day for a hike.

Last night's snow had added six inches to the three feet already on the ground. Daniel knew the new snow meant animal tracks would be fresh. He'd do some tracking along the way.

Soon he was beyond the open fields and deep into the swamp. It was a different world, darker, quieter. The big spruce and fir trees covered up the sky. There was no sound. It was as if this swamp were a noiseless chamber. All Daniel could hear were his snowshoes, whispering, hissing as he moved along. He stopped. Listened. Now there was no sound at all. None. It was as if everything in the world were dead except for one boy who stood silent and alone, deep in a snowy evergreen swamp.

Suddenly, out of nowhere, the sound of galloping broke the silence. Daniel's heart jumped. He crouched down and waited. Then, in a crash of twigs, a shower of snow, three deer burst into a clearing right in front of him—a buck, a doe, and last year's fawn. The three deer stopped. They stood silent in their tracks. Slowly the buck raised his head and sniffed the wind. He caught Daniel's scent. The buck gave a terrible snorting roar, stomped his foot, and away the three went in a muffled thunder of hooves, their sleek, brown bodies plowing through the snow. Daniel stood up and watched the three deer disappear into the dark trees. His heart was still pounding.

He came to a broad open place in the middle of the swamp. Beavers had dammed the swamp brook and made a pond. Daniel could see a large hump in the level snow near the dam. It was a beaver house. As Daniel crossed the pond, he thought about the beavers under all that snow and ice, lazing away the winter, safe in their underwater home. At this very moment there could be a beaver swimming only a few feet below his snowshoes.

When he reached the other side of the beaver pond, Daniel found some rabbit tracks. They weren't really made by a rabbit, even though everybody called them rabbits. They were made by a snowshoe hare, the kind that turns white in the winter and has big, webbed feet for getting around in deep snow. Daniel could tell from the size of the tracks that it was a young rabbit. He followed the tracks up the hill to a place where they stopped abruptly. Here there was a pool of frozen blood and beside the blood on either side, printed neatly in the snow, the marks of two large wings. Daniel knew what had happened.

The hare had been hopping along, when, out of the sky, swiftly, silently, a large hawk had dropped down, his wings set back, his large claws thrust out and down. Thud! Daniel could see the hawk's sharp claws sink into the rabbit's back. He could hear the rabbit scream as it died. Then the hawk beat his wings, leaving the prints there in the snow, and was away, up into the air with his breakfast.

Daniel felt sorry for the rabbit, but he knew this was the way the hawk ate, the way he stayed alive. Last fall Daniel had helped his father slaughter a pig so they could eat meat all winter. The hawk had slaughtered a rabbit so he could eat meat too. But Daniel couldn't help feeling sorry for the rabbit, just as he had felt sorry for the pig. He stood for a long time staring at the rabbit tracks that went nowhere, the frozen blood, the imprint of the hawk's wings. Then he pushed on.

He was out of the evergreen swamp now and starting down the mountain toward the river. Here the trees were all hardwoods, and the sun shone brightly through the bare branches. A chickadee scolded Daniel from a nearby tree.

Daniel saw tiny ruffed grouse tracks everywhere. The grouse had come to the hardwoods to eat the buds off birch trees. Suddenly there was a thundering rush, a wild flutter of wings. Daniel stopped. Grouse were flying everywhere, weaving crazily between the trees. One bird flew right at him. He threw his hands up in front of his face. Then the bird was gone.

Soon Daniel was down the mountain. Otter River was before him. He could see the snow-covered camp on the other side. He walked up and down the riverbank looking for a place to cross. Daniel knew that where the river ran still and deep the ice would

be the thickest. There was a place like that about a hundred yards upstream, but the river looked safe here too and it wasn't quite so wide. Daniel took off his snowshoes. If he fell through with them on, his feet would be trapped under the ice. He stepped out onto the river and jumped up and down a couple of times. The ice was solid. He started across.

When he was almost to the far shore, he heard a loud, thundering crack begin near him and shoot up the river. Slowly, he began to sink. Then more and louder cracks. Then a deep, rumbling roar. He was going down! The whole river was opening up!

Daniel heaved his snowshoes onto the shore and grabbed for solid ice. His boots were full of water, his legs numbed by the cold. Again and again he reached for the edge of solid ice. Each time the ice broke away and bobbed uselessly in front of him. Then his feet struck bottom. He stood waist deep in icy water. He could wade to shore. But there were great slabs of loose ice floating between him and the bank. When he tried to climb on top of them, they sank. When he tried to push them out of his way, they bumped into each other and blocked the way. He was trapped.

Daniel's mind raced. He had to think of something fast. In only a few minutes he would be so cold he'd faint. That would be the end. Quickly he took his pack off his back, undid the top, and grabbed his hatchet. He threw the pack up on the bank. Then, slowly, painfully, Daniel began chopping a channel through the slabs of ice toward the shore.

He reached the bank and pulled himself cold and numb out of the water. He was soaked. The instant his wet clothes met the cold air, they froze. His troubles had only begun.

By now his pants had frozen so hard he could barely bend his knees. He gathered up his snowshoes and pack and limped, stiff-legged, to his camp. Daniel was freezing, not just freezing cold, but actually freezing, freezing to death.

He took the small shovel he and Seth had stashed in the lean-to and cleaned the snow away from the fire pit. He broke an armful of dead branches off a hemlock tree for kindling, took one of the fire starters out of his pack, and lit a fire. He was glad now that last summer he and Seth had stacked dry wood next to the camp.

Soon the fire was burning. Daniel was sleepy and cold, so cold. All he wanted to do was lie down, but he knew he couldn't. Not yet.

He stuck two forked sticks in the snow, one on each side of the fire. Then he laid a long pole between the two sticks above the fire. He propped his snowshoes near the fire, crawled inside the lean-to, and spread his sleeping bag on the bare, dry ground inside the shelter. Then he put more wood on the fire.

When all this was done, he was ready to do the only thing left to do. He couldn't go home. It was too far away. He'd freeze before he got there. He couldn't call for help. There was no one for miles. He'd have to thaw and dry out before he could go any farther.

Although it was below zero, Daniel took off his clothes. He draped his pants and long underwear, socks, and mittens over the long pole. He hung a wool shirt on each snowshoe. He put his boots on a rock near the fire. The snow was so cold on his bare feet that it felt hot. When all his clothes were hung over the fire, he limped into the lean-to and climbed inside his sleeping bag. He shivered violently. He wanted to cry, but he was too cold. Slowly, very slowly, his body heat began to fill the sleeping bag. He

began to warm up. He took the bag of nuts and raisins from his pack and ate. He could see his clothes dripping and steaming over the fire. Daniel was relaxed now. His eyes grew heavy. He fell asleep.

When Daniel woke up, the fire was down to coals. It was warm inside the bag. He had no idea how long he had slept. It may have been an hour or two. He got up and put more wood on the fire. He felt his clothes. They were dry, except for his boots. He got dressed. His clothes smelled like wood smoke. He hung his boots from the pole by their laces and began to fix lunch. He set the bacon to frying in the skillet and put some snow to melt in the quart pail for tea. Since snow water always tasted flat, he added a little salt to the melting snow.

When the water boiled, he added tea and put the pail on a rock at the edge of the fire. He reached into his backpack for the eggs. They were smashed. They must have broken when he threw the pack up on the bank. He dumped the slimy mixture into his metal plate and separated shell from egg as best he could. He took the cooked bacon out of the skillet and put the eggs in, scrambling them with his fork. They cooked quickly. Then he ate. It seemed to Daniel like the best meal he had ever eaten. Crisp bacon, eggs scrambled in bacon grease, good bread with lots of butter, and hot, sweet tea. It was good.

Daniel laughed to himself. Here he was, in the middle of winter, sitting by a fire, by a river he had just fallen into, eating lunch, thinking how good the tea was! It was hard to believe. A couple of hours ago he was almost dead. Now he sat comfortably, his feet warmed by the fire, almost as if nothing had happened.

When the last of the tea was gone, he put his boots on, cleaned and packed his gear, shoveled snow on the fire, rolled the sleeping bag, and started home. This time he headed upstream to where the river moved slowly and the ice was thick. Nobody ever crossed a frozen river more carefully than Daniel did that afternoon.

When he reached the other side, he noticed that the sun was low in the southern sky. It got dark early this time of year, and home was a long way off. He'd have to travel to get there before dark.

He followed his own trail up through the hardwoods, over the brow of the mountain, and down into the swamp.

318

By the time he reached the other side of the beaver pond, the sun was almost down. It was dark in the thick trees of the swamp. Daniel had trouble finding his trail. It got darker and darker. He was hurrying now. Although it was growing colder, he was sweating. Then out of the darkening sky fear dropped down and seized him. He had gotten off the trail. He was lost.

Daniel was running. He had to find his old trail and fast. But the faster he moved, the more confused he got. Then he stopped. He found a log sticking up above the snow, brushed the snow off its top, and sat down. He knew that to get panicky when lost was the worst thing that could happen. He took the bag of nuts and raisins from his pack and ate a handful. He would sit here until he quieted down and decided what to do. But it was hard. He had to force himself to sit on that log. Something inside urged him to get up and run. It didn't matter where, just run! He fought the urge with all the strength he had.

Then he heard the soft rustle of wings. A large white bird floated silently into a tree above him. It was a snowy owl. It seemed to Daniel like a ghost. Its fierce yellow eyes shot through him like needles. Why did that bird sit there, staring? What did it want? Daniel couldn't stand it. He jumped up, made a snowball, and threw it at the owl. The snowball almost hit the owl, but the owl didn't move. He sat there, staring, as if to say, "I'm not the one who is afraid." Then, as if nothing had happened, the snowy owl rolled backward off the branch and disappeared without a sound into the dark trees.

The owl, the noiseless chamber of a forest, the darkness, frightened Daniel more than falling in the river. When he had gone down in the river, he knew what he had to do to save himself. The only question was whether he could do it. But here, in this wild place, there was something unknown, something strange. He felt out of place, alone, deserted. It seemed as if even the trees around him were about to grab him, take him off somewhere, deeper into the swamp, where he would be lost forever.

He decided what to do. He would get up, calmly, and follow his tracks back to where he lost the trail. He'd get back on the trail and go home. It was hard to go back, but he had to do it.

When he found the trail again, he moved along it slowly. It was so dark

now he couldn't afford to get lost again. At last, after what seemed like hours, he found himself standing at the edge of a broad, open field. At the far end of the field he could see his house. The kitchen window glowed warm and orange in the dusky eve-ning light. He struck off across the meadow toward the lighted window.

Daniel took off his snowshoes and stuck them in the snow in front of the house. He dumped his backpack on the porch and stepped into the bright, warm kitchen.

## Reader's Response

Did you feel Daniel's danger as you read? Explain your answer.

# Snowshoe Trek To Otter River

## ◆ Checking Your Comprehension

1. Why was Daniel so careful about the equipment he took on his hike?
2. What was the most important thing Daniel learned from Mr. Bateau?
3. Why did Daniel fall into the river?
4. Summarize the things Daniel did when he emerged cold and numb from the river.
5. What might have happened to Daniel if he had not been able to find the trail? What makes you think this?
6. Do you think Daniel used skill and good judgment in solving his problems? Explain your answer.

## ◆ Writing to Learn

**THINK AND VISUALIZE**  Details make an adventure story realistic and exciting. Below is a list of words the author used to tell about what Daniel wore.

| | |
|---|---|
| wool cap | mittens |
| cotton shirt | long-sleeve undershirt |
| long underwear | heavy wool shirt |
| wool shirt | wool pants |
| two pairs of | leather-top boots |
| heavy wool socks | with rubber bottoms |

**WRITE**  Think of an outdoor experience you have had. On a sheet of paper, list every detail you can remember about what you wore or what you saw or what you did. Then use your list of details to help you write a paragraph describing your outdoor experience.

## Study Skill:
# *Encyclopedia*

In "Snowshow Trek to Otter River," Daniel learned many things about the wilderness from Mr. Bateau, his favorite person. We read that Mr. Bateau "showed him how to fish, build wilderness camps, identify wild flowers and animal tracks, how to talk to birds, call foxes, make coyotes howl." The story is filled with factual details such as these about survival in the north woods.

If you wanted to know more about life in the wilderness, you would not be able to go to Mr. Bateau for your answers. You could, however, go to an encyclopedia for information.

An encyclopedia is similar to a dictionary in the sense that the articles, like the words in a dictionary, are arranged in alphabetical order. Also, most encyclopedias have guide words printed at the top corner of each page, like a dictionary. The guide words help you find the subject of your article quickly.

Most encyclopedias contain far too much information to fit in a single book, so they are divided into several volumes. The volumes are arranged alphabetically, and each volume has guide letters printed on the spine to help you choose the correct one. For example, Volume 1 of an encyclopedia might contain all of the articles about subjects beginning with the letters *A−Ba*, Volume 2 might cover all articles starting with *Be−Ce*, and so on.

To find information about beavers in the encyclopedia, you would locate Volume 2 and look for the article on *Beavers*. However, this article may not provide you with all of the information you need about beavers. For example, it may not provide information on beaver houses or wintering habits.

To find additional information on your topic, you would have to look at the *index*. The index is a separate volume that lists all of the entries that can be found in the encyclopedia for a particular subject. The index entries are arranged in alphabetical order. Guide words at the top of each page help you quickly locate the topic in the index. All related articles are listed under the main entry. The volume number and page number are given after each article listed. For example, an article on page 223 of Volume 3 would be listed as **3**:223. Often, the index will also specify the kinds of illustrations included in the article. Study the sample index below and look for all of these features.

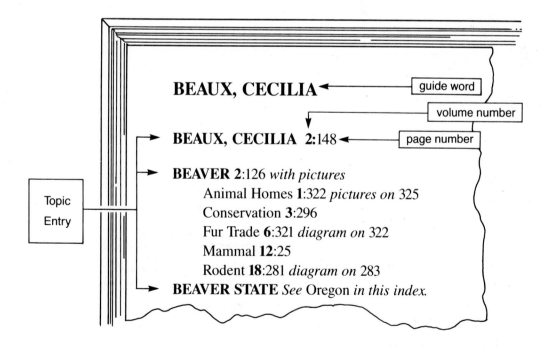

For your research, you may be interested in both the main article *Beaver* in Volume 2, page 126, and *Animal Homes* in Volume 1, page 322. Read the article about beavers in the sample encyclopedia that follows.

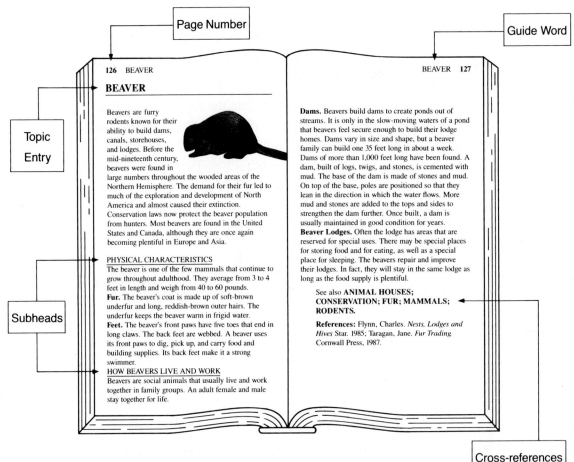

**Page Number**

**Guide Word**

126  BEAVER

BEAVER    127

**Topic Entry**

**BEAVER**

Beavers are furry rodents known for their ability to build dams, canals, storehouses, and lodges. Before the mid-nineteenth century, beavers were found in large numbers throughout the wooded areas of the Northern Hemisphere. The demand for their fur led to much of the exploration and development of North America and almost caused their extinction. Conservation laws now protect the beaver population from hunters. Most beavers are found in the United States and Canada, although they are once again becoming plentiful in Europe and Asia.

**Subheads**

PHYSICAL CHARACTERISTICS
The beaver is one of the few mammals that continue to grow throughout adulthood. They average from 3 to 4 feet in length and weigh from 40 to 60 pounds.
**Fur.** The beaver's coat is made up of soft-brown underfur and long, reddish-brown outer hairs. The underfur keeps the beaver warm in frigid water.
**Feet.** The beaver's front paws have five toes that end in long claws. The back feet are webbed. A beaver uses its front paws to dig, pick up, and carry food and building supplies. Its back feet make it a strong swimmer.
HOW BEAVERS LIVE AND WORK
Beavers are social animals that usually live and work together in family groups. An adult female and male stay together for life.

**Dams.** Beavers build dams to create ponds out of streams. It is only in the slow-moving waters of a pond that beavers feel secure enough to build their lodge homes. Dams vary in size and shape, but a beaver family can build one 35 feet long in about a week. Dams of more than 1,000 feet long have been found. A dam, built of logs, twigs, and stones, is cemented with mud. The base of the dam is made of stones and mud. On top of the base, poles are positioned so that they lean in the direction in which the water flows. More mud and stones are added to the tops and sides to strengthen the dam further. Once built, a dam is usually maintained in good condition for years.
**Beaver Lodges.** Often the lodge has areas that are reserved for special uses. There may be special places for storing food and for eating, as well as a special place for sleeping. The beavers repair and improve their lodges. In fact, they will stay in the same lodge as long as the food supply is plentiful.

See also **ANIMAL HOUSES; CONSERVATION; FUR; MAMMALS; RODENTS.**

**References:** Flynn, Charles. *Nests, Lodges and Hives* Star. 1985; Taragan, Jane. *Fur Trading* Cornwall Press, 1987.

**Cross-references**

When you finished reading this article, you may have noticed the other articles listed near the end of the entry. These are called *cross-references.* You may refer to these additional articles in the encyclopedia for further information on your topic. Also, at the end of the article, there are references to other books that may have more information on your research topic.

## Steps for Using an Encyclopedia

When you use an encyclopedia to research a topic, use these steps.

1. Look up the topic in the encyclopedia index.
2. Select the article or articles that relate to your research. Write down the name of the article, volume number or volume guide letter, and the page on which the article begins.
3. Select the volume or volumes you need.
4. Refer to the page numbers you wrote down to find the article. Use the page guide words to help you find the article more quickly.
5. Skim the article to find the heads and subheads under which you are likely to find the information you need.
6. Use the cross-references at the end of the article to find other encyclopedia articles or books on your topic.

## Using What You Have Learned

Use the sample index on page 323 to answer the following questions.

1. Which volume would you use to find information on trapping beaver for fur? What page would you turn to?
2. Which articles about beavers have diagrams?
3. What topic entry comes before *Beaver* in the index? What volume would you use to find out more information on this topic?

Use the encyclopedia article on page 324 to answer the following questions.

4. If you wanted to find out what types of materials are used to construct dams, which subhead section would you read?
5. Which topic in the list of cross-references would you choose to find out more information on constructing dams and houses?
6. If you wanted to research the importance of the beaver in the Canadian fur trade, which reference would you choose?

326

*Odysseus, the King of Ithaca in ancient times, has been trying to return home from the Trojan War for ten years. On his journey home, he is shipwrecked in the land of the Sea Kings.*

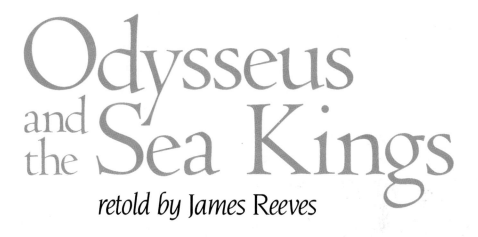

# Odysseus and the Sea Kings

## retold by James Reeves

*"Odysseus and the Sea Kings" retells part of the poet Homer's* Odyssey, *a three-thousand-year-old tale that is one of the most famous epics in all of literature. The Greek king Odysseus, a hero in the ten-year war with Troy, is returning home to Ithaca. But when he blinds the Cyclops Polyphemus, a one-eyed giant, the angry gods make his journey home long and dangerous.*

When Odysseus[1] had finished eating and drinking, Nausicaa[2] spoke to him.

"Let us go to the city, stranger," she said.

"I will take you to my father's palace. As we go through the fields, follow close behind me. But when we come to the city, you must be careful. You will see the walls and the harbour[3] and the market square, through which you must pass. Among our people, I fear, are some rude men who will look with curiosity at a handsome stranger. They will know you are not of this country, and would wonder what I was doing in your presence, when it is thought that I must choose a husband from among our own people.

[1]Odysseus (ō dis′ ē əs)
[2]Nausicaa (nô sik′ ā ə)
[3]Some words in this selection are spelled in the British style.

"This is what you must do. On the way you will find a grove sacred to Athene.[4] There, there are poplar trees and a clear-running spring. Stay there until you think that I and my maidens have had time to reach home. Then go into the city and ask for the house of Alcinous.[5] You will have no trouble in finding it. When you reach it, go straight in to where my mother spins her sea-blue yarn at the fireside; my father sits there beside her. Greet my mother courteously, for, if you win her favour, you will the sooner reach your home."

Nausicaa climbed into the wagon, touched the mules with her whip, and they began to move through the fields towards the city. At sundown they came to the grove of Athene. Here Odysseus bade the Princess farewell; and when the wagon was out of sight, he prayed to the goddess Athene and begged her to help him win favour in the eyes of the Sea Kings, so that they might help him to get home. Athene heard the prayer of Odysseus.

Nausicaa reached home, and her brother unyoked the mules and carried in the clean linen. The Princess was greeted by her old nurse. Meanwhile Odysseus began his journey to the city on foot. In order to protect him from prying eyes, Athene covered him with a mist. Soon he saw the houses and the towers of the Sea Kings. Reaching a little square, he was greeted by Athene in the guise of a maiden carrying a pitcher to fetch water. He asked her where he could find the palace of Alcinous. She said she would show him the way and added:

"Don't talk to anyone, because my people, the proud Sea Kings, are very suspicious towards strangers."

When they got to the palace, Athene told Odysseus to walk boldly in and go straight up to the Queen, whose name was Arete.[6]

"She is held in high honour by her husband and her children," Athene said, "and by all other men. She is wise, and if you can gain her goodwill she will help you as no one else can."

[4]Athene (ə thē′ nē): ancient Greek goddess of wisdom
[5]Alcinous (al sin′ ə wəs)
[6]Arete (ə′ rāt)

328

329

Then Athene, still in the form of the maiden with the pitcher, made her departure, and Odysseus entered the palace. The sight caused him to marvel, for the walls shone like the full moon; they were of bronze and the doors plated with gold. The great hall was lined with seats covered with fine cloths which the women of the house had woven. There were fifty maidservants in the palace of Alcinous, to do the cooking, the spinning and the weaving. They were as skilled at their weaving as the Sea Kings were at managing their swift ships. Outside the palace was a rich and beautiful garden, where grew all manner of fruit—pomegranates, grapes, apples and figs—so that they gave a sweet harvest all the year

round. There were beds full of bright flowers, and two fountains,
one to water the garden and the other for passers-by to drink at.

Dazzled by the beauty of the garden and the splendour of the
palace, Odysseus went through the hall to where the King and
Queen were seated at one end. The Sea Kings and the princess
were sitting round the table; none saw him because of the cloud
of invisibility which Athene had wrapped about him. But when he
reached Queen Arete, the cloud dispersed, and everyone marvelled to see the stranger in their midst. Odysseus knelt before
the Queen and said:

"Great Queen, take pity on me and help a poor, travel-worn

stranger to return to his home and his people. I will pray the gods to send happiness and prosperity to you and all your house."

All were silent, until an old, wise lord said:

"Alcinous, let this stranger be given an honourable place at your table, and let us all drink to his health."

Alcinous led Odysseus by the hand to a place at his side. Servants were commanded to bring water to wash his hands, and food and drink were set before him. When the feast was over, Alcinous told his guests to come to the palace next morning, when they would sit in council and hear the stranger's tale.

"Noble Alcinous," said Odysseus, "I could make a long history of all my griefs and misfortunes, but now all I wish is to return safely to my own country. In the morning, I will beg you to help me on my way."

When the nobles had departed for their houses, Odysseus was left alone with the King and Queen. Now the Queen had been looking closely at the doublet and cloak worn by Odysseus, and she knew that they had been made by herself and her servants.

"Stranger," said Arete, looking into Odysseus' weather-beaten face, "Where do you come from? Who gave you the clothes you are wearing?"

Then Odysseus told the Queen how he had stayed for years on the island of Calypso and how he had made himself a raft and put to sea, for the only thought in his mind was somehow to return to his own country. He told her, how after seventeen days he had been wrecked by the anger of Poseidon[7] and cast up on the coast of the Sea Kings' land. He told how he had passed the night under the bushes, and how next day he had seen Nausicaa and her maidens who had given him food and clothing.

"These are the clothes I am wearing now," he said. "Your daughter told me how to reach your palace, after she herself departed with the wagon and the mules."

[7]Poseidon (pō sīd' ən): ancient Greek god of the sea

"My daughter did well," said Alcinous, "except in one matter. She should have brought you to the palace herself."

"Noble sir," replied Odysseus, "your daughter did right. I had feared that if I had come to your palace in her presence, you might have been offended to see her with a stranger."

"I would not have taken offence," said Alcinous. "If you should choose to stay here and marry my daughter, it would give me the keenest pleasure. You are the sort of man I look to have for a son-in-law. But we will not try to keep you here if you are set on returning to your own country. Stay with us tonight, and tomorrow one of our fastest ships shall be made ready to carry you wherever you desire to go."

So Odysseus went gladly to rest, for he was weary; and in the morning the King roused him and took him to the public square near the harbour. Here they sat down on the stone seats while a herald went round the town bidding the people come and see the lordly stranger. When the square was thronged with townspeople, Alcinous stood up and said:

"My people, I do not know this stranger's name. But yesterday he came to my house and asked for help to sail back to his own country. Let us treat him as is our custom with strangers in our midst. Let us give him the help he asks. Prepare a swift ship and choose fifty of your most skillful sailors. Then come to the palace where we will hold a feast in honour of our visitor."

After a ship was made ready, the princes crowded into the hall. A minstrel came in, led by a herald, for he was blind. He had lost his eyesight, but he had the voice of a great singer. He sang of the siege of Troy and of the heroes who had died there. The minstrel's singing brought bitter tears to Odysseus' eyes. He hid his face in his cloak; only Alcinous knew that he was weeping.

So he ended the feast and told his guests that they ought to give the stranger an exhibition of their skill at games. They threw

quoits, wrestled, boxed and ran races. Then one of the Sea Kings said to the others:

"Let us ask the stranger if he has a particular skill in one or other game. He looks strong and well built."

But when they challenged Odysseus, he shook his head sadly and said:

"I am not in the mood for games. I would rather be left to my sorrow. All I can think of is the wife and the home I left so long ago. All I want from your King and his people is to be helped on my way."

Then one of the young men, whose name was Euryalus,[8] scoffed at Odysseus and said:

"I can well understand why you have no skill in games. I should think you have spent your life as a trader, buying, selling and making bargains. No wonder you will not join in our sports."

Odysseus frowned angrily at the young man and said:

"The gods have given you grace and strength, young man, but they have not given you courtesy. Your rude words have stung me, and I will show you what I can do, stiff and weary though I am with the toils and hardships of my wandering."

So saying, he did not even stop to remove his cloak but stooped and picked up a huge stone quoit. He swung it round and hurled it through the air so that all the onlookers shrank back in fear and amazement. The quoit came to rest far beyond all the others. He smiled as he turned to Euryalus and said:

"There! Make as good a throw as that, young man. Or would you rather I wrestled with you, or boxed, or ran races? I can shoot an arrow too, if that is what you want."

At this there was silence until Alcinous said:

"There is no doubt of your strength and skill, my friend. We have fast ships but, to tell you the truth, games and sports are not our strong point. We like dancing best, so now let two of my sons give you an exhibition of their ability."

[8]Euryalus (yoo rē′ u los)

A space was cleared, a minstrel struck up a lively tune on his pipes, and two princes danced with agility and grace, throwing a crimson ball back and forth between them, catching it in the air and dancing all the while, until Odysseus marvelled at their nimbleness.

When the dance was finished, Alcinous told all the Kings to go and fetch gifts for Odysseus to take with him on his journey home.

"Euryalus," he said, "shall make a special gift, to pay for his rudeness."

The young man readily agreed and presented Odysseus with a handsome bronze sword with a cunningly-wrought scabbard of carved ivory. He smiled at Odysseus in a frank and friendly way and said:

"Pardon me, sir, for my rough words. I beg you, let them be forgotten; and may I wish you a safe and speedy return to your home from which you have been so long away."

Slinging the sword over his shoulder, Odysseus said:

"I thank you for your kindness, friend. May good fortune go with you always, and may you never stand in need of this fine blade!"

Then Alcinous led Odysseus back into the palace. Before entering the hall, Odysseus went to the room that had been set aside for him and bathed. As he entered the hall, he saw that the Princess Nausicaa was standing at the door in all her beauty.

"I have come to say farewell, stranger," she said in a low voice. "When you are home again, think of me, for I was the first to help you when you were cast up on this shore."

"I will never forget you, Princess," answered Odysseus. "You will always be to me like one of the gods, for it was you who brought me back to life after my desperate journey."

Odysseus went and took his seat beside Alcinous, and the minstrel played and sang a song of Troy. Once more Odysseus wept, so that the King told the minstrel to cease singing. He turned to his guest.

"Now, stranger, surely your secret is out. If the tale of Troy causes you such grief, tell us whether you lost a friend or a kinsman in that war. Or what is it that makes you weep?"

So Odysseus told the King and his guests that he was Odysseus. That, from the time of the burning of Troy, he had been away from his home and his people for a full ten years, and that he longed to return. The Princes listened with close attention and wonder as their guest kept them from their beds, telling of all his adventures on the storm-tossed seas—how he had blinded the Cyclops Polyphemus and passed the island of the Sirens, how he had come safely through the straits between Scylla[9] and Charybdis,[10] and how he had lost his ship and all his men and been wrecked on the island of Calypso. He told of his visit to the enchantress Circe; and finally he described his escape from Calypso's island on his raft, and how it was broken to pieces, and of his being thrown up on the Sea Kings' shore when he was almost drowned beneath the waves.

When Odysseus' tale was done, the guests all departed for their homes. In the morning they returned with their gifts, and Alcinous sacrificed an ox to Zeus[11] to ensure a safe journey for Odysseus. All day they feasted and drank, and all the time Odysseus looked towards the sun, longing for it to go down beyond the western wave. That was to be the time for his departure. At last Odysseus turned to King Alcinous and Queen Arete and bade them farewell. He thanked them for all their kindness and their entertainment, and wished them good fortune, happiness and long life.

The heralds led the way to the ship moored in the harbour. The Queen sent her servants with warm clothing for the voyage; the rowers took their places on the benches, while Odysseus lay

[9]Scylla (sil' ə): a six-headed monster

[10]Charybdis (kə rib' dis): a mighty whirlpool

[11]Zeus (zoos): ancient Greek god who ruled the other Greek gods and goddesses

down and stretched himself out in the stern. As the ship left, a deep, sweet sleep fell upon Odysseus. Once out of the harbour, the sailors hoisted sail and the ship sped as fast as a hawk through the dark waters. All through the night the hero who had suffered so much and been buffeted by so many storms slept peacefully and forgot his sorrows.

When the morning star arose, the ship came in sight of Ithaca. Here there was a haven so calm that ships might ride in it without anchor. At the end of the harbour was a great olive tree and a cave where sea-nymphs wove their blue garments. Inside the cave were two springs of clear water. Into this harbour, well known to the Sea Kings, the ship was rowed. The sailors beached the vessel and lifted the still sleeping Odysseus out of the stern. They wrapped him in rugs and laid him gently on the sand. Lastly, they lifted out of the ship all the gifts they had given him and piled them carefully against the gnarled trunk of the olive tree so that he should find them when he woke. Then they dragged the ship into the water, climbed aboard and silently rowed away.

## Reader's Response

After all that he had been through, do you think it was wise or foolish for Odysseus to trust the Sea Kings? Explain your answer.

STORY FOLLOW-UP

# Odysseus
### and the Sea Kings

## Checking Your Comprehension

1. How did Princess Nausicaa help Odysseus?
2. What did Odysseus want more than anything else?
3. What did Odysseus tell his hosts about his adventures?
4. Do you think Odysseus managed to survive so many misfortunes because he was brave or because he was lucky? How did you arrive at this choice?
5. Why was Alcinous willing to go to so much trouble to help Odysseus?
6. What do you think Odysseus would have done if the Sea Kings had not helped him?

## Writing to Learn

**THINK AND PREDICT** When Odysseus awakens, what will he do? Read the two predictions below. Then make one more prediction.

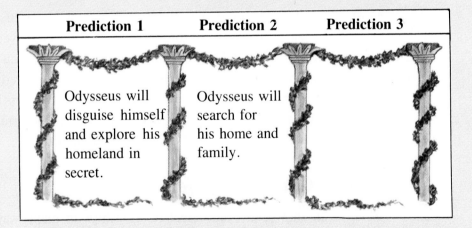

| Prediction 1 | Prediction 2 | Prediction 3 |
| --- | --- | --- |
| Odysseus will disguise himself and explore his homeland in secret. | Odysseus will search for his home and family. | |

**WRITE** Review the predictions and select the one you think is best. Write a paragraph about the future of Odysseus based on the prediction you chose.

*Comprehension:*

# Cause-and-Effect Relationships

**T**hink back to the story "Snowshoe Trek to Otter River." Do you remember when Daniel was tracking the rabbit through the snow? The tracks ended suddenly. At the end of the rabbit's trail, Daniel found the wing marks from a large bird and a pool of frozen blood in the snow.

Do you remember what caused the marks in the snow? Daniel looked at the marks and decided that a hawk had swooped down, captured the rabbit, and carried it off for a meal. Daniel looked at the tracks and the wing marks and figured out what caused the blood in the snow.

Most stories have situations like the one Daniel encountered, in which one event leads to, or causes, another. These connected events are called cause-and-effect relationships. Authors often use cause-and-effect relationships in stories to show how one event is related to another or to show how a character causes something to happen. By recognizing causes and effects in a story, you can better understand why things happen and how one event is related to another.

## *Identifying Cause and Effect*

Writers can show cause-and-effect relationships in many ways. Read the following sentence. When you read, think about what action or event is causing the other event.

> He walked onto the thin ice over the river and, as a result, fell into the icy water below.

First, ask yourself, "What happened?" The answer is, "The boy fell through the ice." That is the effect. Now ask yourself, "Why did this event happen?" He fell through because he walked onto thin ice. That is the cause.

Look at the diagram below. This diagram illustrates the cause-and-effect relationship.

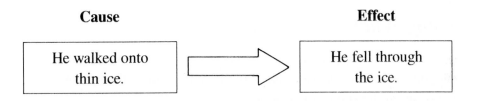

Sometimes cause-and-effect relationships in stories are easy to find because the author uses *signal words*. These are words that signal a cause-and-effect relationship. In this example, the words *as a result* are signal words. Other commonly used signal words include:

so    since    therefore    because

Do you see how signal words can make it easy to find a cause-and-effect relationship and decide which is the cause and which is the effect?

You will often read a sentence or a paragraph with the effect stated first, followed by the cause. Do you remember when Daniel opened his pack and discovered the smashed eggs? The following passage tells what he was thinking.

> He reached into his backpack for the eggs. They were smashed. They must have broken when he threw the pack up on the bank.

Notice that the effect is stated before the cause. What this means is that you have to think carefully when you are looking for cause-and-effect relationships. You can't just look at the order of words in the text.

341

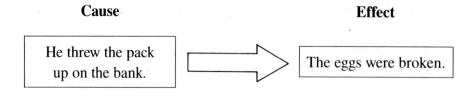

| Cause | | Effect |
|---|---|---|
| He threw the pack up on the bank. | → | The eggs were broken. |

## *Using What You Have Learned*

Read the following passage from "Odysseus and the Sea Kings." As you read, look for cause-and-effect relationships. Then answer the questions at the end of the passage.

When Odysseus' tale was done, the guests all departed for their homes. In the morning they returned with their gifts, and Alcinous sacrificed an ox to Zeus to ensure a safe journey for Odysseus. All day they feasted and drank, and all the time Odysseus looked towards the sun, longing for it to go down beyond the western wave. That was to be the time for his departure. At last Odysseus turned to King Alcinous and Queen Arete and bade them farewell. He thanked them for all their kindness and their entertainment, and wished them good fortune, happiness and long life.

The heralds led the way to the ship moored in the harbour. The Queen sent her servants with warm clothing for the voyage; the rowers took their places on the benches, while Odysseus lay down and stretched himself out in the stern. As the ship left, a deep, sweet sleep fell upon Odysseus. Once out of the harbour, the sailors hoisted sail and the ship sped as fast as a hawk through the dark waters. All through the night the hero who had suffered so much and been buffeted by so many storms slept peacefully and forgot his sorrows.

1. Rewrite this sentence using a cause-and-effect signal word: "When Odysseus' tale was done, the guests all departed for their homes."

**2.** Make a cause-and-effect diagram for the sentence you wrote for question 1.

**3.** What caused the ship to sail "fast as a hawk"?

**4.** Make a diagram for this cause-and-effect relationship.

## As You Read

The next story is "Voyage by Canoe." As you read, ask yourself, "What happened?" and "Why?" Notice any signal words that may indicate a cause and effect.

# from Island of the Blue Dolphins
## By Scott O'Dell

*Some journeys are carefully planned adventures.*
*Others hold unusual surprises. For Karana a journey is a*
*matter of survival.*

An island, shaped like a blue dolphin, lies off the
coast of California. Most of the Indians who lived on the
island were killed in a fierce battle with sea-otter hunters.
Soon the others left with sailors who offered them safe
passage. Twelve-year-old Karana, however, jumped off the
ship and swam back to the island to join her brother
Ramo, who had missed the ship. Soon Ramo was killed by
wild dogs, and Karana was left completely alone.

While Karana waited and hoped for the ship to return
for her, she survived by building a shelter, hunting food,
and making weapons to defend herself against the wild dogs.

Summer is the best time on the Island of the Blue Dolphins. The sun is warm then and the winds blow milder out of the west, sometimes out of the south.

It was during these days that the ship might return and now I spent most of my time on the rock, looking out from the high headland into the east, toward the country where my people had gone, across the sea that was never-ending.

Once while I watched I saw a small object which I took to be the ship, but a stream of water rose from it and I knew that it was a whale spouting. During those summer days I saw nothing else.

The first storm of winter ended my hopes. If the white men's ship were coming for me it would have come during the time of good weather. Now I would have to wait until winter was gone, maybe longer.

The thought of being alone on the island while so many suns rose from the sea and went slowly back in to the sea filled my heart with loneliness. I had not felt so lonely before because I was sure that the ship would return. Now my hopes were dead. Now I was really alone. I could not eat much, nor could I sleep without dreaming terrible dreams.

The storm blew out of the north, sending big waves against the island and winds so strong that I was unable to stay on the rock. I moved my bed to the foot of the rock and for protection kept a fire going throughout the night. I slept there five times. The first night the dogs came and stood outside the ring made by the fire. I killed three of them with arrows, but not the leader, and they did not come again.

On the sixth day, when the storm had ended, I went to the place where the canoes had been hidden, and let myself down over the cliff. This part of the shore was sheltered from the wind and I found the canoes just as they had been left. The dried food was still good, but the water was stale, so I went back to the spring and filled a fresh basket.

I had decided during the days of the storm, when I had given up hope of seeing the ship, that I would take one of the canoes and go to the country that lay toward the east.

I cannot say that I was really afraid as I stood there on the shore. I knew that my ancestors had crossed the sea in their canoes, coming from that place which lay beyond. I was not nearly so skilled with a canoe as these men, but I must say that whatever might befall me on the endless waters did not trouble me. It meant far less than the thought of staying on the island alone, without a home or companions, pursued by wild dogs, where everything re-minded me of those who were dead and those who had gone away.

Of the four canoes stored there against the cliff, I chose the smallest, which was still very heavy because it could carry six people. The task that faced me was to push it down the rocky shore and into the water, a distance four or five times its length.

This I did by first removing all the large rocks in front of the canoe. I then filled in all these holes with pebbles and along this path laid down long strips of kelp, making a slippery bed. The shore was steep and once I got the canoe to move with its own weight, it slid down the path and into the water.

The sun was in the west when I left the shore. The sea was calm behind the high cliffs. Using the two-bladed paddle I quickly skirted the south part of the island. As I reached the sandspit the wind struck. I was paddling from the back of the canoe because you can go faster kneeling there, but I could not handle it in the wind.

Kneeling in the middle of the canoe, I paddled hard and did not pause until I had gone through the tides that run fast around the sandspit. There were many small waves and I was soon wet, but as I came out from behind the spit the spray lessened and the waves grew long and rolling. Though it would have been easier to go the way they slanted, this would have taken me in the wrong direction. I therefore kept them on my left hand, as well as the island, which grew smaller and smaller, behind me.

At dusk I looked back. The Island of the Blue Dolphins had disappeared. This was the first time that I felt afraid.

There were only hills and valleys of water around me now. When I was in a valley I could see nothing and when the canoe rose out of it, only the ocean stretching away and away.

Night fell and I drank from the basket. The water cooled my throat.

The sea was black and there was no difference between it and the sky. The waves made no sound among themselves, only faint noises as they went under the canoe or struck against it. Sometimes the noises seemed angry and at other times like people laughing. I was not hungry because of my fear.

The first star made me feel less afraid. It came out low in the sky and it was in front of me, toward the east. Other stars began to appear all around, but it was this one I kept my gaze upon. It was in the figure that we call a serpent, a star which shone green and which I knew. Now and then it was hidden by mist, yet it always came out brightly again.

Without this star I would have been lost, for the waves never changed. They came always from the same direction and in a manner that kept pushing me away from the place I wanted to reach. For this reason the canoe made a path in the black water like a snake. But somehow I kept moving toward the star which shone in the east.

This star rose high and then I kept the North Star on my left hand, the one we call "the star that does not move." The wind grew quiet. Since it always died down when the night was half over, I knew how long I had been traveling and how far away the dawn was.

About this time I found that the canoe was leaking. Before dark I had emptied one of the baskets in which food was stored and used it to dip out the water that came over the sides. The water that now moved around my knees was not from the waves.

I stopped paddling and worked with the basket until the bottom of the canoe was almost dry. Then I searched around, feeling in the dark along the smooth planks, and found the place near the bow where the water was seeping through a crack as long as my hand and the width of a finger. Most of the time it was out of the sea, but it leaked whenever the canoe dipped forward in the waves.

The places between the planks were filled with black pitch which we gather along the shore. Lacking this, I tore a piece of fiber from my skirt and pressed it into the crack, which held back the water.

Dawn broke in a clear sky and as the sun came out of the waves I saw that it was far off on my left. During the night I had drifted south of the place I wished to go, so I changed my direction and paddled along the path made by the rising sun.

There was no wind on this morning and the long waves went quietly under the canoe. I therefore moved faster than during the night.

I was very tired, but more hopeful than I had been since I left the island. If the good weather did not change I would cover many leagues before dark. Another night and another day might bring me within sight of the shore toward which I was going.

Not long after dawn, while I was thinking of this strange place and what it would look like, the canoe began to leak again. This crack was between the same planks, but was a larger one and close to where I was kneeling.

The fiber I tore from my skirt and pushed into the crack held back most of the water which seeped in whenever the canoe rose and fell with the waves. Yet I could see that the planks were weak from one end to the other, probably from the canoe being stored so long in the sun, and that they might open along their whole length if the waves grew rougher.

It was suddenly clear to me that it was dangerous to go on. The voyage would take two more days, perhaps longer. By turning back to the island I would not have nearly so far to travel.

Still I could not make up my mind to do so. The sea was calm and I had come far. The thought of turning back after all this labor was more than I could bear. Even greater was the thought of the deserted island I would return to, of living there alone and forgotten. For how many suns and how many moons?

The canoe drifted idly on the calm sea while these thoughts went over and over in my mind, but when I saw the water seeping through the crack again, I picked up the paddle. There was no choice except to turn back toward the island.

I knew that only by the best of fortune would I ever reach it.

The wind did not blow until the sun was overhead. Before that time I covered a good distance, pausing only when it was necessary to dip water from the canoe. With the wind I went more slowly and had to stop more often because of the water spilling over the sides, but the leak did not grow worse.

This was my first good fortune. The next was when a swarm of dolphins appeared. They came swimming out of the west, but as they saw the canoe they turned around in a great circle and began to follow me. They swam slowly and so close that I could see their eyes, which are large and the color of the ocean. Then they swam on ahead of the canoe, crossing back and forth in front of it, diving in and out, as if they were weaving a piece of cloth with their broad snouts.

Dolphins are animals of good omen. It made me happy to have them swimming around the canoe, and though my hand had begun to bleed from the chafing of the paddle, just watching them made me forget the pain. I was very lonely before they appeared, but now I felt that I had friends with me and did not feel the same.

The blue dolphins left me shortly before dusk. They left as quickly as they had come, going on into the west, but for a long time I could see the last of the sun shining

on them. After night fell I could still see them in my thoughts, and it was because of this that I kept on paddling when I wanted to lie down and sleep.

More than anything, it was the blue dolphins that took me back home.

Fog came with the night, yet from time to time I could see the star that stands high in the west, the red star called Magat which is part of the figure that looks like a crawfish and is known by that name. The crack in the planks grew wider so I had to stop often to fill it with fiber and to dip out the water.

The night was very long, longer than the night before. Twice I dozed kneeling there in the canoe, though I was more afraid than I had ever been. But the morning broke clear and in front of me lay the dim line of the island like a great fish sunning itself on the sea.

I reached it before the sun was high, the sandspit and its tides that bore me into the shore. My legs were stiff from kneeling and as the canoe struck the sand I fell when I rose to climb out. I crawled through the shallow water and up the beach. There I lay for a long time, hugging the sand in happiness.

## ◆ LIBRARY LINK ◆

*Will Karana ever be able to leave the island? To find out, read all of the book* Island of the Blue Dolphins *by Scott O'Dell.*

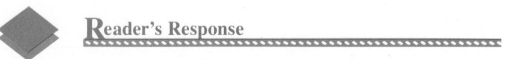

## Reader's Response

What do you think was the most frightening thing that happened to Karana? Explain your answer.

# Voyage by Canoe

## Checking Your Comprehension

1. Why did Karana decide to leave the island?
2. How did Karana keep from losing her way on the ocean?
3. What caused Karana's canoe to leak?
4. Do you think Karana was right to return to the island rather than continue on? How did you arrive at this conclusion?
5. Why did Karana have the feeling that the dolphins took her back to the island?
6. Do you think Karana will ever get off the island? Explain your answer.

## Writing to Learn

**THINK AND ANALYZE**   Karana faces a difficult challenge. She must decide whether to return to the original home of her parents' people. Trace her thinking as you copy and complete the chart below.

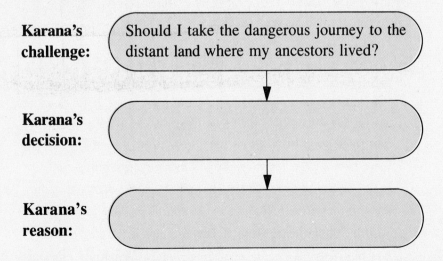

**Karana's challenge:** Should I take the dangerous journey to the distant land where my ancestors lived?

**Karana's decision:**

**Karana's reason:**

**WRITE**   Make a decision map that traces the path of a difficult decision you have made or read about. Explain the challenge you faced, your decision, and why you arrived at this decision.

353

# ISLAND CAMPING

## by Kathryn Lasky

Jem and his father start out on their kayak trip on a course that they had plotted on their chart of Penobscot Bay. But sometimes the best part of a journey isn't found on a chart.

Jem has always heard stories about the kayak trip his father and uncle took twenty-five years ago. Now Jem and his father were planning an overnight kayak trip for the coming summer. All through the winter, Jem planned and dreamed about the trip they were going to take in Penobscot Bay in Maine. With his father's help Jem charted a course in a part of the bay that was filled with interesting islands. When the morning of the trip finally arrived, Jem and his father prepared to set out in their kayak, Wasso.

When the last piece of gear was stowed, Jem and his father pulled on their rubber spray skirts. This was the part that makes kayaking different from any other type of boating. This was the part that made it special for Jem. The spray skirts have an elastic hole to fit around the paddler's waist and an elastic outer edge that fits over the rim of the cockpit. It makes a seal between the paddler and the boat so that no water can get in. But the spray covers do more than keep a paddler dry. The spray skirt made Jem a part of the boat and the boat part of him. The outer and inner edges of the spray skirt formed a double ring. Maybe, Jem thought, it was like the double circle of the compass rose with its true direction and magnetic direction.

Jem and his father climbed into their cockpits. There was always that thrilling first motion that Jem felt when he lowered himself into the seat and felt the water underneath the keel just inches away. It was that instant that the boat came alive for Jem, and he felt an extraordinary connection with the most far-off places, for in the water world everything was one and everything seemed possible. In the stern cockpit Jem fitted his spray skirt over the rim, and his father did the same in the bow cockpit. The seal was made, and with one stroke they glided into deeper water. The white fog swallowed them. Only the dip of their paddles could be heard. There were no splashes. A V of ripples streamed back toward Jem as the bow sliced through the still water.

Jem and his dad paddled silently. The fog was so thick that they could not see the coast to follow it to Dunham Point. Instead, they had to use another compass course that Jem had plotted the night before. The compass was mounted on the deck just in front of his father, and Ben Gray steered by pushing with his feet on a bar that was beneath the deck and attached by wires to the rudder in the stern of the boat. Unless the fog lifted, there would be no way of visually knowing when they rounded the point to pick up the new compass course of 180 degrees south. So Jem had worked out the mileage on this coastal course and knew that they had to paddle 250 degrees west-southwest for exactly forty minutes to clear Dunham Point before turning onto their new course for Isle au Haut. It was Jem's job to keep track of the time and call the course change. Somewhere a lobsterman was hauling traps. Jem could tell that the lobsterman was hauling and not traveling by the rhythmic idling of the engine. But the fog blanketed everything, and the engine sounded like the throb of a great muffled heart.

It was an edgeless world they paddled through, without boundaries or perimeters. The water itself seemed almost the same colorless gray of the fog. It could have been either sky or space through which they moved. It was a timeless world, really, except for the forty minutes that Jem had ordered necessary. Now the throb of the engine was swallowed up too by the fog. There was no sound except for the twin dip of their paddles. Jem could listen to his own heart, his own breathing. His arms held strong. They did not tire as they had last summer. He felt he could paddle forever like this, with the paddle striking the rhythm between him and the sea.

Suddenly there was a raw tidal smell. Unmistakably, it was the strong and slightly sweet odor of wet rocks and seaweed exposed at low tide. It was the smell that scared the daylights out of sailors at night or in fog, but in a kayak with its six-inch draft, or depth, there was little need to fear going aground.

"I can smell the point," Ben said.

"Yep. We're right on schedule." Jem looked at his watch. Thirty-eight minutes had passed, and Dunham Point was off their left, or port, side, probably not more than twenty yards. "We paddle straight for two more minutes and then turn on to 180 degrees south."

Exactly two minutes later, when Jem called, "New course," the fog thinned. The rocky point became softly visible, as if it were behind a screen or gauze. On top of one of the point's rocks, like a teacup on a saucer, a seal arched its back, yawked, and slid into the water.

"Seals all around here," Ben said.

As the fog lifted, Jem and his dad became more talkative. The muffled private world of the gray mist evaporated as the sun burned through, and a new world was revealed, with green islands set like small jewels in the sparkling water. Cormorants and seagulls cruised effortlessly over *Wasso*. Jem and Ben paddled on, picking up their pace, skimming close to steep-shored islands, under cliffs that cascaded with moss and trees that grew straight out from sheer rock faces, defying gravity. With the shallow depth of the kayak, Jem and his father could glide close enough to touch the rock.

At lunchtime they slid into a slight curve of a beach on South Porcupine Island. Small stones, as smooth and round as coins and polished by a million years of lapping water, covered this beach. Jem and his dad sat down to eat their lunch.

"The hardtack looks just like the stone, Dad."

"Probably as hard, too."

Jem tried to crack a biscuit open. "It is. See? Not a crumb."

"Better find a sharper rock. Try over there." Ben pointed to a place at the edge of the beach.

Jem walked over and began looking. Just as he was picking up a sharp-edged rock from amid the debris of driftwood and seaweed, a wise, calm eye seemed to stare up at him. It was a flat piece of driftwood in the perfect contours of a whale's head, with the likeness of a whale's eye set within. Jem drew the wood from its rock ledge. A sculptor could not have carved it better. Gathered in a swirl of wrinkles, the eye was centered at precisely the right spot in the sea-silvered wood, which itself was shaped just like a whale from flukes to head. There were even the fine horizontal lines combing the lower half of the "body," just like the striations on the underside of a blue whale.

Jem munched his hardtack and cheese and looked at the driftwood whale. "For just two people alone on an island," he said, "this is a pretty noisy lunch. Hardtack has to be one of the noisiest foods going."

After lunch they dug some clams. It was near low tide then, and by evening it would be high tide, and they wouldn't be able to dig any. They picked a small pail of berries, too, and each ate a handful. Then they climbed back into *Wasso* and slid away, the driftwood whale tucked in under the spray skirt near Jem's leg. Mark, Scraggy, Sparrow, West Halibut slid by. Then came an island between Halibut and Kimball that had no name. Jem had hardly noticed it on the chart. They rounded its stubby headland, and on the underside a cove opened up, surprising

Jem and his father. Long and crooked as an old person's finger, the cove appeared to channel far into the island.

"Let's go there," Jem said excitedly.

"Let's do!"

A cormorant seemed to be the only inhabitant of the cove. The following tide gave *Wasso* a slight boost. Jem and his father rested their paddles and coasted quietly up the cove that was full of blind corners and secret turns. It was when they passed the last "knuckle," just before the fingertip, that Jem decided that this was where they should camp. Suddenly Kimball Island and Isle au Haut seemed crowded in comparison to this no-name island with its surprise cove.

"I want to camp here, Dad. Is that okay with you?"

"Fine," Ben said and smiled to himself, remembering from twenty years ago that self-discovered things always seemed better and uncharted places more memorable than charted ones.

They coasted to the tip of the water finger. There was a sand beach. Pink ledges on either side sloped into the water, making shallow, tub-size pools just right for swimming. There was a rock just right for cast fishing and a cliff just right for climbing. It was a place you got to and you knew exactly what you wanted to do.

First Jem swam in the pools and then in the larger part of the cove as the sea grass ribboned through his legs.

His dad watched from the shore.

"How can you stand that cold water, Jem?"

"I just keep my feet on the bottom!" Jem whooped and ducked.

After swimming Jem explored the shoreline. Besides the big rock pools, there were several small tidal pools. Glittering in the late afternoon sun, they looked like oddly-cut jewels. Each pool was alive with small plants and seaweeds and some with tiny minnows.

Jem and his father climbed the short cliff. On top of the island was a thick grove of spruce. From the water this grove of trees had looked like a crown on the round flat top of the island. Through the trees and out the other side of the grove the land turned brambly with berry bushes. They picked blueberry, raspberry, and blackberry, dropping them into Ben's hat because they had forgotten the pail. Some islands were "picked out" by hikers and boaters, but "No Name," as Jem had begun to call his island, was not lived on or visited or picked from, except by cormorants and seagulls and whatever four-footed animals lived there.

"Lucky we dug those clams on Porcupine," Jem said, as he watched his father pan-fry a ridiculously small mackerel which ordinarily they would have thrown back.

"This is just an hors d'oeuvre. Those clams will be great!" Ben slid the fish onto a tin plate. It looked even smaller. Jessica might have been right—a steak, just in case. "Hand me the rest of the butter. We'll melt it for the clams."

Jem wondered what Jessica, Michael, and his mother were doing now, that very moment. Eating dinner, he guessed. Maybe chowder, maybe hamburgers. He wondered if they wondered what he was doing. They must. Two places were empty at the table. They didn't have a table here. There was a slab of rock that did fine. They had pulled *Wasso* above the high tide line and turned her upside down, and now they sat leaning against her hull. The cove faced west, just like the Giant's Chair. Jem and his dad shared out the mackerel—all four bites of it—and a heap of clams, and watched the sun slide down behind the horizon like a thin gold coin. It was good thinking that he and his dad, and his mom and Jess and Michael were miles apart but watching the same sun slide on down—Jem and Ben from a beach on an island with no name and a rock for a table, the other Grays from a beach on an island called Deer with a pine table.

They had finished their berries. "Tell me a story, Dad. Tell me an Alaska story."

"An Alaska story? I've told you all of them a hundred times."

"I still like to hear them."

"Alaska was one adventure. This is Maine, another adventure. I'll tell you a Maine story."

"Is it true?"

"You bet."

"Good, let's hear it."

"Once upon a time, a long time ago, on Deer Isle . . ."

"Before the bridge to the mainland?"

"Yes, long before the bridge. If there had been a bridge, this story wouldn't have happened. No, it was before I was born and your grandfather was just a few years older than yourself, maybe seventeen or eighteen at the most. The winters were long on an island without a bridge, especially when it was the kind of winter cold enough to ice the channel but not cold enough to make the ice safe for walking across to the mainland. Too thin for feet, too thick for canoes. You think Cleveland is bad. You ought to try an island in February. Well, March came, and the ice started to break right up, and your grandfather was sure that his charts from the Coast and Geodetic Survey Department had come. He wanted to pick them up."

"The ones for his trip out the St. Lawrence and around the Gaspé Peninsula?"

"That's it, the New England circumnavigation. He'd dreamed of it all winter. He'd ordered the charts just after Christmas, so he was sure they had arrived. That first morning when the ice had just cleared off, no sooner, a herd of low, dark clouds scudded in, and the channel water became choppy as a northeast wind whistled down. My grandfather, your great-grandfather, said, 'Looks like a Northeaster, Pete. You going?' And your grandfather, his son, said he thought he could make it across and back before anything got nasty."

"He let him go?"

"Yes."

"Did he warn him or anything?"

"He asked him if he was going."

"So he just let him go like that?"

"Yes."

"What happened?"

"He made it across fine, but on the way back the wind started to build really fast, and by the time he was halfway across, the channel was boiling white—tops of waves blowing right off. My dad was paddling along. If he'd turned around to go back he would have been caught on the side, abeam, and swamped. He would have lived about two minutes in that water. He had no choice but to paddle right into the teeth of this thing. Somehow he made it. When he walked up from the beach to the old farmhouse where our family lived, his dad was standing there on the front porch. He'd watched him come back. His dad's cheeks were all wet, his eyes red. He'd been crying. He never thought his son would make it back."

"Did he kiss him?"

"No. He wasn't the kissy kind. I think Dad told me that he said something like 'Charts still dry, Pete?'"

"Huh." Jem thought a minute. "Do you think he was right to let him go?"

"You have to let go sometime."

"Would you have let me go?"

Ben paused. "I guess if I thought you were a good enough paddler, I really couldn't stop you."

"Did your parents try to stop you when you and Uncle Pete went to Alaska?"

"No, but all their friends in Cleveland thought they should have, thought they were crazy to let us go." Ben laughed softly. "Come on, let's you and me go for a night glide!"

"A 'night glide'? What's a 'night glide'?"

"You can only do it on a night like this. No wind, and the water is as still as a dark mirror."

They paddled out of the long cove and turned southwest, skimming close to the steep shore. Overhead a million stars chinked the night sky, and as they paddled Jem picked out Orion's Belt: the three bright studs all in a row and the silver point of the sword that dropped below the belt. There were stars, there was the slender mahogany needle, and there was the dip of the paddle. Jem felt part of it all. It was hard to tell where he left off and the boat began. Wood, water, paddler, and stars, they combined for night gliding around the island. Soon Jem noticed a stream of stars streaking back from the bow. Each paddle dip produced a galaxy of small, luminous specks, all sliding smoothly astern.

364

"Phosphorescence!" Ben said. "Stars in the sky! Stars in the water!"

Star paddler, Jem thought, as he dipped his paddle in the water.

They had just rounded the southeast tip of No Name Island when Jem felt the presence of something else in the water. Catching his breath, he saw, amid the galaxies of phosphorescence, a streaking in the night sea like licks of pale fire.

"Dolphins, Dad!" A pair of dolphins swam just off *Wasso's* starboard (right) side. Amid the showering of sparks of phosphorescence, Jem couldn't really see their shapes. Only the trail of water fire that streamed around the dolphins was visible.

"They probably think we're a new fish in the neighborhood," said Ben. "Watch them play around us."

The dolphins divided and arced over one another, braiding the bright water, swimming alongside, just out of the dip of the paddles. A magical energy seemed to surround the kayak.

Jem and his dad did not put up their tent that night. The moon was riding high when they passed the last knuckle of the long-fingered cove. The night air was warm and they decided to sleep out instead of covering up the stars. Jem crawled into his sleeping bag feeling a little bit hungry. He realized suddenly that he had never gone to bed feeling a little bit hungry in his life. Tomorrow he would get up early and try to catch a bigger mackerel for breakfast. He didn't need food now, really. Besides, munching hardtack would be too noisy and he wanted to think about things—like his driftwood whale. Why had the sea made a perfect whale? How had it happened? What joining of water, wind, and current had modeled the wood into the unmistakable folds of a whale's eye? What accidental collision of natural forces had shaped the whale's body? Had it taken eleven years? An old person's lifetime? A century? Or a thousand years for wind and water to make the wooden whale? Jem fell asleep thinking of driftwood whales and paddling the stars.

Mist rose from the still water of the cove. It was the inbetween time, just at the tail end of the last gray of a fading night, but before the first pink of dawn. His father still slept, while Jem stood on a rock with his fishing line. There was a reasonable-sized mackerel in the pail, but Jem was hungry enough that it seemed like a good idea to try for another one. There was a tug on the line. He reeled it in. A plump mackerel thrashed on the end, gilded by the sun that was just slipping up in the east.

Ben was up now, bending over the fire, poking in some kindling to bring it back to life. Jem cleaned the fish on the rock and brought them over to the fire.

"Roe!" That was the first word spoken that morning. "One of them has roe, Dad." Fish eggs were a favorite of Jem's. He usually liked them with bacon. But this wasn't usual, so he guessed he would like them without.

It would be time to go soon, to leave No Name Island, to paddle out of the long-fingered surprise of a cove. There was a part of Jem that wanted to go—to tell Michael and Jessica and his mother about the galaxies in the water, to show them the driftwood whale. But there was a bigger part that wanted to stay, that wanted the trip never to end.

They washed their dishes with sea water and sand. They packed up their sleeping bags, the fishing gear, their plates and pots and pans. The clam shells and fishbones they returned to the sea. The orange peel and empty instant grape juice can they put in a bag to carry with them. They doused the fire with water and a paddleful of sand. Before they left, Ben set up the camera on self-timing and took a picture of the two of them standing with their paddles at the tip of the finger cove called Surprise on No Name Island.

Summer, which always seemed to gallop from August to Labor Day, had briefly stopped for Jem and his dad. Now they put on their spray skirts and slipped *Wasso* into the water.

Jem didn't want to leave. It wasn't just the island he didn't want to leave, it was everything since yesterday morning.

Jem lowered himself into the stern seat. There was that first motion of water under the keel. The thrill was stronger. The boat came alive in a new way for Jem. Everything did seem possible. In that moment he knew that he was not leaving anything behind. None of it—not the peace of the island, not the magic of the dolphins, or the small water galaxies of the night glide, or the skill to chart a course. It was all part of him now, forever, and would be a part of his winter dreams.

As they paddled out of the long-fingered cove, past the first knuckle and the second, Jem began to dream a new dream—the dream for summers to come, when his parents would let go, when he and Michael would be old enough to paddle alone to another island for a day, a week, or maybe a summer of a thousand miles.

◆ LIBRARY LINK ◆

*If you are curious to find out how Jem knew about preparing for his kayak trip, read the rest of* Jem's Island *by Kathryn Lasky.*

**R**eader's Response

What do you think was the most enjoyable part of Jem's journey? Explain your answer.

# ISLAND CAMPING

## Checking Your Comprehension

1. What were Jem's tasks on the journey?
2. Why did Jem want to camp on the island he called No Name?
3. What special meaning did Jem's father's stories have for Jem? How did you figure out your answer?
4. Do you think Jem's great-grandfather was right to let his son go kayaking in bad weather?
5. What descriptions of the "night glide" tell you what it was like?
6. How might the trip have been different if Jem had not discovered No Name Island?

## Writing to Learn

**THINK AND EXPECT**   Boating adventures make for good reading. What expectations do you have when you know you are going to read something about boats? On your paper, fill in the Expectation Chart for "Island Camping."

### EXPECTATION CHART

| | |
|---|---|
| What were your expectations based on the title? | |
| What did you expect based on the author? | |
| What did you expect based on the art? | |
| What did you expect based on the first page? | |

**WRITE**   Write about whether the story "Island Camping" met your expectations.

# Semantic Mapping

In "Island Camping," Jem and his father had *hardtack* for lunch. Do you know what hardtack is? You might guess that it is a kind of food, but what kind of food? *Hardtack* fits in this list of words: hardtack, bread, biscuit, roll, bun. Can you guess what hardtack is?

If you guessed a kind of bread, somewhat like a biscuit, roll, or bun, you are correct. Actually, hardtack is a special kind of biscuit that is made only with flour and water. Sailors often ate hardtack, so it is sometimes called sea bread or sea biscuit.

When you put words together in categories, you are classifying those words. Placing unfamiliar words in categories with words you already know will help you learn their meanings. Classifying also helps you to see how related words are alike and how they are different.

## Constructing a Semantic Map

One way to classify words is to make a semantic map. A semantic map is a group of words that are related to one important or central word. That word is the topic of the semantic map. The other words in the map are then grouped around the topic according to categories. For example, here is a semantic map for several kinds of food that were mentioned in "Island Camping." Look at the map carefully. Notice how the topic word is placed in the middle of the map. Try to determine the different categories, or types, of food that are included in the map.

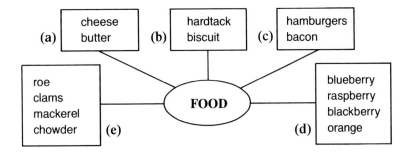

Did you figure out the categories? They are: (a) dairy products, (b) breads, (c) meats, (d) fruits, and (e) seafoods. Did the categories help you understand word meanings? Did the words *clams* and *mackerel* help you realize that *roe* and *chowder* are also examples of seafoods?

To make a semantic map, follow these steps. First, choose a topic word that is familiar to you, like *food*. Second, think of words that are examples of the topic. Third, classify those words into groups, or categories, according to some rule such as types of foods.

## Using What You Have Learned

Make a semantic map of these animals from the story "Island Camping":

| | | | |
|---|---|---|---|
| lobster | seal | cormorant | seagull |
| whale | minnow | mackerel | dolphin |

Use *animals* as the topic word. Arrange the words into these categories: birds, mammals, fish, and shellfish. Next, add words to each category. Finally, expand your map further by adding more categories and words.

## As You Read

As you read "Mars: A Close-Up Picture," look for a word that would make a good topic for a semantic map. If you wish, make the semantic map after you have finished reading.

# THE WORLD OF READING

## The Art of Old Maps

▲
This 1639 map shows that explorers thought California was an island.

Everyone knows what maps are for. They help you get where you want to go or indicate where places are located. We don't expect maps to be beautiful, but we do expect them to be accurate. Map makers in the past, however, did not always have all the information they needed to make maps accurate. Their maps, though, are interesting—and often beautiful to look at.

When explorers first came to North America, they made maps to show what they had discovered. They drew the coastline as they saw it. The problem was that they had no idea what that part of the coastline was connected to. What was north and south of it? Was it a wide continent or a narrow strip of land? They had to draw something, so the only thing to do was imagine what it might be like.

▶
This map of Devonshire, England, by Christopher Saxton dates from 1575.

The result was that they made maps that look very strange to us now. In addition, no two maps were alike. It's fun to look at these old maps now and see what people then thought the world was like.

Many people collect old maps, or copies of them, to decorate their houses or offices. If you have seen some, you know that they have colorful and interesting pictures around the edges or on the map itself. You might see fantastic whale-like creatures or sea serpents roaming the oceans, or fleets of sailing ships being blown by the wind. Sometimes wild animals wander the unknown lands, and people in their native dress decorate the borders of some maps.

At one time, those pictures inspired people to leave their homes for adventures in new and faraway places. Now we can look at them as wonderful works of imagination and art. Today, maps are made with the help of computers and are more accurate than ever. But the old hand-drawn maps have an artistic richness that makes them an historical treasure.

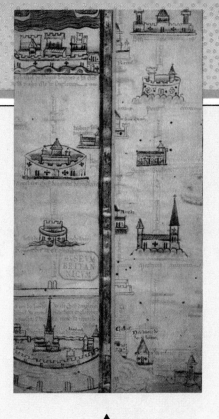

▲
This early English map helped travelers recognize towns along the road between London and Dover.

▶
This map was made in 1876 to commemorate the nation's Centennial.

# ROADS GO EVER EVER ON

*by J. R. R. Tolkien*

Roads go ever ever on,
    Over rock and under tree,
By caves where never sun has shone,
    By streams that never find the sea;
Over snow by winter sown,
    And through the merry flowers of June,
Over grass and over stone,
    And under mountains in the moon.

# MARS

# A Close-Up Picture

*by Patricia Lauber*

*Not long ago, a space journey to Mars could only be imagined. Now, several spacecraft have made the trip and sent surprising information back to Earth.*

Is there life on Mars? Was there ever life on Mars? The possibility catches the imagination. In many ways Mars seems a likely place to look for life, past or present.

## Is Mars Like Earth?

Fourth planet from the sun, Mars is like Earth in many ways. It is smaller than the earth and reddish, because of some kind of rusted iron in its soil. But it has an atmosphere in which white clouds appear, and it has polar ice caps. Since its axis is tilted at the same angle as Earth's, Mars has seasons in its northern and southern hemispheres. They last nearly twice as long as Earth's, because Mars is farther from the sun. It travels a bigger orbit at slower speeds, taking 687 Earth days to make one trip around the sun. Its day, however, is just a little longer than ours.

Mars, like Earth, is a planet on which changes take place with the seasons.

Each ice cap grows in winter and shrinks in summer. Colors change. Seen even blurrily through a telescope, the dark markings of spring and summer turn pale as winter approaches.

Mars is like the earth in another way. Among the inner planets, only Mars and Earth have moons. Mars has two tiny, potato-shaped moons, named Phobos and Deimos.

About a hundred years ago, some astronomers began seeing straight lines on Mars. The more they studied Mars, the more lines they saw crisscrossing the planet in a network. Since straight lines were obviously the work of intelligent beings, imaginations leaped ahead. The lines must be canals, dug to move water from melting polar ice caps to croplands near the equator. What had forced the Martians to dig these canals? There was

**Phobos appears heavily cratered in this photograph taken by the Viking Orbiter.**

only one answer. Mars was slowly drying up. It was a dying planet whose desperate inhabitants had tried to buy time.

Today no one knows what those earlier astronomers were seeing. Modern astronomers have never seen straight lines on Mars—but they have seen changing colors that hinted of plant life.

**Part of the Viking Lander 2 appears in front of the rocky Martian landscape.**

# Is Mars Like Our Moon?

The first exploratory spacecraft put an end to hopes of finding widespread plant life on Mars. Photographs showed a cratered landscape that looked more like the moon than like Earth. But on Mars the craters were flat-bottomed and appeared to be filled with dust. Instruments reported on the carbon dioxide atmosphere. It was very thin; air pressure was less than one one-hundredth the air pressure on Earth at sea level. Because the atmosphere was thin, the carbon dioxide did not create a greenhouse effect.[1] Temperatures on most of Mars were well below the freezing point of water. During a polar winter, temperatures fell below minus 200 degrees. At such levels, carbon dioxide freezes into ice, the kind called dry ice on Earth. A polar ice cap grew on Mars when carbon dioxide froze out of the atmosphere as dry ice. It shrank when temperatures rose, and the ice turned into gas.

Was Mars then, just like the moon, only with ice caps? The answer turned out to be no, not at all. It came from the photographs taken by *Mariner 9*, which went into orbit around Mars, and from those taken by two *Viking* orbiters and the landers that sent back the first pictures from the surface of Mars.

[1]greenhouse effect: the warming effect on the earth's atmosphere produced by the sun

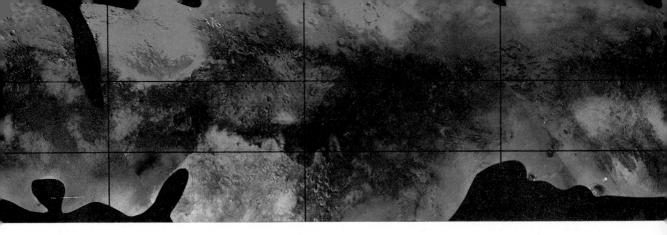

Turquoise areas indicate surface frosts and fogs at the polar ice cap of Mars.

## Surprises on Mars

*Mariner 9* arrived in the middle of a planet-wide dust storm. When the dust finally settled, *Mariner 9* began sending back pictures that took scientists by complete surprise. No one had ever imagined that Mars might look as it did.

The first thing to come into sight was the top of a gigantic volcano, the biggest anyone had ever seen. Named Olympus Mons, this giant is the biggest mountain so far known in the solar system. It towers three times as high as Mount Everest. Its broad, cliff-edged base would barely fit between San Francisco and Los Angeles.

Olympus Mons is one of four huge volcanoes that rise from the Tharsis Plateau at the equator of Mars. Tharsis itself would more than cover the United States from Los Angeles to New York. It is a huge dome-shaped bulge in the crust.

Some 3,000 miles away is another group of big volcanoes. For unknown reasons, most of the volcanoes on Mars are in the northern hemisphere, while most of the craters are in the southern hemisphere. By chance, the first exploratory spacecraft photographed only parts of the southern hemisphere.

This photo taken as Viking came within 348,000 miles of Mars shows volcanoes rising from the Tharsis plateau.

379

To the east of Tharsis is an enormous rift valley, called Valles Marineris. It starts as jumbled land and becomes a canyon that is three times as deep as Arizona's Grand Canyon and so long that it would span the United States from coast to coast.

How did the valley form? One idea is that it marks a place where two huge plates of crust began to move apart. Since Mars is a small planet, it may have lost heat so quickly that nothing more happened. Another idea is that heat inside Mars made it expand, tearing the crust apart. Whatever happened, it is clear that Mars has been—and perhaps still is—hot inside. At times, molten rock has poured out, building giant volcanoes.

*Below,* **Viking approaches the dawn side of Mars.** *Right,* **the great canyon of Mars, Valles Marineris, appears.**

Large parts of Mars are covered with fine dust. In some places the dust forms dunes, like the sand dunes in Earth's deserts. The dust moves with the winds. It has filled in crater bottoms. It erodes and carves rock. And it accounts for the color changes seen on Mars.

Dust storms occur seasonally on Mars. When a storm ends, surface colors have changed. Light-colored dust covers areas that were dark. In other areas, winds have stripped away the dust, revealing darker material.

## Water on Mars

Because the surface of Mars is bone dry, no one expected to see signs of ancient floods. Yet parts of the surface appear to have been shaped by streams and flash floods. There are places that look as if they had once been a sea of mud. This discovery was perhaps the biggest surprise of all.

Where could water have come from? The answer has to be, from Mars itself. There are traces of water vapor in the planet's atmosphere. But even if it could all condense and fall as rain, there's not enough to cause a flood.

There is water ice in the polar ice caps. Each pole has a year-round ice cap to which frozen carbon dioxide is added in winter. The north polar cap is made entirely of water ice, mixed with dust. The south polar cap seems to be made mostly of water ice and perhaps some frozen carbon dioxide.

Much more water is frozen in the ground, near the surface. It is like the permafrost, or permanently frozen layer beneath the surface of Earth's arctic regions.

And recent radar studies seem to show that a few parts of Mars have underground supplies of liquid water.

In one form or another, water does exist on Mars. But at present liquid

This photo from Viking Lander 2 reveals late-winter frost on the rocky ground around the lander.

water cannot exist on the surface. The air pressure is too low and the temperature too cold. Any liquid water would turn to vapor or to ice.

## Temperatures on Mars

Suppose, though, there was a time when Mars was warmer. Less carbon dioxide would be locked up as ice. More would be in the atmosphere, and air pressure would increase. The carbon dioxide in the air would trap most of the sun's heat. The heat would melt water ice and permafrost. Floods of water might then occur. Water could stay liquid with warmer temperatures and greater air pressure.

Two things could make Mars warmer, some scientists suggest. One is an increase in heat from the sun itself; our star is a steady producer of light and heat, but changes do take place in its output. The other is a change in the tilt of Mars's axis; such changes do occur, caused by the pull of Jupiter and other planets. Perhaps in the past some parts of Mars received more heat than they do today. If these scientists are right, then Mars has had periods of being warmer and wetter than it now is.

If Mars has water, has it also had life? We don't know. The *Viking* landers carried out experiments to look for life in the soil. None was found. But that does not prove there has never been life on Mars. It does not prove there is no life on Mars. The landers looked for it in only two places. Besides, the experiments may have asked the wrong questions. They may have looked for the wrong kind of life.

Understanding Mars is important for us. Earth has had warm periods and cold periods. There have been times when, in the cold parts of the earth, more snow fell than the summer sun could melt. The snow packed down into ice that built up into glaciers. And the glaciers advanced over large parts of the earth. No one knows for sure why this happened. But we do know that the tilt of Earth's axis is slightly affected by Jupiter and other planets. We also know that Mars and Earth share the same sun. Our histories are twined together. Clues to our own past and future may lie in the ice caps of Mars, for thick ice holds a record of past climates.

## ◆ LIBRARY LINK ◆

*If you enjoyed this article about Mars and want to find out more about other planets, read the whole book* Journey to the Planets *by Patricia Lauber.*

## Reader's Response

Are you interested in the exploration of Mars? Why or why not?

# MARS A Close-Up Picture

## Checking Your Comprehension

1. What similarities are there between Mars and Earth?
2. If you were writing a fictional story about Mars, how would you explain the straight lines that astronomers saw a century ago?
3. What surprised scientists about the first photographs of the surface of Mars?
4. How did Mariner IX end hopes of finding widespread plant life on Mars?
5. Why would warmer weather have made it possible for life to exist on Mars? How did you think this through?
6. If life were discovered on Mars, how might it be different from life on Earth?

## Writing to Learn

**THINK AND QUESTION**   What would you like your classmates to remember about Mars? Make up a test for them. Write three essay questions about Mars. (An essay question requires at least a one-paragraph answer.)

What would you see if you visited Mars?

**WRITE**   Choose one of the essay questions you wrote. Write your own one-paragraph answer.

*Literature:*

# Science Fiction

**T**hink about the description of our neighboring planet in "Mars: A Close-Up Picture." Although Mars is similar to Earth in some ways, it is also very different. Mars is reddish in color with polar icecaps that swell and shrink with the seasons. It has two moons named Phobos and Deimos. The volcanos on Mars are taller than any mountain on Earth. The valleys dwarf even the Grand Canyon. Dust storms race across the planet's surface and the temperature drops to minus two hundred degrees in the Martian winter.

Now suppose you were writing a story that took place on Mars. From the facts given above, try to imagine different landscapes on Mars. Try to imagine what your characters would look like. Would they be covered in dense fur to withstand the bitter cold? Or would they live in underground cities heated by the fires of volcanos? What would they think about as they marched across the vast polar icefields or gazed up at Phobos and Deimos crossing the night sky in unison?

As you write, you would have to use your imagination, but you also would have scientific facts about Mars as a starting point for the story. This is what some fiction writers do. They try to imagine and describe worlds and creatures and times beyond the limits of our knowledge. But when they imagine, they also use the knowledge that science makes available. By blending imaginary places and characters with scientific facts, writers create a type of literature called *science fiction*.

Four hundred years ago, writers were already imagining what it would be like to fly to the moon. At that time, even short flights were impossible for people, so stories about flying to the moon were science fiction. Today, some astronauts could write about flying to the moon from their own personal experiences. Subjects that were once science fiction are now scientific fact.

In 1783, the hot air balloon was invented, and, for the first time, people could be lifted off the ground. That allowed writers to imagine what flight was like a little more realistically. A hundred years later, Jules Verne, one of the greatest science fiction writers ever, wrote a book entitled *Around the World in Eighty Days* about traveling around the world in a balloon. In *20,000 Leagues Under the Sea*, he wrote about going below the ocean in a submarine. In other books, he wrote about helicopters, airplanes, and television.

You wouldn't be surprised to read about these things in a book today. But Jules Verne was writing a hundred years ago. Submarines and flying machines existed only in his imagination. At that time, pioneers were still crossing the nation in covered wagons. Imagine how astonished a pioneer would have been to look up from the wagon to see a helicopter hovering overhead.

In his fiction, Jules Verne also predicted that a rocket launched in Florida would reach the moon. About a hundred years later, an astronaut walked on the moon. Jules Verne also predicted that astronauts would be weightless in space.

How did he make these predictions that were later proven true? In part, he used the scientific facts that were available to him at the time. Although he took only one ride in a hot air balloon, he used what he learned from that experience to imagine other forms of flying. He used these facts as a starting point for his imagination.

## Read and Enjoy

"Day of the Earthlings" is a science fiction story that takes place on Mars. As you read, see how the author imagined characters and landscapes on Mars. Also, think about what is fact and what is fiction in the story.

# DAY OF THE
# EARTHLINGS
by Eve Bunting

*Cort was the only Earthling living on Mars. Imagine how Cort felt the day he learned a spaceship was on its way to Mars from Earth.*

When Cort was six or seven, he realized that he was not like the other Martians.

"Why am I so much bigger than all my friends?" he asked his father.

"Because you are an Earthling, my son. We Martians are small so that we are well adapted to our wind and our cold and our life underground."

"Is it because I am an Earthling that my eyes are such a strange shape?"

"Yes," his father said.

"Tell me about Earth and how I got here," Cort asked, and his father told him.

"We on Mars are a very advanced people. We took our spaceships to Earth and to Moon and to Saturn before other worlds dreamed of such things. One of our space travellers brought you back once, a long time ago. It was wrong. He should not have done such a thing; but it was done, and we made the best of it."

"Were the people angry with him?"

"They were. Such a terrible thing has never happened again." He reached to touch Cort's hair. "Your mother and I had no children. We took you, and we have loved you always."

"I know," Cort said.

"Do you remember the operations?" his father asked. "Your lungs were Earth lungs and needed oxygen. Our doctors adjusted your body to carbon dioxide. Do you remember it at all, Cort?"

"I don't think so," Cort said slowly.

Yet, somewhere, far far back in time, there was a cloud that spun, and a voice crying, and pain. There must be memories, or else why was there in him this hunger for something he didn't have and didn't know?

The hunger grew with the years. Sometimes at night it would waken him. Sometimes at night, he'd come up to the shining cold of the Martian surfaces, and he'd look into the blackness where the planet Earth lay. That was where he'd been born. The pull of it was as strong as gravity inside him and as strange. He was fifteen years old, and he'd never seen an Earthling; but now the Earthlings were coming.

Cort's father knew what Earth was like. He'd been there twice on a spaceship. He'd taught himself the Earth language by monitoring the space stations, and Cort had learned it from him.

"The sky there is blue, not black like ours," his father said. "They have great wide seas and water that runs in rivers such as we had billions of years ago. In their houses water flows from pipes, and they use it without thought."

That was perhaps the strangest thing of all. Here on Mars water was life and as precious. It was brought from the Polar ice caps by ice-gathering machines or mined underground from the permafrost.

"Their wind does not blow night and day with the strength of ours, and it is warmer there. The Earth men live above ground."

"It sounds . . . it sounds nice." Cort heard the little catch in his voice, and he turned his face from his father.

"It is," his father said. "It should be enough for any people; but the Earthlings would like to take over Mars, too."

"If they come, we could fight them off," Cort said; and he wondered at the falseness of his words. When he spoke of "they" what did he mean? He was one of "them," wasn't he? "We" and "They." How could he separate the two?

Now the Earthlings were coming.

Cosmos 21, their space station, reported *Patriot 1* on its way from Earth. Its touchdown would be on the plain of Nerre.

Nine times already the Earth men had sent their spaceships to Mars in search of life. They had never found it, but this time was more dangerous. This time human men would land to search the Martian planet.

"If they find nothing on this trip, perhaps they will look to Saturn or Venus and leave us alone," Cort's father said; "and since they've chosen Nerre for the touchdown. . . ." He left the sentence unfinished and smiled.

Nerre was a desert and as empty as the Earth's Sahara. The closest Martian underground city was more than two hundred kilometers away. None of their ice-gathering machines worked that zone, and it held none of their telescopes or space antennae. It was good that that was the chosen spot.

A Martian crew travelled to Nerre. In two hours they constructed an underground dugout from which they could watch, unseen. Cort was one of the crew.

When the work was finished, he stood beside his father on the bare plain of Nerre and looked into the day blackness of the sky.

The sun shone through its ice halo, but he saw it speckled by a dust dazzle of blowing sand.

Tomorrow *Patriot 1* would come through that shimmer of sand, it would land, and its doors would open, and . . . Cort's heart beat fast. Cosmos 21 reported two Earth men on the Lander. Soon, soon they would be here.

Ellis Carver huddled in *Patriot 1*'s Lander as it rushed toward Mars. He could see Jonty Johnson's face through the glass of his helmet. The face was lettuce green. He hoped Jonty wasn't going to throw up. He hoped their touchdown would be easy. He hoped they'd live through it.

Sweat rolled down his face, and there was no way to get a finger under his helmet to scratch the itch. It was better to think about the itch than to think about the touchdown.

It had taken eight years and more than a billion dollars to get *Patriot 1* off the ground. So far everything had gone perfectly. They'd cruised 900 miles above Mars taking pictures. Whatever happened now, that part of the mission had been a success. The pictures had already been beamed back to Earth. Whatever happened now! The words echoed in his mind and seemed to bounce off his space helmet. All they needed was one big rock, and the Lander would topple. Suppose . . . no, don't suppose.

He'd been training for four years, ever since he was eighteen. "Reacts well under stress." That's what his very first NASA report had said. Ellis licked his lips. He tried to catch the sweat trickle with his tongue. Reacts well under stress. It wasn't that he was scared. It was just that everything was unknown and so much depended on them.

There was a loud, plopping noise—the rocket engines firing, bringing them on a downward path. That soft, swishing sound was their parachute unfurling. Six miles an hour—that's what their speed should be now. The red light flashed on the control panel. Thirty seconds till

touchdown. Why did they call it a control panel? They didn't have control of anything. Everything was pre-programmed. They were on a computer course with no way to change it.

The light blinked and blinked. Twenty-seven, twenty-six. Ellis watched the flashing red eye as it ticked away the seconds.

Each of the Martian crew men had a telescopic periscope. It was reed-thin, crafted to be almost invisible from ground level. Their dugout was five kilometers from the touchdown zone.

Cort watched the small ship coming silver through the black dust-dazzle of the sky. Above it the detached parachute hung wispy as a cloud. The three landing legs were down, and a shower of sparks shot from the ship's side.

"The braking rockets," his father muttered.

Slowly, delicately the Lander eased down. One foot pad touched Martian ground. The wind gusted, and the metal trembled. Then the other two feet took hold, and the craft swayed and settled. Cort held his breath. His heart-sound was loud in his ears. Soon he would have his first glimpse of Earthlings—his own kind, his very own. Soon now.

Inside the Lander, Ellis and Jonty Johnson carried out their first tasks. Ellis relayed their safe touchdown to the orbiting mother ship. Jonty used the remote scoop to pick up soil samples and store them in the thermal vault. The Lander's camera moved down below the ship to photograph the foot pads and the ground around them. The high television camera on top of the craft activated and began rolling. It was time to leave the Lander. But whatever happened now, this much had been accomplished. Whatever happened now!

Jonty swung the side hatch up and let down the runway. His wave to Ellis said, "You first."

Ellis stood by the side of one of the small mobile Rovers and looked through the dust at the Red Planet. It wasn't red. He felt awe and a sense of something of tremendous importance. His eyes were seeing what no human eyes had seen before.

Ahead of him lay desert, more lifeless than anything on Earth. No shrub grew—no plant. There was only a broad, barren plain, the wind whipping its rocky sand knee high, flinging it against the Lander as if sensing an alien object. In the distance he could see a rim of sharp-edged craters. Ellis drew a deep breath. They'd been lucky. Suppose they'd tried to land there?

Mars! He said the word under his breath. For this second he was Columbus on the deck of the *Santa Maria*, seeing the New World for the first time.

Jonty tapped his shoulder, and Ellis nodded. He checked his air tanks and tubes. Then he climbed behind the Rover's wheel, his body awkward in his heat-controlled suit. The sound of the Rover's engines was lost in the whine of the wind. His headlights gilded the dust that snapped through the air. Slowly the Rover rolled on its tractor treads down the runway.

He would travel due North; Jonty due South. Tonight they'd re-charge their air tanks and refuel the Rovers. Tomorrow they'd head East and West. The Rover's control panel would buzz at the return point. When the buzzer sounded, half the air and half the fuel were gone. There was a half-volume reserve tank.

Ellis sat in the Rover at the foot of the Lander and looked up at it. It was like a great silver beetle on a rock, a dragonfly maybe. Its searchlight shone reassuringly from above, giving light for the television camera—light for them too, a hope in the dark to look back to. Ellis took a shivery breath. Air wasting. Time to start.

The strange stone desert stretched ahead and to either side. From time to time he stopped to gather and store a strange, glittering rock, a blackened, burned-out lump of stone. From time to time he checked his space compass. There was no sign of life, but Ellis felt no disappointment. He knew now that he had not expected to find any. "Why do we climb mountains?" he asked himself.

"Because they are there."

"Why do we look for other worlds?"

"Because we must always reach for new knowledge." He looked back at the Lander, and it was a beacon that would guide him home.

The Rover rolled slowly up to one of the craters. Ellis stopped it. What had caused this round, black hole? A meteor, crashing into Mars billions of years ago? An ancient volcano? He should have a soil sample. He got out of the Rover and stepped close to the crater's rim. Then suddenly, unbelievably he wasn't standing on rock; he was standing on sand. Then he was standing on nothing, and he was falling, tumbling into what looked like a grey snowdrift below.

Cort saw the Earth man fall. His periscope brought everything close enough to touch, and Cort had been watching hungrily. He wanted to press his face close to the window on that space helmet. He wanted to see Earth eyes, to touch Earth skin; and then the Earth man fell.

Cort heard the gasps, the faint hissing of breath as the Martians realized what had happened. His father raised his periscope to get a down-view into the crater.

"He can't get up," he said sadly.

Cort wound his periscope high. The Earthling lay face down on top of the powder sand. Somehow he had sense not to struggle. With the weight of his tanks and thermal suit, to struggle would be to sink and suffocate.

Cort wet his lips and looked at his father.

"What will we do?"

His father's eyes held the same sadness as his voice. "There is nothing we can do. To help him we would have to reveal ourselves. Perhaps the other Earth man will come to his rescue." He spoke so softly that Cort could scarcely hear him. "Perhaps he'll be in time."

Cort swallowed. "How much air does he have?"

"I see the red light on his Rover. The warning buzzer is on. One Earth hour left. Perhaps a half-hour emergency oxygen, no more."

Cort looked at the stranded Earthling one more time and could bear to look no longer. "You taught me that life is precious," he told his father. His anger burned inside him. "Is an Earth life not precious?"

"It is," his father said. "But we must count the cost."

Cort sat by himself and tried to understand his feelings. The pull was back, drawing him strongly, surely toward the Earth man. Leave him to die? How could they do that? And yet . . . and yet . . . Cort chewed at his underlip till he felt the sting of blood.

The other Martians watched intently through their periscopes. No one saw Cort take the coil of woven rope and slip away.

Ellis listened to the Rover's buzzer and made his time calculations. Then he accepted the fact that he was going to die.

The shock of the rope dropping over his shoulders made him flounder and sink several inches.

"Don't move," a voice said.

Ellis' heart fluttered wildly. Jonty . . . it must be Jonty! Cautiously he raised his head.

What? Who?

A boy stood at the crater's rim holding the end of the rope. "Slowly. Put it under your arms," the boy said in halting English.

Ellis got his arms through the loop and held on to the rope with all his strength. He felt dazed, in some sort of shock where he knew this was happening and knew too that it couldn't be.

"Good." The boy wore Eskimo clothes of some glowing fabric, but that was a human face under the hood and that was a human voice. There was a drop of dried blood on the boy's lower lip.

The boy stepped back out of sight, and Ellis panicked and moved. He felt himself sink. "Hey," he called; but his word was hollow inside his helmet. Then he heard the Rover's motor start, and the rope under his arms tightened. He was dragged like a big fish through the sand drift and up the edge of the crater. On level ground he lay gasping, too stunned to move as the boy wrapped the rope round and around him, trussing him like a chicken.

"I will let you go," the boy said. "But first you must give me your word. No one is to know that you saw me. No one is to know what happened. Do you give me your word as an Earth man?"

Ellis looked at the face so close to his own. A human, breathing Martian air, living here. It couldn't be. It couldn't.

"Promise, or I will throw you back in."

Ellis managed to move his head in a nod. He mouthed, "I promise." Reacts well under stress, the report had said. Reacts well.

"You saw nothing. You got yourself out." The voice was fierce. The human face was pressed close against his helmet window. Their eyes met and held.

"Who are you?" Ellis begged silently. "How are you here?"

Shadows like clouds moved behind the boy's eyes. To Ellis it seemed as though he stared at him forever. The boy raised his hand and gently touched the side of Ellis' helmet. Then he unwound the rope, bunched it loosely, and edged back.

Ellis struggled to his knees. He held on to the side of the Rover and pulled himself up. The boy had disappeared. Should he try to follow him through the speckled dark? Which way had he gone? Had there been a boy at all? There must have been. Someone, something had dragged him from death.

Ellis shook his head. For a few seconds he stared into the emptiness; then he climbed behind the Rover's wheel and turned it toward the light of the Lander.

His mind was a jumble of unanswered questions. He'd promised. . . . What had he promised? But this was the cosmic discovery of all time, and he was a scientist. Nothing should stand in the way of this truth.

It could be that they wouldn't believe him. It sure wasn't easy to believe. And he'd promised the boy. Ellis thought of the boy's eyes, the way he'd touched his helmet as if saying goodbye.

Now he was under the Lander. He looked up at it and remembered what he'd forgotten, and he knew that the decision wasn't his to make.

Cort leaned against the outside wall of the dugout. He had disobeyed his father and gone against the will of his people. The race across the rocky ground was like a dream now, the running so fast that there had been no time to think. The Earth man's face, so like his own and yet so different! For a second, as he'd looked down at that face, his mind had been filled with impossible thoughts. He could ask the Earthling to take him back with him. The operations could be reversed. He'd be with his own people. He'd leave Mars forever. He'd looked down, and there had been a moment of choice, and for the first time he'd known what that choice was. *These* were his people. He belonged here with the known things, with the acceptance, with the love. There was a sadness in finally knowing who he was, and a relief too.

Now his hands trembled as he pushed open the door. His father and the others must have seen him through their periscopes as he ran to help the Earth man. They hadn't tried to stop him. There was some hope in realizing that.

They faced him as he stood against the door, and he saw at once that there was no anger. But there was something else.

"He won't tell," Cort said shakily. "He gave me his word as an Earth man."

The room held silence, and something else.

Cort spoke to his father, "I had to go."

"I know," his father said. "But there was one thing you didn't know, my son, or didn't remember." He spread out his hands. "We saw you running; and we could have brought you back, but it was already too late. The Lander has a television camera with a dark-view eye. You are there, my son, on film. The pictures must already be on their way back to Earth."

Someone pulled down his periscope, and the click of it was the only sound in the room.

"It will take them many years to build another space-ship," his father said, "but nothing will stop them now. We will leave here, move to the opposite side of our planet, but they will find us."

"What have I done?" Cort heard his voice rising out of control.

"Not you alone," his father said. "What happened tonight was started many years ago when you were brought here. The fault is also ours."

There was the crackle of static. Cosmos 21.

They froze, listening.

The words that came from the box were slurred with excitement, but no one in the room failed to understand.

"*Patriot 1* reports life found on Mars," the space voice said. "Repeat. *Patriot 1* reports life found on Mars."

### Reader's Response

Do you think that Cort was courageous? Explain your answer.

# WRITING ABOUT READING

## Writing a Description

In this unit you read stories about journeys to fascinating places. An author's imagination can travel anywhere—to the outer limits of space or to unexplored islands on earth.

Write two paragraphs of description of an imaginary place and share it with the members of your class. The words you choose will help your readers picture a place in their minds.

### Prewriting

Read this description from "Snowshoe Trek to Otter River." Notice how the author's words convince you that you are there.

> Soon he was beyond the open fields and deep into the swamp. It was a different world, darker, quieter. The big spruce and fir trees covered up the sky. There was no sound. It was as if this swamp were a noiseless chamber. All Daniel could hear were his snowshoes, whispering, hissing as he moved along. He stopped. Listened. Now there was no sound at all. None. It was as if everything in the world were dead except for one boy who stood silent and alone, deep in a snowy evergreen swamp.

In your mind, explore your imaginary place and record your observations. Draw a chart like the one on the next page. Then write what you see, hear, smell, taste, and feel in your imaginary place.

## Observation Chart

| *See* | *Hear* | *Smell* | *Taste* | *Feel* |
|-------|--------|---------|---------|--------|
| big spruce | whisper | | | alone |
| fir trees | hiss | | | |
| evergreen | | | | |
| ·swamp | | | | |
| snow | | | | |

### Writing

Use your chart to write your two paragraphs of description. Begin by telling where your imaginary place is located. Are you at the edge of a river or on the top of a mountain? Then tell what you see and hear. Your readers will want to know how you feel. If you smell or taste anything, mention these details also.

### Revising

Read your description to a partner. Ask your partner to make a list of the details in your description. Review the list. Would your details be more effective if they were organized in another way? Add more details to make your writing real.

### Proofreading

Correct spelling, punctuation, and capitalization mistakes. Make a clean copy of your description.

### Publishing

Use your descriptions to create a class book called *Visions from Another World*.

# WORKING TOGETHER

## Making a Map of a Journey

The stories in this unit described travels to real and imaginary places. For example, Daniel in "Snowshoe Trek to Otter River," made a winter journey to one of his favorite places. Your group will make a map that shows the route taken by one of the story characters in this unit.

Your group will do well by sharing these responsibilities.

♦ Contributing ideas

♦ Using people's names during group discussion

♦ Recording people's ideas

♦ Making sure the group finishes on time

Begin by reviewing the travels described in the stories in this unit. If you could choose one place, where would you like to go? Which trip or voyage was most interesting to you? Together, agree on one story for which you will make a map. Discuss which places or landmarks to include. Keep a list. Choose one person to start the map, and then take turns adding and labeling landmarks and important places described in the story. As you work, connect the places with dotted lines to show where the journey started, where it continued, and where it ended. Ask other classmates to guess which story your map illustrates.

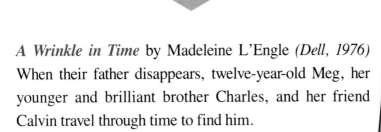

# BOOKS TO ENJOY

*A Wrinkle in Time* by Madeleine L'Engle *(Dell, 1976)* When their father disappears, twelve-year-old Meg, her younger and brilliant brother Charles, and her friend Calvin travel through time to find him.

*Alice's Adventures in Wonderland* by Lewis Carroll *(Putnam, 1986)* After falling into a rabbit hole, Alice meets the White Rabbit, the Dormouse, the Mad Hatter, and others during her strange adventures.

*The Promised Year* by Yoshiko Uchida *(Harcourt, 1959)* When Keiko journeys from Japan to California, she can only guess what life will be like when she lives with her aunt and uncle for a year.

*The Search for Delicious* by Natalie Babbitt *(Farrar, 1969)* When no one at the castle can agree on which food should define *delicious* in the Prime Minister's dictionary, Gaylen is sent off to poll the entire kingdom.

*When Hitler Stole Pink Rabbit* by Judith Kerr *(Dell, 1973)* Anna, Max, and their parents flee from Hitler's Germany first to Switzerland and then to France. Their journey is both difficult and exciting as they adjust to both new places and new languages.

# THE
# HOME
## OF
# THE BRAVE

*There are all kinds
of houses in all
kinds of places.*

---

*What is the special
something that makes
a house a home?*

---

QUILT WITH SCENES OF WYOMA,
MASSACHUSETTS,
*quilt by Celestine Bacheller, American, ca. 1850–1900*

407

# IF YOU SAY SO, CLAUDE

written by Joan Lowery Nixon
illustrated by Lorinda Bryan Cauley

*Shirley and Claude want to settle down in Texas.
However, Shirley's idea of home is not quite the same as
Claude's.*

In the spring, after the last of the big snows, Shirley and Claude drove down from the silver-mining towns of the Rocky Mountains. They headed for that great state called Texas.

Claude was as short as he was broad, with a curly gray beard that waggled when he talked. Shirley was as tall as a doorpost, and almost as thin, with hair and skin the color of prairie dust with the sun on it. They drove in a covered wagon pulled by two sway-backed, but good-natured, horses.

"I can't abide those minin' towns any longer, Shirley," Claude said. "All that shootin' and yellin' is too rough a life for me. I've heard there's plenty of peace and quiet to be found in that great state called Texas."

"If you say so, Claude," Shirley said. But she missed the mountains and the forests and the plumb good looks of the Colorado Territory.

They followed a trail that cut south and turned east into upper West Texas, where long canyons dug deep into the hard rock.

"Will you look at that!" Claude cried. He eased the horses and wagon down a trail to the bottom of a narrow, rocky canyon. The purple shadows lay over them, and the silence lay around them.

"Shirley, I do believe this is the peaceful place we've been lookin' for," Claude said.

"I hope not," Shirley said. "I don't really take to this place, Claude. I feel like I'm in a four-sided box."

"Never mind. This land will grow on you, Shirley," Claude said. "For now, why don't you take the rifle and see if you can hunt up some meat for the table. I'll get our sleepin' pallets out of the wagon and tend to the horses."

So Shirley unfolded her long legs and stuck her feet in her boots, hiked up her skirts, and climbed down from the wagon. She took the rifle and edged past the back of the wagon. Right off she spied a fat, lop-eared rabbit sitting on a rock ledge just across the narrow canyon; so she raised the rifle and fired.

Shirley's aim never was very good, so she missed the rabbit; and that old bullet bounced off the rock and back and forth across the canyon, whanging and banging, zinging and zanging, making a terrible racket. Shirley and the rabbit just froze, staring wide-eyed at each other.

Well, Claude took that moment to stick his head out the back of the wagon to see what that awful noise was, and the bullet tore right through the top of his hat, dropping it in the dust at Shirley's feet.

Claude looked across the canyon just in time to see the rabbit hightail it behind the ledge. He thought on it for a moment. Then he said, "Shirley, get back in the wagon. I don't think we want to live in a place where we can't go out to get meat for the table without the rabbits shootin' back. We're gonna have to move on."

Shirley picked up Claude's hat, climbed back into the wagon, and gave a happy sigh of relief.

"If you say so, Claude," she said.

For two days Shirley and Claude headed south, farther down into that great state called Texas. The sun was mean enough to sizzle lizards and curl up the cracks in the dried-out earth, when Claude pulled the sweating, but good-natured, horses to a stop.

He said, "Shirley, I do believe this is the peaceful place we've been lookin' for."

Shirley gazed at the flat landscape that stretched before her gray and bleak, broken only by clumps of scrubby mesquite. And she said, "I hope not, Claude. This land has got the worst case of the uglies I've ever seen."

"Never mind. It'll grow on you, Shirley," Claude said. "For now, why don't you go see what you can find in the way of firewood. I'll get our sleepin' pallets out of the wagon and tend to the horses."

So Shirley unfolded her long legs, stuck her feet in her boots, hiked up her skirts, and climbed down from the wagon. She walked back aways, among the clumps of mesquite. Suddenly she heard an angry rattle. She looked down, and her right boot was planted square on the neck of a mad five-foot diamondback rattler that had stretched out in the shade to take a nap.

Before she could think what to do, she heard another noise. She looked over to her left to see a mean little wild hog. Its beady eyes glared, its sharp tusks quivered, and its small hooves pawed the ground, getting ready to charge.

411

Quick as she could, Shirley stooped down, grabbed the snake careful like around the neck, and, using it as a whip, flipped its tail at the wild hog. That tail, rattle and all, wrapped itself tight about the neck of the hog.

But the hog was coming fast, and all Shirley could do was hang onto the snake and use all her strength to twirl the hog clear off his feet and round and around her head. With a zap she let go. The snake fell to the ground, done for. But the hog flew off, squealing and snorting and carrying on something awful.

Shirley's aim never was very good, so it happened that just as Claude climbed down from the wagon to see what was making the terrible racket, that hog sailed right past his face, nearly brushing the end of his nose.

Claude watched the hog until he was out of sight, way yonder past a far clump of mesquite, and he thought on it for a moment.

"Shirley," he called, "get back in the wagon. It seems to me a man has a right to set foot outside his wagon without gettin' bad-mouthed by a wild hog who wants the right of way. Especially," he added, "when that hog's in a place no hog ever ought to be. We're gonna have to move on."

Shirley climbed back into the wagon and gave a happy sigh of relief.

"If you say so, Claude," she said.

For the next few days Shirley and Claude headed east in that great state called Texas. The dusty trail rose and took them into land that was strewn with rocks and boulders of all sizes.

Claude pulled the stumbling, but good-natured, horses to a stop and said, "Shirley, I do believe this is the peaceful place we've been lookin' for."

Shirley gazed out at the ridges and rocks and the stubby trees whose roots clung to the patches of soil. And she said, "I hope not, Claude. This land is nothin' but bumpy-lumpy and makes me feel dry enough to spit cotton."

"Never mind. This place will grow on you, Shirley," Claude said. "For now, why don't you set things to right around here. I'll get our sleepin' pallets out of the wagon and tend to the horses."

So Shirley unfolded her long legs, stuck her feet in her boots, hiked up her skirts, and climbed down from the wagon. She strung a line between the rim of the wagon and a branch of a nearby tree, and on it she hung out to air Claude's long johns and his other shirt, and her petticoats and second-best, store-bought dress.

She was just finishing this chore when she heard a crackle of a broken twig. She turned around to see a large, mangy wolf creeping closer and closer. His eyes were narrow slits, his ears were laid back, and he was up to no good.

Shirley grabbed the nearest thing at hand, the frying pan that was hanging on the back of the wagon, and she let fly at the wolf.

Shirley's aim never was very good, so the frying pan hit the clothesline instead, sweeping it down, just as the wolf leaped forward.

Unfortunately for the wolf, he dove right inside the skirt and on up through the bodice of Shirley's second-best, store-bought dress. His head poked out of the sweetheart neckline, and his front paws were pinned so he couldn't use them.

Well, he set up a snarling and a yelping, meanwhile bouncing around on his back legs and making a terrible racket.

Just as Claude came around the front of the wagon to see what was going on, that old wolf bounced and leaped right on past him, carrying on something awful.

Claude watched the wolf until he disappeared around a far boulder, then he thought on it for a moment.

"Shirley," he said, "get back in the wagon. I don't know why that pointy-nose lady has got her dander up, but I sure don't want any near neighbors that mean and noisy. We're gonna have to move on."

414

Shirley gathered up their things, put them into the back of the wagon, and climbed up on the seat next to Claude. She gave a happy sigh of relief and said, "If you say so, Claude."

The trail into that great state called Texas curled east and southeast into its heartland. And as it rose it softened into rolling hills, with meadows cupped between. Splashes of blue and gold and red wildflowers dotted the grassy hillsides, and great oaks spread their branches to make deep pools of shade.

Upward they went, until they crested a gentle hill.

Shirley put a hand on Claude's arm and said, "Stop the wagon, Claude."

He pulled the tired, but good-natured, horses to a stop under a stand of oaks, and she said, "Take a look around us. Breathe in that pure air. How's this for a place of peace and quiet?"

"I don't know," Claude said. "Any place that looks this good is bound to get filled up with people afore long. And then we wouldn't remember what peace and quiet were all about."

"Down at the foot of the hill is a stream, probably just jumpin' with fish," Shirley said. "And you can look far enough in both directions goin' and comin' so you could spot a traveler and think on him two days afore he got here."

"I don't know," Claude said again. "Get down from the wagon, Shirley, and see what you can put together for supper. I'll get our sleeping pallets out of the wagon and tend to the horses."

Shirley unfolded her long legs, stuck her feet in her boots, hiked up her skirts, and climbed down from the wagon. She took out the stew pot and set it on the ground under an old and gnarled oak tree. Then she took down the rifle. She was going into the woods to find some fresh meat for the table.

Suddenly she heard the rustle of small leaves, and she looked up to see a big bobcat on a branch near her head. His narrow eyes were gleaming, his lips were pulled back in a snarl, and his tail was twitching. Shirley knew he was getting his mind set to spring.

Well, Shirley stared that bobcat square in the eyes and said to him, "I've found my peaceful place, and you're not goin' to spoil it for me." She raised her rifle, aimed it dead center at the bobcat, and pulled the trigger.

Shirley's aim never was very good. The shot hit that old tree branch, snapping it with a crack that flipped the bobcat in an arc right over the wagon. He came down so hard against a boulder that the force knocked it loose, and it rolled down the hill, tearing up the turf.

Behind it came the screeching bobcat, all spraddle-legged, with every pointy claw digging furrows in the soil as he slid down the hill.

*Splat!* went the boulder into the stream, knocking two good-sized, unsuspecting trout up on the bank and dam-ming up a nice little pond. The bobcat flew over the stream and ran off so fast that Shirley knew she'd seen the last of him.

Claude came running and said, "Shirley, what was makin' all that racket?"

"Nothin' much," Shirley said. "Just a few things gettin' done around here after a branch fell off that tree."

Claude peered at the tree. "Seems there's something oozin' out of that tree into our stew pot," he said.

"What pure good luck!" Shirley said. "Looks like when that branch broke, it opened a honey cache, Claude. You'll have somethin' good on your biscuits tonight."

She took his arm and pointed him toward the sloping hillside. "Take notice that my vegetable garden's already plowed, and there's two good-sized trout down by the stream that are goin' to be pan-fried for supper."

Claude thought on this a moment. Then he said, "Shirley, get back in the wagon and start pullin' out the stuff we'll need. If you can just learn to do your chores without makin' so much noise, then I think we've found us our place of peace and quiet."

Shirley leaned against the wagon and gave a happy sigh of relief. She looked down at the stream that was sparking with pieces of afternoon sunlight, and she gazed out over the hills and the meadows that were soft and pleasing to the eyes.

She gave Claude the biggest smile he'd ever seen anyone come up with, and she said, "If you say so, Claude."

## Reader's Response

What do you think was the funniest thing Shirley
did? Explain your answer.

# IF YOU SAY SO, CLAUDE

## Checking Your Comprehension

1. Why were Shirley and Claude moving to Texas?
2. Which place made the best home for Shirley and Claude? Explain your answer.
3. What didn't Shirley like about each of the first three places she and Claude found?
4. How did Shirley get Claude to leave the places that she did not like?
5. How did Shirley get Claude to stay in the place that she chose? How did you reach your answer?
6. Do you think Shirley meant it when she said, "If you say so, Claude"? Explain your answer.

## Writing to Learn

**THINK AND ANALYZE**  Over and over again in this story, Claude and Shirley do and say similar things. Claude starts each adventure with the same words, and Shirley ends each adventure with the same words. Note the things Claude and Shirley say and do in the puzzle pieces.

BEGINNING

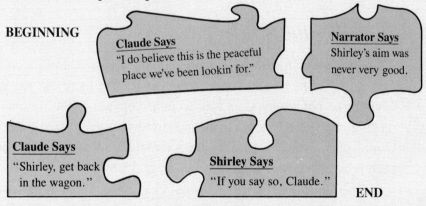

**Claude Says**
"I do believe this is the peaceful place we've been lookin' for."

**Narrator Says**
Shirley's aim was never very good.

**Claude Says**
"Shirley, get back in the wagon."

**Shirley Says**
"If you say so, Claude."

END

**WRITE**  Compose an original Claude-and-Shirley adventure. Include some of the Claude-and-Shirley comments and actions shown here, or use others you identified in the story.

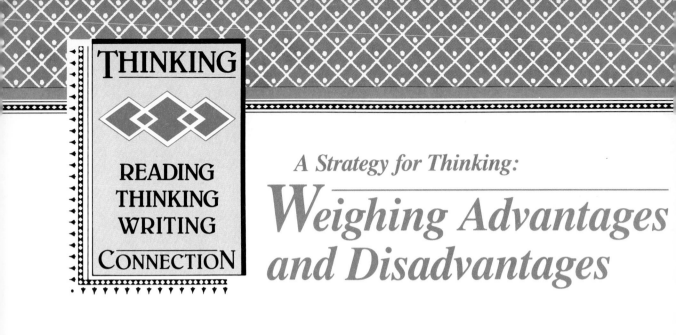

*A Strategy for Thinking:*

# Weighing Advantages and Disadvantages

**L**ife is full of choices. Think about a difficult decision you may have faced. Maybe you had to choose between two activities, such as learning to play the guitar or trying out for the soccer team. How do you make this kind of decision?

Anytime you make a decision, you probably study your choices, then weigh and balance the advantages and disadvantages of each option. The same is often true of the people you read about. They face choices or find themselves in situations that have advantages and disadvantages to be considered. Being able to evaluate advantages and disadvantages can make you more sympathetic and understanding toward the people you read about.

## Learning the Strategy

Suppose you were asked to be one of the first colonists on Mars. You might want to know what it's like to live there as you decide whether or not to go. One way to help you weigh the options is to make a chart of the advantages and disadvantages of living on Mars. On the chart, you can list the characteristics and then decide whether each is an advantage or a disadvantage, and why.

The following chart lists several characteristics of Mars based on "Mars: A Close-Up Picture." Each characteristic is given a plus sign (+) if it is an advantage or a minus sign (−) if it is a disadvantage. Then the reason for each rating is stated.

420

| Characteristic | Advantage or Disadvantage | Reason |
|---|---|---|
| Mars has seasons like Earth. | + | I enjoy watching seasons change. |
| A year on Mars is twice as long as a year on Earth. | − | Fewer birthday parties. |
| Temperatures as low as −200 degrees in winter. | − | Too cold. |
| Two moons. | + | More full moons. |

Different people will not always agree on whether a characteristic is an advantage or a disadvantage. Do you agree with the reasons given in the chart above?

## *Using the Strategy*

Make a chart of the advantages and disadvantages of the planet Earth as a home. First, list four or five characteristics of Earth. Decide whether you think each characteristic is an advantage or a disadvantage.

## *Applying the Strategy to the Next Selection*

The next selection, "Sea of Grass," is about a pioneer family. You will be asked to think about, then make a chart of, the advantages and disadvantages of the family's home.

The writing connection can be found on page 453.

*In 1872 in Nebraska, a home could be a shelter built with bricks cut from sod. Life in such a home wasn't easy.*

# A Sea of GRASS

## by Duncan Searl

For six generations, the Davidson family has farmed the flat and fertile soil of the Nebraska plains. With a fleet of trucks and tractors, the family plants and harvests more than a thousand acres of wheat each year. Barns, sheds, houses—the farm has enough buildings for a small village. Miles of fences and farm roads stretch in all directions to connect the pieces.

When twelve-year-old Keith Davidson scans the horizon, he wonders what the farm was like long ago, when the first Davidsons arrived on the land.

Grandpa Davidson has told him that the farm began as "a sea of grass and a hole in the ground."

The first time Keith heard this, he had to accompany his grandfather to a nearby creek to understand. There, Grandpa pointed toward a place in the streambank which appeared to have been scooped out. That, Grandpa told Keith, was where the Davidson farm began.

## The Dugout

Early in April of 1872, the Davidsons' covered wagon rolled onto their 160-acre land claim in eastern Nebraska. There was no shelter waiting for them. Like most settlers on the Great Plains, the Davidsons had to build their own shelter. At first, the family lived in the covered wagon. That was all right for a while. But by fall, they needed more protection from Nebraska's cold and windy climate.

Back east, the Davidsons had lived in a wooden farmhouse. They would have liked to build a wooden house on the Plains, too. But there wasn't a tree in sight. Lumber for building wasn't available in Nebraska, even if the family had been able to afford it.

There wasn't time for building, anyway. As farmers, the Davidsons knew they had to get on with the all-important work of plowing and planting. Only then would their new land provide enough harvest to see them through the winter.

Rabbits and foxes dig their burrows and dens in hillsides, and that's what the Davidsons did too. The settlers chose the streambank location because it was conveniently close to water. There were no building materials to buy or skilled workers to hire. After two days of digging, the Davidsons' new home was ready.

What were the advantages of the dugout house?

Earth formed three walls, the roof, and the floor of the dugout. The fourth wall was the opening. The Davidsons covered it with canvas from the top of their covered wagon. A small hole dug overhead allowed smoke from the kitchen fire to escape.

Most people believe in the old saying, "There's no place like home." The Davidsons, however, might not have felt that way about their dugout. The cramped dwelling was damp and dark, even on sunny days. Dirt from the roof sifted down into bedding and food. Insects and snakes were constant house guests. ◄❖►

◄❖►

**What were the disadvantages of the dugout house?**

Hoping their new shelter would be a temporary one, the Davidsons began to plow and plant. But this wasn't as easy as they had expected. In the early 1870s, more than a foot of thick sod covered almost every inch of the territory. Held together by a mass of tangled roots, this sod was almost impossible to cut through. It could take weeks to plow a single acre. Settlers like the Davidsons became known as "sodbusters."

The sod's toughness gave the settlers an idea. Why not build with it? The new fields were covered with long ribbons of sod that had been plowed up. It would be a simple matter to cut these into smaller pieces and use them as building blocks. The settlers even had a nickname for this unusual building material—"Nebraska marble."

### Building with Sod

At first, the Davidsons weren't sure whether they should build with sod. But a sudden summer rainstorm made up their minds. The downpour sent a wall of water racing along the side of their streambank. This flash flood poured into their dugout, sweeping away some of the family's few possessions. After rescuing what they could of their muddy clothing and food supplies, the Davidsons began work on a safer, better shelter.

The next home site was on a gently-sloping hillside far from the stream. Into the slope, the family dug a level floor about ten feet wide and twelve feet long. Fortunately, the Davidson children had found some cottonwood trees growing along a river a few miles away. From this precious wood, their father cut a few beams to use as a frame for their new house.

The frame of the house was simple. In front, two poles were sunk into the ground. A third beam was nailed across the tops of them. From this crosspiece, other beams were stretched back to the hillside to form the frame of a roof.

The whole family worked to cut and move the heavy blocks of prairie grass. To form walls, the sod was stacked like bricks. Each "brick" was about two feet long, one foot wide, and six inches thick. Loose dirt was used between the layers to keep them level. Every fourth layer was laid crosswise of the others to bind the wall more firmly.

The Davidsons used sod for the front of their house and on each side to fill the triangular space between the roof and the slope of the hillside. The roof was also sod, laid atop a layer of branches and poles that stretched across the roof beams. The rear part of the house was dug out. The front was sod. So the house was called a dugout soddy.

When building the front of their new home, the Davidsons included a frame for a door and a window. There weren't enough boards for a wooden door, though. So the family used a flap of

deerskin instead. Plate glass for windows was a luxury few settlers could afford. So the Davidsons used a piece of oiled paper to fill the window opening. It let in light but kept wind and water out.

The dugout soddy was an improvement of a plain dugout. It was drier and airier than the dugout. It was larger and more comfortable. Outside, wildflowers and grass grew out of the roof, giving the home a happy, carefree appearance. ◄◆►

**What were the advantages of the dugout soddy?**

The Davidsons lived in their dugout soddy for almost ten years. During this time, they struggled to improve their farm. They plowed more land and planted more crops. They built a sod barn for their horses and cow. They bought some new farm equipment. The family enjoyed good harvests and even saved money from the crops they sold.

But everyday life in a dugout soddy was difficult. Chunks of dirt fell from the walls and ceiling, making house-cleaning an impossible chore. Mice and insects lived in the walls. During heavy rains, the roof was sure to leak. The Davidsons often had to drape a sheet of canvas next to the ceiling to catch the dripping rain and mud. Wet and muddy, the roof beams soon began to rot. Part of the roof almost caved in one winter under the weight of the snow. ◄❖►

◄❖►

**What were the disadvantages of the dugout soddy?**

About this time, many of the Davidsons' neighbors were building free-standing sod houses to replace their dugouts. The Davidsons thought about building one of these roomy and sturdy sod houses, too. But they all had their hearts set on another kind of shelter. Without speaking about it, everyone in the family knew what they were saving for.

**A New House**

In the late spring of 1881, three wagonloads of lumber from the East arrived at the Davidson farm. That was just enough for a one-room house, about twenty feet long and sixteen feet wide.

428

The family built it themselves, using stones from a nearby river for the foundation. The house had a wooden door and three glass windows.

Inside, the fireplace was the center of the house. It provided warmth, light, and heat for cooking. In the evening, the family would gather around this hearth to talk, read, sew, and plan for the future.

The house was furnished simply with homemade chairs and tables. Two sleeping lofts were built below the roof. There was no plumbing in the building. Until the well was dug, water had to be carried from the nearby stream. By today's standards, the house was small and rough. But after living in a dugout soddy, the Davidsons thought the new house was a palace.

Eventually, that "new house" became only one room in the modern-day Davidson farmhouse. As the family and farm grew, so did the farmhouse. Rooms were added to meet the needs of each generation. But it all started with that one room, called the "family room" by the Davidsons today. Not a bad name for a place where one family has lived for over 100 years! ◄✦►

◄✦►

**Make a chart of the advantages and disadvantages of the Davidsons' new house.**

# DAKOTA DUGOUT

*written by Ann Turner*
*illustrated by Ronald Himler*

Packing all your belongings, moving to the Dakota prairie, settling the land, and building a home all required hard work . . . and courage.

Tell you about the prairie years?
I'll tell you, child, how it was.
When Matt wrote, "Come!"
I packed all I had,
cups and pots and dresses and rope,
even Grandma's silver boot hook,
and rode the clickety train

to a cave in the earth,
Matt's cave.
Built from sod, you know,
with a special iron plow
that sliced the long earth strips.
Matt cut them into bricks,
laid them up, dug into a hill
that was our first home.

431

I cried when I saw it.
No sky came in that room,
only a paper window
that made the sun look greasy.
Dirt fell on our bed,
snakes sometimes, too,
and the buffalo hide door
could not keep out the wind
or the empty cries in the long grass.

The birds visited me,
there was no one else,
with Matt all day in the fields.
A hawk came, snake in its claws,
a heron flapped by with wings like sails,
and a sparrow jabbered the day long
on a gray fence post.
I jabbered back.
Winter came sudden.

432

Slam-bang! the ground was iron,
cattle breath turned to ice,
froze their noses to the ground.
We lost twelve in a storm
and the wind scoured the dugout,
*whish*-hush, *whish*-hush.
Spring, child, was teasing slow
then quick,
water booming in the lake,

geese like yarn in the sky,
green spreading faster than fire,
and the wind blowing
*shoosh*-hush, *shoosh*-hush.
First summer we watched the corn grow,
strode around the field clapping hands.
We saw dresses, buggies, gold in that grain
until one day a hot wind baked it dry
as an oven, *ssst-ssst, ssst-ssst.*

433

willows our roof under the earth.
I pasted newspaper on the walls,
set bread to bake on the coals,
and the wind was quiet.
Corn grew finally,
we got our dresses, buggies, some gold,
built a clapboard house
with windows like suns,
floors I slipped on,
and the empty sound of too many rooms.
Didn't think I'd miss
the taste of earth in the air.
Now the broom went *whisp*-hush,
and the clock tocked like a busy heart.
Talking brings it near again,
the sweet taste of new bread
in a Dakota dugout,
how the grass whispered like an old friend,
how the earth kept us warm.
Sometimes the things we start with
are best.

Matt sat and looked two whole days,
silent and long.
Come fall we snuggled like beavers
in our burrow, new grass on the floor,

## ◆ LIBRARY LINK ◆

*Would you like to know more about life on the prairie? Try* My
Prairie Year *by Brett Harvey or* Chancy and the Grand Rascal
*by Sid Fleishman.*

## Reader's Response

In your opinion, what was most difficult about living in a
pioneer home?

A Sea of
GRASS

DAKOTA
DUGOUT

◆ **C**hecking Your Comprehension

1. Why did the Davidson family live in a dugout?
2. Why did the Davidsons build a dugout soddy, instead of a free-standing sod house, for their second home?
3. List the various types of shelters in which the six generations of Davidsons lived.
4. How would you describe the Davidson family? What words came to mind? Of all the words that came to mind, which did you keep and which didn't you keep?
5. If the Davidsons told their own story, do you think their feelings would be similar to those of the woman in ''Dakota Dugout''? Explain your answer.
6. The woman in ''Dakota Dugout'' said many things about her dugout home. Which statements are facts, and which are opinions?

◆ **W**riting to Learn

**THINK AND PLAN**   It is a long road from a sod dugout to a modern farmhouse. Make a time line that identifies some of the steps on that journey. Copy and complete the time line below. At each step, list the date, the type of structure, and descriptive details.

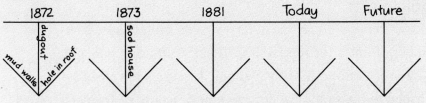

**WRITE**   Now add a future stop on the time line. Think about the kind of home you would like to live in when you grow up. Write the date, the kind of home, and descriptive details. Then write a real estate ad (FOR SALE: — ) describing the future home of your dreams.

## Libraries: Homes for Books

TREASURES OF THE
**Library of Congress**
*By CHARLES A. GOODRUM*

"**E**very student welcome if he does not enter in wet clothing, or bringing ink, or a knife, or a dagger." You have probably never seen a sign like this in any library you've been to. But it really did appear in the Oxford University Library six hundred years ago. There was a good reason for it, too. The library owned a grand total of sixty-seven books. Each had been copied by hand because the printing press had not yet been invented. In those years, the 1300s, each book was chained to a desk and carefully watched so students wouldn't damage or steal it.

Libraries have changed greatly since those days. Even the smallest library has thousands of books. The Library of Congress in Washington, D.C., the largest library in the world, has more than 84 million items. In addition to books, it has musical works, photographs, movies, maps, and manuscripts, such as Abraham Lincoln's handwritten Gettysburg Address.

Some libraries today have very special collections. The Schomberg Center for Research in Black Culture is part of the New York Public Library System. Libraries have been established to house the papers and other records of former U.S.

▲
Libraries can be fascinating subjects in themselves for books.

This is part of the Library of Congress.
▼

436

◄
Book wagons took
books to people in
rural America.

presidents. John F. Kennedy and Gerald Ford are among the
presidents who have had libraries built in their honor.

Modern librarians have ways of protecting and preserving
books that early librarians did not. Air conditioning in libraries
keeps mold from growing on books, and special chemicals are
used to kill insects that eat the starch in book bindings.

A continuing problem is space. Thousands of
books, magazines, and newspapers are published
each year. Microfilm and microfiche help libraries store printed materials in a tiny fraction of
their original space.

The library of today looks nothing like
the library of long ago with its sixty-seven
books chained to desks. Comparing those
libraries with ours makes us wonder what
the library of the future will look like.

▶
The Library of Congress keeps track of
its books in both a card catalog and a
system of computers.

# A FAMILY HOME

## by Mary Calhoun

*The whole family is very excited about the book Katie John's father is writing. Katie John's enthusiasm turns to misery, however, when she learns that they will have to sell their big, old family home. They need money to live on until her father can finish and sell his book.*

It was November-cold as Katie John walked home from the library. Dusk had sifted down from the gray sky, and the street lights were already lit. The wind, whipping through bare branches, made Katie huddle deep into her coat. She clutched a pile of library books to her chest, smiling at the warm feeling she got from them. She'd picked out such good ones this time. Another one about Jane, a new book of fairy tales, and a book about a girl in Revolutionary War times that looked exciting. She could hardly wait to curl up in the big chair and start reading. Which one, though? They all looked so good. The one about Jane, she decided. The Moffats were so cozy, just right for a cold winter evening.

Katie rounded the corner onto her block, and the wind pushed straight at her now. At the end of the block, at the top of the hill, she could see her house, one light shining yellow out of an upstairs window. The tree branches around the house flung about in the wind, but the house itself rose square and solid above them.

It's like a ship, riding out a storm, Katie thought. No, more like a great lighthouse, standing steady as a rock with all the storm swirling around it. And the light is a beacon for me.

In a spurt against the wind, Katie ran up the hill and into the house. She pushed the door shut and stopped in the hall. How quiet the house was, after the noise of the wind outside. So still and warm. Yet alive with a murmur of little sounds. Katie stood there, holding her books, soaking in the warmth, listening. That soft rumble under her feet was the stoker in the furnace coming on. That distant tap-tap-tap was her father working at his typewriter upstairs . . . tap-tap-tap, ping, went the bell faintly. A rattle of a pan lid said Mother was back in the kitchen. Katie sniffed. Oh good! Hamburgers and onions, with mashed potatoes and gravy, her favorite supper.

Now in the stillness she heard the tock-tock of the old marble clock in the parlor. It's like the sound of the house, ticking away at its business, she thought. She turned to look in at the clock on the mantelpiece. Why, it had been ticking there for almost a hundred years, ever since Great-Grandpa brought it home in the wheelbarrow.

Lovingly, Katie looked at all the signs of the Clark family, gleaming in soft lamplight or shadowy in corners—the polished dark woods, the vases and china collected over the years, Great-Grandfather's paintings on the walls, Great-Aunt Emily's crocheted doilies on Katie's reading chair. Her fingers smoothed the yellow wood of the doorframe. The good house that Great-Grandfather built. The good home.

Suddenly Katie John knew why Aunt Emily had never left this house, never gone away for new adventure when it was clear that she wouldn't marry.

Because this was home.

As simple as that. Because this was where she belonged.

The next thought came as surely as summer follows spring: *This is where I belong, too.*

Katie felt such a spreading in her chest that she wanted to stretch out her arms. Oh, she loved this house! She loved Barton's Bluff. She even loved her neighbor Miss Crackenberry, and that crazy dog Prince. Because they were all a part of living here.

She dropped her books on the big chair and tossed her coat at the hall hat-rack as Dad came clattering down the stairs.

"Oh, Dad!" She ran to him. The words for all that she wanted to say choked in her throat. "Dad, come quick!"

She pulled him back to the kitchen. She had to say it to both of them.

"Dad, Mother, the house—let's stay! Let's not sell the house. Let's just stay here. Let's live here always!"

"Oh now, Katie," Dad began, laughing.

But Mother looked at her with a sad little smile. "I know, Katie. I know. If only we could—"

Dad wasn't laughing now. "I'd like to stay, too. It's a good house, and we're happy here. I don't have to live in New York to write. But—"

The facts hadn't changed. They still needed the sale money from the house to live on until he started earning money from his books.

Dad rubbed his face. "There's something else. This is a bad time to tell you. But we'll just have to face it."

Someone wanted to buy the house. It was the man who had wanted to turn it into a rooming house. He wanted to squeeze in lots of roomers. Make some money from the house before it fell apart, he said.

"He made a pretty good offer," Dad was saying. "Came near our asking price. I'm afraid we'll have to—"

"No!" Katie cried. "No no no!"

He wouldn't take care of the house. He said he didn't want to spend money on repairs. And an old house needed lots of care. Dad had said the house needed a new roof. With all those people, the place would get rattletrap and dirty, start to fall apart. She'd seen some of the old homes that were now rooming houses, boardinghouses. Crumbling steps, broken windows, paint cracked, washing flapping on the porches. No!

Katie argued. She begged. At last she cried. She stopped when she saw that Mother and Dad looked almost ready to cry, too.

All through the miserable supper that no one ate, Katie's thoughts wound drearily. So they'd leave the house. Go live in some dinky little New York apartment. Oh, a person could be happy anywhere. Sure. But this was home. And then to think of the hordes of people moving in and out and none of them loving it, and it crumbling away.

The hamburger tasted like soggy cardboard in her mouth, and she could hardly swallow it. Money. Hateful, horrible stuff. Where could they get some money, so they could stay?

If only she and her friend Sue could have found a sack of gold hidden away somewhere in the house when they were looking for secret places. Or if

Great-Aunt Emily had left some money. But all she'd left was the house. And old houses were so big and expensive to keep up, they weren't good for anything any more but to rent out rooms.

Oh, if only the man even loved the house, Katie thought in despair. Then at least he might take care of it.

Wait. What was that? Rent out rooms but take care of the house. Ye-es-s, yes! Why couldn't they do it instead of that man?

Katie started to blurt it out. Then she stopped. Dad might say, "No, Katie," and not really understand the idea. Better to think it all out and then tell them.

After supper Katie hurried right off to bed, leaving her parents sighing because they thought she was so unhappy. But she had to be alone, now, and in bed was the best place for thinking things through. Now she must be careful. She couldn't go whizzing at this idea in her usual way. This was serious business. Their last chance. She had to get it just right, so it would make sense to grown-ups.

As Katie threw off her clothes, though, she felt a doubt. Was it worth it? Would it be the same, would the house still be home with renters in it? She didn't want to share her home with a lot of other people.

It's better than nothing, she told herself firmly. It will still be our house.

She scrambled under the covers and began to figure. Now it was clear they'd have to rent out most of the house, if they were to make enough money to live on. They must live on just the first floor. She'd have to give her pretty bedroom to her folks, she realized with a twinge of regret. She could sleep in the little room off the kitchen.

Then they could rent all the rooms on the second and third floors. And the basement, too. Yes, the little servants' apartment, where the dumbwaiter ended up, would be nice for someone.

And oh, what a lucky thing that Aunt Emily had put in so many bathrooms!

But would anyone want to rent rooms in an old house? They should get nice people who would take care of their rooms. What could be special about the rooms?

Why, the fireplaces! Every room had a fireplace. So far Dad had lit the little fireplace in the kitchen, and Katie loved dressing before the open brick hearth on cold mornings.

Everyone loves a fireplace, she reasoned, and here they could have one of their own even in a rented room. Some of the fireplaces were really beautiful, too, with carving around the edges and lacy iron or painted fire screens. Yes, the fireplaces could be the drawing card.

Katie John was getting sleepy now; her plans were fuzzy at the edges. Tomorrow she'd tell Mother and Dad about it . . . so good to know things were working out. So good that the house had bathrooms and fireplaces and big rooms for renters. The house would save itself, after all . . . or maybe it was Great-Grandfather who was saving it, because of the way he'd built the house, she thought drowsily. And Aunt Emily. All the Clarks had put so much into the house. Because they loved it.

And what had she herself put into the house? The thought woke her up a little. Nothing, really. Well, she was probably the only person outside of the builder who knew what the inside of the dumbwaiter walls looked like. But that wasn't doing anything. She would, she promised herself. Someday she'd do something for the old house.

The next morning Katie decided not to tell her folks yet. It was a good plan. But grown-ups had such a habit of saying "No, Katie" to good plans. Better if they could actually see it working out. Upon waking up, it had been quite plain what she must do: find a renter.

What's more, she knew just the person. Her teacher, Miss Howell. Not long ago Miss Howell had been saying that soon she and her sister must move into town from their farm for the winter. They lived out on a hill above the river in their old homeplace. Now that she understood so much more, Katie guessed they must love their house as she did hers. But it was too cold and icy for the two of them to live out there alone in the winter. So, as Miss Howell had been telling her when she was helping after school the other day, every winter they moved into an apartment in town. And they hadn't found one yet.

As Katie walked to school she grew more and more excited as she figured how a little kitchen could be put in one of the rooms upstairs, so that Miss Howell could have a big two-room-and-bath apartment. She was so wrapped up in plans that she forgot to stop for Sue. Later at school she explained to Sue that she had something very big brewing, and she'd tell her tonight if it worked out.

Katie almost burst before recess time. When the bell rang she stayed in the room and told Miss Howell all about it. About loving the house and wanting to stay and renting out rooms. Then she was afraid it sounded as though she were begging. So as not to put Miss Howell on the spot, she said hastily:

"Of course, you mustn't do it just to help us out. You shouldn't rent the apartment unless you really like it." And couldn't help adding honestly, "But I hope you do."

Miss Howell, who had listened carefully, smiled now. "I understand, Katie John. Of course I want to help you. But I promise you I won't rent it unless it will suit Julia and me. After all, we're the ones who will have to live there all winter."

Miss Howell pointed out that it would also depend on how much the rent would be. She thought that Katie should talk it over with her parents first. But Katie had her plans fixed.

"Please, just look at the rooms first," she said. "Then if you're already interested, Mother and Dad will think about it more seriously."

So Miss Howell said that she'd come home with Katie after school. Katie could hardly keep her mind on schoolwork for the rest of the day. She made all the circles in penmanship slant the wrong way because she was thinking about the one last important detail. How would she work out that part? Maybe she shouldn't—it might make Mother and Dad mad . . . But it would make everything so perfect. Katie pushed at her bangs. She just had to do it. If only her folks would be out, just once, when she got home from school.

As it happened, Miss Howell had to stay after school for a parent conference. She said she'd drive down to Katie's house afterward. But that was fine. It would give Katie plenty of time to finish that last detail.

"Got to hurry," she told Sue after school. "I'll run on ahead and see you later. Tell you all about it then."

Sue looked disappointed but nodded patiently. Oh, what a joy it was to have a good friend like Sue! Another reason for staying in Barton's Bluff. Let Miss Howell like the rooms, Katie prayed, as she ran.

Mother and Dad were just coming out the front door when Katie got home. They were going down to Mr. Follensbee's real estate office to talk over plans for selling the house to the man.

"You're not going to sign anything already?" Katie cried.

Dad shrugged unhappily. "Honey, you know it's got to be done. But no, we won't be signing anything today. We'll be right back."

"Be sure you don't," Katie said. "We may not have to sell the house yet!"

She heard Mother say as they went down the walk, "Poor child. She's hoping for a miracle." And Katie giggled, almost about to burst with excitement. Little did they know!

She ran down to the basement for the things she needed and took them upstairs. When she had that all ready, she set about making the apartment look as handsome as possible, dusting, opening curtains, taking dust covers off the furniture. She'd chosen two big rooms with a connecting bathroom. The front room overlooked the river, and the back room could be partitioned into a bedroom and kitchen, she'd decided. It already had a washbowl that could be used for washing dishes.

The doorbell rang. It must be Miss Howell. Katie did the last important thing. Then she raced down the stairs and brought her teacher in.

"Mother and Dad went to the real estate office, but they'll be right back," Katie told her. "I'll show you the apartment."

Katie's hands were suddenly cold and she clasped them in front of her as she led Miss Howell up the stairs. Miss Howell's warm voice was saying nice things about how beautiful the house was, but now Katie couldn't answer. The important thing was, what would she think of the apartment?

Along the hall . . . open the door . . . Katie gasped.

Smoke! Black smoke billowed in the room and poured out the doorway.

"The house is on fire!" Katie screamed. "Quick! Water!"

She ran to get water from the bathroom somehow. And then she saw that the room wasn't on fire, after all. The wretched black smoke was pouring from the fireplace—the beautiful fireplace, where she'd worked so hard laying wood. That had been the important thing that was to make it all perfect. She wanted Miss Howell to be greeted by a homey blaze when she looked into the room. Just before she'd run downstairs she'd lit the fire.

And now look! Smoke filled the room, and more was coming out all the time. The wood was burning, but the smoke wasn't going up the chimney.

"We must put out the fire quickly!" Miss Howell scooped up the empty coal bucket from the hearth and ran to the bathroom for water.

Katie ran after her, sobbing and getting in the way.

"No, you open the windows," Miss Howell said, hurrying back to the fireplace.

Fortunately, the fire hadn't gotten well started yet, and the blaze died under the water.

"Oh, look at the room!" Katie wailed. "It'll be black with smoke!"

She beat at the smoke, trying to push it out the window before it settled on the walls and the white curtains. The fire reduced to wet black ashes, Miss Howell rushed to help Katie, fanning the smoke with a sheaf of school papers.

"What in the world!"

Katie turned and saw her horrified parents coming into the room.

"It's all my fault!" she cried in despair. "I wanted to make a nice fire, but the smoke didn't go up the chimney."

"Because the chimney is capped! All of them are except the one for the kitchen." Dad's face was angry. "Young lady, I—"

"Oh, wouldn't you know!" Katie sobbed. "Everything I do goes wrong!"

"Let's get the smoke out of here first," Mother suggested.

She and Dad joined Miss Howell in fanning smoke out the windows while Katie poured out the whole story.

"I knew I shouldn't have lit that fire," she ended miserably, "but it seemed like such a wonderful idea. And now look."

She stared at the soupy mass of ashes in the fireplace.

"Well," Dad said slowly, "of course you shouldn't have lit the fire without a grown-up around—you do get carried away with your ideas, Katie. But basically you had a pretty good plan, at that."

In fact, he'd been thinking about renting out apartments, too, he said. He'd figured that from the rents they could pay for the upkeep of the big house and have a little left over.

"We can't do it, though, Katie," he added quickly. "I soon realized that running an apartment house would throw entirely too much work on your mother. And we couldn't afford to hire help."

"I just don't see how I could do it all alone," Mother sighed, "and I won't have you leave your writing to do it," she told her husband.

He shook his head sadly. "I could do the repair work and take care of the furnace. But it would still leave too great a burden on you. We'll just have to forget it."

Katie had been looking from one parent to another. Well, for goodness' sakes! So she had been on the right track, with her idea about renting. For once she'd thought something through almost like a grown-up would! Her chest stopped feeling so tight.

But still, it didn't do any good. They had to leave, just the same. Renting rooms meant too much work for Mother. Katie sighed. It was just too bad that she wasn't big enough to help.

And then Katie began to get all hot inside, the way she always did when she was about to have a wonderful idea. Just how big did she have to be to help? How big, to sweep down the stairs that renters would dirty, to make beds, hang sheets on the line, dust furniture, vacuum floors? She could do those things.

But all that work! Katie shuddered. I'm just a little girl. I hate housework. It would take so much time.

"I could do it," she heard herself saying. "I could help. I could work after school and on Saturdays."

Mother smiled but shook her head. "It's really sweet of you, Katie. But you're just a little girl. I have to stand over you even to get you to dust your room."

"I know! I know!" Katie cried desperately. "But I can change! Now I want to work. If only we can stay here!"

She had to make them understand. To make them know how much she wanted to stay, enough to do all that work. The words tumbled out until Mother interrupted.

"Why, you've really made up your mind, haven't you!" She laughed. "And I know you, Katie John. When you set your mind on something, you stick to it. I do believe I can depend on you!" She turned to Dad. "Dear, let's try it!"

Dad looked from Mother to Katie John. He threw up his hands and laughed. "It's all right with me. You women will be doing all the work!"

All the tensely held breath went out of Katie. "Oh, Daddy!" She flung herself at him.

While he hugged her he said that after he started earning money from his book they could hire a cleaning person. And Mother said they'd get things organized so Katie wouldn't have to work all the time. But Katie hardly heard. All she could think was: We're staying! We're staying!

Miss Howell had been wandering around the rooms, and now she came back to the Tuckers.

"May I have the honor of being your first renter?" she asked with a twinkle in her smile.

Despite the smoky fireplace, she said—and Dad hastily said he'd uncap the chimneys—she liked the rooms and was sure her sister would, too. •

That made things perfect, but all Katie could do was reach out and squeeze her teacher's hand. Dad and Mother and Miss Howell went off to the second room to discuss how they could partition it and put in a stove and refrigerator. Katie walked out into the hallway.

And so they would stay. The old Clark house would go on, with the Tucker family in it. And the renters, too. Wonder who they'd be? Why, it could be fun, Katie realized with a little prick of excitement, having all sorts of people—nice ones and maybe ornery ones—coming to live here. And she and Mother would take care of them.

A warm, satisfied feeling spread through Katie, clear down to her stomach, because everything had worked out so well. Even the answer to that question that had been bothering her last night: What could she do for the old house to match the loving care of Great-Grandfather and Great-Aunt Emily? Her work. All that pesky housework that would help them keep the house.

Katie John looked up the stairwell to the top of the house, then down to the hall below. She started down the stairs, sliding her fingers along the banister.

"Hello, home," she said softly.

♦ LIBRARY LINK ♦

*"A Family Home" is from the book* Katie John *by Mary Calhoun. To find out if Katie John's plan for the boarders works out, read* Depend on Katie John *by the same author.*

**R**eader's Response

Could you identify with Katie John's feelings about her home? Explain your answer.

# A FAMILY HOME

## ◆ Checking Your Comprehension

1. What do you think Katie John meant when she compared her home to a ship and a lighthouse?
2. Why didn't Katie John want her parents to sell their home?
3. How did Katie John's plan for renting rooms differ from that of the man who wanted to buy her home?
4. Why did Katie John think she needed a renter before she told her parents her plan?
5. Do you think Katie John's behavior was selfish or unselfish? What did you consider in reaching your answer?
6. Do you think that Katie John will be happy with the new arrangements for her home? Explain your answer.

## ◆ Writing to Learn

**THINK AND ANALYZE**   In deciding between moving and renting out rooms in their house, Katie John's family had to consider the advantages and disadvantages of each option. On the chart is one advantage of renting. Complete the chart on another paper.

| Characteristic | Advantage or Disadvantage | Reason |
|---|---|---|
| Extra money from renting | + | The money can be used for house repairs |
| | | |
| | | |

**WRITE**   Think of a decision you had to make. Write a paragraph about the advantages and disadvantages you thought about in making your decisions.

*Comprehension:*

# Drawing Conclusions

**F**or a moment, think about Mary Calhoun's story, "A Family Home." Do you remember how Katie John felt about where she lived? The author wrote, "Oh, she loved this house. She loved Barton's Bluff." Even before the author said so, perhaps you had already drawn that conclusion. How could you have done this?

Ms. Calhoun first describes how Katie John thought of her house as a ship, riding out a storm. Then she goes on to describe the house as being "so still and warm," filled with the Clark family treasures. From the author's description, you can conclude that this house is a wonderful place to live in and a place to love.

## How to Draw Conclusions

Imagine that you are about to discuss something important with your family. Read the following passage. As you read, use your own family experiences to draw conclusions.

> But Mother looked at her with a sad little smile. "I know, Katie. I know. If only we could—"
>
> Dad wasn't laughing now. "I'd like to stay, too....But—

What do you conclude from reading the above passage? It seems that Katie's parents are about to tell her that they must move. Your own experience, as well as the information in the story, leads to that conclusion, as the following diagram demonstrates.

454

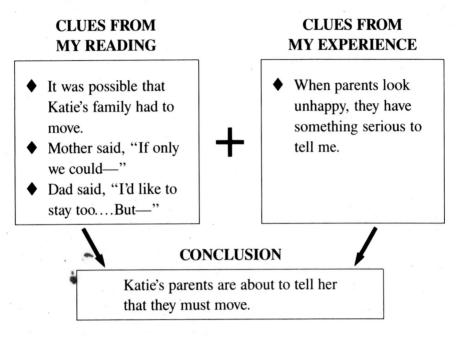

**CLUES FROM MY READING**

♦ It was possible that Katie's family had to move.
♦ Mother said, "If only we could—"
♦ Dad said, "I'd like to stay too....But—"

**+**

**CLUES FROM MY EXPERIENCE**

♦ When parents look unhappy, they have something serious to tell me.

**CONCLUSION**

Katie's parents are about to tell her that they must move.

## Using What You Have Learned

Read the following passage and draw a conclusion about how Katie's mother and father feel about Katie's hopes for the house.

> Dad shrugged unhappily. "Honey, you know it's got to be done. But no, we won't be signing anything today."
> "Be sure you don't," Katie said....
> She heard Mother say as they went down the walk, "Poor child. She's hoping for a miracle."

1. Tell how Katie's parents feel about Katie's hopes for the house.
2. Make a diagram like the one above. Show how the clues from your reading and your experience help you draw your conclusion.

## As You Read

In the next story, "Thinking About Home," Roosevelt Grady's home is only a dream. As you read the story, use clues from your own experience to draw conclusions about Roosevelt's goals.

# THINKING ABOUT
# HOME

*from Roosevelt Grady*
*by Louisa Shotwell*

There is an old saying that "Home is where the heart
is." For Roosevelt Grady, home is a dream that he holds in
his heart.

*Roosevelt Grady's family earns a living picking crops. They must move from farm to farm, following the crops as they ripen. As a result, Roosevelt must move from school to school. At one school, Roosevelt tells his teacher that he wants to learn how to do division, which he calls "putting into." The teacher promises to teach division the next day. But when the next day comes, Roosevelt and his family are on the road again.*

Roosevelt bunched his sweater underneath him to soften the jouncing floor of the moving truck. He leaned his head back against his mother's arm. If the air got any chillier, he'd have to take his sweater out from under him and put it on to keep warm, but it wasn't quite that cold. Not yet.

Along with three other families, the Gradys rode in the back of the truck. All but Papa, who sat up front to spell Cap Jackson. Cap was the regular driver and he was the crew leader, too. He owned the truck and in it he carried the people to places where crops were ready for picking.

"We're heading for beans and cucumbers," Cap Jackson said.

Roosevelt's mother sat straight up on the flat side of the family's suitcase. It was made of metal and it was slippery, so she had her feet planted wide apart and flat on the floor to brace herself. On her lap she held Princess Anne, sleeping.

Between Mamma's feet lay Sister. She was seven years old and dainty, with dimples. Her smile, Papa always said, could charm a snake out of a tree.

"Honest, could it?" Roosevelt asked him once.

"Well, I tell you, Roosevelt," Papa said, "the first time we find a snake in a tree, we'll get Sister to smile at it and we'll see what happens." So far they hadn't found a tree with a snake in it.

On the other side of Mamma slumped Matthew, who was only five and chubby. Matthew had a lame foot, but that didn't keep him from enjoying life. He was great on making jokes, and he didn't miss a thing.

The truck had a canvas roof. The roof sloped up on each side to a peak like the top of a barn, and it kept you from seeing the sky. Anyway, it was dark outside. It was the middle of the night, but the truck kept right on going.

Between sleeping and waking, Roosevelt thought about putting into. He thought about that special thing he wanted to know. The question kept running around his head the way a mosquito teases you in the dark.

This was his question: When you put something into something else and it doesn't come out even, what do you do with what's left over?

What happened yesterday was exactly what had happened at the school where he'd first heard about putting into. The teacher came to where it seemed she must explain it the very next day. And then what? That time it wasn't beans that ran out. It was celery, but it didn't matter what the crop was. If it ran out, it ran out, and that was the end. The whole family packed up and piled into Cap Jackson's sputtery old truck and away they went to find a place where onions or tomatoes or some old thing was coming along ready to harvest. And same as yesterday, Roosevelt never got back to school to hear what the teacher had to say.

Some places there wouldn't be any school at all. Or

else there'd be a school and the bean-picker boys and girls didn't get to go to it. The school would be for residents, and bean-picker families weren't residents. They didn't belong.

Once there was a school and it was closed when they got there. It was closed because the crop was ripe. A crop vacation, folks called this, and everybody picked, young ones and grown-ups and old people. Everybody except, of course, Princess Anne. Over in Louisiana she sat by herself in a fruit crate at the end of the strawberry rows and sucked her thumb, cute as a bug.

Roosevelt rubbed his eyes, leaned his head against Mamma's knee, and tried hard to go to sleep. He'd almost made it when buzz went that old mosquito again, nagging at him about putting into. Like 3 into 17. You can't say 17's got six 3's in it, because six 3's need 18. So the answer has to be five 3's. But that's only 15. So what do you do with the poor little 2 that gets left over?

Roosevelt liked to have things come out even. He liked to have a place to put every piece of whatever it was he had. He liked to pick all the ripe beans quick and clean off one plant and then move along that row to the next. He liked to fill his basket just full enough so it was even across the top. If one bean stuck up in the air, he'd pull it out and make a little hole among the other beans and poke it carefully down in. He liked to make a pan of corn bread and cut it into exactly enough squares to make one piece for everybody in the family. Except Princess Anne. Her teeth hadn't come through far enough yet to chew anything crusty. Sometimes Mamma would break off a little of her piece of corn bread and dunk it in her coffee to soften it. Then she gave it to Princess Anne.

Bouncing along through the dark, Roosevelt got to thinking more about numbers. Take nine. Right now nine was an important number in his life. He was nine years old. His birthday was the ninth day of September, and if you began to count the months with January one and February two and so on, what did September turn out to be? Why, nine!

To be perfectly sure, he whispered the months over to himself, counting on his fingers. Sure enough, nine came out to be September.

How many different schools had he been to in his

lifetime? He counted to himself. Six, seven, eight . . . and nine. There was nine again. Different schools, that is. If you counted twice the schools he'd been to and then gone back to, they made thirteen, but Roosevelt didn't want to count that way. He didn't like the number thirteen. Papa said thirteen was unlucky. Mamma said she didn't believe in lucky or unlucky, but there was no use tempting fate.

One day a while back, Roosevelt had asked Papa about putting into and the poor little leftover number. He had laughed and said: "Just throw it away."

But Roosevelt couldn't feel right doing that. What would become of it?

Another day he had asked Mamma. She said: "Save it till you need it."

"What do you do with it," Roosevelt wanted to know, "while you're waiting to need it?"

Mamma didn't laugh nearly so often as Papa did, but she laughed that time.

"Put it in your pocket," she said, "and go fetch me a bucket of water."

The truck jerked to a stop, and the motor coughed and went still. From the driver's seat, Cap Jackson called out:

"Anybody want a drink? There's a spring here at the edge of the woods."

The people stirred. Cap came around and let down the tailgate and put up the ladder. Roosevelt experimented with a swallow and his mouth felt dry, so he clambered down. The stars were bright. The air was cold and it had a piney smell, clean and fresh. He waited his turn in line in front of a pipe with water bubbling out of it. In the starlight the pipe looked rusty. The men had to stoop over to reach it, but it was exactly the right height for Roosevelt. He didn't have to bend down or stand on his toes, either one.

When his turn came, the water was cool and he took a big gulp, but it didn't taste good. Not good at all. It tasted like a bad egg.

"Sulphur water," said one of the men.

Roosevelt spit his mouthful out on the ground. He shivered. When he climbed back into the truck, he put his sweater on and sat right flat down on the boards.

As the motor wheezed and the truck began to move, Sister and Matthew both woke up and wiggled. Roosevelt was glad they'd waked up. He felt like having company.

"Talk to us, Mamma," said Matthew. "Tell us a story."

"Hush," said Mamma. "Other folks want to go to sleep."

"Talk to us soft-like," begged Matthew. "Whisper to us about . . . you know . . ."

Roosevelt knew what was coming. Matthew always asked for the same story. It was Roosevelt's favorite story, too.

". . . about the olden days. And the dog run."

"All right," said Mamma. "Lean close and I'll tell it to you short. Then you go to sleep."

And she did. She didn't make it too short either. About the little house in the cotton field in Georgia, how it sat up on stilts and was a house in two parts like, with this comfortable sitting-out place in between and a roof over the whole thing. The sitting-out place was the dog run, and it had a rocking chair like President Kennedy's.

The Gradys had a dog there too, a hound, sort of. Named Nellie. She had short tan hair and floppy ears and brown eyes. Her eyes were wistful.

"What's wistful?" Matthew demanded.

"Wistful is you want something and you don't know what," said Mamma.

They had chickens, too, and two big pigs and a litter of little pigs. And a goat. And growing out back they had sweet potatoes and collards and mustard greens.

Roosevelt moved his tongue around to see if he could make himself remember the taste of a sweet potato. He couldn't.

Now it was Sister's turn. Was she still awake? She was.

"Take us back to your wedding day, Mamma," she said. "Tell us about your white dress and what Papa said."

"There was this magnolia tree," said Mamma, "right outside the Pink Lily Baptist Church. And it was brim full of waxy white blossoms. I wore a shiny white dress with a green sash and long streamers and I had a veil, all cloudy, made of net. Your papa told me I was almost the prettiest thing in the whole county.

" '*Almost* the prettiest? Why *almost*?' I said, kind of sniffy and jealous."

"Jealous," said Sister. "Tell us what's jealous."

"Jealous is you're scared somebody you like likes somebody else better than you," Mamma explained.
"Now don't interrupt me any more. And your papa said,

464

'You or that magnolia tree. I can't make up my mind which is prettier. But I'll pick you.' So off we went to live in the little house in the cotton field."

"Now tell us why we left the little house in the cotton field," insisted Matthew. "Why did we go away and leave our dog Nellie and the little pigs and the dog run all behind us?"

"Why we left? Why, honey, the machines came along. The tractors got bigger and bigger and they did more and more of the work the people used to do. Mr. Wilson let us stay on a while and your papa got some work in the sawmill six miles off. But pretty soon Mr. Wilson had to tear down our house to plant more cotton. So that's when we went on the season, looking for work wherever we could find it."

She stopped a minute. When she went on, her voice sounded different. Angry, almost.

"Some folks say now they've even got a machine that knows how to pick cotton. A big red monster. With fingers."

Sister sighed, a long whishy sigh that meant she was on her way to sleep again. Roosevelt waited. When Matthew breathed so even it seemed certain he must be asleep too, Roosevelt sat up close to Mamma's ear.

"Now let's you and me talk about our secret," he whispered.

"Hush," said Mamma.

"Please," said Roosevelt.

Mamma didn't say anything right away, and Roosevelt sat stiff and still. Then she spoke, not whispering but still so low he could hardly hear. She said just what he knew she'd say.

"Someday we'll find ourselves a house in a place where there's work for your papa every one of all twelve months in the year. Maybe the house won't have a dog run, but it'll sure enough be a home. And you and Sister and Matthew will go to school, the same school right along, day in, day out, fall and winter and right on to the end of spring."

"And Princess Anne?" asked Roosevelt.

"Princess Anne, too, soon as she's big enough. You'll go right along with the children that belong. Because we'll be in a place where we'll all belong. We'll be right out of this bean-picking rat race and we'll stay put."

"How will we find this place?" asked Roosevelt anxiously, even though he'd asked this before and knew what the answer would be.

"I don't know how," said Mamma, "but we'll know it when we see it. There'll be something about it so we'll know it. And don't forget. This is our secret."

"It's our secret," said Roosevelt, and he dropped his head in the crook of Mamma's elbow and fell sound asleep.

## ◆ LIBRARY LINK ◆

*This story is one chapter from a book about Roosevelt Grady and his family. To find out if the Gradys do find a permanent home, look in the library for* Roosevelt Grady *by Louisa Shotwell.*

## Reader's Response

Which character in the story did you find most admirable? Explain your answer.

# THINKING ABOUT
# HOME

## Checking Your Comprehension

1. Why didn't Roosevelt Grady's family have a permanent home?
2. How did Roosevelt feel about always changing schools? How can you tell how he felt?
3. Roosevelt liked to make things come out even. What does this tell you about his character?
4. Why did Roosevelt and Matthew like to hear the story about the family's old house?
5. Do you think it was a good idea for Roosevelt and his mother to have a dream about a home? Explain your answer.

## Writing to Learn

**THINK AND DECIDE**  You read about the Grady family's dreams and expectations for a home they will have some day. Decide what the Gradys' home will be like when they find one. Draw a picture of the outside of that home.

The Grady Home

**WRITE**  Now imagine that you are inside the home you drew. Write a story about a typical day in the new Grady home.

467

# Reading Diagrams

**S**ome science textbooks deal with the workings of our planet. They teach about weather, plants and animals, and the role of humans on the planet. Science textbooks teach about these and other topics in a variety of ways. They often use photographs, graphs, and charts. Another useful tool for presenting scientific ideas is the diagram. It is important to be able to read and understand diagrams because they often contain information that is not presented in paragraph form.

A diagram is a kind of drawing, or illustration, that shows how something works or what parts it has. For example, one diagram may explain how the water cycle works while another may show how a jet flies.

All diagrams contain elements such as labels, captions, and arrows to help you understand the diagram. Words or phrases that identify the parts of a diagram are called *labels*. Each label may be connected by a line, or pointer, to the part of the diagram it identifies. A diagram may also have a caption. Captions are words near illustrations that name or explain the illustrations.

Often, parts of diagrams are numbered or marked with arrows. These markings show the order, or sequence, in which things happen in an illustration. Arrows may also be used to show the direction in which something in a diagram moves or flows.

# How to Read a Diagram

Follow these steps to understand the diagrams used in your science textbooks.

1. Study the illustration, and read the caption and labels.
2. Follow any numbers or arrows marked on the diagram.
3. Read any descriptions or explanations included in the book.
4. Check to see if you understand the diagram by summarizing, in your own words, what it tells you.

The diagram below describes the water cycle. Study the diagram. What does the entire diagram picture? What do the labels show? What do the arrows represent? Now read the written explanation on the next page. How does the diagram help you understand the written explanation?

## The Water Cycle

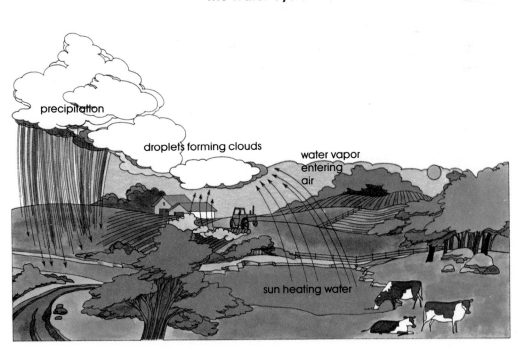

precipitation

droplets forming clouds

water vapor entering air

sun heating water

As described in the diagram, water on the surface of the earth is warmed by the sun. As this water is heated, some of it escapes into the air in the form of a gas. This gas is known as **water vapor.**

When air containing water vapor is cooled, the vapor begins to condense—it becomes liquid water. Tiny water droplets are formed. Countless numbers of these small droplets make up a cloud. In the cloud the tiny droplets may come together to form bigger, heavier droplets. These heavier droplets fall to the ground as rain. Water that falls to the ground is known as **precipitation.** Much of this water flows back to rivers, lakes, and oceans. Thus, the water cycle continues.

What part of the diagram does the author write about first? The very first sentence mentions how water is warmed by the sun. This sentence refers to the part of the diagram labeled "sun heating water." You may wonder why there are no arrows leading from the sun to the pond to show this. The arrows in this diagram show only the direction and movement of forms of water.

Do any words in the paragraphs also appear in the diagram? The words in dark type, **water vapor** and **precipitation,** are also used in the diagram. Paragraphs in science books will *tell* you what many important words mean. Diagrams in science books will *show* you what many important words mean.

**As You Read**   Read the following pages from a science textbook. Use the diagrams to answer the questions on page 477.

# Water Pollution

## What causes water pollution?

Most of the water on the earth is in the oceans. Because of the salt in the oceans, this water cannot be used for drinking. It also cannot be used in industry or in farming. People must depend on fresh water for their needs. Most fresh water comes either from under the ground or from lakes, rivers, and streams. It is important to take care of the limited supply of water.

Watering crops

How much water do you use each day? Some studies show that each person in the United States uses nearly 400 L a day. Some people have guessed that industries in the United States use about 10 billion L of water a day. Large amounts are also needed to water farmland in certain parts of the country. Most of this water comes from lakes, rivers, and reservoirs.

If the freshwater supply is polluted, there is less water left for people, farms, and industries. Polluted water means there is also less water for fishing and swimming.

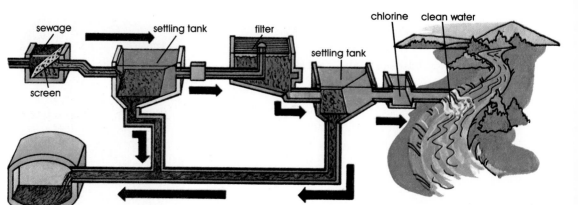

sewage
settling tank
filter
chlorine   clean water
settling tank
screen

collection
of heavy
materials

Sewage treatment plant

## WATER TREATMENT

Water can be polluted when sewage (sü'ij) is dumped into it. Sewage contains waste from sinks, toilets, and showers. Most sewage comes from homes and businesses. Sewage in water can cause disease in people who drink the water. What other problems are caused by sewage?

Many large cities have sewage-treatment plants that remove many of the pollutants from water. The water must pass through several steps. Follow these steps in the drawing.

First, sewage that enters these plants must pass through screens. These screens filter and remove large objects. The water then passes to a settling tank. Light materials float to the top, where they are skimmed off. Heavier materials sink and are removed. The water is pumped through a filter and then to a second settling tank. Then it is treated with the chemical chlorine (klôr'ēn). The chlorine kills certain harmful living things in the water. After the water has been treated, it is returned to lakes, streams, rivers, and finally to the oceans.

Water can be polluted by fertilizers and chemical sprays. Many farmers use chemical fertilizers (fèr′tə lī zərz) on their crops. A **fertilizer** is a substance that helps plants grow. Chemical sprays are often used to kill insects and weeds that damage crops. Chemicals from the fertilizers and sprays soak into the soil when it rains. In time water carrying these chemicals drains into streams and rivers. The streams and rivers then empty into lakes and oceans. This is how these waters become polluted.

Fertilizers entering the water increase the growth of small plants called algae. When the algae die, they pile up on the bottoms of ponds and lakes. As the dead plants decay, they may use oxygen from the water. As the oxygen supply decreases, fish and other animals that get oxygen from the water may die. This kind of pollution is shown in the drawing.

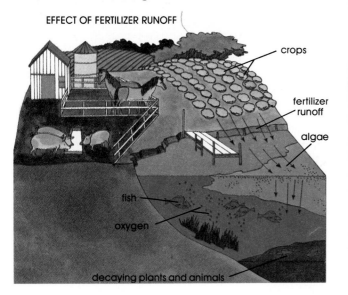

EFFECT OF FERTILIZER RUNOFF

crops

fertilizer runoff

algae

fish

oxygen

decaying plants and animals

Algae covering water

Chemicals from insect and weed sprays can poison fish and other living things in the water. The sprays can even affect living things that live near the water. This happens through a food chain. For example, a small fish may take in the poison when it eats small plants. The small fish may be eaten by a larger fish. The larger fish may be eaten by a large bird. The poisons build up in the bird as it eats more fish. In time the bird dies from the poison.

POISON IN THE FOOD CHAIN

Runoff with poisonous materials

Pollution from fertilizers and insect sprays can be reduced by using less of these chemicals. Sometimes farmers plant shrubs and grasses near water. These plants help prevent soil erosion. In this way, soil carrying chemicals will not enter the water.

Taking water samples

Industries can also pollute water. When industries make products, they may dump liquid or solid wastes into bodies of water. Many of these wastes poison the water. The poison wastes make the water unsafe for drinking and swimming.

Many industries have built their own waste-treatment plants. These plants remove many harmful substances from water before it enters rivers, lakes, streams, or oceans.

Some industries also release hot water into streams and lakes. The dumping of heated material into water is called **thermal** (ther′məl) **pollution.** Hot water cannot hold as much oxygen as cold water. With lower amounts of oxygen, certain plants and animals cannot live in the water.

There are ways in which industries and power plants can stop thermal pollution. Instead of re-

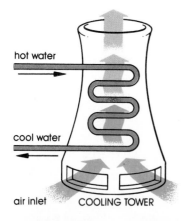

hot water

cool water

air inlet    COOLING TOWER

leasing heated materials into lakes and rivers, the heat can be released into the air. For example, some nuclear power plants have large cooling towers like the one shown. Hot water from the power plant is pumped to the cooling tower. In the tower, the hot water passes through coiled pipes. Cool air is then blown over the pipes. The air, which is now heated, is released through the top of the tower. The cooled water is returned to the power plant for reuse.

In recent years a new problem has developed. This problem is oil spills. Huge ships are used to carry oil across the oceans. Sometimes the tanks in these ships leak oil into the ocean. Another source of oil spills is offshore drilling for oil. Long stretches of beach have been damaged because of oil spills from these offshore wells. Fish and other wildlife have been killed by oil spills. The bird in the picture is being cleaned up after an oil spill. The people are tossing straw to stop the spread of oil.

Cooling tower

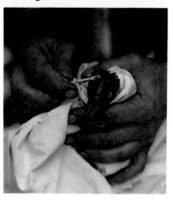

Bird rescued from oil spill

Cleanup after oil spill

## Using What You Have Learned

1. What is a diagram? What does a diagram show?

2. What elements are used to make a diagram clear?

3. What happens first in the diagram on page 472? How does the text on that page give you a clue? What in the diagram tells you what happens next?

4. List three of the labels used in the diagram on page 473. How do you know which things these labels identify?

5. How does the diagram on page 474 show the effects of poison on the eagle's food chain?

6. What is the object in the diagram at the top of page 476 called? How do you know?

7. Use the list below to draw a diagram showing the path of energy from the sun. Use arrows to represent energy coming from the sun. Give your diagram a caption and labels.
   a. energy from the sun shining down on and then bouncing off of low clouds
   b. energy from the sun being absorbed into the ground
   c. energy from the sun bouncing off the surface of the ground
   d. energy from the sun bouncing off the leaves of a tree

Examples and excerpts are from *Silver Burdett & Ginn Science,* © 1987.

*All her life Jean Guttery has yearned for this journey. She is on her way home from China to an America she has never seen, and to a grandmother she knows only through letters.*

## ON MY WAY HOME
*by Jean Fritz*

*from Homesick: My Own Story*

*Jean Guttery was an American who enjoyed growing up in China. Her parents taught the Chinese about American ways. Jean especially loved Lin Nai-Nai, who helped raise her. In 1927, the Gutterys crossed the Pacific Ocean on a journey to America with their friends, the Hulls, and their children, Andrea, David, and Edward.*

It took twenty-eight days to go from Shanghai to San Francisco, and on that first morning I thought I'd be content to lie on my deck chair and stare at the ocean and drink beef tea the whole time. Not Andrea. She thought the ocean was one big waste. We should be watching the people, she said, and sizing them up as they went by. So we did. We found that mostly they fit into definite types. There were the Counters, for instance: fast-walking men, red-cheeked women, keeping score of how many

times they walked around the deck, reveling in how fit they were. Then there were the Stylish Strollers, the Huffers and Puffers, the Lovebirds, leaning on each other, the Queasy Stomachs who clutched the railing and hoped for the best.

"You notice there's no one our age," Andrea said.

That was true. We had seen young people who were probably in their twenties, children who were Edward's age, and of course the majority who were our parents' age or older. But not one who might be in seventh or eighth grade or even high school.

Andrea jumped from her chair. "I'm going to explore."

Normally I would have gone with her but I hadn't had a chance yet to get my fill of the ocean. It was the same ocean as I'd had in Peitaiho,[1] and I looked and looked. I walked up

[1]Peitaiho (bāē di' hu): a city in China where Jean and her family usually spent the summer

479

to the top deck where I could see the whole circle of water around me. I was smack in the middle of no place, I thought. Not in China, not in America, not in the past, not in the future. In between everything. It was nice.

By the time I went back to my chair, Andrea had returned from her explorations.

"There really is no one our age on board," she reported.

"Well, we can play shuffleboard and deck tennis. There are lots of things we can do."

Andrea sighed. "I was hoping for some boys."

I knew that Andrea had begun to like boys. She said everyone at the Shanghai American School had a crush on someone else and when your love was requited—well, that was the cat's. What I couldn't understand was how someone could be in love with John Gilbert[2] and a kid in knickers at the same time.

I suppose Andrea could see that I was trying to figure out the boy business. She gave me a curious look. "Just how do you picture your school in Washington, P.A.?" she asked.

Well, I knew exactly what it would be like, so I told her: I'd be an American in a class with nothing but Americans in it. When we fought the American Revolution, we'd all fight on the same side. When we sang "My country' tis of thee," we'd yell our heads off. We'd all be the same. I would *belong*.

"There'll be boys in your class," Andrea pointed out.

"Naturally. I've seen boys before. So what?"

"Well, I think you're going to be surprised."

I didn't want to be surprised. For years I'd planned my first day at school in America.

"So how do you picture your school in Los Angeles, California?" I asked.

Andrea looked out at the ocean as if she expected to see her school sitting out there on the water. Then suddenly she shut her eyes and dropped her head in her hands. "Oh, Jean," she whispered, "I can't picture anything anymore. All I keep thinking about is my father. Alone in Shanghai."

This was as close as I'd ever seen Andrea come to crying. I put my hand on her shoulder. "I'm sorry," I said. Sorry! Such a puny word. You'd think the English language could give you something better. "I'm so sorry," I repeated.

[2]John Gilbert was a movie star at the time of this story.

480

Andrea dropped her hands and took a deep breath. "Well, let's play shuffleboard," she said.

From then on we played a lot of shuffleboard. Sometimes David joined us, but mostly he stayed in the ship's library, reading books about boys with real families. Edward kept busy in programs planned for children his age and the grown-ups made friends and talked their usual boring grown-up talk.

On the whole, Andrea and I had a good time on the *President Taft*. In the evenings we often watched movies. In the afternoons we made pigs of ourselves at tea where we had our pick of all kinds of dainty sandwiches, scones, macaroons, chocolate bonbons, and gooey tarts. Actually, I even liked going to bed on shipboard. I'd lie in my bunk and feel the ship's engines throbbing and know that even when I fell asleep I wouldn't be wasting time. I'd still be on the go, moving closer to America every minute.

Still, my "in-between" feeling stayed with me. One evening after supper I took Andrea to the top deck and told her about the feeling. Of course the "in-betweenness" was stronger than ever in the dark with the circle of water rippling below and the night sky above spilling over with stars. I had never seen so many stars. When I looked for a spot where I might stick an extra star if I had one, I couldn't find any space at all. No matter how small, an extra star would be out of place, I decided. The universe was one-hundred-percent perfect just as it was.

And then Andrea began to dance. She had slipped off her shoes and stockings and she was dancing what was obviously an "in-between" dance, leaping up toward the stars, sinking down toward the water, bending back toward China, reaching forward toward America, bending back again and again as if she could not tear herself away, yet each time dancing farther forward, swaying to and fro. Finally, her arms raised, she began twirling around, faster and faster, as if she were trying to outspin time itself. Scarcely breathing, I sat beside a smokestack and watched. She was making a poem and I was inside the poem with her. Under the stars, in the middle of the Pacific Ocean. I would never forget this night, I thought. Not if I lived to be one hundred.

Only when we came to the international date line did my "in-between" feeling disappear. This is the place, a kind of imaginary line in the ocean, where all ships going east add an extra day to that week and all ships going west drop a day. This is so you can keep up with the world turning and make time come out right. We had two Tuesdays in a row when we crossed the line and after that when it was "today" for me, I knew that Lin Nai-Nai was already in "tomorrow." I didn't like to think of Lin Nai-Nai so far ahead of me. It was as if we'd suddenly been tossed on different planets.

On the other hand, this was the first time in my life that I was sharing the same day with my grandmother.

*Oh, Grandma, I thought, ready or not, here I come!*

It was only a short time later that Edward saw a couple of rocks poking out of the water and yelled for us to come. The rocks could hardly be called land, but we knew they were the beginning of the Hawaiian Islands and we knew that the Hawaiian Islands were a territory belonging to the United States. Of course it wasn't the same as one of the forty-eight states; still, when we stepped off the *President Taft* in Honolulu (where we were to stay a couple of days before going on to San Francisco), we

wondered if we could truthfully say we were stepping on American soil. I said no. Since the Hawaiian Islands didn't have a star in the flag, they couldn't be one-hundred-percent American, and I wasn't going to consider myself on American soil until I had put my feet flat down on the state of California.

We had a week to wait. The morning we were due to arrive in San Francisco, all the passengers came on deck early, but I was the first. I skipped breakfast and went to the very front of the ship where the railing comes to a point. That morning I would be the "eyes" of the *President Taft,* searching the horizon for the first speck of land. My private ceremony of greeting, however, would not come until we were closer, until we were sailing through the Golden Gate. For years I had heard about the Golden Gate, a narrow stretch of water connecting the Pacific Ocean to San Francisco Bay. And for years I had planned my entrance.

Dressed in my navy skirt, white blouse and silk stockings, I felt every bit as neat as Columbus or Balboa and every bit as heroic when I finally spotted America in the distance. The decks had filled with passengers by

now, and as I watched the land come closer, I had to tell myself over and over that I was HERE. At last.

Then the ship entered the narrow stretch of the Golden Gate and I could see American hills on my left and American houses on my right, and I took a deep breath of American air.

483

" 'Breathes there the man, with soul so dead,' " I cried,

" 'Who never to himself hath said,
This is my own, my native land!' "

I forgot that there were people behind and around me until I heard a few snickers and a scattering of claps, but I didn't care. I wasn't reciting for anyone's benefit but my own.

Next for my first steps on American soil, but when the time came, I forgot all about them. As soon as we were on the dock, we were jostled from line to line. Believe it or not, after crossing thousands of miles of ocean to get here, we had to prove that it was O.K. for us to come into the U.S.A. We had to show that we were honest-to-goodness citizens and not spies. We had to open our baggage and let inspectors see that we weren't smuggling in anything illegal. We even had to prove that we were germ-free, that we didn't have smallpox or any dire disease that would infect the country. After we had finally passed the tests, I expected to feel one-hundred-percent American. Instead, stepping from the dock into the city of San Francisco, I felt dizzy and unreal, as if I were a made-up character in a book I had read too many times to believe it

wasn't still a book. As we walked the Hulls to the car that their Aunt Kay had driven up from Los Angeles, I told Andrea about my crazy feeling.

"I'm kind of funny in the head," I said. "As if I'm not really me. As if this isn't really happening."

"Me too," Andrea agreed. "I guess our brains haven't caught up to us yet. But my brains better get going. Guess what?"

"What?"

"Aunt Kay says our house in Los Angeles is not far from Hollywood."

Then suddenly the scene speeded up and the Hulls were in the car, ready to leave for Los Angeles, while I was still stuck in a book without having said any of the things I wanted to. I ran after the car as it started.

"Give my love to John Gilbert," I yelled to Andrea.

She stuck her head out the window. "And how!" she yelled back.

My mother, father, and I were going to stay in a hotel overnight and start across the continent the next morning, May 24, in our new car. The first thing we did now was to go to a drugstore where my father ordered three ice-cream sodas. "As tall as you can make them," he said. "We have to make up for lost time."

My first American soda was chocolate and it was a whopper. While we sucked away on our straws, my father read to us from the latest newspaper. The big story was about America's new hero, an aviator named Charles Lindbergh who had just made the first solo flight across the Atlantic Ocean. Of course I admired him for having done such a brave and scary thing, but I bet he wasn't any more surprised to have made it across one ocean than I was to have finally made it across another. I looked at his picture. His goggles were pushed back on his helmet and he was grinning. He had it all over John Gilbert, I decided. I might even consider having a crush on him—that is, if and when I ever felt the urge. Right now I was coming to the bottom of my soda and I was trying to slurp up the last drops when my mother told me to quit; I was making too much noise.

The rest of the afternoon we spent sight-seeing, riding up and down seesaw hills in cable cars, walking in and out of American stores. Every once in a while I found myself smiling at total strangers because I knew that if I were to speak to them in English, they'd answer in English. We were all Americans. Yet I still felt as if I were telling myself a story. America didn't become completely real for me until the next day after we'd left San Francisco and were out in the country.

My father had told my mother and me that since he wasn't used to our new car or to American highways, we should be quiet and let him concentrate. My mother concentrated too. Sitting in the front seat, she flinched but she never said a word. I paid no attention to the road. I just kept looking out the window until all at once there on my right was a white picket fence and a meadow, fresh and green as if it had just this minute been created. Two black and white cows were grazing slowly over the grass as if they had all the time in the world, as if they knew that no matter how much they ate, there'd always be more, as if in their quiet munching way they understood that they had nothing, nothing whatsoever to worry about. I poked my mother, pointed, and whispered, "Cows." I had never seen cows in China but it was not the cows themselves that impressed me. It was the whole scene. The perfect greenness. The washed-clean look. The peacefulness. Oh, *now*! I thought. Now I was in America. Every last inch of me.

By the second day my father acted as if he'd been driving the car all his life. He not only talked, he sang, and if he felt like hitching up his trousers, he just took his hands off the wheel and hitched. But as my father relaxed, my mother became more tense. "Arthur," she finally said, "you are going forty-five."

My father laughed. "Well, we're headed for the stable, Myrtle. You never heard of a horse that dawdled on its way home, did you?"

My mother's lips went tight and thin. "The whole point of driving across the continent," she said, "was so we could see the country."

"Well, it's all there." My father swept his hand from one side of the car to the other. "All you have to do is to take your eyes off the road and look." He honked his horn at the car

in front of him and swung around it.

At the end of the day, after we were settled in an overnight cabin, my father took a new notebook from his pocket. I watched as he wrote: "May 24. 260 miles." Just as I'd suspected, my father was out to break records. I bet that before long we'd be making 300 miles or more a day. I bet we'd be in Washington, P.A., long before July.

The trouble with record breaking is that it can lead to Narrow Squeaks, and while we were still in California we had our first one. Driving along a back road that my father had figured out was a shortcut, we came to a bridge with a barrier across it and a sign in front: THIS BRIDGE CONDEMNED. DO NOT PASS. There was no other road marked DETOUR, so obviously the only thing to do was to turn around and go back about five miles to the last town and take the regular highway. My father stopped the car. "You'd think they'd warn you in advance," he muttered. He slammed the door, jumped over the barrier, and walked onto the bridge. Then he climbed down the riverbank and looked up at the bridge from below. When he came back up the bank, he pushed the barrier aside, got in the car, and started it up. "We can make it," he said.

It hadn't occurred to me that he'd try to drive across. My mother put her hand on his arm. "Please, Arthur," she begged, but I didn't bother with any "pleases." If he wanted to kill himself, he didn't have to kill Mother and me too. "Let Mother and me walk across," I shouted. "Let us out. Let us OUT."

My father had already revved up the motor. "A car can have only one driver," he snapped. "I'm it." He backed up so he could get a flying start and then we whooped across the bridge, our wheels clattering across the loose boards, space gaping below. Well, we did reach the other side and when I looked back, I saw that the bridge was still there.

"You see?" my father crowed. "You see how much time we saved?"

All I could see was that we'd risked our lives because he was so pigheaded. Right then I hated my father. I felt rotten hating someone I really loved but I couldn't help it. I knew the loving would come back but I had to wait several hours.

There were days, however, particularly across the long, flat stretches of Texas, when nothing out-of-the-way happened. We just drove on and on, and although my father reported at the end of the day that we'd gone 350 miles, the scenery was the same at the end as at the beginning, so it didn't feel as if we'd moved at all. Other times we ran into storms or into road construction and we were lucky if we made 200 miles. But the best day of the whole trip, at least as far as my mother and I were concerned, was the day that we had a flat tire in the Ozark Mountains. The spare tire and jack were buried in the trunk under all our luggage, so everything had to be taken out before my father could even begin work on the tire. There was no point in offering to help because my father had a system for loading and unloading which only he understood, so my mother and I set off up the mountainside, looking for wildflowers.

"Watch out for snakes," my mother said, but her voice was so happy, I knew she wasn't thinking about snakes.

As soon as I stepped out of the car, I fell in love with the day. With the sky—fresh, blotting-paper blue. With the mountains, warm and piney and polka-dotted with flowers we would never have seen from the window of a car. We decided to pick one of each kind and press them in my gray geography book which I had in the car. My mother held out her skirt, making a hollow out of it, while I dropped in the flowers and she named them: forget-me-not, wintergreen, pink, wild rose. When we didn't know the name, I'd make one up: pagoda plant, wild confetti, French knot. My mother's skirt was atumble with color when we suddenly realized how far we'd walked. Holding her skirt high, my mother led the way back, running and laughing. We arrived at the car, out of breath, just as my father was loading the last of the luggage into the trunk. He glared at us, his face streaming with perspiration. "I don't have a dry stitch on me," he said, as if it were our fault that he sweat so much. Then he looked at the flowers in Mother's skirt

and his face softened. He took out his handkerchief and wiped his face and neck and finally he smiled. "I guess I picked a good place to have a flat tire, didn't I?" he said.

The farther we went, the better mileage we made, so that by the middle of June we were almost to the West Virginia state line. My father said we'd get to Washington, P.A., the day after the next, sometime in the afternoon. He called my grandmother on the phone, grinning because he knew how surprised she'd be. I stood close so I could hear her voice.

"Mother?" he said when she answered. "How about stirring up a batch of flannel cakes?"

"Arthur!" (She sounded just the way I knew she would.) "Well, land's sakes, Arthur, where are you?"

"About ready to cross into West Virginia."

My grandmother was so excited that her words fell over each other as she tried to relay the news to my grandfather and Aunt Margaret and talk over the phone at the same time.

The next day it poured rain and although that didn't slow us down, my mother started worrying. Shirls Avenue, my grandparents' street, apparently turned into a dirt road just

before plunging down a steep hill to their house and farm. In wet weather the road became one big sea of mud which, according to my mother, would be "worth your life to drive through."

"If it looks bad," my mother suggested, "we can park at the top of the hill and walk down in our galoshes."

My father sighed. "Myrtle," he said, "we've driven across the Mohave Desert. We've been through thick and thin for over three thousand miles and here you are worrying about Shirls Avenue."

The next day the sun was out, but when we came to Shirls Avenue, I could see that the sun hadn't done a thing to dry up the hill. My father put the car into low, my mother closed her eyes, and down we went, sloshing up to our hubcaps, careening from one rut to another, while my father kept one hand down hard on the horn to announce our arrival.

By the time we were at the bottom of the hill and had parked beside the house, my grandmother, my grandfather, and Aunt Margaret were all outside, looking exactly the way they had in the calendar picture. I ran right into my grandmother's arms as if I'd been doing this every day.

"Welcome home! Oh, welcome home!" my grandmother cried.

I hadn't known it but this was exactly what I'd wanted her to say. I needed to hear it said out loud. I was home.

## ♦ LIBRARY LINK ♦

*"On My Way Home" is one chapter from a book about Jean. To find out how Jean enjoys life in Pennsylvania, read* Homesick: My Own Story *by Jean Fritz.*

## Reader's Response

At the end of the selection, Jean writes, "I was home." How do you feel about her calling a place that she'd never seen "home"?

# ON MY WAY HOME

## Checking Your Comprehension

1. What were Jean's and Andrea's final destinations in America?
2. What meaning did Andrea's dance have for Jean?
3. Why did Jean recite a poem when she saw the Golden Gate?
4. Why was Jean's father in such a hurry to cross the United States?
5. Why were her grandmother's words, "Welcome home," so important to Jean? How did you decide what was important about them?
6. How do you think Jean's experiences of America compared with the way she had imagined America to be?

## Writing to Learn

**THINK AND ANALYZE**   Once, Jean "fell in love with a day." Have you ever fallen in love with a day? Look at the model below that tells about an incident in Jean's story. Then write the who, what, when, where, and why of a day you enjoy remembering.

| Who? | Jean and her mother |
|---|---|
| What? | picked wild flowers |
| When? | on the journey from San Francisco |
| Where? | from a hillside |
| Why? | because a tire was flat |

**WRITE**   Write a paragraph about the day in your life that you "fell in love with." Use your answers to the who, what, when, where, and why questions to help you write your paragraph.

491

# THIS IS MY ROCK

This is my rock,
And here I run
To steal the secret of the sun;

This is my rock,
And here come I
Before the night has swept the sky;

This is my rock,
This is the place
I meet the evening face to face.

*David McCord*

# HOME SWEET HOME

'Mid pleasures and palaces though we may roam,
Be it ever so humble, there's no place like home;
A charm from the sky seems to hallow us there,
Which, seek through the world, is ne'er met with
    elsewhere.
        Home, Home, sweet, sweet Home!
There's no place like Home! there's no place like Home!

To there I'll return, overburdened with care;
The heart's dearest solace will smile on me there;
No more from that cottage again will I roam;
Be it ever so humble, there's no place like home.
        Home, Home, sweet, sweet Home!
There's no place like Home! there's no place like Home!

*John Howard Payne*

493

# READING NON-FICTION

## Vocabulary:
# Context Clues

The next selection you will read is called "Today's Immigrants." Think for a moment: What is an immigrant? If you don't know, here are some sentences that can help you figure out the answer.

> The *immigrants* had come from many lands. These newcomers gazed curiously at their new country.

From reading these sentences, you know that *immigrants* are newcomers from other lands. Context clues—the related words and sentences around the unfamiliar word *immigrants*—help you understand its meaning. In the sentences above, three context clues are: "come from many lands," "newcomers," and "their new country."

Sometimes context clues give you a definition. For example, the following sentence gives you a definition for the word *sweatshops*.

> Often the new arrivals could only find work in the city's *sweatshops*, the factories where workers toiled from dawn until dark for poor wages.

Other times, you can figure out the meaning of a word because a word or phrase with the opposite meaning is in that sentence or in a nearby sentence.

> The immigrants' quietness at a job was in sharp contrast to the *volubility* of the workers who already knew the language.

In the sentence, the word *quietness* means the opposite of *volubility.*

Still other times, context clues indicate what class or category a word belongs to. This kind of context clue is in the next sentence.

At the baggage center, the traveler said his trunk and suitcase had arrived, but his *valise* had not.

What category of objects is the sentence about? Think about that category in order to guess what a valise is. If you guessed that it is a piece of luggage, you are correct.

## *Using What You Have Learned*

In the following examples, identify the context clues for the words in italics. Then write a definition of each word.

1. Wouldn't it be exciting to visit every *continent*: North and South America, Europe, Asia, Africa, Australia, and Antarctica?
2. The driver said, "Let me *concentrate*. I must pay attention to where I'm going."
3. Immigrants value many experiences that natives are likely to *eschew.*

## *As You Read*

As you read the next selection, "Today's Immigrants," look for context clues to help you figure out the meaning of a word you don't know.

# Today's Immigrants

## by Luz Nuncio

*From the earliest years of this country's existence, immigrants have been coming to the United States. Today, immigrants continue to come to America, and they share the same dream as immigrants of the past—to make a new home and a better life for themselves and their children.*

On the weekend of July 4, 1986, all Americans were invited to New York City for a special birthday party. The Statue of Liberty, one of the city's most famous monuments, was turning one hundred years old. Six million people came, and many million more across the United States watched the celebration on television. For four days and nights, people enjoyed concerts, parades, speeches, and fireworks in honor of the newly renovated statue. That special Fourth of July weekend became known as "Liberty Weekend."

During the celebration, Americans were not just honoring the statue's age or beauty. They were especially proud of what the Statue of Liberty stands for. For the last century, the Statue of Liberty was the first glimpse of America for the millions of European immigrants entering the country through New York harbor. With her torch raised high, the Statue of Liberty symbolizes a welcome to immigrants from all over the world. It symbolizes a chance to make a better life in the United States.

## Early Newcomers

Immigrants have been coming to the United States from the time of its founding. During the first century of immigration, most of the newcomers were English, Irish, Scottish, German, and Scandinavian.

During this time, people were also brought to the United States from Africa against their wishes. Blacks have been in the United States since colonial times and have served their country and contributed to its culture like other groups of newcomers. But until the end of the Civil War, most blacks were slaves. They were not free to make a better life for themselves and their children. Like other newcomers, they had their own hopes and dreams of freedom. But unlike European immigrants, blacks had no opportunity when they were brought here to make those dreams come true.

## Later Immigrants

During the second century of the United States' existence, especially from 1880 until 1920, most immigrants to the United States were Italian, Greek, or eastern European. A small but important wave of Chinese and Japanese immigrants was recruited to come to America from the 1850s until the end of the nineteenth century. They worked as miners, farm laborers, and for the fishing and railroad industries. In fact, much of the Western link of the Trans-Continental Railroad was built by Chinese workers.

The European immigrants came to America to escape poverty or violence in their own countries. They survived hard and often heartbreaking journeys to make America their new home. When they arrived, life for nearly all of them was very difficult and different from the life they had known in their old homelands. America was a country of big cities and new ways. Many of the immigrants came from farms and villages where ways of life had not changed much over time.

All immigrants struggled to adapt themselves to their new home. They learned English and worked hard to make life better and easier for their children. They *assimilated*, which means that they changed some of their ways and ideas to blend into the ways and ideas of people in their new home.

But in changing themselves to become American, these immigrants also changed America. They brought with them not only different foods and different music from their homelands, but talent, special knowledge, and skills. They brought the best of their old home to their new home for everyone to share.

## Today's Immigrants

Like immigrants before them, some recent immigrants have had to suffer a long, dangerous voyage across an ocean in order to reach America. But most immigrants today come by plane. Others come by train, car, or by foot. When they arrive, many of them are not as surprised at what they find in America as earlier immigrants were. Modern means of transportation and communication have made the world a smaller place, so many of today's immigrants already know something about American culture when they arrive.

Today's immigrants are different from earlier immigrants in another way. Most of the immigrants who came to the United States over the last two centuries were western, southern, or eastern European. They were, for example, from England and Germany, Italy and Greece, and Poland and Romania. Today, most of the immigrants come from non-European countries. They come mostly from countries in Latin America and Asia.

## Immigrants from Latin America

Today's immigrants from Latin America come mainly from Mexico and countries in Central America such as Guatemala and El Salvador. They also come from islands in the Caribbean such as

Cuba and Puerto Rico, and from South American countries such as Argentina and Peru. However, the number of South American immigrants is not as great as that of immigrants from Mexico, Central America, and the Caribbean.

Although most Latin American immigrants see themselves as Hispanics sharing the same Spanish language and culture, there are many differences among Hispanic groups. Some Hispanic immigrants choose to come to the United States. Others come because war, economic hardship, or political trouble in their own countries leaves them no choice but to leave. Some have visited the United States before and may have friends or relatives in this country. Others come to settle in America sight unseen, knowing nobody.

Hispanic immigrants also come from different economic backgrounds. Many immigrants come to the United States for whatever jobs they can find, no matter how low the pay and how hard the work. But other immigrants have received much training for the work that they do. These immigrants are doctors, lawyers, professors, or business people. They come to the United States because they believe it is a better place to carry on their work. Some of these immigrants also come because of civil war or other political unrest in their countries.

## One Hispanic Immigrant

Teresa Fraga[1] had worked as a migrant worker in the farms and ranches of the United States for years before coming to settle in Chicago in 1966. She had come legally to the United States at a time when Mexicans were being encouraged by the American government to come and fill the demand for migrant farm workers and other kinds of laborers.

As a migrant worker, Teresa worked in the fields, caring for and harvesting fruit and vegetable crops. She received very low pay, and the workday was long and hard. Her husband also worked in the fields. They could only work for a few weeks at each place,

[1]Teresa Fraga (te re′ sä  frä′ gä)

**Teresa Fraga, at left, enjoys talking with her family in the dining room of their Chicago home.**

since that was how long it took to complete the work. When they finished working on one farm or ranch, they would move on to another. They never knew where they would find work next, or how long it would last, or what it would pay.

Teresa and her family decided to go to Chicago to find work that would last more than just a few weeks. They settled in the Mexican neighborhood in the Pilsen-Little Village area of Chicago. Teresa's husband found a job as a construction worker, and their family grew.

The Pilsen-Little Village area where Teresa and her family settled is a large and established Mexican neighborhood in Chicago. It has been home for Mexicans coming to Chicago since the beginning of this century. Like the European immigrants before them, Mexican immigrants have made their first home in communities where their language is spoken and where friends and relatives may already live.

In spite of the harsh Chicago winters, Teresa and her family felt at home in the Pilsen-Little Village neighborhood. The streets in this neighborhood are lined with Mexican restaurants and bakeries. There are also several supermarkets and grocery stores that sell food and newspapers from Mexico. These restaurants and stores are usually decorated with piñatas and streamers in the colors of the Mexican flag: red, white, and green. Murals on the outside walls of buildings portray scenes from Mexican history or famous Mexican patriots.

*Above*, Teresa joins in a celebration in front of one of the colorful murals in her neighborhood. *Left*, Teresa greets a former student.

As the years passed for Teresa and her family in the Pilsen-Little Village part of Chicago, Teresa became more involved in efforts to improve her neighborhood. She joined groups that were pressing to have a new high school built in the area because the schools they had were old and overcrowded. She became a member of the neighborhood council.

502

Many Mexican immigrants dream of returning to their homeland. Others dream of staying in the United States but moving closer to Mexico, to one of the southwestern states that borders on Mexico and has a large Mexican population. These immigrants miss the warm weather and the ways of their culture.

Teresa and her family shared this dream. For years they went to Texas each winter, to check on the house that they were having built. But when the house was finally finished, it stood empty for eleven years. The Fraga family did not go.

Somehow, over the twenty years the Fraga family had lived in Chicago, they had quietly decided to stay. The Fraga children had grown up and gone to school in their neighborhood in Pilsen-Little Village. Teresa had worked hard to make it a neighborhood that made her feel proud. Her husband had found a good job to support the family.

The Fraga family made friends and found a stable life in the city after traveling up from Mexico through the fields of the United States as migrant workers. They came to America looking for work, but they found a home.

## Immigrants from Asia

Like Latin American immigrants, Asian immigrants coming to the United States today are from different countries, social classes, and backgrounds. They also come for different reasons.

Many recent Asian immigrants, such as those from Vietnam, Cambodia, and Laos, fled their countries during the period from 1960 to the late 1970s because of war and violence there. Many were fishermen or farmers in tiny Asian villages. For these immigrants, the journey and the process of getting used to a new life in America have been very hard. Other Asian immigrants who came to the United States during this time were professionals. They came to the United States also seeking to escape the violence and to further their careers in American universities, medical centers, and technical fields.

## One Asian Immigrant

Nghi Lu[2] came to the United States from Vietnam in 1984, when she was seventeen. She had lived in the small town of Bac Lieu,[3] in South Vietnam, with her father, mother, four brothers, and three sisters.

A few years earlier, one of Nghi Lu's sisters had come to the United States and had settled in Chicago. As soon as she was able, Nghi Lu's sister applied to the American Immigration and Naturalization Service as a *sponsor* to help the rest of her family come to the United States. A *sponsor* is someone who asks the United States government to allow other people who are not United States citizens to come live in the United States. Usually, a sponsor is a member of the family of the future immigrants. The sponsor agrees that he or she will provide for the immigrants and help them make their new life in America.

Nghi Lu remembers clearly the day when she arrived in Chicago. The weather was bitterly cold and there was snow on the ground. Nghi Lu and her family were not prepared for the harsh winter weather. They were wearing the same light clothes they had worn at home in Vietnam. But Nghi Lu's sister was prepared. She met her family at the airport with coats, sweaters, scarves, and gloves. The only thing she forgot, laughs Nghi Lu, was boots!

Nghi Lu remembers hurrying to get out of the cold, feeling the sharp sting of the wind, but also feeling very happy and excited at having her family together again.

The first few months in Chicago were hard for Nghi Lu and her family. They not only had to get used to the cold weather, but to a new way of life. In Vietnam, Nghi Lu and her family had lived in an airy, two-story building with the living quarters on the upper floor and a variety store on the lower floor. Nghi Lu and her brothers and sisters went to a school with large classrooms that held up to seventy students.

In Chicago, Nghi Lu's family lived in a brick apartment building

[2]Nghi Lu (ngē lu-oo)    [3]Bac Lieu (bä lē'-oo)

***Above***, new stores open as Nghi Lu's neighborhood attracts more immigrants from Southeast Asia. ***Right***, a recent photo shows Nghi Lu.

on a busy street. At school, the classes Nghi Lu and her brothers and sisters attended were smaller, but they were made up of students from all over the world who had also just come to America. Like these students, Nghi Lu and her brothers and sisters took classes both in English and their native language.

Nghi Lu felt the most homesick the first time her family

celebrated Chinese New Year in Chicago. Like many of their neighbors in Vietnam, Nghi Lu's family had adopted Chinese holidays. Although Nghi Lu and her family were able to find most of the things they needed for their celebration in Chicago's Chinatown, New Year was just not the same as it had been in Vietnam. Like other immigrants they loved their new country, but their old home remained a part of them, and they still missed it very much.

Today, Nghi Lu speaks three languages: Vietnamese, Chinese, and English. Although it was hard for Nghi Lu to learn English and to get used to her school in the big city, she worked very hard and was helped by her teachers and counselors. In June 1987, she graduated from high school. Because of her hard work, she earned tenth place in a class of 490 students. Nghi Lu plans to go on to college, where she will study nursing.

Nghi Lu says that she would like to return to Vietnam some day. She would like to see aunts and uncles who are still there. She would also like to spend time using her education to help her people. Nghi Lu believes that the freedom she has found here to keep learning, the chance to get a good education, and her own hard work will open many new doors for her. Nghi Lu has her family in America, and little by little, she is making America her home.

Today's immigrants are like all previous immigrants in one very important way. Their coming to America, no matter how difficult or painful, is a celebration of the chance to make a better life and a new home in America.

## Reader's Response

In what ways has life in America been influenced by its immigrants? Explain your answer.

# Today's Immigrants

## Checking Your Comprehension

1. Instead of the Statue of Liberty, what other famous national symbol might the author have used, and why?
2. How are today's immigrants similar to earlier immigrants to America?
3. What were the differences between the lives of African newcomers and European newcomers during the first century of immigration?
4. What made life difficult for many immigrants during the second century of immigration? What details led you to your answer?
5. What do Teresa Fraga and Nghi Lu have in common?
6. What have Teresa Fraga and Nghi Lu been able to accomplish since coming to America?

## Writing to Learn

**THINK AND IMAGINE**   Many years ago, Emma Lazarus wrote a poem that appears on the base of the Statue of Liberty. In the poem, the Statue of Liberty speaks to the other nations of the world. Read these lines from that poem.

> Give me your tired, your poor,
> Your huddled masses
>     yearning to breath free. . . .
>
> — Emma Lazarus

**WRITE**   What would the Statue of Liberty say to people of today who want to immigrate to the United States? Write the words you think she would speak.

*"Moving" isn't usually a scary word, but when it applies to you, it can cause fear and uncertainty. Luke finds this out firsthand.*

# A Good Chance

## by Ianthe Mac Thomas

The train was coming. Luke could hear it whistling and rumbling through the tunnel that cut into the side of the mountain. Clouds of thick, black smoke dotted the sky behind it. It was coming fast.

As on other days, the train made Luke feel like running. He liked to race with the train, no matter how far away. To him, the train was movement and excitement, a part of the world whizzing past.

But today was different. Today Luke was going places, but not with the train. After running only a short distance, he gave up. He reached the point where the tracks curved around his family's old peach orchard. Then, gasping for breath, he threw himself on the grass. He lay there for some time, breathing in the sweetness of the blades around him.

"Luke?" It was his father's voice. "We're ready."

Luke got up slowly and walked to the driveway with his dad. Today he and his parents were moving out of Esperanza, the little town they had always called home. His friends Jesse and Alberta had come to see him off, but he couldn't even bring himself to wave goodbye to them. He tried to lift his hand, but it felt *so* heavy! As he quickly ducked into the waiting station wagon, he felt his heart jump in his chest.

Once in the car, Luke closed his eyes. He could picture the streets they'd be taking out of town. He knew every one of them by heart. He could see the small cluster of one-story shops that seemed to hug each other along the four blocks of Main Street.

Everything he had ever needed was close by: Colby's Fish Market, where Mr. Colby had saved fish heads for Luke's cat; Sara's Bake Shop, where all the cakes for his family's special events had been baked. Even the Old Lawson house, now the town's public library, held special memories for Luke. Luke had spent many happy times reading there last summer.

Across the street from these places was the town square. It had green park benches, clipped hedges and a two-hundred-year-old oak tree. Luke and Jesse loved that tree. Luke's dad had once helped them hang a swing from it, and all the little kids in town still used that swing.

Most of the town's buildings, stores, and houses were small and old, but each was painted and neat. Every sidewalk, though cracked, was carefully swept each morning. Luke knew every crack, every lawn, every swinging gate, every scraggly rosebush in town.

Now it seemed to Luke that his dad was taking too much time driving out of town. The car moved more slowly than he expected. Soon, though, the ride became smooth, and Luke knew they were on the highway. Luke kept his eyes pressed shut, as if in this way he could also shut out his parents' conversation.

"I hope—" he heard his mother say, "I just hope it won't be too hard for me to find a place to park every morning. And . . . oh," her voice trailed off.

"I know," said Luke's father. "There will be so much to do! Moving to a new place is never easy. But how could we pass up a good chance?"

Luke remembered the Friday night when his father had come home with a big smile on his face. He had grabbed

Luke's mother around the waist and they had put on music and done a dance called the "tango" across the living room floor.

Luke still couldn't believe it. He felt his whole life had turned upside down the moment his father began telling about his big promotion. The family would have to move to San Francisco, his dad had said. Shortly after that, his mother had also landed a good job there. All was set. The family was going to move to San Francisco.

From the very first, Luke had said he wouldn't move. He couldn't even *imagine* it. What would a day be like without his friends Jesse and Alberta?

And what would his life be like if he didn't wake up in his old room? For one thing, he'd miss the brown carpet with the horse design on it. It was tacked down in his room and too old, his mother had said, so they wouldn't be taking it.

Luke loved that carpet. He liked to pretend that the horses came to life at night and visited wonderful new places he had read about. Sometimes he dreamed they were galloping across some wide prairie, sometimes through deep canyons. But his horses were always there in the morning when he woke up.

Now it was Luke who was going to a new place, and going away for good. As the car rolled down the highway, he could feel his father looking at him in the rearview mirror. The next time his father spoke, Luke felt that his dad was trying hard to explain something not just to him, but to himself as well.

"We knew it wouldn't be easy," his father continued, "but how could I *not* accept the promotion?" He turned to his wife. "How could *you* turn down your new job? It's not just *one* good chance, but *two*, and we have to take advantage—"

"Yes . . . I guess so," Luke's mother said. Her words came out slowly, almost sadly.

On hearing this, Luke straightened up in the back seat. His ears tingled as he waited for what she might say next, what he hoped she would say. His mouth felt dry. His hands were damp.

He wanted his mom to tell his father to turn around and go back to Esperanza. Maybe his father would agree. Maybe this whole move would become nothing more than a bad dream.

But it wasn't anything like a dream when Luke heard his mother's next words. "Yes, you're right," she continued. "Sometimes I think how much I'll miss my friends and the town and . . . well, everything. Things will be *so* different! But you're right. We couldn't pass up a good chance like this."

When she said this, the matter seemed settled. Luke sank back against the seat. He felt all his energy seep out of him. All his hope was gone.

Luke's mom turned in her seat and gently squeezed his chin. "You awake, honey?" she said. "Luke?"

He kept his eyes closed, but he could feel her fingers stroking his cheek.

"It's not going to be so bad, Luke, you'll see. San Francisco is beautiful. It has that fantastic Golden Gate Bridge, remember? And, Luke . . . Luke?" Her voice was playful and soft, almost pleading.

It took all of Luke's effort to keep his eyes shut. He knew his mom was trying to cheer him up, but he didn't care. He only wanted to go back home where he felt comfortable, where he knew everyone and everyone knew him. He turned his face away from her and looked out the open window. The wind whipped his face, and he soon fell asleep.

"Hey, move it, mister!" someone called out to Luke's father. Luke awakened to the man's sharp voice. He rubbed his eyes and looked out the car window.

So *this* was their welcome to the big city, thought Luke. He had never seen so many buildings in his life. They seemed to crowd over them, too close for comfort. They seemed like monsters about to swallow people whole. A police or ambulance siren screamed somewhere in the distance. The traffic inched its way into the city.

Luke could see that both his parents were concentrating hard as they drove through the traffic. He thought they looked a little like new kids at school trying to find their classroom. He shook his head and smiled. He didn't know why, but then and there he decided he would be easier on them.

As Luke looked around, he caught sight of flower boxes on the balconies of modern apartment buildings, high above the street. It shocked him to see them. They looked so pretty against the concrete and steel.

The next sight surprised Luke even more. Beyond a cluster of buildings Luke could see the tops of trees. Trees!

For the first time that long day, Luke said something to his parents: "Hey, there are trees here."

The remark made them all laugh. His father answered, "Yeah, trees! And a park where we can ride horses. Not so bad, huh?"

When they reached the apartment building that was to be their new home, Luke tried not to look very interested. Yes, the place *was* big, but it hadn't swallowed them whole, as Luke had expected. Its bigness seemed to promise something, but just what, Luke couldn't imagine.

Luke and his parents were standing at a door exactly like all the others, except this one had a name plate with their last name printed on it. His father had just inserted the key in the lock when another door down the hall opened.

A woman stuck her head out, smiling cheerfully. She said, "Welcome, I'm your neighbor, Mrs. . . .", but she didn't get a chance to finish her sentence. A boy about Luke's own age pushed past her.

"Excuse me, Ma," he said. Then he saw Luke and said, "Hi, I'm Mark. What's your name?"

Luke looked at him and answered shyly, "I'm Luke."

Mark said, "Do you play stickball? There's a game going on over in the park. Want to come?"

Luke shuffled his feet, which already seemed to be answering for him. He looked at his father. His father laughed and said, "Go ahead. We'll wait for the movers in the meantime. Just be careful crossing the streets."

Luke decided that it was much easier to hit a ball with a bat instead of the sawed-off broomstick they'd given him. But he did manage to bunt the ball once with the stick, and he soon found himself absorbed in the game.

He, Mark, two girls with bright red hair, and a boy with a bandage on his knee were one team. The park had a real, regulation baseball diamond with canvas bases and a slate scoreboard. Luke's side lost, but when he and Mark were leaving, the other kids shouted after them, "Hey, Mark, you and the new kid coming back tomorrow? We'll beat you again." Luke laughed, surprised at this sudden invitation to return for another game.

When Luke got back to the apartment, his father was opening a large pizza carton. His mother was standing in the living room amid some partially unpacked boxes. She looked tired and confused.

"Come and get it!" Luke's father said. He held the box of steaming pizza out for her to see. "Leave that for now. Let's eat!"

His mother looked at his father and sat down on one of the boxes. "I'm almost too tired to eat," she said.

To Luke, her voice sounded like she really meant it. Suddenly he wasn't upset with his mother *or* father anymore. He thought maybe they were feeling more scared about all the "newness" than he was.

At that moment, Luke thought he understood what his parents meant when they talked about not missing a good chance. Sometimes, reaching for a good chance might mean having to give something up—even something you loved.

Luke walked over to his mother and put his arm around her shoulders. "Come on, Mom," he said, and led her to the table.

They all sat in silence for a minute, munching on their slices of pizza. When his mother asked him how he'd liked the game in the park, Luke answered slowly, "It's okay. But they don't have real bats, just sticks."

Then he remembered how he and his friend Jesse had sanded their own bats and used cardboard for bases back home. Thinking of Jesse made Luke feel sad. Suddenly he didn't feel like eating anymore.

But that pizza smelled *so* good! Luke finished his slice, then ate two more. He couldn't help it. The pizza was delicious.

That night, as Luke lay in bed, the noises of the city drifted up to his window. He couldn't hear any crickets, but someone in their building was playing a recording. He perked his ears and recognized the song, one of his favorites. Alberta used to sing it while they gathered fallen peaches in the orchard. Luke turned in bed and hummed a few bars of the song.

He thought about the two red-haired girls. They must be twins, he decided. They were good at stickball. Not better than Alberta, but they were good.

Luke's thoughts continued to pile up. It didn't seem possible that the day was over. His eyelids felt so heavy, he had to close his eyes. Tired as he was, he couldn't sleep. He wondered if Jesse was sleeping.

He remembered the delicious pizza he'd had that day. Jesse would have loved it. "Jesse *will* love it," Luke corrected himself, "when he comes to visit."

"Yes, Jesse, Mark, and me." Luke murmured as he fell asleep.

 **R**eader's Response

How did you feel about the way in which the writer described the experience of moving to a new city?

# A Good Chance

## Checking Your Comprehension

1. Why did Luke and his parents move to San Francisco?
2. Luke's new home in San Francisco was very different from his home in Esperanza. Describe how his old home and his new home were different.
3. At what point in the story did you know that Luke had begun to adjust to his new home? What signals in the story told you this?
4. What did Luke's remark at the end of the story, "Yes, Jesse, Mark, and me," tell you about how Luke felt?
5. Compare the advantages and disadvantages of life in a small town like Esperanza versus a big city like San Francisco.
6. What do you think would be another good title for this story?

## Writing to Learn

**THINK AND ANALYZE**   What did Luke expect, and what did Luke discover? Copy and complete the expectations chart below.

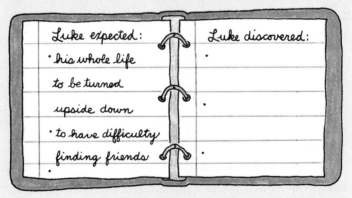

**WRITE**   Have you ever had an experience that turned out differently from what you expected? Write an expectations chart like the one above for your adventure. Then use the chart to help you write a story about your adventure and its unexpected ending.

**"D**id you ask him," your sister whispers, "or was he in a bad mood?" We all have moods: good ones, bad ones, medium ones. When you're in a great mood, everything you look at seems great. The sun seems to be shining just for you. The air feels good on your skin. You smile and you feel little bursts of happiness.

But when you're in an awful mood, everything seems to go wrong. Your best friend hates you. The sun is too bright and makes you squint. You scowl and feel rotten about everything around you. The way you feel inside affects how you see the world outside. And what you see and experience in the outside world may make the feelings you have stronger.

## Mood in Writing

In poems and stories, writers can create moods, too. By carefully choosing details, an author can create a light, humorous mood or a dark, somber mood. This mood will sometimes reflect how the characters are feeling. You can determine the mood of a story by looking at the details the writer has chosen.

"Dakota Dugout" and "If You Say So, Claude" are both about the prairie. Both are told from the point of view of women who had to settle there. But the mood of "If You Say So, Claude" is entirely different from the mood of "Dakota Dugout."

The author of "Dakota Dugout," Ann Turner, shows you how she feels about her first prairie home. Read her description at the beginning of the poem:

Matt's cave.
Built from sod, you know,
with a special iron plow
that sliced the long earth strips.
Matt cut them into bricks,
laid them up, dug into a hill
that was our first home.
I cried when I saw it.

The author creates a somber mood to tell you how she felt. You can almost sense her feelings of loneliness and despair as she huddled in her "cave" of a house.

Contrast the mood of "Dakota Dugout" with this description of the landscape in "If You Say So, Claude":

The trail into that great state called Texas curled east and southeast into its heartland. And as it rose it softened into rolling hills, with meadows cupped between. Splashes of blue and gold and red wild-flowers dotted the grassy hillsides.

The mood of the description is completely different from that in "Dakota Dugout." Phrases like "rolling hills," "blue and gold and red wild-flowers," and "grassy hillsides" create a mood of warmth and happiness.

Sometimes there is a shift in the mood of a story or poem, reflecting a change in the feelings of the characters or the author. For example, when spring finally arrives in "Dakota Dugout," the mood becomes much more hopeful, and the author remembers "geese like yarn in the sky, / green spreading faster than fire." The mood of the poem has changed from somber to warm and joyful.

## Read and Enjoy

The next story is "Can She Sing?" As you read it, notice the details the author includes. Then try to figure out the mood of the story.

Anna and Caleb love their home on the prairie. But something is missing that only a special person can provide.

# Can She Sing?

*from Sarah, Plain and Tall*
*written by Patricia MacLachlan*
*illustration by Maria Sewall*

"Did Mama sing every day?" asked Caleb. "Every-single-day?"
He sat close to the fire, his chin in his hand. It was dusk, and the
dogs lay beside him on the warm hearthstones.

"Every-single-day," I told him for the second time this week.
For the twentieth time this month. The hundredth time this year?
And the past few years?

"And did Papa sing, too?"

"Yes, Papa sang, too. Don't get so close, Caleb. You'll
heat up."

He pushed his chair back. It made a hollow scraping sound
on the hearthstones, and the dogs stirred. Lottie, small and
black, wagged her tail and lifted her head. Nick slept on.

I turned the bread dough over and over on the marble slab
on the kitchen table.

"Well, Papa doesn't sing anymore," said Caleb very softly. A
log broke apart and crackled in the fireplace. He looked up at me.
"What did I look like when I was born?"

"You didn't have any clothes on," I told him.

"I know that," he said.

"You looked like this," I held the bread dough up in a round pale ball.

"I had hair," said Caleb seriously.

"Not enough to talk about," I said.

"And she named me Caleb," he went on, filling in the old familiar story.

"*I* would have named you Troublesome," I said, making Caleb smile.

"And Mama handed me to you in the yellow blanket and said. . . ." He waited for me to finish the story. "And said? . . ."

I sighed. "And Mama said, 'Isn't he beautiful, Anna?' "

"And I was," Caleb finished.

Caleb thought the story was over, and I didn't tell him what I had really thought. He was homely and plain, and he had a terrible holler and a horrid smell. But these were not the worst of him. Mama died the next morning. That was the worst thing about Caleb.

"Isn't he beautiful, Anna?" Her last words to me. I had gone to bed thinking how wretched he looked. And I forgot to say good night.

I wiped my hands on my apron and went to the window. Outside, the prairie reached out and touched the places where the sky came down. Though winter was nearly over, there were patches of snow and ice everywhere. I looked at the long dirt road that crawled across the plains, remembering the morning that Mama had died, cruel and sunny. They had come for her in a wagon and taken her away to be buried. And then the cousins and aunts and uncles had come and tried to fill up the house. But they couldn't.

Slowly, one by one, they left. And then the days seemed

long and dark like winter days, even though it wasn't winter. And Papa didn't sing.

*Isn't he beautiful, Anna?*

*No, Mama.*

It was hard to think of Caleb as beautiful. It took three whole days for me to love him, sitting in the chair by the fire. Papa washing up the supper dishes. Caleb's tiny hand brushing my cheek. And a smile. It was the smile. I know.

"Can you remember her songs?" asked Caleb. "Mama's songs?"

I turned from the window. "No. Only that she sang about flowers and birds. Sometimes about the moon at nighttime."

Caleb reached down and touched Lottie's head.

"Maybe," he said, his voice low, "if you remember the songs, then I might remember her, too."

My eyes widened and tears came. Then the door opened and wind blew in with Papa, and I went to stir the stew. Papa put his arms around me and put his nose in my hair.

"Nice soapy smell, that stew," he said.

I laughed, "That's my hair."

Caleb came over and threw his arms around Papa's neck and hung down as Papa swung him back and forth, and the dogs sat up.

"Cold in town," said Papa. "And Jack was feisty." Jack was Papa's horse that he'd raised from a colt. "Rascal," murmured Papa, smiling, because no matter what Jack did Papa loved him.

I spooned up the stew and lighted the oil lamp and we ate with the dogs crowding under the table, hoping for spills or handouts.

Papa might not have told us about Sarah that night if Caleb hadn't asked him the question. After the dishes were cleared and washed and Papa was filling the tin pail with ashes, Caleb spoke up. It wasn't a question, really.

"You don't sing anymore," he said. He said it harshly. Not because he meant to, but because he had been thinking of it for so long. "Why?" he asked more gently.

Slowly Papa straightened up. There was a long silence, and the dogs looked up, wondering at it.

"I've forgotten the old songs," said Papa quietly. He sat down. "But maybe there's a way to remember them." He looked up at us.

"How?" asked Caleb eagerly.

Papa leaned back in the chair. "I've placed an advertisement in the newspapers. For help."

"You mean a housekeeper?" I asked, surprised.

Caleb and I looked at each other and burst out laughing, remembering Hilly, our old housekeeper. She was round and slow and shuffling. She snored in a high whistle at night, like a teakettle, and let the fire go out.

"No," said Papa slowly. "Not a housekeeper." He paused. "A wife."

Caleb stared at Papa. "A wife? You mean a mother?"

Nick slid his face onto Papa's lap and Papa stroked his ears.

"That, too," said Papa. "Like Maggie."

Matthew, our neighbor to the south, had written to ask for a wife and a mother for his children. And Maggie had come from Tennessee. Her hair was the color of turnips and she laughed.

Papa reached into his pocket and unfolded a letter written on white paper. "And I have received an answer." Papa read to us:

**"Dear Mr. Jacob Witting,**

**"I am Sarah Wheaton from Maine as you will see from my letter. I am answering your advertisement. I have never been married, though I have been asked. I have lived with an older brother, William, who is about to be married. His wife-to-be is young and energetic.**

"I have always loved to live by the sea, but at this time I feel a move is necessary. And the truth is, the sea is as far east as I can go. My choice, as you can see, is limited. This should not be taken as an insult. I am strong and I work hard and I am willing to travel. But I am not mild mannered. If you should still care to write, I would be interested in your children and about where you live. And you.

"Very truly yours,
"Sarah Elisabeth Wheaton


"P.S. Do you have opinions on cats? I have one."


No one spoke when Papa finished the letter. He kept looking at it in his hands, reading it over to himself. Finally I turned my head a bit to sneak a look at Caleb. He was smiling. I smiled, too.

"One thing," I said in the quiet of the room.

"What's that?" asked Papa, looking up.

I put my arm around Caleb.

"Ask her if she sings," I said.

Caleb and Papa and I wrote letters to Sarah, and before the ice and snow had melted from the fields, we all received answers. Mine came first.


Dear Anna,

Yes, I can braid hair and I can make stew and bake bread, though I prefer to build bookshelves and paint.

My favorite colors are the colors of the sea, blue and gray and green, depending on the weather. My brother William is a fisherman, and he tells me that when he is in the middle of a fogbound sea the water is a color for which there is no name. He catches flounder and sea bass and bluefish. Sometimes he sees whales. And birds, too, of course. I am enclosing a book of sea birds so you will see what William and I see every day.

Very truly yours,
Sarah Elisabeth Wheaton

Caleb read and read the letter so many times that the ink began to run and the folds tore. He read the book about sea birds over and over.

"Do you think she'll come?" asked Caleb. "And will she stay? What if she thinks we are loud and pesky?"

"You *are* loud and pesky," I told him. But I was worried, too. Sarah loved the sea, I could tell. Maybe she wouldn't leave there after all to come where there were fields and grass and sky and not much else.

"What if she comes and doesn't like our house?" Caleb asked. "I told her it was small. Maybe I shouldn't have told her it was small."

"Hush, Caleb. Hush."

Caleb's letter came soon after, with a picture of a cat drawn on the envelope.

Dear Caleb,

My cat's name is Seal because she is gray like the seals that swim offshore in Maine. She is glad that Lottie and Nick send their greetings. She likes dogs most of the time. She says their footprints are much larger than hers (which she is enclosing in return).

Your house sounds lovely, even though it is far out in the country with no close neighbors. My house is tall and the shingles are gray because of the salt from the sea. There are roses nearby.

Yes, I do like small rooms sometimes. Yes, I can keep a fire going at night. I do not know if I snore. Seal has never told me.

Very truly yours,
Sarah Elisabeth

"Did you really ask her about fires and snoring?" I asked, amazed.

"I wished to know," Caleb said.

He kept the letter with him, reading it in the barn and in the fields and by the cow pond. And always in bed at night.

One morning, early, Papa and Caleb and I were cleaning out the horse stalls and putting down new bedding. Papa stopped suddenly and leaned on his pitchfork.

"Sarah has said she will come for a month's time if we wish her to," he said, his voice loud in the dark barn. "To see how it is. Just to see."

Caleb stood by the stall door and folded his arms across his chest.

"I think," he began. Then, "I think," he said slowly, "that it would be good—to say yes," he finished in a rush.

Papa looked at me.

"I say yes," I told him, grinning.

"Yes," said Papa. "Then yes it is."

And the three of us, all smiling, went to work again.

The next day Papa went to town to mail his letter to Sarah. It was rainy for days, and the clouds followed. The house was cool and damp and quiet. Once I set four places at the table, then caught myself and put the extra plate away. Three lambs were born, one with a black face. And then Papa's letter came. It was very short.

**Dear Jacob,**

**I will come by train. I will wear a yellow bonnet. I am plain and tall.**

**Sarah**

"What's that?" asked Caleb excitedly, peering over Papa's shoulder. He pointed. "There, written at the bottom of the letter."

Papa read it to himself. Then he smiled, holding up the letter for us to see.

*Tell them I sing* was all it said.

Sarah came in the spring. She came through green grass fields that bloomed with Indian paintbrush, red and orange, and blue-eyed grass.

Papa got up early for the long day's trip to the train and back. He brushed his hair so slick and shiny that Caleb laughed. He wore a clean blue shirt, and a belt instead of suspenders.

He fed and watered the horses, talking to them as he hitched them up to the wagon. Old Bess, calm and kind; Jack, wild-eyed, reaching over to nip Bess on the neck.

"Clear day, Bess," said Papa, rubbing her nose.

"Settle down, Jack." He leaned his head on Jack.

And then Papa drove off along the dirt road to fetch Sarah. Papa's new wife. Maybe. Maybe our new mother.

Gophers ran back and forth across the road, stopping to stand up and watch the wagon. Far off in the field a woodchuck ate and listened. Ate and listened.

Caleb and I did our chores without talking. We shoveled out the stalls and laid down new hay. We fed the sheep. We swept and straightened and carried wood and water. And then our chores were done.

Caleb pulled on my shirt.

"Is my face clean?" he asked. "Can my face be *too* clean?" He looked alarmed.

"No, your face is clean but not too clean," I said.

Caleb slipped his hand into mine as we stood on the porch, watching the road. He was afraid.

"Will she be nice?" he asked. "Like Maggie?"

"Sarah will be nice," I told him.

"How far away is Maine?" he asked.

"You know how far. Far away, by the sea."

"Will Sarah bring some sea?" he asked.

"No, you cannot bring the sea."

The sheep ran in the field, and far off the cows moved slowly to the pond, like turtles.

"Will she like us?" asked Caleb very softly.

I watched a marsh hawk wheel down behind the barn.

He looked up at me.

"Of course she will like us." He answered his own question. "We are nice," he added, making me smile.

We waited and watched. I rocked on the porch and Caleb rolled a marble on the wood floor. Back and forth. Back and forth. The marble was blue.

We saw the dust from the wagon first, rising above the road, above the heads of Jack and Old Bess. Caleb climbed up onto the porch roof and shaded his eyes.

"A bonnet!" he cried. "I see a yellow bonnet!"

The dogs came out from under the porch, ears up, their eyes on the cloud of dust bringing Sarah. The wagon passed the fenced field, and the cows and sheep looked up, too. It rounded the windmill and the barn and the windbreak of Russian olive that Mama had planted long ago. Nick began to bark, then Lottie, and the wagon clattered into the yard and stopped by the steps.

"Hush," said Papa to the dogs.

And it was quiet.

Sarah stepped down from the wagon, a cloth bag in her

hand. She reached up and took off her yellow bonnet, smoothing back her brown hair into a bun. She was plain and tall.

"Did you bring some sea?" cried Caleb beside me.

"Something from the sea," said Sarah, smiling. "And me." She turned and lifted a black case from the wagon. "And Seal, too."

Carefully she opened the case, and Seal, gray with white feet, stepped out. Lottie lay down, her head on her paws, staring. Nick leaned down to sniff. Then he lay down, too.

"The cat will be good in the barn," said Papa. "For mice."

Sarah smiled. "She will be good in the house, too."

Sarah took Caleb's hand, then mine. Her hands were large and rough. She gave Caleb a shell—a moon snail, she called it—that was curled and smelled of salt.

"The gulls fly high and drop the shells on the rocks below," she told Caleb. "When the shell is broken, they eat what is inside."

"That is very smart," said Caleb.

"For you, Anna," said Sarah, "a sea stone."

And she gave me the smoothest and whitest stone I had ever seen.

"The sea washes over and over and around the stone, rolling it until it is round and perfect."

"That is very smart, too," said Caleb. He looked up at Sarah. "We do not have the sea here."

Sarah turned and looked out over the plains.

"No," she said. "There is no sea here. But the land rolls a little like the sea."

My father did not see her look, but I did. And I knew that Caleb had seen it, too. Sarah was not smiling. Sarah was already lonely. In a month's time the preacher might come to marry Sarah and Papa. And a month was a long time. Time enough for her to change her mind and leave us.

Papa took Sarah's bags inside, where her room was ready

with a quilt on the bed and blue flax dried in a vase on the night table.

Seal stretched and made a small cat sound. I watched her circle the dogs and sniff the air. Caleb came out and stood beside me.

"When will we sing?" he whispered.

I shook my head, turning the white stone over and over in my hand. I wished everything was as perfect as the stone. I wished that Papa and Caleb and I were perfect for Sarah. I wished we had a sea of our own.

The dogs loved Sarah first. Lottie slept beside her bed, curled in a soft circle, and Nick leaned his face on the covers in the morning, watching for the first sign that Sarah was awake. No one knew where Seal slept. Seal was a roamer.

Sarah's collection of shells sat on the windowsill.

"A scallop," she told us, picking up the shells one by one, "a sea clam, an oyster, a razor clam. And a conch shell. If you put it to your ear you can hear the sea." She put it to Caleb's ear, then mine. Papa listened, too. Then Sarah listened once more, with a look so sad and far away that Caleb leaned against me.

"At least Sarah can hear the sea," he whispered.

Papa was quiet and shy with Sarah, and so was I. But Caleb talked to Sarah from morning until the light left the sky.

"Where are you going?" he asked. "To do what?"

"To pick flowers," said Sarah. "I'll hang some of them upside down and dry them so they'll keep some color. And we can have flowers all winter long."

"I'll come, too!" cried Caleb. "Sarah said winter," he said to me. "That means Sarah will stay."

Together we picked flowers, paintbrush and clover and prairie violets. There were buds on the wild roses that climbed up the paddock fence.

"The roses will bloom in early summer," I told Sarah. I looked to see if she knew what I was thinking. Summer was when the wedding would be. *Might* be. Sarah and Papa's wedding.

We hung the flowers from the ceiling in little bunches. "I've never seen this before," said Sarah. "What is it called?"

"Bride's bonnet," I told her.

Caleb smiled at the name.

"We don't have this by the sea," she said. "We have seaside goldenrod and wild asters and woolly ragwort."

"Woolly ragwort!" Caleb whooped. He made up a song.

*"Woolly ragwort all around,*
*Woolly ragwort on the ground.*
*Woolly ragwort grows and grows,*
*Woolly ragwort in your nose."*

Sarah and Papa laughed, and the dogs lifted their heads and thumped their tails against the wood floor. Seal sat on a kitchen chair and watched us with yellow eyes.

We ate Sarah's stew, the late light coming through the windows. Papa had baked bread that was still warm from the fire.

"The stew is fine," said Papa.

"Ayuh." Sarah nodded. "The bread, too."

"What does 'ayuh' mean?" asked Caleb.

"In Maine it means yes," said Sarah. "Do you want more stew?"

"Ayuh," said Caleb.

"Ayuh," echoed my father.

After dinner Sarah told us about William. "He has a gray-and-white boat named *Kittiwake*." She looked out the window. "That is a small gull found way off the shore where William fishes. There are three aunts who live near us. They wear silk dresses and no shoes. You would love them."

"Ayuh," said Caleb.

"Does your brother look like you?" I asked.

"Yes," said Sarah. "He is plain and tall."

At dusk Sarah cut Caleb's hair on the front steps, gathering his curls and scattering them on the fence and ground. Seal batted some hair around the porch as the dogs watched.

"Why?" asked Caleb.

"For the birds," said Sarah. "They will use it for their nests. Later we can look for nests of curls."

"Sarah said 'later,'" Caleb whispered to me as we spread his hair about. "Sarah will stay."

Sarah cut Papa's hair, too. No one else saw, but I found him behind the barn, tossing the pieces of hair into the wind for the birds.

Sarah brushed my hair and tied it up in back with a rose velvet ribbon she had brought from Maine. She brushed hers long and free and tied it back, too, and we stood side by side looking into the mirror. I looked taller, like Sarah, and fair and thin. And with my hair pulled back I looked a little like her daughter. Sarah's daughter.

And then it was time for singing.

## ◆ LIBRARY LINK ◆

*To enjoy more episodes about Sarah, read the rest of the book* Sarah, Plain and Tall *by Patricia MacLachlan.*

## Reader's Response

What quality would you look for in a person who was going to play an important role in your life?

## *Writing an Explanation*

In this unit you learned that homes can change. Can you predict what homes of the future will be like? What new inventions will be part of future homes?

Build on your knowledge of homes today and write a prediction of what homes will be like in the future. In two paragraphs, tell what a home of the future might be like. Your use of specific statements and exact details will help your classmates picture a new and interesting house of the future.

### *Prewriting*

Prepare to write by making a chart. Your chart should show differences between present-day homes and a home of the future. Look at the chart that has been started for you. Copy it and add more information. You will use the details from the chart when you begin writing about the future home of your grandchildren's grandchildren.

### *Writing*

Ideas from the chart will help you write about an imaginary home of the future. Pretend you are on the doorstep of the home. Imagine that you have rung the bell and asked the owner for a tour. Tell what you see, hear, and experience as you walk through the home.

## Houses

|  | *Now* | *In the Future* |
|---|---|---|
| *Heat* | oil burner | solar heat |
| *Windows* | small windows | large windows cover one side of house |
| *Cleanliness* | moderately clean | hospital-clean with air filters and continuous cleaning machines on floors and windows |

### Revising

When you revise, look for details. Try to use exact words and give precise information. Room measurements, temperature-control methods, size and location of windows, construction materials, and the size of gardens are only a few of the specific details that you could include.

### Proofreading

Check for spelling, punctuation, and capitalization mistakes. Make a clean copy.

### Publishing

Make a *Homes of the Future* class book. Add drawings or other illustrations.

# WORKING TOGETHER

## *Presenting a Scene*

Stories in this unit focused on the different places people refer to as "home." The authors of these stories could have chosen to write their ideas in the form of a play. Below is part of a scene, in script form, from the story "On My Way Home." A narrator has been added to give the background information an author usually provides. Notice that characters' names are followed by a colon, and that quotation marks around the dialogue are not necessary.

Now your group will write a script and present a scene from a story in this unit.

The members of your group should do these things to help the group work:

> Presenting a Scene
>
> NARRATOR: Jean and Andrea imagine what their new school would be like.
> ANDREA: There will definitely be boys in your class.
> JEAN: Naturally. I've seen boys before. So what?

- Encourage everyone to share their ideas
- Help the group reach agreement
- Show appreciation for everyone's contribution
- Agree or disagree in a pleasant way

You may want to look at the stories again to help everyone think of ideas. Discuss scenes that would make interesting scripts. As a group, decide on one scene to use. Then, agree on what information is important to the script and what can be omitted. Make a list of the cast of characters, and don't forget to add a narrator. Take turns writing lines for the script.

When the script is finished, agree on who will play each part and present your scene to the class.

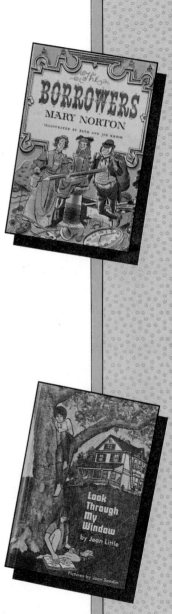

***The Borrowers*** by Mary Norton *(Harcourt, 1986)* Have you ever noticed that pins, rubber bands, and pencils seem just to disappear? If so, there may be borrowers living in the walls of your house.

***The House of Dies Drear*** by Virginia Hamilton *(Macmillan, 1968)* The whole family knows that their new home had been a stop on the Underground Railroad. But Thomas and his father are determined to uncover the mystery that surrounds the house.

***Building a House*** by Ken Robbins *(Four Winds, 1984)* A house does not just appear! From the planning stages through construction and on to the final touches, this book describes each step of the way.

***Look Through My Window*** by Jean Little *(Harper, 1970)* Home for Emily Blair has always been an apartment with her parents. Life changes abruptly when the Blairs, joined by Emily's four younger cousins, move to an eighteen-room house.

***Owls in the Family*** by Farley Mowat *(Bantam, 1981)* Billy's pets already include a dog, pigeons, gophers, and white rats! How will his family feel about adding owls to the household?

# Browsing for Books

## *Your Own Library*

How many books are there in your house that are your own? You probably have many more than you think, especially if you count all your picture books, and the early readers that you read when you were very young.

In fact, you may even have enough books to start your own library. The most important thing about a library isn't to have lots of books. It's having just a few good books that you really like. If you have those, there are only two other things you need for a library. The first is a place to keep your books. A shelf or even a space at the back of your desk could be a fine place to start. Or, perhaps you could stack some boxes in a convenient corner. It doesn't have to be fancy as long as it is your own special place—a place that says, ''These are my books. This is my library.''

The second thing you need is a way to organize your books—some categories to keep the different kinds of books separate. For one person, that could mean different sections for baseball, football, and basketball stories. For another, there would be books by each of several science-fiction writers.

A question you might have is, ''Why start my own library?'' One good reason is that it's fun, and it's an easy way to start a collection. So, if you've always wanted to have a collection but didn't know what to collect or how to get started, or if you didn't think you could afford to collect expensive coins, stamps, or dolls, try starting a library. With just a few books and a place to keep them, your collection will be well on the way. And the books will always be there to remind you of the great experience you've had reading them.

# The Comeback Dog

## Jane Resh Thomas

drawings by
Troy Howell

"I don't want another dog! I hate dogs!" Daniel shouted. "I wish I'd never laid eyes on Captain!"

"Daniel, you've done nothing but mope around this house since Captain died," said his mother. "A month is long enough."

The canary at the window had stopped singing. Daniel put his head down on the table and played with his fork. "You and Pa don't even care," he said.

"Of course we care," said his mother. She removed the hairpin from the knot at the back of her neck, twisted her lank hair several turns tighter, and jabbed the pin back into place. "We knew Captain fourteen years—five years longer than we've known you. We even knew his mother when *she* was a pup."

"You act as if you don't care," repeated Daniel.

"Stop it!" his mother snapped. "I miss Captain so much I dream about him at night."

Daniel jumped up, overturning his chair. He left it there and ran out into the cold February morning. He jumped the porch steps, with his parka in one hand, and started down the walk. His teeth were chattering, but not from the cold. He jammed his fists into the parka's sleeves, ripping the lining at one armhole, and kicked a chunk of ice that sat on the walk. The ice had melted enough in yesterday's sun to freeze fast to the cement during the night, and it didn't yield when Daniel kicked it. For a minute, he thought he had broken his toe. He hoped he had. The pain in his foot helped him forget the other pain.

As his anger cooled, Daniel thought of what he had lost. It was like feeling the socket with his tongue when he'd lost a tooth, tasting the blood, stroking the tender spot, measuring the empty space.

No more Captain, who had pulled Daniel out of the water when he was a baby and had chased a frog into the pond. No more Captain, who had waited with Daniel at the school bus stop every dark winter morning and met him there every afternoon; who slept beside his bed and woke him snuffling with a cold nose at Daniel's ear.

He wandered across the farmyard, stepping in the footprints that pocked yesterday's mud. Overnight, water had frozen in the foot-shaped pools. As the ice crackled and shattered under his boots, he enjoyed the small destruction.

He picked up a fragile wafer of ice from a puddle and held it up before one eye. Through the ice, the world looked crooked and blurry. The straight lines of the windmill, with its blades going like sixty as the wind gusted, seemed broken and disconnected. Daniel could distinguish only masses of color: the dusty red of the barn and the silvery gray of the chicken coop. But the world *felt* crooked and blurry whether he was peering through ice or not. He dropped the glassy pane and watched it break into crystals at his feet.

A muddy red pickup truck with a noisy muffler pulled into the yard. Daniel looked up and nodded at the veterinarian who kept the cows healthy. Usually he enjoyed watching the vet deliver a calf or give the cows their shots. Today he didn't want to talk. Doc might ask where Captain was.

Daniel scooped up a handful of stones in the driveway and limped to the roadside ditch. He liked to throw stones through the culvert that carried the ditch water under the drive, liked the *doink, doink, doink* sounds they made as they bounced through the steel tube. He threw the first stone sidearm as hard as he could, but it made no sound. He threw a bigger rock, this one the size of an egg, but the culvert swallowed it as silently as if it were a cotton ball.

He brushed the ground clear of snow and glass that had splintered in the ditch last fall when a pair of deer hunters had shot bottles off the mailbox. Daniel had plugged the holes in the box with sticks to keep the rain out; the buckshot was still embedded in the weathered wooden post. Pa said it was a wonder the ignoramuses hadn't shot a cow or mistaken the house for a deer.

Daniel knelt in the ditch and looked down the tunnel. A dirty bundle filled the end of the culvert. As his eyes adjusted, he could see that the bundle was not rags or papers, but an animal with matted, dirty hair.

"It must be dead," he thought, "or it would have yelped when the stones hit it. That's all I need—another dead critter to bury."

Daniel sighed and looked out across the fields where he and Captain had played. He looked back at the animal blocking the culvert. If he left it there, when the snow melted, the runoff in the ditch would back up and flood the yard. He

reached in and felt the cold metal and the cold stones he had thrown. The warmth of the body surprised him as he heaved it out into the ditch.

"You're a dog, and you're breathing," he said. "Just barely."

The dog's eyes were open but dull. Mud clotted its white fur and made the black patches indistinct. It bared its teeth, but it didn't growl, as if moving its lips took all its strength.

Light though it was for its size, it was too big and awkward for Daniel to carry. He ran to get his rusty wagon from under the back porch and put a couple of old gunny sacks in the bottom. Powdery earth from the potatoes that had been stored in the bags sifted into the air, but the dog was so dirty and sick that Daniel thought it wouldn't notice a little dust.

He ran back to the culvert with the wagon clattering and bouncing behind him. Hurry. Load the bag of bones into the wagon. Cushion its head. Ease across the ruts the tractor had made yesterday in the sun-softened mud that now was frozen hard again. Hurry past the chicken coop. Past the corncrib.

Up the concrete ramp they went and into the barn, where Pa and Doc stood, shining a light into the mouth of a cow. Though Daniel was panting too hard to speak, the men took in everything at a glance and moved immediately to help.

"Let's get her off this cold steel so's I can look her over." Doc lifted the dog into a manger that was half full of fragrant hay. "Where'd you find her?"

"In the culvert at the end of the drive. Do you suppose she was hit by a car and crawled in there to get shelter?"

"I don't know, but she's in bad shape," said Doc. He sucked his front teeth, as he always did when he worried. Gently he flexed the dog's joints. He prodded her belly and shone the flashlight in her eyes. He listened to her chest through his stethoscope. All the while, the dog lay still and unresisting.

"Well, you got yourself a young female here," said Doc. "She looks sound. Don't think she's been in any accidents, but she's near starved to death. Run your hand along those slats."

Daniel felt the dog's ribs.

"There's no meat to pad the bone. Doubt she'll make it through the day, Dan." The vet thought for a moment, rubbing his whiskered jaw. "I'm a cow man, of course, no expert in small animals."

"She's a full-grown English setter," said Pa, sizing her up, gauging her quality. "Look at those big paws. Nice broad muzzle. Tall at the shoulder. A rangy, heavy-boned dog like this is a powerful hunter. She could have run all day. What a shame for a fine animal to come to such grief."

"You talk as if she was already dead," said Daniel. "Can't we do something for her?"

"She's sick to death," said Doc. "We can speed her along. I've got some stuff in my bag. One shot will put her

out nice and easy. She won't feel a thing but the prick of the needle. It would be a mercy, Dan."

"No!" Daniel shouted. The stanchions creaked as all of the black-and-white cows swung their heads in unison to stare at him. "I found her," he said in a quieter voice. "I'll take care of her."

Doc looked at him over his glasses. "Okay. You can try to bring her back. Put her by the stove and try to feed her a spoonful of broth every quarter hour or so. You can try, but don't expect any miracles."

Daniel took off his parka. With Doc's help he wrapped it around the big dog and buttoned it. His father picked up the bundle in his arms, cradling it like a baby. The dog's face was white as a skull in the shadows of the hood. Her scraggly, almost hairless tail hung down like an icy rope.

"I'll finish up here on my own," said Doc. "You call me tomorrow morning early and tell me how you're doing, Daniel. Hear?"

The boy nodded. He felt thin and small, shivering there in his shirt-sleeves, surrounded by things bigger than himself— the tall, muscular men, the hulking cows, the hugeness of the barn itself. High overhead in the rafters, a pigeon flapped. The cows chewed their hay, noisy and wide-eyed, as if a full mouth were all the world to them. With the same oblivious gaze, they would stare at the wall or whisk flies with their tails or step unawares on a kitten.

Daniel opened the door for his father. "Come on, dog," he said. "You're not dead yet."

Crossing the yard they leaned against the wind. Daniel's thin shirt billowed, baring his chest to the cold, but he kept his hand like a lifeline on the dog's flank. He noticed how smoothly his father moved and how easily the big dog lay in his arms.

"Guess we got too smug and comfortable yesterday in that thaw," said Daniel's father, glancing at the heaped gray clouds at the end of the sky. "Winter's going to remind us who's boss. He'll pick us up and shake us and set us down again when he's good and ready."

"A north wind like this swoops right through the culvert," said Daniel. "She wouldn't have lasted much longer, that dog."

"We'll put her by the stove and see what happens."

They avoided the broken board in the creaky steps.

"You were going to fix that Thursday, and here it is Saturday morning already," Daniel's father said. "Those steps have got to be fixed before something worse than a board gets broken, and I don't have the time."

"They'll be right when you come back to the house," said Daniel.

As the kitchen door slammed behind them, his mother looked up from the dishes she was washing and smiled. "Well, I see you came back," she said. "Who's that wearing your parka?"

Daniel's father laid the dog gently on the floor. "She's all yours, Son. I'll be in the barn," he said.

Daniel pushed back the hood of the parka. "I'll need some rags, Mama. She's sick, but Doc says there's always hope."

His mother shook the soapsuds on her hands into the sink and reached for the rag bag that hung on a hook in the pantry. "Lord knows we've got plenty of rags. I can hardly tell the difference between the rags and the clothes we're wearing." She sighed. "We'll put her by the wood stove."

"I'm afraid she'll stink."

"I've smelled worse than wet dog," his mother said. "We can always air the house."

"Doc said to give her a little broth every fifteen minutes."

"Then I'll put a tough old hen on to stew, and we'll have creamed chicken and peas for supper." She hugged the boy. "I'm glad for your kind heart, Daniel."

Arranging the faded rags behind the stove in the dining room, between the woodbox and the couch, the boy noticed that the wood was nearly gone. On such bitter windy days, the oil furnace made too little heat, and the stove gobbled logs faster than Daniel could chop them and carry them in.

As he moved the dog to her bed, she half opened her eyes, but they looked dull and blind. He and his mother dried the dog's coat with towels. She groaned, as if the gentlest touch hurt her bones.

"What's her name?" said Mama.

"I'm afraid to name her."

"How about something contrary, like Fang? Or Wolf? Maybe we can scare off death with a joke," said his mother.

"Lady," said Daniel. "That's what I'm going to call her."

"All right, then. Lady she is."

When the broth was ready, Daniel filled a medicine dropper and emptied it inside the dog's cheek. Twice the broth dribbled out of her muzzle, but she swallowed the third dropperful.

"Let her rest now," said Mama. "More than a few drops

at a time might make her throw up. Then she'd be worse off than she was without us."

As Daniel knelt beside the dog, he thought of Captain. He jumped up before the tears could get a good start.

"Your parka's in the washing machine," said Mama. "It was smeared with mud inside and out. Wear this for now."

She helped him into his father's old flannel-lined denim jacket. He let her put one hand on the back of his head and hug him close for a moment. She was all bone and muscle and hard spots, but her touch was gentle.

"Help her the best you can, Daniel. Then the rest is out of your hands," she said. "I see the woodbox is empty."

"Couldn't you let me off chores just once?" said Daniel.

"We've all got as much work as we can do," said Mama. "Who's going to do yours, if you don't?"

"Can't I watch the dog? Just once, couldn't the rules be changed?"

"Vigilance won't cure that dog. What's going to keep her warm, or us, if we run out of wood?"

Daniel pulled away and flung himself out the back door. At the woodpile, he picked up the knotty chunk of oak that had fought the ax all winter and set it angrily on the chopping block. He chopped and chopped with all his strength, and every time the ax fell, the knot squirted off the block.

Furious, he sharpened the ax on the hand-turned grindstone Pa kept in the woodshed, wedged the knot between two logs, and chopped some more. By the time he had worn himself out, the wood lay in irregular pieces at his feet. Too tired to be angry anymore, he carried them into the house, avoiding the broken step again, and laid them on the fire. When he clanged the stove door shut, he saw the dog jump slightly.

He gave her another dropper of broth. This time she opened her eyes fully.

"Nice dog," said Daniel. His words sounded clumsy. Was he forgetting how to talk to a dog? he wondered.

He carefully smoothed her head, as his mother had caressed his own. She slept again. Daniel thought she was breathing more deeply, with less effort.

He went outside, determined to fix the back steps before Pa caught him with the job undone. He could smell the wood smoke in the air. The gray clouds were moving in rapidly; soon the blizzard would drive him indoors. He hauled out the lumber Pa had stored under the porch and assembled his tools—a crowbar for loosening the broken board, a folding measuring stick, a saw and hammer, and a handful of two-inch nails.

He pried the old board off, carefully saving the rusted, bent nails in his jacket pocket; they could be straightened when he had more time, and used again. He measured one of the planks in the steps and marked the new lumber with a pencil. Again he measured, checking the board against the step. His father had trusted him with expensive wood; a plank sawed too short was a wasted plank.

For his fifth birthday, Daniel's father had given him a red toolbox filled with tools fit for a man's use, not just toys that bent and broke in real work. Now, four years later, Daniel could saw a straight line or drive a spike straight and true. He could drill a hole or sand a board silky smooth. Last fall he had built a table for his mother's Christmas present.

He sawed the board where he had marked it, set it in its place, and drove two nails, one at each end, to attach it. Worried about Lady, he dragged a crate to the dining-room window, so he could keep an eye on her. Standing there on his tiptoes, he saw the canary hopping in its cage. The dog lay behind the stove where he had left her. She lay as still as stone. Dreading that she had stopped breathing, he went indoors but found that she was only asleep. She roused and accepted more broth.

Mama came into the dining room with an armload of folded laundry. It still smelled fresh from blowing in yesterday's warm wind.

"Don't fret—I'm keeping watch over her too," she said. "You've done just the right things for her, Daniel." She set the stack of clothes on the table and shook out a heavy red and black shirt. "Pa's jacket is so big on you, I fixed your heavy hunting shirt."

"Thanks," said Daniel, "but I'd rather wear Pa's." Daniel liked wearing his father's clothes, even though they hung on him like tents. He buttoned the comforting jacket tighter around his neck, rolled up the sleeves almost to his elbows, and went back to his work.

Snow stood in droplets on his oiled saw, but now he would soon be finished. He drove seven more nails; that made three at each end and three in the middle. Painting would have to wait for a warmer, drier day. Back to the toolshed he went again to wipe the tools with an oily cloth and hang them in their proper places on the rack. When he tried the step, he found that he had nailed it firm, without a wobble in it. He would feel good every time he stepped on that board.

Daniel slept on the couch by the stove that night, while the antique, handmade clock ticked time away. He forced himself to awaken when the clock chimed the hours. Since Lady seemed more alert, he had gradually increased her ration of broth with each feeding, so that both of them could sleep for longer intervals.

At three o'clock, he woke in confusion. The fire shone through the isinglass windows in the stove door and reflected on the opposite wall in moving red shapes and shadows that terrified him. He leaped off the couch, thinking that he was in his own bed and the room was afire.

Behind the stove, Lady whined. In an instant, Daniel awoke completely, remembering where he was and why. The dog awkwardly shifted her position, raised her head, and struggled to her feet. She looked straight at Daniel with begging eyes, whining.

"What do you want? Do you need to go out?"

She whined again. Daniel carried her to the newspapers he had spread in the enclosed back porch. She made a small dark puddle on the papers. Daniel was jubilant. If her body was working, maybe the broth had helped. Maybe she was better.

"You're paper-trained," he said, "so you must have been a house dog somewhere. I wonder where you came from?"

She whined again as he carried her back to her bed.

"Yes," he said, "you can have all the broth you want. Hold on a minute, dog, and I'll warm it for you. It gets thick when it's cold."

Returning with the warm broth, he found her no longer outstretched on her side, but lying with her chin between her paws. She pushed the medicine dropper away with her nose and snuffed the side of the bowl in Daniel's hand.

"I'm not fast enough for you?" Daniel held the soup bowl under the dog's nose. She lapped and slurped the broth until she had licked the bowl dry. Then she pricked her ears and looked expectantly at Daniel.

He laughed. "For a dead dog, you sure are hungry! You're going to make a monkey out of Doc."

He pushed the lace curtains aside to look out at the blizzard that had shrieked around the house since dinner. Snow still fell so thickly that all he could see of the yard lamp was a glowing swirl. The wind had dropped, and the snow was coming down in big soft flakes. Spruce trees and hedges planted as windbreaks partially protected the farmyard.

Elsewhere, snowdrifts had closed country roads by now, buried fences and mailboxes, and filled ditches.

Daniel thought with satisfaction—as if he had planned and organized the snowstorm himself—that the school bus would be kept away from his house for several days. That would be long enough for him to get Lady back on her feet.

He imagined himself teaching her to herd the cows as Captain used to do, running across the meadow on cold spring mornings with his breath visible in gusts. In his mind, Daniel saw her playing Captain's old games. She would bring him sticks to throw and bark at him until he cooperated. She would sleep under his covers on winter nights and lie with her chin on his foot while he did his homework.

Then he looked at the skinny dog that lay by the stove, already sleeping again. Her big feet and starved legs were like clubs. Her coat was so sparse he could see her knobby spine and her ribs.

Even if she lives, he thought, she may not stay here. I didn't want a new dog. Maybe she doesn't want a new boy. Maybe she'll go back home where she belongs.

The snow blocked the road to school for three days. By the time the county plow cleared a path for the milk truck and the mail on Tuesday afternoon, Daniel thought he had shoveled a ton of snow.

He had dug out the mailbox and mounted a red bandanna on a long stick above it so the snowplow wouldn't shear off the post. The plow buried the mailbox again, bandanna and all. Daniel dug it out once more.

He had helped his parents clear the driveway and barnyard and had made paths from the house to the outbuildings. Where the drifts were deepest, the snow was piled higher than his head on both sides of the path. He wanted to dig a hideout, but he had no time for play.

Every morning, even before he dressed, Daniel had put out fresh water and food for Lady. "You'll have to take care of yourself, dog," he said. "I'm lucky they'll give me time off to eat." Every evening her dishes were empty.

On Wednesday, Daniel and his father came into the house together for breakfast. They had fed and watered the chickens, gathered the eggs, and milked the cows before the sun rose. Manure from the barn and chicken coop stuck to their boots, so they changed into house shoes on the porch.

Daniel gave the wire basket full of eggs to his mother, who would keep a few, sort the others for size and freshness, and sell them at the crossroads store.

"Thank you, Daniel," she said. "The chickens are laying better since I changed their mash."

She handed Daniel a jar of homemade applesauce and a serving spoon. He dished up the sauce as she spooned fried potatoes and side pork from the iron skillet onto three large plates. Daniel's mouth watered as they carried the plates into the dining room, where Pa was opening mail and listening to the radio.

"They say the roads are open. School today," said Pa.

"Did you hear that, dog? School will be a vacation from all this work," Daniel dropped down on his knees beside the stove, where Lady was watching them out of the corner of her eye, her ears laid back.

As he lunged happily toward her, Lady bared her teeth and snarled. She jumped to her feet and crawled under the couch. She cowered in the darkest corner, shivering and watchful.

"What's the matter with her?" said Daniel.

"Something more than starvation ails that dog," said Mama, pouring two cups of steaming coffee and a mug of cocoa for Daniel.

"Looks like she's taken some beatings from somebody," said Pa. "Sometimes people's meanness ruins dogs. She may never be any good."

"I'll train her," said Daniel. "Now that we've caught up on the work, I'll take her outdoors after school. I'll throw sticks for her."

"You'd better put her on a leash," said Pa. "If you don't control her until this place seems like home, she'll run."

In the weeks that followed, Lady looked healthier every day. With Doc's advice, Daniel gradually changed her diet from liquids to bland foods to meat. After her appetite returned, she was constantly hungry. The weight she gained was visible. He eyes were bright, and her coat began to shine.

When Daniel thought no one was looking, he tried to train her. He dragged her out from her place under the couch and held her head between his knees while he stroked her silky hair. He forced her to lie under the table while he did his homework, and jabbed her with the toe of his boot when she inched away. He shut her in his room at night and held her in his bed with his arm locked around her neck. He even tried to make her lick his hand.

But inevitably his grip relaxed when he fell asleep. In the morning, he found her in the closet, squeezed under the low shelf, or far under the bed, with fluffs of dust caught in her whiskers and eyebrows.

Lady never snarled at Daniel again, but she wouldn't wag her tail either. She merely submitted.

One day after school, when Daniel found her under the couch as usual, he lost all patience. As he grabbed her hair and yanked at her, she yelped and whined.

"What's the matter with you?" he said. "I'm the one who fed you when you were half dead."

"You can't squeeze blood out of a turnip, Daniel," said his mother quietly at the kitchen door.

"What's that supposed to mean?"

"You can't get love by force, if she's not willing."

Daniel let Lady go, and she crawled back under the couch.

"She's not a bit like Captain," he said. "He followed me everywhere. I had to lock him up to get rid of him."

His mother knelt beside him and put her arm around him. "Every dog has ways of its own," she said.

"She let me touch her when she was sick because she couldn't get away." He wiped his eyes on his flannel sleeve. "Now she won't come near me."

His mother nodded.

"Maybe she thought I didn't want another dog. Maybe it's my fault she doesn't like me."

His mother patted his head.

"She's worse than nothing!" Daniel cried. "I wish she had died that first day. I wish I'd never found her!"

The last week of March brought robins and weather so warm the family worked outdoors without jackets. The remaining snow melted suddenly. The runoff overflowed the creek and flooded the fields near the house. Within a few days, the water receded, and warm winds and sun dried the ground.

After the chores were done and breakfast was over on Saturday morning, Daniel's father said, "Take this morning off, Daniel. You and Lady can check all the fences around the west meadow, while I muck out the barn."

"I'd rather walk fences than shovel manure any day," said Daniel.

His father watched as the boy pulled Lady from under the couch, fastened the choke-chain around her neck, and snapped the leash onto the ring. The chain ran through a larger ring, like a slip knot, so that tension on the leash would tighten the chain around the dog's neck.

Daniel pulled the leash. Lady sat back, stubbornly stiffened her front legs, and leaned in the opposite direction. Daniel jerked the leash. She coughed and gagged as the chain pinched her windpipe.

"A choke-chain can be a brutal thing, Daniel," said his father, in a voice so soft it was almost a whisper.

"Oh, you know I won't hurt the dumb dog," Daniel said. He put his head down so his father couldn't see the redness in his hot cheeks as he pushed Lady across the dining room, through the kitchen, and out the back door.

They walked side by side across the yard, past the windmill and the chicken coop, but they were not companions. Lady skulked along, close to the ground, watching Daniel, leaning as far as she could against the leash.

"You don't trust me one bit, do you, dog?" Daniel said. "I saved you, but now you can't wait for the thinnest chance to get away."

As they crossed the lane between the farmyard and the fields, Daniel picked up a short stick, thinking Lady might chase it. She shied away so fearfully she fell over on her side, whimpering, and pawing at the ground as if she wished she could crawl into the earth. She rolled on her back, with her feet in the air in a gesture of surrender.

Furious, Daniel threw the stick with all his strength over last year's chopped-off cornstalks. He slipped the choke-chain off Lady's neck and ran as fast as he could across the soft earth. Looking back, he saw Lady creeping on her belly down a corn row, watching him distrustfully over her shoulder.

"Go, then! Starve to death!" he shouted. "I never wanted you anyway!"

When he certainly could not have caught her, even if

he had tried, she bolted. With her tail curled under her legs, she dashed for the woods at the far end of the field. In a moment, Daniel lost sight of her as she plunged into the creek bed, still filled with cottony morning fog.

The creek divided the cornfield, with banks that were now two or three feet above the water. As Daniel approached it, with a sick feeling in his stomach and tears dripping from his chin, he bent automatically to pick up a field stone. Although he and his father had carried off wagonloads of rocks from that field, every spring the frost had heaved up more.

Looking down, he noticed the claw of a dead crayfish and nearby another. The claws were everywhere, no longer the clay-green color of the living animal, but blue as could be, with red edges on the pincers.

Daniel was amazed by their number and their beauty. He knew that the flood had washed them out of the creek, but they might have been carved purposely for miniature decorations and polished by hand. Daniel imagined the multitudes of creatures living unnoticed in the creek. He filled the pockets of his windbreaker and jeans with the claws. In the distance, he could see Lady where she sat at the edge of the woods, watching him. He watched back until she fled into the brush. She was gone for good now, he was sure.

He walked back to the flower garden at the side of the house where he and his father and mother had taken turns breaking the frozen ground with a pickax, to bury Captain among the hybrid iris and rambler roses. He carefully coiled the choke-chain and the leash on the bare earth and put the crayfish in a mound beside them. Then, trying not to look toward the woods, where nothing lively moved, he walked quickly out to the barn to help his father clean the stalls.

Every day for a week Daniel pressed his cheek against the cool glass and watched from the school bus window until his eyes hurt, searching the countryside for a glimpse of white fur. Every evening, as he sat in the pool of warm lamplight at the dining-room table, trying to think about math problems, he listened for Lady, scratching like Captain to come in.

He woke up once in the middle of the night, thinking he had heard her bark. When he opened the back door, a startled raccoon ran for cover across the moonlit yard; he knew that no coon would come near if a dog were about. Daniel picked up a stick of kindling and threw it into the darkness after the coon.

566

Back in bed, he shivered under blankets that had chilled while he was off fooling himself, looking for Lady. He wouldn't be tricked again by wishful thinking, he told himself. She was gone, and good riddance. He would forget her.

After that, when he caught himself with his mind wandering, looking out the bus window, searching the fields, he made himself open his books and study his homework. "There are six kinds of simple machines," he read. He shut his eyes and tried to list them without looking at the book: "the wheel, the lever, the inclined plane. . . ." But he couldn't concentrate. His thoughts returned to Lady. He worried that she might be trapped in some culvert just down the road from his house. She might have gone back to the place where somebody beat her.

Then, one chilly morning nineteen days after Lady had run off, Daniel went to the barn with his father to do the chores before school. Violins were playing a love song on the radio that ran all day to soothe the cows so they would give more milk.

As the door creaked open, a shaft of sunshine lit a pile of hay in the corner, and there crouched Lady. Daniel saw that her nose and lips and even one eyelid bristled with broken white needles.

"Look at her!" said Daniel. "What a mess."

"She's tangled with a porcupine," said Pa. When he reached for her, she snarled. "She wants nothing to do with me."

"She can cure herself then," said Daniel. He pulled down the bill of the green and yellow cap the machinery dealer had given him, until it all but covered his eyes.

"For heaven's sake, Daniel, what do you want of that dog?" said Pa. "You've been grieving for nearly three weeks because she ran away. Now you're mad because she's come back."

Lady struggled to her feet and limped to Daniel's side. She raised her ragamuffin head high, erect and stately as a show dog, looking at him imploringly with her uninjured eye.

Daniel turned his back on her and kicked a pail so hard it bounced and banged halfway across the barn, rolled into the straw, and bumped a cow in the shins. The cow jumped back, surprisingly nimble, but with her head fastened in the stanchion, she couldn't go far. The whole herd shifted, frightened by the noise.

"Daniel, stop and look at yourself." Pa rarely spoke so sharply. "No matter how you feel, I won't have you disturbing the cows."

"I didn't mean to kick it so hard," said Daniel.

As he retrieved the bucket and patted the insulted cow on the nose, Lady followed him. He tried not to look at her, but she whined and nudged him and stood on his foot.

"It's now or never, Son," said Pa. "She's yours if you want her."

Tears spilled down Daniel's cheeks. He knelt beside her, put his arms around her shoulders, and whispered in her ear, "Of course I'll help."

"Hold on, and I'll get the pliers," said Pa.

Daniel sat on a crate with the dog's head in his lap. "You're a good dog," he whispered, as he gripped the porcupine quills close to the skin with the narrow-nosed pliers. Then he drew them out one by one. "Good Lady. We're halfway done."

Her whole face was swollen and infected. She trembled in his lap, moaning and watching his every move with her good eye, but she sat still. When Daniel had pulled out all of the quills, first from her eyelid and then from her muzzle, he took a deep, shuddering breath. His hands were shaking.

"Look her over carefully," said Pa. "Your grandfather

569

claimed that porcupine needles move into an animal's body. He said they might kill a bear if they lodged in a place the bear couldn't reach."

Together Daniel and Pa gently made the dog lie down. She lay patiently still as they combed through her hair with their fingers and inspected every part of her body.

"Look at her paws," said Daniel. "Sores all over the pads of her feet."

"She must have tried to clean her face and pierced her paws with the needles," said Pa, "but she could pull those out with her teeth."

"I don't know how she could walk," said Daniel.

The door swung open as Mama came into the barn, hugging herself in a heavy knitted sweater. "What's happened? Breakfast is getting cold," she said, squinting in the dim light of the barn. "Why, it's Lady!"

"She's come back," said Daniel.

His mother saw the porcupine needles at Daniel's feet and the pliers in his hand and Lady's hurt face. "I begin to doubt that dog's sense," she said. "Bring the old pincushion up to the house and we'll put some salve on her face."

Lady wouldn't let Pa pick her up but cringed and clung to Daniel.

"It's a good thing we weren't quick to get rid of her bed," said Mama.

"Look how bedraggled she is," said Daniel. "We'll have to start fresh, fattening her up again. What a pain in the neck you are, dog."

He turned away from her and walked into the morning sunshine. "I can't carry you," he said, "and I got rid of the leash. You'll have to make it on your own power."

Slowly Lady followed the boy through the barn door and limped across the yard. The windmill swung and squeaked in the rising breeze. The tulips Daniel had planted along the sidewalk last fall had broken through the ground, and the yellow cups bobbed on stiff stems. The air was alive with a robin's song.

Footsore and stiff and muddy as on the day Daniel had first seen her, the dog wagged her tail and licked his hand.

Overcome by the morning, he took off his cap and skimmed it into the branches of the oak he climbed in summer. "Lady's come back on her own," he said to the birds.

He bent and kissed the dog on her hot, dry nose. "Maybe this time," he said, "you'll stay."

# GLOSSARY

**Full pronunciation key**\*   The pronunciation of each word is shown just after the word, in this way: **abbreviate** (ə brē′vē āt).

The letters and signs used are pronounced as in the words below.

The mark ′ is placed after a syllable with a primary or heavy accent as in the example above.

The mark ′ after a syllable shows a secondary or lighter accent, as in **abbreviation** (ə brē′vē ā′shən).

| SYMBOL | KEY WORDS | SYMBOL | KEY WORDS |
|---|---|---|---|
| a | ask, fat | b | bed, dub |
| ā | ape, date | d | did, had |
| ä | car, father | f | fall, off |
|  |  | g | get, dog |
| e | elf, ten | h | he, ahead |
| er | berry, care | j | joy, jump |
| ē | even, meet | k | kill, bake |
|  |  | l | let, ball |
| i | is, hit | m | met, trim |
| ir | mirror, here | n | not, ton |
| ī | ice, fire | p | put, tap |
|  |  | r | red, dear |
| o | lot, pond | s | sell, pass |
| ō | open, go | t | top, hat |
| ô | law, horn | v | vat, have |
| oi | oil, point | w | will, always |
| oo | look, pull | y | yet, yard |
| o͞o | ooze, tool | z | zebra, haze |
| yoo | unite, cure |  |  |
| yo͞o | cute, few | ch | chin, arch |
| ou | out, crowd | ŋ̑ | ring, singer |
|  |  | sh | she, dash |
| u | up, cut | th | thin, truth |
| ɹr | fur, fern | *th* | then, father |
|  |  | zh | s in pleasure |
| ə | a in ago |  |  |
|  | e in agent | ′ | as in (ā′b'l) |
|  | e in father |  |  |
|  | i in unity |  |  |
|  | o in collect |  |  |
|  | u in focus |  |  |

\*Pronunciation key and respellings adapted from *Webster's New World Dictionary, Basic School Edition,* Copyright © 1983 by Simon & Schuster, Inc. Reprinted by permission.

# A

**a·bide** (ə bīd') *verb.* to put up with: I really can't *abide* carrots. **abided, abiding.**

**a·brupt·ly** (ə brupt'lē) *adverb.* happening in a sudden way; quickly and unexpectedly.

**ab·sorb** (əb zôrb' *or* ab zôrb') *verb.* **1.** to suck up. **2.** to take one's full attention: The book *absorbed* me so much I didn't hear the doorbell. **absorbed, absorbing.**

**ac·claim** (ə klām') *verb.* to greet with praise or applause. —**acclaimed** *adjective.* recognized as a special talent: The crowd mobbed the *acclaimed* singer.

**a·dapt** (ə dapt') *verb.* **1.** to change something so it fits. **2.** to change oneself to life in a new situation: I expect to *adapt* quickly to my new school.

**ad·mi·ra·tion** (ad'mə rā'shən) *noun.* a feeling of delight at something beautiful or well done: I was filled with *admiration* for her paintings.

**ad·ver·tis·ing** (ad'vər tī zing) *noun.* **1.** public announcements that give information or persuade people to buy things: I saw *advertising* for a new toy. **2.** the work of preparing advertisements.

**air pres·sure** (er' presh'ər) *noun.* the force that the earth's atmosphere exerts on everything on the earth.

**a·maze·ment** (ə māz'mənt) *noun.* great surprise: Imagine my *amazement* when the dog began to sing!

**an·ces·tor** (an'ses tər) *noun.* a person who lived before you in your family line: My *ancestors* came from Ireland. **ancestors.**

**an·noy** (ə noi') *verb.* to bother: The loud noises *annoyed* me as I studied. **annoyed, annoying.**

**ap·plause** (ə plôz') *noun.* the act of clapping one's hands to show approval.

**ar·chi·tect** (är'kə tekt) *noun.* a person who draws plans for and oversees construction of buildings and other structures.

**ar·ray** (ə rā') *verb.* **1.** to put in correct order. **2.** to dress up in fine clothing. **arrayed, arraying.**

**as·sis·tant** (ə sis'tənt) *noun.* a person who helps someone: The zookeeper's *assistant* held the panda cub.

**as·ton·ish·ment** (ə ston'ish mənt) *noun.* wonder; great surprise: Our *astonishment* grew as the circus act continued.

**at·mos·phere** (at'məs fir) *noun.* **1.** the air that surrounds the earth. **2.** the gases around any planet or star. **3.** the general feeling of a place or thing.

**au·di·tion** (ô dish'ən) *noun.* a time when an actor or musician gives a short performance to try to get a job. —*verb.* to take part in an audition: She plans to *audition* for a major part in the school play.

**au·thor·ize** (ô'thə rīz) *verb.* to allow: The club treasurer *authorized* us to buy the supplies. **authorized.**

**au·to·graph** (ôt'ə graf) *noun.* something written in a person's handwriting, especially the person's name. —*verb.* to write one's name on: The actor was *autographing* our programs. **autographed, autographing.**

**a·wak·en** (ə wāk"n) *verb.* to arouse; to wake someone up. **awakened, awakening.**

**ax·is** (ak'sis) *noun.* a real or imaginary line around which something turns: The earth's *axis* goes through the North and South Poles.

Absorb comes from a Latin word that means "to swallow or soak up."

**advertising**

Autograph is made up of *auto*, meaning "self" or "same," and *graph*, which means "to write." Together they mean "signed with one's own hand."

# B

**beacon**

**bag·gage** (bag'ij) *noun.* suitcases taken on a trip; luggage: We had too much *baggage* to fit in the car's trunk.

**bal·co·ny** (bal'kə nē) *noun.* **1.** a platform that sticks out from the side of a building. **2.** an upper floor of a theater. **balconies.**

**ban·is·ter** (ban'əs tər) *noun.* a railing for people to hold on to, often along a staircase.

**bar·ri·er** (bar'ē ər) *noun.* something that blocks the way: The piles of rocks were *barriers* across the path. **barriers.**

**bash·ful·ness** (bash'fəl nəs) *noun.* a feeling of shyness: The baby always shows *bashfulness* with strangers.

**bat·ten** (bat' 'n) *noun.* **1.** a strip of wood placed over a seam between boards. —*verb.* **1.** to fasten with battens: The crew *battened* down the hatches. **battened, battening.**

**bea·con** (bēk''n) *noun.* **1.** a strong light used for warning or guarding. **2.** a tower with beams of light.

**bed·rock** (bed'rok') *noun.* the solid rock that lies under the soil on the earth's surface: They dug down to *bedrock* when they built this building.

**ben·e·fit** (ben'ə fit) *noun.* a help: The lights on the path were a *benefit* for guests who arrived at night. —*verb.* **1.** to do good for. **2.** to be helped.

**bleak** (blēk) *adjective.* **1.** not sheltered; bare: We looked out at the *bleak,* harsh plains. **2.** gloomy.

**bliz·zard** (bliz'ərd) *noun.* a heavy snowstorm with strong winds.

**board·ing·house** (bôrd'ing hous') *noun.* a house where people pay to live and eat their meals: Some of the large

Boardinghouse is a combination of the root words *board* and *house*. Board refers to the daily meals that could sometimes be purchased in a house that rented rooms. This use of the word *board* goes back to a time when meals were served on rough planks of wood, or boards. In time, the meals themselves came to be known as *board*.

**cable**

homes on our street have been turned into *boardinghouses.* **boardinghouses.**

**bod·ice** (bod'is) *noun.* the upper part of a woman's dress.

**boul·der** (bōl'dər) *noun.* a large rock made smooth by the wind and water.

**bow** (bou) *noun.* the front part of a ship or boat: We stood in the *bow* of the ship and watched the water ahead.

**bunk·house** (bungk'hous') *noun.* a building on a ranch or in a camp where people sleep. **bunkhouses.**

**bunt** (bunt) *verb.* to hit a baseball lightly, on purpose, so that it does not go far: The coach told me to *bunt.* —*noun.* a baseball hit so lightly, on purpose, that it does not go out of the infield.

**bur·row** (bʉr'ō) *noun.* a hole that an animal digs in the ground: Some rabbits live in *burrows.* **burrows.**

# C

**ca·ble** (kā'b'l) *noun.* **1.** a thick wire made of other wires twisted together: The bridge is held up by *cables.* **2.** the wires through which electricity can be sent. **cables.**

**cache** (kash) *noun.* **1.** a place where things are hidden or stored: The pirate had a secret *cache* of gold. **2.** anything hidden like this.

**cal·cu·la·tion** (kal' kyə lā'shən) *noun.* **1.** the act of finding out an answer through arithmetic. **2.** the answer found through arithmetic: Our *calculations* show that the club lost money this year. **calculations.**

**can·vas** (kan'vəs) *noun.* a strong, heavy cloth made of hemp, cotton, or linen used for tents or sails. —*adjective*. of heavy cloth.

**cap·i·tal** (kap′ə t'l) *noun*. **1.** the form of a letter used to begin a sentence. **2.** the city or town where the government is located.

**cap·tive** (kap′tiv) *noun*. a person caught and kept as a prisoner. —*adjective*. held as a prisoner: The *captive* fish struggled against the net.

**car·bon di·ox·ide** (kär′bən dī ok′sīd) *noun*. a gas made up of carbon and oxygen: People breathe in oxygen and breathe out *carbon dioxide*.

**cast** (kast) *verb*. **1.** to throw or toss. **2.** to choose actors for a play. —*noun*. **1.** a throw. **2.** a stiff form made of plaster which is placed on a broken arm or leg to keep it in place while it heals. **3.** the actors in a play.

**ca·the·dral** (kə thē′drəl) *noun*. **1.** the principal church of a district, headed by a bishop. **2.** any large, important church. **cathedrals.**

**cel·e·bra·tion** (sel′ə brā′shən) *noun*. a special party in honor of an event.

**cen·ten·ni·al** (sen ten′ē əl) *adjective*. **1.** lasting one hundred years. **2.** happening once in one hundred years. **3.** of a hundredth anniversary. *noun*. a hundredth anniversary or its celebration.

**chan·nel** (chan′'l) *noun*. **1.** the path of a river or stream. **2.** the deeper part of a river or harbor. **3.** a passage through which something moves: We cut a *channel* through the weeds in the stream. **4.** a band on which a television or radio station sends out its programs. —*verb*. to make a channel in something: The icebreaker will *channel* through the heavy ice in the harbor.

**chart** (chärt) *noun*. **1.** a map, especially one for a ship: The sailors used a *chart* to plan their route past the

rocks. **2.** a table or graph. —*verb*. **1.** to make a map of. **2.** to show on a chart.

**chuck·le** (chuk′'l) *verb*. to laugh softly: We *chuckled* at the puppy's silly behavior. **chuckled, chuckling.**

**clap·board** (klab′ərd *or* klap′bôrd) *noun*. a thin board used as siding for a wooden house. —*adjective*. of thin board.

**clap·per** (klap′ər) *noun*. the tongue of a bell that claps against the side of the bell to cause the ringing sound.

**clat·ter** (klat′ər) *noun*. **1.** sharp, loud sounds. **2.** noisy talking. —*verb*. to make a clatter: The students *clattered* through the halls at noon. **clattered, clattering.**

**clus·ter** (klus′tər) *noun*. a number of things growing or seen together: A *cluster* of flowers grew at the edge of the lake.

**coast·al** (kōs′t'l) *adjective*. of, near, or along a coast: Savannah, Georgia, is a *coastal* city.

**com·e·dy** (kom′ə dē) *noun*. **1.** a story that is funny. **2.** a funny event: The mix-up of the packages turned out to be a real *comedy* in the end.

**com·mis·sion·er** (kə mish′ə nər) *noun*. a member of a group chosen to do a certain thing: Ten *commissioners* were appointed by the governor. **commissioners.**

**com·pa·ra·ble** (kom′pər ə b'l *or* kəm par′ə b'l) *adjective*. more or less the same: My grades are not *comparable* to hers because she studies harder than I do.

**com·pass** (kum′pəs) *noun*. an instrument that shows direction with a needle that always points to magnetic north.

| a fat | ơi oil | ch chin |
| ā ape | ơơ look | sh she |
| ä car, father | ōō tool | th thin |
| e ten | ou out | *th* then |
| er care | u up | zh leisure |
| ē even | ur fur | ŋ ring |
| i hit | | |
| ir here | ə = a *in* ago | |
| ī bite, fire | e *in* agent | |
| o lot | i *in* unity | |
| ō go | o *in* collect | |
| ô law, horn | u *in* focus | |

**Clapboard** is a variation on the German word *klappholtz*. *Klappen* means "to fit together," and *holtz* means "wood."

**clapper**

575

crate

**com·pel** (kəm pel′) *verb.* to make someone do something: The guards *compelled* everyone to leave the museum at 5:00. **compelled, compelling.**

**con·cen·trate** (kon′sən trāt) *verb.* to gather all one's efforts: You must *concentrate* on keeping your eyes on the ball.

**con·dense** (kən dens′) *verb.* **1.** to become thicker or denser: Steam will *condense* into water drops on a cold window. **2.** to make shorter.

**con·fi·dent** (kon′fə dənt) *adjective.* sure, certain: I am *confident* that I can win the race.

**con·fuse** (kən fyo͞oz′) *verb.* to mix up in one's mind: He was *confused* by the difficult instructions. **confused, confusing.**

**Con·gress** (koṅg′grəs) *noun.* the group of people in the government of the United States that makes laws: *Congress* is made up of the Senate and the House of Representatives.

**con·scious·ness** (kon′shəs nis) *noun.* awareness of one's own feelings or of what is happening around one: Her *consciousness* of all the nighttime noises kept her awake for hours.

**con·sul·ta·tion** (kon′səl tā′shən) *noun.* a meeting to talk over a problem.

**con·ti·nent** (kont″n ənt) *noun.* any of the large land areas on earth: Asia is the largest *continent*.

**cour·age** (kur′ij) *noun.* being able to control fear and face danger; bravery.

**course** (kôrs) *noun.* **1.** a path along which something moves. **2.** the direction in which something moves: The explorers set their *course* toward the mountains. **3.** a part of a meal served at one time.

**cove** (kōv) *noun.* a small bay.

**crate** (krāt) *noun.* a wooden box used for packing things.

**crew** (kro͞o) *noun.* **1.** all the workers on a ship, train, or airplane. **2.** any group of people who work together: The cleanup *crew* stayed after the school party to clean the rooms.

**crop** (krop) *noun.* any farm product, such as wheat or fruit: The cherry *crop* was so large that we needed more pickers.

**crum·ble** (krum′b′l) *verb.* to break into small pieces. —**crumbling** *adjective.* breaking into crumbs.

**cul·ture** (kul′chər) *noun.* **1.** the use of soil for crops. **2.** improvement by study of the mind or manners. **3.** the ideas, skills, arts, and tools of a certain people; way of life: We studied the *culture* of the Native Americans during the 1700s.

**cu·mu·lus** (kyo͞om′yə ləs) *noun.* a kind of cloud in which round masses are piled on each other.

**Congress** comes from a Latin word that means "a coming together; a friendly meeting."

cumulus

# D

**dan·der** (dan′dər) *noun.* **1.** tiny bits from feathers or hair that may cause allergies. **2.** anger or temper. —**get one's dander up.** to become angry: They were rude, and that *got her dander up.*

**daz·zle** (daz″l) *verb.* **1.** to be so wonderful as to cause admiration. **2.** to make nearly blind with a bright light. **dazzled.** —**dazzling** *adjective.* nearly blinding.

**de·ceit·ful** (di sēt′fəl) *adjective.* lying or misleading: I think he was *deceitful* about the missing money.

**del·i·cate** (del′i kit) *adjective.* **1.** pleasant because of its lightness or mildness. **2.** easily hurt; not strong: Be careful of the *delicate* glassware.

**de·scend·ant** (di sen′dənt) *noun.* a person who comes after you in your family: My children and grandchildren will be my *descendants.* **descendants.**

**de·scent** (di sent') *noun.* the act of moving down to a lower place: Be careful on your *descent* from the top of the tower.

**de·sert** (di zurt') *verb.* to leave someone or something when one should not. **deserting.** —**deserted** *adjective.* abandoned.

**de·sign** (di zīn') *verb.* to think of and draw plans to make: She is *designing* all her own clothes. **designed, designing.**

**de·spair** (di sper') *verb.* to give up hope: I *despaired* of ever finding my lost keys. **despaired, despairing.**

**de·tain** (di tān') *verb.* to hold back: I must *detain* you for a few more minutes.

**de·tour** (dē'toor) *noun.* a route used when the usual route is closed to traffic.

**di·a·logue** or **di·a·log** (dī'ə lôg) *noun.* **1.** a talking together to try to understand each other's views. **2.** a speech between two people in a play or television program.

**di·a·mond** (dī'mənd *or* dī'ə mənd) *noun.* **1.** a very hard, valuable, clear stone. **2.** a four-sided figure having four equal sides and equal opposite angles. **3.** a baseball playing field.

**di·a·ry** (dī'ə rē) *noun.* **1.** a day-by-day record written about things in a person's life. **2.** a book in which someone writes such a record.

**di·lem·ma** (di lem'ə) *noun.* a problem in which someone must choose between two things that are equally unpleasant or dangerous: We faced the *dilemma* of continuing on even though we were lost, or stopping and waiting in the bitter cold.

**dis·ci·pline** (dis'ə plin) *noun.* **1.** training that teaches one to control one's behavior. **2.** self-control.

**3.** punishment. —*verb.* **1.** to train to self-control: If you *discipline* yourself, you can practice playing the piano every day. **2.** to punish.

**dis·grace** (dis grās') *noun.* shame; loss of respect: I am in *disgrace* due to my bad behavior.

**dis·trib·ute** (dis trib'yoot) *verb.* **1.** to give out in parts. **2.** to spread or scatter: We have to *distribute* these notices all over town.

**doc·u·ment** (dok'yə mənt) *noun.* a printed or written record, often used to prove something: Birth certificates are important *documents.* **documents.**

**dou·ble-bit·ted axe** (du"l bit"d aks) *noun.* a tool for chopping wood, having two blades pointing in opposite directions on the end of the handle.

**doze** (dōz) *verb.* to take a nap; sleep lightly. **dozed, dozing.**

**dread** (dred) *verb.* to look forward to fearfully. —*noun.* great fear of an event that is about to happen: I feel real *dread* about tomorrow's test.

**drift·wood** (drift'wood) *noun.* wood that has been drifting in the water.

**dug·out** (dug'out) *noun.* a shelter that is dug in the ground.

**dumb·wait·er** (dum'wāt'ər) *noun.* a small elevator used to send food and small things from one floor to another.

**dune** (doon *or* dyoon) *noun.* a small hill made of sand. **dunes.**

**dusk** (dusk) *noun.* the part of twilight just before the night's full darkness.

**dwell·ing** (dwel'ing) *noun.* a house; home: Some Native Americans lived in a kind of *dwelling* called a "hogan."

| a fat | oi oil | ch chin |
| ā ape | oo look | sh she |
| ä car, father | ōo tool | th thin |
| e ten | ou out | *th* then |
| er care | u up | zh leisure |
| ē even | ur fur | n͠g ring |
| i hit | | |
| ir here | ə = a *in* ago | |
| ī bite, fire | e *in* agent | |
| o lot | i *in* unity | |
| ō go | o *in* collect | |
| ô law, horn | u *in* focus | |

**driftwood**

◇

**Dumbwaiter** came into being because people wanted to be able to have dinner without the services of a waiter. *Dumb*, in this case, means "silent" or "speechless." Dumbwaiters, unlike human servants, were silent and also could not listen in on their employers' conversations.

# E

**ea·glet** (ē′glit) *noun*. a young eagle. **eaglets.**

**e·co·nom·ic** (ē′kə nom′ik *or* ek′ə nom′ik) *adjective*. having to do with managing money: We studied the president's *economic* policy.

**ed·i·tor** (ed′ə tər) *noun*. **1.** someone who prepares pieces of writing for publication by correcting and changing them. **2.** someone who is in charge of a newspaper or magazine and decides what will be printed in it.

**ed·u·cate** (ej′ə kāt) *verb*. to teach; train: He *educated* himself in current events by reading three newspapers every day. **educated, educating.**

**ef·fec·tive·ly** (ə fek′tiv lē) *adverb*. in a way that produces a wanted result: They used their practice time *effectively.*

**el·der** (el′dər) *noun*. **1.** a person who is older. **2.** certain church, temple, or town officials: The *elders* of the village make the rules. **elders.**

**el·e·vate** (el′ə vāt) *verb*. to raise or lift up. **elevating.** —**elevated** *adjective*. raised up.

**em·bar·rass** (im ber′əs) *verb*. to make feel uncomfortable. **embarrassing.** —**embarrassed** *adjective*. worried.

**em·brace** (im brās′) *verb*. to hold closely in one's arms in order to show love; hug. **embraced, embracing.**

**e·merge** (i mʉrj′) *verb*. to come out: A butterfly *emerged* from the chrysalis. **emerged, emerging.**

**en·cir·cle** (in sʉr′k'l) *verb*. to make a circle around; surround. **encircled, encircling.**

**en·dure** (in dŏŏr′ *or* in dyŏŏr′) *verb*. **1.** to put up with; to hold up under difficulties: She *endured* the long, lonely winter. **2.** to last; to continue to exist. **endured, enduring.**

**eaglets**

**figurine**

**en·gi·neer** (en′jə nir′) *noun*. **1.** a person who is trained in the science of building machinery, roads, bridges, etc. **2.** a person who drives a railroad locomotive.

**en·tail** (in tāl′) *verb*. to require or make necessary: The party *entailed* a lot of work. **entailed, entailing.**

**en·vi·ous** (en′vē əs) *adjective*. full of jealousy.

**e·qua·tor** (i kwāt′ər) *noun*. an imaginary circle around the middle of the earth, exactly halfway between the North and South Poles.

**es·cort** (es′kôrt) *verb*. to go along with someone for protection: She *escorted* the small boy home. **escorted, escorting.**

**ex·ec·u·tive** (ig zek′yə tiv) *noun*. any of the people who manage the business of an organization. —*adjective*. having to do with managing: She has strong *executive* talents and runs the business well.

**ex·hi·bi·tion** (ek′sə bish′ən) *noun*. a public show: We went to the art *exhibition.*

**ex·te·ri·or** (ik stir′ē ər) *adjective*. of or on the outside. —*noun*. the outside or outer part: The *exterior* of the building is painted white.

# F

**false·hood** (fôls′hŏŏd) *noun*. a lie.

**fan·tas·tic** (fan tas′tik) *adjective*. **1.** very strange or weird. **2.** seeming to be beyond belief: The hero in the story had *fantastic* strength.

**fer·tile** (fʉr′t'l) *adjective*. able to grow much fruit or large crops: The land along the river was very *fertile.*

**fig·u·rine** (fig yə rēn′) *noun*. a small statue: There was a china *figurine* of a dog on the mantlepiece.

**flash flood** (flash′ flud′) *noun.* a sudden overflowing of water after a heavy rain.

**flex·i·ble** (flek′sə b'l) *adjective.* that bends easily without breaking.

**flush** (flush) *verb.* **1.** to become red in the face: Her cheeks were *flushed* from the heat. **2.** to empty out with water. **flushed, flushing.**

**folk·lore** (fōk′lôr) *noun.* the stories and beliefs told by a people: We listened for hours to Grandma's Finnish *folklore.*

**for·bid** (fər bid′) *verb.* to order that something not be done: Customers are *forbidden* to go behind the counter. **forbade, forbidden, forbidding.**

**foun·da·tion** (foun dā′shən) *noun.* the bottom part that supports a building.

**found·ry** (foun′drē) *noun.* a place where metal is melted and poured into molds to cool.

**frost·bit·ten** (frôst′bit″n) *adjective.* damaged by exposure to extreme cold.

**fu·ri·ous** (fyoor′ē əs) *adjective.* very angry: He was *furious* at the mistake.

**fur·nace** (fur′nəs) *noun.* a structure in which heat is produced for warming a building.

**fur·row** (fur′ō) *noun.* a long, thin, shallow trench made in the dirt by a plow: The tractor made all the *furrows,* and we planted corn seeds in them. **furrows.**

---

# G

---

**gear** (gir) *noun.* **1.** a part of a machine having wheels with teeth that fit into each other. **2.** tools and equipment needed to do something: I packed my camping *gear* in the car.

**gen·er·ous** (jen′ər əs) *adjective.* willing to give; not selfish.

**ge·nius** (jēn′yəs) *noun.* **1.** great natural talent: His paintings showed his artistic *genius.* **2.** a person who has such a talent. **3.** a person with a very high IQ.

**gi·gan·tic** (jī gan′tik) *adjective.* very big; huge: An elephant is *gigantic* when compared to a mouse.

**good·will** (good′wil′) *noun.* a feeling of kindness or friendliness.

**grad·u·al·ly** (graj′oo wəl lē) *adverb.* happening in such a slow way that changes can hardly be noticed: The sun crept *gradually* over the horizon.

**gram·mar** (gram′ər) *noun.* the rules for speaking and writing a language: We studied English *grammar.*

**grat·i·tude** (grat′ə tood *or* grat′ə tyood) *noun.* being grateful or thankful for a favor.

**grief** (grēf) *noun.* a deep sorrow: He had many *griefs* in his long life. **griefs.**

**guar·an·tee** (gar ən tē′) *noun.* a promise to replace something if it does not work. —*verb.* **1.** to give a guarantee. **2.** to promise: The clerk *guaranteed* that the radio would work. **guaranteed, guaranteeing.**

**guise** (gīz) *noun.* **1.** a costume. **2.** the way something looks, often a false appearance: In the story, the prince appears in the *guise* of a poor man.

**gui·tar** (gi tär′) *noun.* a musical instrument having six strings: You play the *guitar* by plucking the strings.

---

# H

---

**hail** (hāl) *verb.* to welcome with a shout: We *hailed* the arrival of the President. **hailed, hailing.**

| a fat | oi oil | ch chin |
|---|---|---|
| ā ape | oo look | sh she |
| ä car, father | ōō tool | th thin |
| e ten | ou out | *th* then |
| er care | u up | zh leisure |
| ē even | ur fur | ŋg ring |
| i hit | | |
| ir here | ə = a *in* ago | |
| ī bite, fire | e *in* agent | |
| o lot | i *in* unity | |
| ō go | o *in* collect | |
| ô law, horn | u *in* focus | |

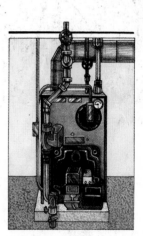

**furnace**

**guitars**

**hearth**

**hard·ship** (härd′ship) *noun.* something hard to bear; trouble or pain. **hardships.**

**hard·wood** (härd′wood) *noun.* a wood such as oak, walnut, or maple that is hard and closely grained. **hardwoods.**

**harsh** (härsh) *adjective.* **1.** rough; not pleasing. **2.** cruel: The punishment was unusually *harsh.*

**har·vest** (här′vist) *noun.* **1.** the gathering of a ripe crop. **2.** the crop gathered in one season. —*verb.* to gather a ripe crop: We must *harvest* the beans before they are too ripe.

**hatch·et** (hach′it) *noun.* a small axe; a tool for chopping or splitting wood.

**ha·ven** (hā′vən) *noun.* **1.** a harbor. **2.** a safe place.

**hearth** (härth) *noun.* **1.** the brick or stone floor of a fireplace. **2.** the life of the home.

**heart·land** (härt′land′) *noun.* a central area of a country, especially one that is thought to be very important to the country.

**hem·i·sphere** (hem′ə sfir) *noun.* **1.** half of a sphere or globe. **2.** one of the halves into which the earth is divided in geography.

**her·ald** (her′əld) *noun.* a person in earlier times who made public announcements.

**he·ro·ic** (hi rō′ik) *adjective.* **1.** like a hero: The legend speaks of many *heroic* men and women. **2.** showing great bravery.

**her·o·ine** (her′ə win) *noun.* **1.** a woman or girl who has done something brave. **2.** the most important woman or girl character in a play or story: She was cast as the *heroine,* which was the most important role in the play.

**hes·i·tant** (hes′ə tənt) *adjective.* waiting because one has doubts or feels unsure: I was *hesitant* to answer the question because I feared that I might be wrong.

**his·tor·i·cal** (his tôr′i k'l) *adjective.* **1.** having to do with history: Many *historical* records are stored in this library. **2.** actually happened in history; not fictional.

**hob·by** (hob′ē) *noun.* something that a person likes to do in spare time: My *hobby* is collecting stamps.

**hoist** (hoist) *verb.* to lift or raise up: Can we *hoist* that heavy box onto the truck?

**home·site** (hōm′sīt) *noun.* a place where a house is or will be built: The pioneer family chose a flat area for its *homesite.*

**hon·or·a·ble men·tion** (on′ər ə b′l men′shən) *noun.* an award given to something or someone not winning a prize but still considered very fine: My drawing received an *honorable mention* from the judge.

**hor·i·zon·tal** (hôr′ə zon′t'l) *adjective.* parallel to the horizon; not vertical; flat and even; level.

**hor·ri·fy** (hôr′ə fī) *verb.* **1.** to fill with fear. **2.** to disgust. —**horrified** *adjective.* shocked. **horrifying.**

**hud·dle** (hud′'l) *verb.* **1.** to crowd close together: We *huddled* under the umbrella. **2.** to hunch oneself up. **huddled, huddling.**

**hu·mil·i·ate** (hyoo mil′ē āt) *verb.* to make feel ashamed. **humiliated** —*adjective.* had feeling of embarrassment or shame.

**hur·tle** (hurt′'l) *verb.* to move or throw with great speed: The wagon *hurtled* down the path, endangering its passengers. **hurtled, hurtling.**

# I

**i·den·ti·cal** (ī den′ti k′l) *adjective.*
exactly the same: The two chairs are
*identical.*

**id·i·o·ma·tic** (id′ē ə mat′ik) *adjective.*
using phrases that have meanings
different from what the words usually
mean, such as "Drop everything," to
mean "Stop what you are doing":
The character's *idiomatic* speech was
enjoyable to hear.

**il·le·gal** (i lē′gəl) *adjective.* against the
law.

**ill·ness** (il′nis) *noun.* a sickness or
disease.

**il·lus·tra·tion** (il′ə strā′shən) *noun.*
**1.** a picture used to explain or
decorate: I liked the colorful
*illustrations* in the book. **2.** an
example. **illustrations.**

**i·mag·i·nar·y** (i maj′ə ner′ē) *adjective.*
only in the imagination; not real: A
unicorn is an *imaginary* animal.

**im·i·tate** (im′ə tāt) *verb.* **1.** to copy
someone's appearance or actions,
etc.: Some children *imitate* the way
their heroes act. **2.** to make fun of
someone by acting like that person.
**imitated, imitating.**

**im·mi·grant** (im′ə grənt) *noun.* a
person who comes to a new country
to live.

**im·pa·tient·ly** (im pā′shənt lē) *adverb.*
not in a patient way; unwilling to
wait.

**im·print** (im′print) *noun.* a mark that is
made by pressing: When she awoke,
her face had the *imprint* of the
wrinkled blanket on which she had
slept.

**im·prob·a·ble** (im prob′ə b′l) *adjective.*
not likely to happen; not likely to be
true: The story had an *improbable*
ending.

**im·prov·i·sa·tion** (im prov′ə zā′shən)
*noun.* something that is made up as
one goes along, as with a speech,
song, or act: Because the play was
not written ahead of time, it was
presented as *improvisation.*

**in·de·pen·dence** (in′di pen′dəns) *noun.*
freedom: The colonists wanted their
*independence.*

**in·scrip·tion** (in skrip′shən) *noun.*
something written or carved on a
coin, statue, building, or book: We
read the *inscription* in the stone
above the doorway.

**in·sert** (in surt′) *verb.* to put something
into something else: He *inserted* the
key into the lock. **inserted, inserting.**

**in·sig·nif·i·cant** (in′sig nif′ə kənt)
*adjective.* of no importance: I forget
*insignificant* facts quickly.

**in·te·ri·or** (in tir′ē ər) *noun.* the inside
or inner part of something.
—*adjective.* inside; inner: The *interior*
lining of the box is red velvet.

**in·ter·rupt** (in tə rupt′) *verb.* **1.** to
break in on talk or action. **2.** to stop:
She had to *interrupt* her meal to
answer the phone.

**in·vi·ta·tion** (in′vi tā′shən) *noun.* **1.** the
asking of someone to come
somewhere or do something. **2.** a
special letter asking someone to come
somewhere: I mailed him an *invitation*
to visit us.

# J

**jour·nal·ist** (jur′n′l ist) *noun.* a person
who works on a magazine or
newspaper as a writer or editor.

**jour·ney** (jur′nē) *noun.* a trip.

| a fat | oi oil | ch chin |
|---|---|---|
| ā ape | oo look | sh she |
| ä car, father | ōō tool | th thin |
| e ten | ou out | *th* then |
| er care | u up | zh leisure |
| ē even | ur fur | ng̈ ring |
| i hit | | |
| ir here | ə = a *in* ago | |
| ī bite, fire | e *in* agent | |
| o lot | i *in* unity | |
| ō go | o *in* collect | |
| ô law, horn | u *in* focus | |

**immigrants**

**Immigrant** is based on the word
*migrate,* which comes from Latin. It
means "to move from one place to
another."

# K

**kay·ak** (kī'ak) *noun.* a canoe that is covered all over with skins except for an opening for the person or people who paddle. **kayaking.**

**kelp** (kelp) *noun.* a large, coarse brown seaweed: The beach was covered in *kelp* washed to shore by the storm at sea.

**kayak**

*Kayak* is one of many words that have come unchanged into English from another language. *Kayak* is the name for one of the kinds of boats used by Eskimos in the Arctic. The boat has been changed slightly, but the word *kayak* remains the same.

**mansion**

# L

**land·scape** (land'skāp) *noun.* **1.** an area of scenery: The mountain *landscape* stretched out in front of her. **2.** a picture showing such a view.

**launch** (lônch) *verb.* **1.** to hurl, throw, or send off into space. **2.** to set afloat; to cause to slide into the water. **launched, launching.**

**lean-to** (lēn'tōō') *noun.* a small building with a slanted roof built against the side of another building.

**Li·brar·y of Con·gress** (lī'brer'ē uv koṅg'gres) *noun.* the United States national library in Washington, D.C.

**log·ger** (lôg'ər) *noun.* a person who works at cutting down trees and taking the logs to a sawmill.

**life pre·serv·er** (līf pri zɜrv'ər) *noun.* a jacket, belt, or large ring that can keep a person floating on the surface of a body of water.

**lone·ly** (lōn'lē) *adjective.* unhappy because of being alone: He felt *loneliest* at night, although he was alone all day as well. **lonelier, loneliest.**

**loy·al·ty** (loi'əl tē) *noun.* quality of being faithful to one's family, country, etc.: He proved his *loyalty* to his country by defending it.

**lu·mi·nous** (lōō'mə nəs) *adjective.* **1.** giving off light. **2.** glowing in the dark: The *luminous* paint on the fenders makes my bicycle safer to ride at night.

**lux·u·ry** (luk'shə rē *or* lug'zhə rē) *noun.* anything that gives comfort or pleasure but that one does not need to survive: A new dress is a *luxury* that I can't afford.

# M

**mag·no·li·a** (mag nō'lē ə *or* mag nōl'yə) *noun.* a tree or shrub with large white, pink, or purple flowers.

**man·sion** (man'shən) *noun.* a large house.

**mar·vel** (mär'v'l) *noun.* a wonderful thing. —*verb.* to wonder; be astonished: We *marveled* at the athlete's skill. **marveled, marveling.**

**mas·ter·piece** (mas'tər pēs) *noun.* **1.** a thing made with great skill. **2.** the best thing a person has ever done: Many people consider the "Mona Lisa" to be Leonardo da Vinci's *masterpiece.*

**match·stick** (mach'stik) *noun.* a slender piece of wood that is coated at one end with a chemical that catches fire when rubbed hard.

**me·di·um** (mē'dē əm) *noun.* a way of communicating with the public: Television is today's most popular *medium*.

**mem·oirs** (mem'wärz) *plural noun.* the story of a person's life written by that person; autobiography: I read the *memoirs* of a famous artist.

**mem·o·rize** (mem'ə rīz) *verb.* to fix exactly in one's memory; learn by heart.

**mem·o·ry** (mem'ər ē) *noun.* **1.** the ability to remember. **2.** something that is remembered: I have good *memories* of my visits to your house. **3.** the part of a computer that stores information. **memories.**

**mile·age** (mīl'ij) *noun.* **1.** the total number of miles: The *mileage* from San Francisco to Los Angeles is less than from San Francisco to Phoenix. **2.** the average number of miles a car will go on a gallon of fuel.

**mim·e·o·graph** (mim'ē ə graf) *noun.* a machine for making copies of written material using a stencil. —*verb.* to make copies on such a machine: Our teacher *mimeographed* our exercise for the day. **mimeographed, mimeographing.**

**min·strel** (min'strəl) *noun.* in earlier times, an entertainer who sang, played an instrument, and recited poems.

**mir·a·cle** (mir'ə k'l) *noun.* **1.** something that seems to go against the laws of nature. **2.** a surprising or remarkable thing: It will be a *miracle* if we win.

**mod·ern·ist** (mod'ərn ist) *noun.* **1.** one who likes modern things, practices, or ideas. **2.** in recent architecture, one who designed buildings in a spare, simple style. **modernists.**

**monk** (muŋk) *noun.* a man belonging to a religious group of men who live according to very strict rules.

**mon·u·ment** (mon'yə mənt) *noun.* a statue or building put up in honor of a famous person or event: Washington, D.C., has *monuments* that honor past presidents. **monuments.**

**moor** (moor) *verb.* to tie a boat in place with ropes or anchors: We *moored* the boat at the dock. **moored, mooring.**

---

# N

---

**na·tion·al** (nash'ə n'l) *adjective.* having to do with the whole nation: We have a *national* election for president every four years.

**na·tive** (nāt'iv) *adjective.* **1.** having to do with the place where someone was born: The United States is my *native* land. **2.** born in or belonging to a certain country. —*noun.* a person born in a certain place.

**neg·lect** (ni glekt') *verb.* **1.** to fail to do something because of carelessness. **2.** to pay too little attention to: He *neglected* to water the dying plant. **neglected, neglecting.**

**nui·sance** (noo's'ns *or* nyoo's'ns) *noun.* an act, thing, or person that is a bother or causes trouble: Sometimes a younger brother can be a *nuisance*.

---

# O

---

**of·fi·cial·ly** (ə fish'əl lē) *adverb.* in a formal way; in the manner of someone who has authority or power: We were told *officially* by the committee about the plans for the new building.

| | | |
|---|---|---|
| **a** fat | **oi** oil | **ch** chin |
| **ā** ape | **oo** look | **sh** she |
| **ä** car, father | **ōo** tool | **th** thin |
| **e** ten | **ou** out | **th** then |
| **er** care | **u** up | **zh** leisure |
| **ē** even | **ur** fur | **ŋ** ring |
| **i** hit | | |
| **ir** here | **ə** = a *in* ago | |
| **ī** bite, fire | e *in* agent | |
| **o** lot | i *in* unity | |
| **ō** go | o *in* collect | |
| **ô** law, horn | u *in* focus | |

◇

**Mimeograph** is a modern word based on two Greek words. *Mimeo* means "to imitate or copy"; *-graph* means "to write."

the Washington **Monument**

**o·men** (ō′mən) *noun.* an event that is supposed to be a sign of something good or bad to come: I took the dark clouds as an *omen* that I would have a bad day.

**om·i·nous** (äm′ə nəs) *adjective.* of or like a sign of something bad to come; threatening. An *ominous* silence followed the loud crash.

**or·bit** (ôr′bit) *noun.* the path followed by a planet or moon around another planet or the sun: The earth completes an *orbit* around the sun every 365 days.

**o·rig·i·nal** (ə rij′ə n′l) *adjective.* **1.** the first or earliest. **2.** not copied; new: His *original* idea solved the problem.

**or·tho·dox** (ôr′thə doks) *adjective.* keeping to the usual or traditional beliefs or customs in religion or politics.

orbit

pavilion

pedestal

# P

**pal·let** (pal′it) *noun.* a bed or mattress of straw that is used on the floor. **pallets.**

**par·tial·ly** (pär′shəl lē) *adverb.* not totally: The work is *partially* done.

**par·tic·i·pate** (pär tis′ə pāt) *verb.* to take part in an activity with others: They are *participating* in our field day activities. **participated, participating.**

**par·ti·tion** (pär tish′ən) *noun.* a wall that separates two rooms. —*verb.* to divide into parts: We *partitioned* the attic to make small bedrooms. **partitioned, partitioning.**

**pa·vil·ion** (pə vil′yən) *noun.* a building used for exhibits at a fair or park.

**peace·ful** (pēs′fəl) *adjective.* **1.** free from noise; quiet: I love the *peaceful* seashore at dawn. **2.** not fighting.

**ped·es·tal** (ped′is t′l) *noun.* the base that holds up a statue or lamp.

**per·ma·frost** (pur′mə frôst′) *noun.* soil under the earth's surface that is always frozen.

**per·mis·sion** (pər mish′ən) *noun.* the act of allowing: I have received *permission* to go on the trip.

**pe·ti·tion** (pə tish′ən) *noun.* a formal request signed by a number of people: We sent the governor a *petition* for more funds.

**phos·pho·res·cence** (fos′fə res″ns) *noun.* **1.** the power of giving off light without heat or burning. **2.** such a light: We watched the *phosphorescence* from the seaweed glow on the sea.

**pit·y** (pit′ē) *noun.* a feeling of sadness for someone's troubles: It was a *pity* to see the hungry animals. —*verb.* to feel sorry for. **pitied, pitying.**

**plain** (plān) *adjective.* **1.** open; clear. **2.** without luxury. **3.** simple; easy. **4.** not good-looking. **5.** not fancy. —*noun.* a large area of flat land: The pioneers crossed the *plains.* **plains.**

**plank** (plangk) *noun.* a long, wide board. **planks.**

**play·wright** (plā′rīt) *noun.* a writer of plays: We congratulated all the *playwrights* on the success of the drama festival. **playwrights.**

**plead** (plēd) *verb.* to request in a serious way; beg. —**pleading** *adjective.* in a begging and serious manner: She used a *pleading* voice to ask her father's permission.

**plot·ter** (plot′ər) *noun.* a person who makes secret plans with other people: The crew caught the *plotters* before they could capture the ship. **plotters.**

**plumb·ing** (plum'iṅg) *noun.* **1.** the pipes, sinks, and drains of a building's water or gas system. **2.** the work of a plumber.

**po·lar** (pō'lər) *adjective.* **1.** near the North or South Pole. **2.** near either end of a sphere like the earth or other planets: They studied the *polar* areas of Mars.

**po·lit·i·cal un·rest** (pə lit'i k'l un rest') *noun.* a condition in which people are unhappy with their government and are struggling to change it.

**pon·der** (pon'dər) *verb.* to think deeply and carefully about: He was *pondering* their offer of a new job. **pondered, pondering.**

**port·a·ble** (pôr'tə b'l) *adjective.* able to be carried or easy to be moved: I can take my *portable* computer to school.

**por·trait** (pôr'trit *or* pôr'trāt) *noun.* a drawing or painting of a person.

**pov·er·ty** (pov'ər tē) *noun.* being poor or not having enough to live on: Many people live in *poverty*.

**prai·rie** (prer'ē) *noun.* a large, flat area of grassy land with few trees.

**prank·ster** (praṅk'stər) *noun.* someone who plays tricks, often causing mischief: A *prankster* must have put soap in the fountain.

**pre·cious** (presh'əs) *adjective.* **1.** having great value. **2.** much loved: The grandmother's ring was *precious* to her granddaughter.

**pro·claim** (prō klām') *verb.* to announce: The governor *proclaimed* a special holiday. **proclaimed, proclaiming.**

**proc·tor** (prok'tər) *noun.* a person in a school or college who keeps order and watches over students taking tests.

**pro·jec·tion** (prə jek'shən) *noun.* something that sticks out: The cat sat on a *projection* near the top of the wooden fence.

**pro·mot·er** (prə mō'tər) *noun.* one who helps increase the popularity, growth, or sales of something: Our coach is a *promoter* of regular exercise for children.

**pro·mo·tion** (prə mō'shən) *noun.* a raising to a higher rank or grade: He received a *promotion* from clerk to supervisor.

**pros·per·i·ty** (pro sper'ə tē) *noun.* being wealthy or successful.

**pro·test** (prə test') *verb.* to speak out against; object to: She *protested* that her grade was unfair. **protested, protesting.**

**pu·ma** (pyoo'mə *or* poo'mə) *noun.* a large animal of the cat family, with a slender, tan body and a long tail; another name for cougar.

# R

**rab·bi** (rab'ī) *noun.* the spiritual leader of a Jewish temple or synagogue.

**rack·et** (rak'it) *noun.* loud noise or clatter: Skateboards make a *racket!*

**rag·ged** (rag'id) *adjective.* **1.** shabby. **2.** rough and uneven: The paper tore, leaving a *ragged* edge.

**rav·e·nous·ly** (rav'ə nəs lē) *adverb.* in a very hungry way: We ate the meal *ravenously.*

**raw·hide** (rô'hīd) *noun.* cattle hide that is not yet tanned into leather.

**re·al es·tate** (rē'əl ə stāt' *or* rēl' ə stāt') *noun.* a piece of land and whatever is on it, such as buildings or trees.

**rea·son·a·ble** (rē'zən ə b'l) *adjective.* **1.** sensible. **2.** fair: I set a *reasonable* price for my old bike.

| a | fat | oi | oil | ch | chin |
|---|---|---|---|---|---|
| ā | ape | oo | look | sh | she |
| ä | car, father | oo | tool | th | thin |
| e | ten | ou | out | th | then |
| er | care | u | up | zh | leisure |
| ē | even | ur | fur | ṅg | ring |
| i | hit | | | | |
| ir | here | ə | = a *in* ago |
| ī | bite, fire | | e *in* agent |
| o | lot | | i *in* unity |
| ō | go | | o *in* collect |
| ô | law, horn | | u *in* focus |

**puma**

**Puma** came to our language from the Inca Indians of Peru. The Spanish conqueror Pizarro learned the Inca name for this American cougar when he came to Peru in the 1500s.

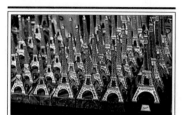

replicas

rig

**re·cep·tion** (ri sep′shən) *noun.* **1.** a receiving or being received. **2.** a party at which guests are received: We went to the wedding *reception* after the ceremony.

**reck·on** (rek′ən) *verb.* **1.** to count. **2.** to think of as being. —**reckoned with** to have thought about; considered: We *reckoned with* her probable reaction as we made our plans.

**re·cruit** (ri krōōt′) *verb.* to get new members: We *recruited* members for the soccer team. **recruited, recruiting.**

**re·fuge** (ref′yōōj) *noun.* shelter; protection: We looked for *refuge* from the storm.

**reg·u·la·tion** (reg′yə lā′shən) *noun.* a rule or law. —*adjective.* done according to rules: We wore *regulation* scout uniforms on our hikes.

**re·ject** (ri jekt′) *verb.* to refuse to agree to: to turn down. **rejected, rejecting.**

**re·lay** (rē′lā *or* ri lā′) *verb.* to receive and pass on: We will *relay* the message to her.

**re·li·a·ble** (ri lī′ə b′l) *adjective.* that can be depended on; trustworthy.

**re·lief** (ri lēf′) *noun.* **1.** lessening of pain, trouble, or worry: The people came inside to get *relief* from the cold. **2.** help given to victims of disasters.

**rem·e·dy** (rem′ə dē) *noun.* **1.** a treatment that cures or relieves a disease: We have no perfect *remedy* for the common cold. **2.** anything that corrects a problem.

**ren·o·vate** (ren′ə vāt) *verb.* to make like new; repair: We *renovated* the old house. **renovated, renovating.**

**rent·er** (rent′ər) *noun.* someone who pays money at regular times to live in a house or apartment: This house is occupied by a *renter.*

**rep·li·ca** (rep′li kə) *noun.* an exact copy of something, such as a painting.

**re·sem·ble** (ri zem′b′l) *verb.* to look like: Two houses on the block *resemble* our house, but both are smaller.

**res·i·dent** (rez′i dənt) *noun.* someone who lives in a place. **residents.**

**re·sign** (ri zīn′) *verb.* to give up a membership or job: I will *resign* as club president after this meeting.

**re·sound** (ri zound′) *verb.* **1.** to echo over and over. **2.** to become filled with sound. **resounded, resounding.**

**re·spect·a·ble** (ri spek′tə b′l) *adjective.* **1.** proper; correct. **2.** fairly good: The team got a *respectable* score, although they lost the game.

**re·ward** (ri wôrd′) *noun.* **1.** something given for good work or a good deed: We were given a *reward* for helping out. **2.** money offered in return for something, especially something lost or stolen.

**rhyth·mic** (ri*th*′mik) *adjective.* having a regular pattern of beats coming at fixed times: Your heart beats in a rhythmic way.

**rid·dle** (rid″l) *noun.* a puzzle, often in the form of a question with a tricky meaning or answer.

**rig** (rig) *noun.* **1.** the arrangement of sails on a ship. **2.** a truck tractor with the trailer attached to it: They loaded the *rig* with fruit for the cross-country trip.

**rig·id** (rij′id) *adjective.* **1.** unbending; stiff: The cast held his arm *rigid.* **2.** strict; not changing.

**rot** (rot) *verb.* to spoil from dampness or other causes: The tomatoes will *rot* on the vine if the rain continues.

**rus·tle** (rus″l) *verb.* to move with a soft, rubbing sound. —*noun.* a soft, rubbing sound: We heard the *rustle* of her long, silk dress.

# S

**sand·spit** (sand′spit′) *noun.* a ridge of sand formed in a river or along the seashore.

**scale** (skāl) *noun.* **1.** an instrument or machine for weighing. **2.** one of the thin, small plates covering the body of a fish or reptile. **3.** a series of spaces marked off by lines and used for measuring distances or amounts. **4.** a system for grouping or classifying by size, importance, or perfection: The director always made his movies on a very grand *scale*.

**sce·ner·y** (sē′nər ē) *noun.* **1.** the view in an outdoor area: We love mountain *scenery*. **2.** the painted background used for a play: The *scenery* made the stage look like an ancient castle.

**scent** (sent) *noun.* **1.** smell: I love the *scent* of lilacs. **2.** the sense of smell. **3.** a smell that an animal leaves.

**script** (skript) *noun.* **1.** handwriting. **2.** a copy of a play, movie, or television show, used by the cast of the play, movie, or show.

**sea·wall** (sē′ wôl) *noun.* a wall built to protect an area of shoreline from being washed away by waves.

**seep** (sēp) *verb.* to leak slowly through small openings; ooze: Water was *seeping* from that old hose into the ground. **seeped, seeping.**

**self-pit·y** (self′pit′ē) *noun.* a feeling of sorrow for oneself: He is full of *self-pity* since his accident.

**self-re·li·ance** (self′ri lī′əns) *noun.* trust in one's own efforts, judgment, and abilities: Because she had always taken care of herself, she had great *self-reliance*.

**ser·pent** (sur′pənt) *noun.* a large snake.

**set** (set) *noun.* **1.** scenery and furniture used on a theater stage: Our drama club has several *sets* to use for different plays. **2.** a group of things that go together. **3.** a number of parts put together in a cabinet, as in a television set. **4.** a group of six or more games in tennis won by a margin of two or more games. **5.** in mathematics, any group of units, numbers, etc. **sets.**

**sher·iff** (sher′if) *noun.* the chief law officer in a county: In Western movies, the *sheriff* wears a badge shaped like a star.

**shrug** (shrug) *verb.* to pull up one's shoulders to show that one does not care or does not know something: He only *shrugged* when we asked where she was. **shrugged, shrugging.**

**shuf·fle** (shuf′l) *verb.* **1.** to walk or dance with a dragging motion of the feet: He *shuffled* slowly along the hall. **2.** to mix playing cards. **shuffled, shuffling.**

**shuf·fle·board** (shuf′l bôrd) *noun.* a game in which long sticks are used to push pucks onto numbered sections of a triangle painted on the ground or some other surface.

**siege** (sēj) *noun.* the surrounding of a city or other place by an army trying to capture it.

**sketch** (skech) *noun.* **1.** a simple drawing without much detail: His *sketch* of the mountains was shown to the whole class. **2.** a short, often funny, scene in a show. —*verb.* to make a simple drawing of. **sketched, sketching.**

**skill·ful·ly** or **skil·ful·ly** (skil′fəl lē) *adverb.* in an expert way; in a well-trained or practiced manner.

| a fat | oi oil | ch chin |
|---|---|---|
| ā ape | o͞o look | sh she |
| ä car, father | o͞o tool | th thin |
| e ten | ou out | th then |
| er care | u up | zh leisure |
| ē even | ur fur | ng ring |
| i hit | | |
| ir here | ə = a *in* ago | |
| ī bite, fire | e *in* agent | |
| o lot | i *in* unity | |
| ō go | o *in* collect | |
| ô law, horn | u *in* focus | |

**sandspit**

Sandspit is a combination of *sand* and *spit*. *Spit*, in this case, is a noun, meaning "a small, sandy point of land extending into water."

**snowshoes**

**stilts**

**slab** (slab) *noun.* a flat, broad, thick piece: There were big *slabs* of marble in the artist's studio. **slabs.**

**slick·er** (slik′ ər) *noun.* a loose fitting, waterproof coat, originally made of oil-treated cloth. **slickers.**

**snarl** (snärl) *verb.* **1.** to growl fiercely, showing the teeth: The dog was _ *snarling* at the man at the gate. **2.** to speak in an angry voice. **snarled, snarling.**

**snout** (snout) *noun.* the nose and jaws projecting from the head of an animal, as on a pig. **snouts.**

**snow·shoe** (snō′shoo) *noun.* a wooden frame with leather strips that is worn on the shoes to keep a person from sinking into the snow. **snowshoes.**

**soar** (sôr) *verb.* to fly high in the air: The eagle *soared* above the clouds. **soared, soaring.**

**sod** (sod) *noun.* the top layer of earth that contains grass and its roots: The pioneers' plows broke the *sod.*

**sod·bus·ter** (sod′bus′tər) *noun.* a farmer on the frontier in the American West who broke through the sod to plant a crop. **sodbusters.**

**so·lar sys·tem** (so′lər sis′təm) *noun.* a sun and all the planets, moons, and other bodies that move around it.

**span** (span) *noun.* **1.** the part of a bridge between two supports: The main *span* of the bridge is more than ninety yards long. **2.** a certain period of time. **spans.**

**spec·i·fi·ca·tion** (spes′ə fi kā′shən) *noun.* a detailed description. —**specifications** *plural noun.* a description of all the necessary details for something, including sizes and materials: The engineer had the *specifications* for the new building.

**splen·dour** or **splen·dor** (splen′dər) *noun.* **1.** great brightness. **2.** the quality of being beautiful in a grand way: We admired the *splendour* of the room.

**spout** (spout) *verb.* to shoot out in a forceful way: Spray was *spouting* from the whale's airhole. **spouted, spouting.**

**sput·ter** (sput′ər) *verb.* **1.** to spit out drops from the mouth, as when talking too fast. **2.** to talk in a confused way. **3.** to make hissing sounds. **sputtered, sputtering.** —**sputtery** *adjective.* hissing, spitting out.

**sta·bil·i·ty** (stə bil′ə tē) *noun.* steadiness; firmness: I don't trust the *stability* of that chair.

**stan·za** (stan′zə) *noun.* a group of lines in a poem or song; verse. **stanzas.**

**star·va·tion** (stär vā′shən) *noun.* the condition of dying or suffering from lack of food: Deer may die of *starvation* in a cold, snowy winter.

**stash** (stash) *verb.* to hide in a secret, safe place. **stashed, stashing.**

**stern·ly** (sturn′lē) *adverb.* in a strict way; harshly: He looked at me *sternly* when I came in late.

**stilt** (stilt) *noun.* **1.** a long pole with a place partway up for one's foot. **2.** a tall pole used to support something above the ground: The house was built on *stilts* above the marsh. **stilts.**

**strand** (strand) *noun.* **1.** a thread or wire twisted together with others to make a rope or cable. **2.** something that is like a string or rope: She twisted a *strand* of her hair as she talked. **strands.**

**struc·ture** (struk′chər) *noun.* something that is built, such as a house or building.

**sub·mit** (səb mit′) *verb.* **1.** to give to others to look over or to decide about: We *submitted* our papers to

the teacher. **2.** to give in to.
**submitted, submitting.**

**sub·side** (səb sīd′) *verb.* **1.** to sink or
fall to a lower level; go down. **2.** to
become less active or intense.
**subsided, subsiding.**

**su·per·vi·sion** (sōō′pər vizh′ən) *noun.*
direction or management: The
employees all work under her
*supervision.*

**sup·port** (sə pôrt′) *verb.* **1.** to hold up.
**2.** to provide money for. —*noun.*
**1.** being supported. **2.** a person or
thing that holds up. *adjective.* weight
carrying.

**sur·vey** (sər vā′) *verb.* **1.** to look over
carefully. **2.** to measure the size or
shape of a piece of land using special
instruments. **surveyed.** —*noun.* **1.** a
study of the general facts. **2.** a
measurement of size and location of
land. —**surveying** *adjective.*
measuring the land: The *surveying*
task was made difficult by the hilly
land.

**sus·pen·sion** (sə spen′shən) *noun.*
**1.** something held by support from
above. **2.** the act of keeping out or
away from because of unacceptable
behavior.

**swamp** (swomp) *noun.* a piece of damp
land; bog.

**sway·backed** (swā′bakt) *adjective.*
having a spine that sags in the middle:
The old horse was *swaybacked.*

**swell** (swel) *verb.* to become larger or
increase in volume. —*noun.* a part that
swells, as a large, rolling wave or a
piece of rising ground. **swells.**

**sym·bol·ize** (sim′b′l īz) *verb.* to stand
for something: The flag *symbolizes* the
United States. **symbolizes, symbolized,
symbolizing.**

**sym·met·ri·cal** (si met′ri k′l) *adjective.*
balanced; right half like the left half.

# T

**tem·po·rar·y** (tem′pə rer′ē) *adjective.*
lasting for a short time; not
permanent: The bad weather is only
*temporary.*

**ten·e·ment** (ten′ə mənt) *noun.* an
apartment house that is old and
crowded.

**text** (tekst) *noun.* **1.** the words on a
page, not including pictures. **2.** the
actual words a writer uses in a book,
speech, or other writing: He read the
*text* of his speech one last time.

**tex·tile** (teks′tīl *or* teks′t′l) *noun.* woven
fabric. —*adjective.* clothlike.

**thaw** (thô) *verb.* to melt: The ice on the
lake will *thaw* by spring.

**the·o·ry** (thē′ə rē) *noun.* **1.** an
explanation of why something
happens. **2.** the general rules
followed in a science or an art. **3.** an
idea, guess, or opinion. **theories.**

**thrive** (thrīv) *verb.* **1.** to become
successful; to do well. **2.** to grow in a
strong and healthy way: The baby
*thrived* on homemade baby food.
**thrived, thriving.**

**ti·dal** (tīd′l) *adjective.* having to do
with the regular rise and fall of ocean
waters: The *tidal* waters moved up the
shore.

**tilt** (tilt) *verb.* to tip to one side: The
flowers *tilt* toward the sun.

**toil** (toil) *verb.* to work hard. —*noun.*
hard work: We read about the
workers' *toils* in building the railroad.
**toils.**

**tra·di·tion·al** (trə dish′ən′l) *adjective.*
handed down from older people to
younger ones: We sang the *traditional*
holiday songs.

| a fat | oi oil | ch chin |
|---|---|---|
| ā ape | oo look | sh she |
| ä car, father | ōō tool | th thin |
| e ten | ou out | *th* then |
| er care | u up | zh leisure |
| ē even | ur fur | ṅg ring |
| i hit | | |
| ir here | ə = a *in* ago | |
| ī bite, fire | e *in* agent | |
| o lot | i *in* unity | |
| ō go | o *in* collect | |
| ô law, horn | u *in* focus | |

**textile**

**Thrive,** which comes from
Norwegian, has a selfish
early meaning, which was "to seize
or grasp for oneself." Perhaps in
times gone by, if people didn't *seize*
what they needed, they didn't *thrive.*

**Tutor** has friendly roots. It started out meaning "defender" or "guardian." It has come to mean "a person showing friendliness to someone." Next time you tutor someone, think of yourself as a friendly helper.

**vessel**

**trag·e·dy** (traj′ə dē) *noun.* **1.** a serious play that has a sad ending. **2.** something that is very sad: The loss of his dog was a *tragedy* to him.

**trans·late** (trans lāt′ *or* trans′lāt) *verb.* to put the words of one language into the words of a different language: I can *translate* Spanish stories into English.

**tri·umph** (trī′əmf) *noun.* **1.** a victory in a battle. **2.** great joy about a successful event: We cheered in *triumph* as our team won.

**turf** (turf) *noun.* the top layer of the ground; sod.

**tu·tor** (tōōt′ər *or* tyōōt′ər) *noun.* a teacher who teaches one student at a time in a certain subject.

# u

**un·con·scious** (un kon′shəs) *adjective.* **1.** unable to feel and think: He fainted and was *unconscious* for a minute. **2.** not aware of something.

# v

**vast** (vast) *adjective.* very large.

**ve·loc·i·ty** (və läs′ ə tē) *noun.* speed; rate of motion in a particular direction. The wind *velocity* of 20 miles per hour made biking against the wind very difficult.

**ven·ture** (ven′chər) *noun.* an activity in which there is some risk of losing something: The orange juice stand is a new *venture* for its owner.

**ves·sel** (ves″l) *noun.* **1.** any hollow utensil for holding something as a pot, bowl, etc. **2.** a boat or ship, especially a large one. **3.** any of the body's tubes through which blood flows.

**ves·tige** (ves′tij) *noun.* a part or mark left from something that is no longer there: The snowbank was the last *vestige* of the big storm.

**vi·brate** (vī′brāt) *verb.* to move back and forth quickly.

**vig·il** (vij′əl) *noun.* a time when someone stays awake to watch at night.

**vi·o·lence** (vī′ə ləns) *noun.* **1.** a force used to hurt or cause damage: The demonstrators protested without violence. **2.** great strength.

**vol·un·teer** (vol ən tir′) *noun.* a person who offers to do something without being forced to do so: We asked for several *volunteers* to clean up after the party. **volunteers.**

**voy·age** (voi′ij) *noun.* **1.** a trip by water: We went on an ocean *voyage.* **2.** a trip through the air or outer space.

when he saw the man dressed in a bear costume.

**whine** (hwīn) *verb.* to make a long, high feeble sound or cry, as in complaining. **whined, whining.**

**wist·ful** (wist′fəl) *adjective.* showing a wish or a longing: She had a *wistful* look on her face as she looked at the toys in the store window.

**worth** (wurth) *noun.* **1.** the quality that makes something have merit. **2.** the value of something: She sold the car for less than it's *worth.*

| a fat | oi oil | ch chin |
|---|---|---|
| ā ape | oo look | sh she |
| ä car, father | ōo tool | th thin |
| e ten | ou out | *th* then |
| er care | u up | zh leisure |
| ē even | ur fur | n͡g ring |
| i hit | | |
| ir here | ə = a *in* ago | |
| ī bite, fire | e *in* agent | |
| o lot | i *in* unity | |
| ō go | o *in* collect | |
| ô law, horn | u *in* focus | |

## W

**wade** (wād) *verb.* to walk through water, mud, or anything that slows one down. **waded, wading.**

**wal·rus mus·tache** (wôl′rəs mə stash′) *noun.* a long, full mustache or hair that men grow on their upper lip that droops down on both ends.

**wea·ry** (wir′ē) *adjective.* very tired; worn out.

**whim·per** (hwim′ pər) *verb.* to make low, broken sounds, as in crying or in fear. The little boy started to *whimper*

## Y

**yank** (yaṅk) *noun.* a sudden, strong pull. —*verb.* to pull or jerk. **yanked, yanking.**

**year·book** (yir′book) *noun.* a book published at the end of a year that tells about events during that year.

**wade**

# ABOUT THE AUTHORS

*The authors listed below have written some of the selections that appear in this book. The content of the notes was determined by a survey of what readers wanted to know about authors.*

### GENEVIEVE BARLOW

Genevieve Barlow was born in Gardena, California, where she still lives. In addition to being a writer, she has also been a schoolteacher and a translator for the Red Cross in Puerto Rico. Her book *Latin American Tales* was chosen as a Junior Literary Guild selection. *(Born 1910)*

DAVID BUDBILL

### DAVID BUDBILL

David Budbill is a playwright, a poet, and an author of stories for young people. He, his wife, two children, and several pets live in a small town in Vermont in a house that he and his wife built. His wife, Lois Eby, is a painter and has illustrated some of her husband's books of poetry. The Dorothy Canfield Fisher Award and Kirkus Choice Book are two of the honors David Budbill has received for his books. *(Born 1940)*

CLYDE ROBERT BULLA

### CLYDE ROBERT BULLA

Although Clyde Robert Bulla never had any formal training in writing, he learned his art by reading. "Reading was a kind of magic," he says. "By the time I was ready for the third grade, I had read most of the books in the school library." From the time he was a young boy, Bulla wanted to be a writer. When he was in the fourth grade, he won a prize for a story he wrote. As an adult, he has continued to win prizes and awards for his writing. *(Born 1914)*